PEACE, POWER, and PRESENCE

April 2009

Beloved Tilah & Tawlia,

Every moment within my Heart,
forever present, & remembered in
Love. I give thanks...

With Heart,

Jonathan

Books in the
Wisdom for a Life of Freedom series

VOLUME I
Peace, Power, and Presence

VOLUME II
The Seven Empowerments

VOLUME III
Empowering Relationships

VOLUME IV
The 'I' of God

Peace, Power, and Presence

A Guide to Self Empowerment, Inner Peace, and Spiritual Enlightenment

Wisdom for a Life of Freedom
VOLUME I

Jonathan Evatt

INSPIRED EARTH
PUBLISHING HOUSE,
NEW ZEALAND

PEACE, POWER, *and* PRESENCE: A Guide to Self Empowerment, Inner Peace, and Spiritual Enlightenment — by Jonathan Evatt

Copyright © 2008 by Jonathan Evatt

All rights reserved. No part of this book may be reproduced or transmitted in any form or by any means without written permission from the author. Extracts of up to 450 words (in total within any one published work) may be quoted and shared in a non-commercial fashion on the proviso the author is first notified in writing, and the full title and author name are clearly identified with every extract. Any request made by the author to remove such extracts supersedes any rights granted here.

To reproduce any content herein for any other purpose, you must email the author outlining intentions, and await receipt of permission to do so.

ISBN 978-1-877492-00-6 (Paperback)
ISBN 978-1-877492-01-3 (Hardback)

North American Edition (1st)

Published in New Zealand by:
Inspired Earth Publishing House
PO Box 556, Shortland Street
Auckland, NEW ZEALAND.
Phone: +64 (28) 892-436   Fax: +64 (28) 892-437

www.inspiredearthpublishing.com

National Library of New Zealand Cataloguing-in-Publication Data
Evatt, Jonathan, 1975-
Wisdom for a life of freedom / Jonathan Evatt.
North American ed. (1st)
Includes bibliographical references and index.
ISBN 978-1-877492-00-6 (pbk. : v. 1)
ISBN 978-1-877492-01-3 (hbk. : v. 1)
Contents: v. 1. Peace, power and presence.
1. Self-realization. 2. Peace of mind. 3. Spirituality. 4. Conduct of life. 5. Toltec philosophy. I. Title.
158—dc 22

Editorial:	Diana Christine
Interior Design:	Jonathan Evatt
Cover Artwork & Design:	Dan Vlad, Jonathan Evatt

*In loving dedication to all my Relations throughout Infinity, throughout all the many wondrous dimensions of Life.
May freedom blossom deep within your hearts and expand throughout your world.*

Acknowledgements

Special thanks goes to Diana for her ceaseless support in the form of editing and encouragement, both so fundamental in the creation of this book. In my world you are a living miracle. Simply amazing.

I give thanks to Andrew Forrest, Andrew Gonzalez, Jim Warren, Professor Philip Rubinov Jacobson, and Jonathan Earl Bowser for lovingly sharing their exquisite artwork. It's an incredible gift.

My gratitude also goes to Dan Vlad for helping with the cover graphics.

With deep respect and love I give thanks to Yolande for courageously walking a path of Freedom, for being by my side, and for providing the perfect mirror as I do the same for you.

Thanks to my family in Finland for giving me the time, support, and space to complete this publication. Thanks to Arun in Aotearoa for the same.

...and my heartfelt gratitude goes to all those Men and Women of Knowledge throughout the Ages — the Toltec, the Ka'huna, the mystics, sages, spiritual masters, and Yogis — through whom I have received countless blessings, it's more than I can put into words. Together, may we dream the dream of a Luminous World — a world that accurately reflects our Divinity.

Contents (Concise)

Illustrations 13
Preface 15
Introduction 17

Part One: Establishing A Common Perspective
1. I Am the Dreamer of a Dream 31
2. The Laying of New Foundations 51
3. The Dreamer and the Dreamed... Who Am I? 73
4. Your Dream Configuration 115
5. Your Personal L.O.R.E. 127
6. The Stories We Tell 137
7. Your Realm and the King Who Fell 151

Part Two: Your Immaculate Conception
8. Unraveling the Stories We Tell 173
9. Beyond Duality 189
10. Authentic Power 199
11. Inner Peace 225
12. Reclaiming Your Attention 237
13. Life as Medicine 255
14. Healing Your Beliefs and Perception 267

Part Three: The Rebirth Of Now
15. Peace, Power, and Presence 291
16. Koyaanisqatsi – Life Out of Balance 301
17. Loving What Is 331
18. Setting the World Free 343
19. Resurrecting Your Highness 353
20. The Intelligent Universe 373
21. Healing Principles and Perspectives: An Overview 391
Ω. From Now to Infinity 401
Appendix 404
Index 410

Contents

Illustrations	13
Preface	15
Introduction	17

Part One: Establishing A Common Perspective

1. I Am the Dreamer of a Dream — 31
- *Illusion* 32
- *Life is but a Dream* 34
- *The Projector and the Light That Shines Through* 37
- *An Issue of Mistaken Identity* 39
- *The Light of God is in All Things* 40
- *The Warrior as an Archetype* 43
- *The Warrior's Challenge* 46
- *The Dreamer's Purpose* 47

2. The Laying of New Foundations — 51
- *Time* 53
- *Separation* 55
- *Illusion* 56
- *Healthy Denial* 59
- *Holy Ground* 60
- *Establishing Our Common Ground* 61

3. The Dreamer and the Dreamed... Who Am I? — 73
- *The Collective Dream Configuration* 75
- *Your Tri-part Self Within the Dream* 77
- *The Body-mind* 82
- *The Attentive-mind / Attention* 86

	The Spirit-mind	89
	The Much-Talked-About Ego	90
	Greater Incorporation Through the Heart	95
	The Deeper 'I' of Life	97
	The Unfolding of Self Over Time	103
	Malu, Entities, and Non-Self	105
	The Dreamer	107
	The Ego and the Dreamer	111
4.	**Your Dream Configuration**	**115**
	Your Personal Dream Configuration	123
5.	**Your Personal L.O.R.E.**	**127**
	Recognising Your Lore	129
	From Lore to Love	130
	Inner Peace and Inner War	132
6.	**The Stories We Tell**	**137**
	Receiving the Gift of the Present	138
	The Silent Stories Within	140
	The Love Story	141
	The Never-ending Story	144
	Replacing the Story – An Experiment	145
	Stories Within the Tri-part Self	147
7.	**Your Realm and the King Who Fell**	**151**
	The World and the Earth	151
	Perception	153
	Collective World Views	153
	Hand in Hand	154
	Objective Reality? Perhaps Not	155
	I Know Nothing	156
	There's Life, Jim, but Not as We Know It	157
	Corruption and Denial	158
	Humanity's Old Mental Blocks	159
	The King and His Realm	162
	The Fall	164

Part Two: Your Immaculate Conception

8. Unraveling the Stories We Tell   173
- *The Moral of the Story* 174
- *You – The Path of Your Perfection* 175
- *Regaining Objectivity* 176
- *We Internalise the Stories Already Within Us* ... 178
- *The Process of Unraveling a Story* 179
- *The Folly of Self Reflection* 181
- *Two Sides to the Story* 183
- *The Taste of Chocolate* 186

9. Beyond Duality   189
- *The Duality of the Person and His Behaviour* ... 192
- *It's All Relative* 194
- *No Opposition* 195

10. Authentic Power   199
- *True Power is Within* 202
- *False Power* 204
- *A Fresh Perspective on the Nature of Success* ... 205
- *The Illusion of Cause and Effect* 207
- *Power and Perception* 208
- *Gaining Power* 209
- *The Folly of Powerlessness* 211
- *Losing Power* 214
- *Power and Disease* 215
- *Collective Disease* 216
- *A Challenge from Infinity* 217
- *Power Within the Tri-part Self* 219
- *There is Only One Power* 220

11. Inner Peace   225
- *The Seed of Discontent* 227
- *Minding the Gap* 229
- *Two Sides to Inner Peace* 231
- *Revisiting the Projector* 233

12. Reclaiming Your Attention   237
- *The Who, Where, What, and Why of Things* 240

	The Nature of Attention	241
	Attention and Energy	247
	Reclamation	248
	Self Reflection	250
	The Cosmic Mystery of One	252
13.	**Life as Medicine**	**255**
	Letting the Victim Go Now	257
	An Agent of Healing	260
	Energy and Issues	260
14.	**Healing Your Beliefs and Perception**	**267**
	Victims and Blame	268
	For You and Not To You	270
	Stalking Your Power	273
	BE-AWARE of Your (De)fences	274
	Selfishness and Self-centeredness	277
	The Word "Selfish"	278
	A Deeper Look	281
	Know Thy Self	283
	Selfishly Saving the World	285

PART THREE: THE REBIRTH OF NOW

15.	**Peace, Power, and Presence**	**291**
	You Are the Path of Peace, Power and Presence	293
	Our Task	294
	Presence	295
	Stillness	296
	Being Present to Now	298
16.	**Koyaanisqatsi – Life Out of Balance**	**301**
	The Sixth Extinction	303
	Perspective and Context	304
	Consumption	306
	Cultural Blindness	308
	The American Dream	310
	Capitalism and the Superstition of Materialism	312
	Extremes – Showing the Middle Way	315

    Philosophical Skepticism *316*
    Dissolving the Extremes That Hold Us Back *318*
    The Purpose of Extremes *322*
    Just What on Earth are We Creating? *324*
    Bringing It All Home *326*
    Taking Flight *327*

17. Loving What Is — **331**
    Exploring What Is *332*
    Is It True? *334*
    Turning It Around *335*
    A Symbolic Perspective *335*
    The Quickening *337*
    The Illusion of Progress *338*

18. Setting the World Free — **343**
    Forgiveness – The Master Key *344*
    The Ego & Separation *347*
    Practicing Forgiveness *349*

19. Resurrecting Your Highness — **353**
    Chaos & Decline *354*
    The Resurrection *364*
    Restoring Balance *366*

20. The Intelligent Universe — **373**
    Cosmic Self-Awareness *374*
    The "I" of Infinity *376*
    Love and Truth *377*
    Intelligent Co-Operation *379*
    The Book of Life *381*
    The Story of Truman *382*

21. Healing Principles and Perspectives: An Overview — **391**
    The Way of No Way *393*
    You are the Path of Your Awakening *394*

Ω. From Now to Infinity — **401**
    About the Author *403*

Appendix — **404**

Index — **410**

ILLUSTRATIONS

Magia of the Heart, *by Andrew Gonzalez* *27*
The Oracle of the Pearl, *by Andrew Gonzalez* *30*
The Fire Flower, *by Prof. Philip Rubinov Jacobson* *50*
Dreamwalker, *by Jim Warren* *72*
Kingdom of the Solar Logos, *by Andrew Forrest* *114*
Spellbound, *by Andrew Forrest* *126*
Living in a Jim Warren Painting, *by Jim Warren* *136*
Sibling Rivalry, *by Jonathon Earl Bowser* *150*
The King's Daydream, *by Prof. Philip Rubinov Jacobson* ... *172*
One, *by Andrew Forrest* *188*
Authentic Power, *by Jonathan Evatt & Wahcana* *198*
Earthshrine, *by Andrew Forrest* *224*
The Master & His Pet, *by Jonathon Earl Bowser* *236*
In the Very Eye of the Muse, *by Prof. Philip Rubinov Jacobson* *246*
Majesty of Gaia, *by Andrew Forrest* *254*
Albido Sublimus, *by Andrew Gonzalez* *266*
Spirit Wind Creation Myth, *by Andrew Forrest* *290*
World Out Of Balance, *by Jonathan Evatt* *300*
The Secret Rapture, *by Andrew Gonzalez* *330*
He is Free, *by Prof. Philip Rubinov Jacobson* *342*
Fravashi, *by Andrew Gonzalez* *352*
The Fall, *by Jonathon Earl Bowser* *363*
Council of the Elohim, *by Andrew Forrest* *372*
Old Man River, *by Jim Warren* *390*
Stairway to Heaven, *by Jim Warren* *400*

Please refer to the Appendix for information about these artists and their web sites where you can see more of their beautiful artwork.

Self Responsibility

The author of this book does not dispense medical advice or prescribe the use of any technique as a form of treatment for physical, emotional, psychological or medical conditions without the advice of an appropriate health practitioner or physician, either directly or indirectly. The intent of the author is only to offer information of a general nature to help you in your quest for emotional and spiritual well-being. In the event you use any of the information in this book for yourself, which is your sovereign right to do so, the author and the publisher assume no responsibility for your actions.

Preface

Several days ago my granddaughter said that she cannot imagine my ever being angry, that she cannot form an image of me upset or frustrated. In a moment I realized how profound has been the learning and deepening of my own life, how during the past several years I have become more peaceful, more authentic, more present to my own self and to those around me. Later, alone in my home, I considered what those things are that have contributed most to how I have become.

I have worked with my New Zealand friend Jonathan as his editor for the past three years, and *Peace, Power, and Presence* has become part of who I am. My perception of the world around me is more conscious; my state of inner power is more balanced. I cannot say it could not have happened without Jonathan's writing (were it not for the writings of Jonathan, the Universe would have provided another means of discovery), but for me very much of my own realization has come through *Peace, Power, and Presence.*

You and I, we are but dreamers of a dream.... Jonathan opens chapter 1 with these words and we begin to unravel the many beliefs that create our sense of powerlessness, the same beliefs that distort our presence and take away our peace.

We live in a world of beliefs, so many beliefs that we have become unaware that everything is a belief. When I was born I was told my name is Diana Christine and it became the beginning of my set of beliefs—it just so happens everyone agreed to share this same belief, and that made me Diana Christine to the rest of the world. I was told I am an American—America is merely a shared belief, too, and has been for 232 years. I was then told what it means to be an American, what it means to be a girl in America, and from there my beliefs began to become more individual. Someone told me I was pretty and someone told me I was ugly; I believed one of them and called it the truth (or I believed both of them and called myself confused). I then began to create emotions attached to my beliefs, and to complicate it all, I believed my emotions were outside my control, that they simply came from how I felt (not realizing how I feel originates from a belief). My beliefs and emotions shaped my sense of worth and my sense of power.

In *Peace, Power, and Presence* Jonathan shows us how our beliefs and emotions become the stories we tell ourselves and tell the world around us. He takes us on a journey to discover how to restore ourselves to a deep sense of peace and a place of authentic power.

People often ask me how can it be possible not to be furious, anguished, depressed, enraged, or devastated by things that happen to you. One of the greatest awakenings for me in *Peace, Power, and Presence* was the understanding that nothing happens "to" me, but instead, everything happens "for" me. I have transformed my sense of helpless subjection to one of powerful presence, but the concept is difficult for me to explain in quick casual conversations. Jonathan's writing will open this door of understanding for you and you will begin your journey toward authentic power.

An underlying cause of pain in our lives is the belief in duality and separation. Jonathan's writing opened this understanding to me quite beautifully—imagine for a moment in the beginning with God (whatever your concept of God might be). In the beginning was only God, and God was all there was. In the beginning God created, and what God used to create with was all there was, which was God. How can we not clearly see that all that is is part of the same One thing, and that we all are this same One? *Peace, Power, and Presence* makes it all so clear for me.

I would like to suggest that you read *Peace, Power, and Presence* more than one time, and even read parts of it again and again. Every reading of it will pull you a little more out of the stories you tell and bring you more in alignment with your own self.

I wish you many blessings as you commence the journey with Jonathan in your reading of *Peace, Power, and Presence*.

Diana Christine
Director, Spirit First
Washington, D.C.

Alpha

INTRODUCTION

"One cannot help but be in awe when he contemplates the mysteries of eternity, of life, of the marvellous structure of reality. It is enough if one tries merely to comprehend a little of this mystery every day."
Albert Einstein

Isn't it incredible the way each moment—moments such as the one we are in the midst of right now—unfolds into our experience and then just as magically passes away? There is such deep mystery within and woven through all *things* and all life, that when I fully engage myself with that which is around me and within me, it is as if I am stepping into a deep nurturing relationship with a close and intimate lover. Perhaps you have also felt a sense of intimacy in your relationship to life, now or in the past? As you read and understand what is within the pages of this book I am certain your experience of the profundity of life will dive and rise even deeper and higher than it is right now.

As I write these words (in your apparent past), your Essence is already in agreement to be, in this moment, reading what I have written. Beyond the reach of our ordinary perception, you and I have already agreed to impart what is contained on these pages from me to you in this particular form. Such is the unfathomable mystery called Life and the profundity of our unavoidable and absolute interconnectedness.

Welcome.

It's been quite a journey for both of us, I am sure, to be here now, and yet it is precisely Now that our journey truly begins...

My Journey Here

For the past 33 years and beyond I have devoted my life to remembering, recognising, and integrating principles and perspectives that support liberation from the suffering that, for most people, is an inherent part of the human experience. As a child it was apparent to me that "people in this world are truly free and magnificent, yet they believe otherwise, and most people don't seem to recognise this." I realised "I too do not fully experience and recognise here in the flesh the truth of my freedom, of my essence beyond form. My mind is under the influence of a falsity, a lie, and it must be undone. Only then can I serve all my relations to help them realise their freedom."

I've never felt inspired to pursue worldly achievements, or any*thing* in this world, for the sake of pursuit of that thing alone. My freedom was what mattered most, and therefore if I was to pursue any*thing* in this world, it was folly to do so unless it was in some way an active step to uncovering and experiencing that freedom.

By my mid-teens I discovered that the pursuit of spiritually based freedom has been with humankind since our inception—since the beginning of time. I discovered many names for this pursuit and its eventual outcome, such as enlightenment, liberation, moksha, nirvana, et cetera. I also came across many of the concepts behind these words and the way in which this freedom is traditionally and typically portrayed. I realised that in my experience I was seeking something subtly yet profoundly different from the ordinary human perspective on freedom. I couldn't help but feel that many of the so-called spiritual paths and teachings pertaining to liberation often seemed to emphasize "pulling away from the world," and also to propose the idea that "I am somehow not perfect right now" and must therefore *work my way toward* some state that is perfect, or "Enlightened," and away from the so-called sins and trappings of this world. I've realised—often with difficulty, and even sadness—that many of the paths purporting to result in such liberation are, in fact, just another form of bondage and limitation. Perplexed, and inspired, I continued the journey of discovery—of uncovering the direct perception of my own Self.

Nearly every religion I have studied creates at a fundamental level a chasm of separation between Man and Earth, between Man and God, even between Man and Life itself. Many also seem to place an unhealthy degree of emphasis on blindly *believing* in specific teachings or concepts; following particular teachers or Gurus, often despite their obvious shortcomings; and engaging in particular spiritual practices in order to *become* enlightened. It seems to me now, as it did when I was a child, that all of this is about **doing something outside the context of simply being who and what I Am right Now, and failing to use the power of That to wake up to what is real in each moment as it manifests through and around me in all that I perceive.**

Emphasis on the notion that there is somehow something "wrong" with the human condition all too often implies or outrightly states there are certain "unwholesome" or "bad" *things* about ourselves we must squash, deny, change, or repress in order to not get led astray on the path to "God" and liberation. Some religions call these bad things "sins" and arrogantly try to impress upon people's minds that we are born with something called "original sin" like some kind of tainted stain on our soul. Others speak of these being dark and evil times that can be transcended only by the small glimmer of hope afforded to man by their particular religion, teacher, and beliefs.

Since my childhood I have felt these approaches to spirituality and life typically further strengthen the core illusions the average person maintains within his or her mind, and which hold us in an experience of bondage to forces of which we are wholly unaware. The illusion that *I am separate from all things*. The illusion that *That which I Am somehow became less than what The Source created That as*. The illusion of worldly evolution from a condition that is *worse* into one that is *better*. I felt that these lies, to name but a few, served only the people, organisations, and institutions that perpetuate them. Of course it is a valid experience to get involved in that sort of contracted perception of life and its magnificence, to then feel and experience the pain of that contraction, and to then one day make the conscious choice to break away into something new and more inclusive toward all Life as One. Valid, yes, but not something I felt compelled to experience myself in this lifetime.

It felt to me that many of the teachings pertaining to spiritual and human freedom invariably had subtle forms of control woven into them, through and through. I felt that on some level the result of a person subscribing to these sorts of teachings was one of ongoing disempowerment, further duality, control by something "out there," and deeper bondage to illusions and lies—what was previously garden-variety human bondage was all too often transformed by religion into some kind of deep spiritual bondage, potentially much harder to unravel because it had slipped into a level of subtlety that only a very lucid and sober mind would discern and see. Such lucidity is hard to come by when a person is confused about the true nature of Life and is hypnotised by such deeply ingrained thought-forms as those I experienced in my peers, the human world around me, and within my own conditioning.

Unable to ignore these feelings, since my early teens it has been my primary focus and concern to realise what is "True" for me, and what constitutes true freedom.

What you have in your hands is timeless wisdom. I can assure you there is nothing *new* here. There is nothing here that you won't find hidden and dispersed in the pages of other books, scriptures, and teachings all over the world and throughout time. More importantly, there is no-thing here that you don't already know at some level somewhere within your own heart and mind. Yet, in honouring that I am here to share That which I Am and That which I know, these words have sprung forth onto these pages—from this unit of the universal Mind, the totality of Life, into the one you identify as your self.

Defining the Topic

During the writing of this book people have asked, oftentimes in passing or during what is obviously going to be a brief conversation, "So, tell me, what are your books about?" Typically my answer has gone something like this: "This is a series of books about *power*, how we manage (or mismanage) our power, how energy is afforded to us by power, how Inner Peace results from embracing such power in a life-giving way, and how we can approach life in such a way that our experience constitutes a life of freedom."

The best way I have been able to define life thus far is that it is the unfolding of Forever Expanding Awareness in Liberation. Put another way, we could say it is for the purpose of e-volving awareness. The key here is that life for each of us as units of the Totality is also the unfolding of Forever Expanding Awareness in Liberation. It is the mystery we call power that enables us to operate in this grand unified purpose of life, and it is our personal power that enables us to operate in our individual purpose as human beings. One archetype that is particularly well suited to explaining the most suitable approach to life's purpose is that of the Warrior. The Warrior re-cognises that each of life's challenges is in fact a call to power—a gift of power waiting for him or her to claim. Yet it is not a gift that is given up easily and for this reason a battle or hunt of one kind or another is necessary.

The Warrior is not unlike a traditional hunter who must go out into nature, which for him always embodies and represents the unknown, in order to stalk his pray so he can eat and survive. He does not wage a war on nature, for that is folly at best. Rather he uses the skill, knowledge, and power that life has afforded him to make the best of his situation in what is ultimately an act of co-operation with nature. I wish to emphasize that when I refer to the archetype of the Warrior I am not referring to the image of the warmonger that some people might otherwise associate with this archetype. The battles fought by the Warrior I am familiar with are for the most part fought in silence, in secret, and within the confines of her body, mind, and spirit.

THE FIRST IN A SERIES

As you may have noted, this book is the first in a series of at least four volumes. In this first volume we will take a condensed yet relatively broad look at what I ultimately intend to impart and share with you through the collected works *Wisdom for a Life of Freedom*. It is not my intention to weigh this work down with too much technicality and metaphysical complexity, although in places a little of this will be called for. I will therefore keep my explanations as simple as I feel I can, without losing the depth of field that is necessary to impart a clear sense of feeling to you for the topics at hand.

In this first volume of *Wisdom for a Life of Freedom* we shall explore the basic yet essential principles that will make the content of the volumes to follow easier to grasp and assimilate. It is here we do the groundwork, preparing the fertile soils within for growing the seeds that are already contained there. A large part of the groundwork in any garden—if I may continue with that metaphor—is about uprooting and coming to understand the things already growing in these soils that no longer directly support the purpose we have for this patch of earth as defined by our intention as gardeners. They do, of course, indirectly support our purpose insofar as it is through the uprooting, composting, and eventual reintegration of our assumed knowledge that we become aware of what we really do and don't know—thus gaining a feeling for the unlimited potential in the field of the *unknown* and a feeling for what is presently on the verge of bursting forth from the unknown into that patch of dirt called the known.

In *The Seven Empowerments* (the second volume) we shall look at seven essential perspectives and the principles associated with them, which will, when incorporated into your approach to Life, lead to true empowerment and liberation. These seven empowerments will surely help you—just as they have helped me—in turning every event, situation, relationship, and person in your world into a source of empowerment, into a deeper experience of love, and into that which is truly life-giving.

The third volume, *Empowering Relationship*, will address all of the above from within the context and sacredness of relationship. Relationship, in all its many forms, is an unavoidable element of life and the world in which we experience that life. It is in our relationships—and the state of relatedness we maintain within ourselves when we approach or avoid those relationships—where are to be found some of our greatest gifts of power.

Further information on the fourth volume was not available at the time of printing this title.[1]

A Path of Freedom

Here is perhaps the most important part of my introduction to you, for it is here that this book and the series of books being published hereafter are put into context with regard to their purpose and intent. It is here I shall endeavour to introduce the subject matter pertaining to *a Life of Freedom*. I say *endeavour* for the simple fact that it's not something I feel can truly be put into words. Of course that won't stop me from having a go at it! But first I must clarify the following point. Because every *step* we take and every choice we make in our lives

---

1   You can visit my web site and easily join my online "Updates" mail list if you want to receive updates on Vol. 4 and other news. Please refer to the appendix.

establish a path of one kind or another, I shall primarily refer to this subject matter as a *Path of Freedom*. Life simply *Is*, yet as our awareness and subsequent attention move through life in its linear fashion—at least whilst we experience ourselves as human beings—we create and walk what may be defined in the simplest term as a *path*. To ensure the impeccability of the path we are each creating, there is only one pertinent question to ask ourselves in any given moment, namely: "Is this a path with Heart?"

A Path of Freedom has consistently been sought out, explored, mapped, defined, and lived by a relatively small number of people throughout human history—to my knowledge, dating back at least 30,000 to 40,000 years. First and foremost it is a Path with Heart, the Heart being that all-inclusive capacity centered within Man and Woman—within each and every human being. "Inclusive toward what?" one might ask. The answer is simple, and yet profound. Inclusivity toward all Life—as One Life—both the manifest (form side) and the non-manifest (formless) side of Life. It is the Heart that enables us to incorporate the unknown into the known, and only through our utilisation of this capacity do we fulfil our purpose in the evolution of Awareness.

The Path of Freedom is in many regards unique to each individual human being, for it is a path made up of the steps we take and the choices we make in response to our unique challenges in life, and more precisely our own unique ways of facing those challenges. Do I face each challenge in a way that sets me free—in a way that accurately reflects and portrays my true nature as a Divine and free Being—or in a way that propels me deeper into bondage with something that is not real?

A Path of Freedom does not require belief, dogma, fanaticism, or an external authority figure for you to walk and live it. Each of these things may have its place, in time, yet only insofar as it plays its part in enabling you to awaken from an unconscious sleep into the realisation of your own Divine sovereignty. Far from requiring lofty beliefs and fanatical one-sided ideologies, a Path of Freedom calls on those who walk it to make a fresh choice, moment to moment, in what action best serves the fulfilment of their purpose and the wellbeing of the totality to which they are a part.

Inherent to a Path of Freedom is deep unfailing recognition that there is only One Life, and all Life is therefore completely and absolutely interconnected, interrelated, and interdependent. This is a Path that calls for all human beings to stand up and learn to think for themselves, to ask questions about everything, to make assumptions about nothing, and to remain inclusive not only toward all things, but also toward the Unnamable, Indefinable, and Unknowable aspect of Life permeating and animating the totality. Call It Infinity. Call It the Great Eagle. Call It God. Call It Brahman. Call it Great Spirit. Call It the Tao. Call It by any name you like, just so long as you are clear that "I (the one walking this path) humanly have no idea what It actually is."

I observe and wish to acknowledge that many religions—and more especially the mystical traditions within those religions—have at their core a seed of a Path of Freedom. I don't know, however, of any religion that has not at some point been hijacked and distorted by the institutions that inevitably arise around those adhering to such paths. Thusly, what so often started out as a seed of Freedom is eventually cultivated and hybridised in the mind of Man and Woman into something that bears intoxicating fruit. When eaten, this fruit blinds us to who and what we truly are and leaves us in a drunken stupor doing our best to navigate our way through the resulting pain and suffering.

A Path of Freedom is a path made up not of beliefs, but of principles and perspectives that each person can recognise as true for him or herself. If such recognition does not take place in one area—with regard to some particular principle or another—one on this path is free to put his attention to where it both makes sense and proves itself to be of practical benefit for himself and for all his relations. It is, therefore, a path based on the recognition that we each have within us all that we require to wake up and to live in service to Life itself.

Those attached to and identified with the many manifestations of separation in this world—be they religious beliefs, cultural beliefs, political factions, or spiritual beliefs—may at first find true comprehension of a Path of Freedom and its ramifications quite formidable and perhaps entirely unimaginable. Just as Johann Wolfgang von Goethe[2]

---

2 Johann Wolfgang von Goethe (1749-1832) – A German poet, dramatist, novelist, and scientist who embraced many fields of human endeavour including an interest in mysticism and alchemy, who is by many considered to be the greatest of all German poets. It is also said that of all modern men of genius, Goethe is the most universal.

said, "Few people have the imagination for reality." Fortunately for us all, imagination is a capability every one of us has to some degree, great or small, and like all capabilities, it can be strengthened, developed, and mastered.

As you read this book and as you explore the life you are living, dare to have an open mind. Dare to have a wild and fanciful imagination. Dare to step completely out of any boxes you might find yourself within. Dare to let go of the chains you might one day notice around your ankles. Dare to be yourself.

Dare to be free.

> *"One must know that one is ignorant before one can begin to know."*
>
> Sri Aurobindo
> *A Practical Guide to Integral Yoga*

Your Journey Here

I can only imagine the journey that has led you to where you are right now, here, holding this book, reading these words. Within my imaginings I envision someone who knows or at the very least has an un-ignorable suspicion that there is more to life than what society led you to believe. I imagine you've seen and heard enough to know that this human world is full of contradictions and you may have even noticed the consistent hypocrisy evident in almost every human endeavour you have cared to explore. I imagine you feel either cursed or blessed by a gnawing feeling inside that you somehow have to break free. From what exactly, you may not be entirely sure.

In my imagination, I picture you, the reader, as someone with a deep heartfelt compassion for life and other beings. I imagine you are someone who cares and loves and dreams, yet you also may be someone who hurts and hides in one way or another from small personal nightmares that just don't seem to go away. You may have also discovered that it is this hurting that faithfully propels you toward wholeness, and your hiding that propels you toward greatness—toward dreaming and living a life that is true to who and what you are, deep down inside now, in that place only you know and feel.

I imagine your journey here has been long, challenging, and at times arduous, and yet most certainly not without many moments of great joy, excitement, and optimism. I imagine your journey, and mine, have had much in common, and you and I share more similarities than we might ever humanly recognise. It is this, I imagine, that is playing out through the crossing and intertwining of our paths here within this book, within the pages now in your hands, and within the intention that has brought these words into being.

I also imagine you to be someone with an open mind and a receptive heart, and it is largely this receptivity that has led you here today, moved you to pick up this book from where it was previously situated, and inspired your choice to be reading and comprehending these very words right now.

Before we move on to the pages that follow, I wonder what answer will arise within your heart and mind in response to asking yourself the following pertinent question:

"On my own path of Freedom, in my own life at this time, what is the most life-affirming step I could take right now?"

*"My story is not a pleasant one;
it is neither sweet nor harmonious, as invented stories are; it has the taste of nonsense and chaos, of madness and dreams—like the lives of all men who stop deceiving themselves."*

Hermann Hesse
from his novel, Demian

PART ONE

ESTABLISHING A COMMON PERSPECTIVE

establish, *verb*
1. Set up or lay the groundwork for
2. Use as a basis for
3. To cause to be recognised and accepted

common, *adjective*
1. Belonging to or shared by two or more parties

perspective, *noun*
1. A way of regarding situations or topics etc.

Chapter One

I AM THE DREAMER OF A DREAM

> *"Have you ever had a dream...that you were so sure was real? What if you were unable to wake from that dream? How would you know the difference between the dream world and the real world?"*
>
> Morpheus, in The Matrix (movie)

You and I, we are but dreamers of a dream....

Imagine this...if you will.

You lie down to rest one night and you slip into a vivid and realistic dream, a dream so absorbing and so engaging to your senses that you entirely forget it's all just a dream. Just as Morpheus pointed out to Neo in the movie The Matrix, you may have experienced the occasional dream like this, whereby when you awaken it takes some minutes, or even much of the day, for the realisation to sink into your feeling world that this was in fact all just a dream.

I ask you to consider an important though perhaps unusual question that is seldom asked, for the answer is one most people make a massive life-long assumption on.

Are you absolutely certain you woke up this morning—that you are not still just dreaming? If your answer is "yes," on what basis do you derive such certainty? Ask yourself this, and really feel, now, into the answer—both in the mind and in the heart. *How do you know you are not dreaming? Further to this, what if the "you" you think I am referring to—the* one reading this book—*is actually within the dream of another higher aspect of you? Can you be certain you are not within a dream right now? What if all your living memory is derived solely from that dream, and therefore you have no objective point of reference to say whether this is a dream or not?*

What if you did wake up this morning and yet the physical world you perceive is actually also a dream? Suppose the real You—your essential Self—is dreaming up all of this in some kind of vast and ineffable Mind that you are perhaps entirely unaware of—whilst your attention is completely fixated on that very same dream as real?

To the rational mind these questions may seem odd or even pointless, yet there are various cultures and spiritual traditions that perceive exactly this—that the world is simply a dream, that our nocturnal dreams are closer to reality than our waking world, and we are dreaming everything we experience. Even today's theories of quantum physics—heading toward becoming the most contemporary form of metaphysical and spiritual inquiry—suggest that the whole phenomenon known as *the universe* and often times referred to as *Creation* is, as far as scientific inquiry can determine, something akin to a thought arising within a vast Mind.

In the words of Max Planck (Nobel Prize-winning Father of Quantum Theory);

"All matter originates and exists only by virtue of a force...We must assume behind this force the existence of a conscious and intelligent Mind. This Mind is the matrix of all matter."

ILLUSION

There are many cultures and spiritual traditions that have referred to this world as *Maya* or *illusion*. I've met quite a few people who upon hearing "the world is an illusion" react rather strongly because they think what is implied is that *the world does not exist* or that the world they experience is being invalidated or denied its place in the cosmic scheme of things. There is the misguided notion that to call the world an illusion is to say it is nothing, that it does not exist. Quite obviously, it is some*thing*; otherwise we would not be able to perceive it. In my experience, this is not what is meant by describing the world as an *illusion*. I have found various definitions for the word "illusion" in the dictionary. Let's take a look at a few of them:

- An erroneous perception of reality
- An erroneous concept or belief
- An erroneous mental representation
- Perception of something objectively existing in such a way as to cause misinterpretation of its actual nature

In the statement "the world is an illusion," the emphasis is not on describing the nature of the objective world itself, but rather is shedding light on the nature of our subjective perception of the world. The world is as it is—yet our perception of the world is, according to some, erroneous and misconceived. The way you perceive *things* to be differs from how they actually are.

> *"Reality is merely an illusion, albeit a persistent one."*
>
> Albert Einstein

Let's take a look at this word *illusion* from another angle. The root of the word *illusion* goes back to the Latin word illudere, which literally means "to play with," or "at play." From this root word was also derived the classic Latin word *illusionem*, which referred to "a mocking, jesting, irony." That every*thing* is an illusion implies to me the understanding that it's all a Divine play, both in the theatrical sense and in the sense of playfulness. So as you can see, when we get to the root of the word "illusion," it implicates not only our subjective experience of reality, as suggested by me above, but also the adjective nature of reality—it is literally an ironic play, dance, or—as we will explore soon—a story.

I first started seriously pondering the nature of reality in my early teen years (though I did so in a more passive way even when I was a young child). Since that time, I have been referring to the world as "a *dream*." I diverged for a while and referred to it as "an illusion," yet I have since realised that describing it as "a *dream*" is more accurate and meaningful. We all understand, in one way or another, what it means to dream whilst asleep in bed, yet many of us don't have an intrinsic feeling for what it means to bear witness to an illusion. So, to make use of this inherent comprehension we have of what it means to *dream*, I will use this term to describe reality as it is perceived by most people.

Perhaps the children's nursery rhyme started me thinking along these lines—"Row, row, row your boat, gently down the stream. Merrily, merrily, merrily, merrily, life is but a dream." Perhaps it was something else. What I can say is that the Path of Freedom within me is one I have been exploring for as *far* and as *long* back as I have been able to remember—which extends beyond the memory of what most people would refer to as "this lifetime."

LIFE IS BUT A DREAM

"We are such stuff as dreams are made on, and our little life is rounded with a sleep."

William Shakespeare
From The Tempest

So, what is the *dream* I am referring to?

Well, you're actually looking right at it. These words, this book, your hands, the room around you—everything around you is all a part of the *dream*, including your sense of who and what "you" are. The *"you"* that you think I am referring to is also the *dream*. Perhaps it is necessary for me to elaborate.

Simply put, "the *dream*"—or Maya as it was referred to in various Eastern spiritual traditions—is everything you perceive through the five senses (or six senses, if you use that many).

The above definitions of the word *illusion* do a fairly good job of describing the situation at hand. Most of us think the world is "real," solid and permanent, and is the product of physical forces interacting with physical "stuff." Yet this is not how it is. My spiritual ancestors knew this. I also know this. Various mystics, Yogis, and native cultures also know, or knew, this. Yet our five senses tell us otherwise. Our five senses present us with an illusion—an erroneous perception of reality.

The reason our perception of reality is erroneous is simple. Ancient mysticism and modern psychology both recognise that everything we perceive is nothing more than a construct within the human brain.

The brain receives electrical impulses from the sensory faculties of the body—the eyes, ears, skin, and so forth—and then constructs an *internal* image or re-presentation of the world *out there*. Each human being has his own particular and oftentimes peculiar way of constructing this internal re-presentation of the world *out there*. Each person's internal re-presentation is molded by his particular biased view on life—by his beliefs, by what I refer to as his personal Lore (his truth regarding *the way things are*)[1].

There is a deeper reality at play here, which the above description of perception does not take into account, namely that this whole process is taking place the other way around. What I described in the last paragraph is a one-way process of stimuli from the world reaching the human senses, being converted into electrical impulses, and triggering the human brain to construct a re-presentation of the world. The deep mystery at play here is that this all occurs the other way around— completely back-to-front from what we are led (by our senses) to believe. The world *out there*, including the body and the brain, is in fact a projection from the profundity of our Being, which creates the apparition of a material universe with the Mind—a Mind that is independent of the human form. If that has fried your noodle it's okay; one is not to worry—we'll explore this topic in more detail in just a moment.

In this moment, before you move on, I invite you to reread the last few paragraphs. Skip back up to the definition of "illusion." Yet this time read it more slowly. Allow the words to sink in a little, and to open you to *feeling* the meaning of the statement "the world is an illusion." Give some time and space to consider just what it is you have read, and its implications. Consider this question, "What if I am dreaming right now? What implications would that have on this moment, on my life, on me, and on who and what I perceive myself to be?"—and *who* exactly is this "*I*" we are referring to?

That then was the simple explanation. It says it all, yet the nature of the average human ego is such that by now you have probably had a lot of thoughts and feelings thrown up into your perception that are trying to make sense of just what the implication of the above statements really amounts to. So, here's some further explanation for those who want it or believe they require it in order to get a clear feeling of

---

1   Personal Lore is a topic we will be exploring in Chapter Five

what I have just explained.

It is possible, even likely, that one will find it difficult to understand the nature of reality as a dream through simply reading these words. Truly understanding the illusionary nature of so-called "reality" must be experienced. That experience may first come as a concept, a vision, a revelation, or inspiration. As that perception works its way down into your body, it starts to come across as a feeling—one that very often contradicts what your rational mind, and senses, are telling you. Essentially the Truth can be authentically realised only when it is unveiled within you. For some my words may simply support the early steps toward that unveiling. Through this book I intend to impart knowledge and wisdom that will also assist you in the journey to seeing through the illusion.

Words and language are a phenomena arising within the *dream* and therefore can never be used to define accurately that which is *Real*. They are a symbolic re-presentaion of what we perceive and therefore can only at best point *toward* the perception of what is real. Communication (the act of communing or coming together as one) does not take place at the level of language and words. Our oneness and unity are already present—already a fact, behind the veil of our human perception. When employed to impart wisdom about Truth, words will always obstruct a clear experience of the realities they might vainly attempt to explain. Therefore, it is important not to take my words at face value. Read into them, feel into them, read between the lines, and use your instinct and your intuition. Let the words be nothing more than pointers with which to guide and direct your Awareness and feelings. Taking my words at face value is likely to create further illusion within your mind—enmeshed in ever-deeper veils as you walk down an interesting yet confusing hall of mirrors.

"You create your own universe as you go along. The stronger your imagination, the more variegated your universe. When you leave off dreaming, the universe ceases to exist."

Winston Churchill
Known chiefly for his leadership of Great Britain during World War II, he was Prime Minister of the United Kingdom from 1940 to 1945 and again from 1951 to 1955

THE PROJECTOR AND
THE LIGHT THAT SHINES THROUGH

As mentioned above, as far as I have been able to ascertain, the world we appear to live in is a projection from within a deep level of our collective "mind." The greater totality of manifest creation has been Dreamed up within what I will be referring to as *Mind*[2] or Infinite Mind within this book. The universe is a projection from within this Infinite Mind. The best way I can describe the tangible universe as we know it is as something the Ego has *dreamt up*. That which I AM is the Creation of God[3] — an extension of God, created by God. God created that I AM in His — or "Her" if that works better for you, but for simplicity I will use either — likeness. Hence the Creation of God has the same power to create that God has. They are in essence one and the same, except that one is the source AND the creation — the totality — and the other extends out from that source. One analogy I have come across that I feel accurately illustrates this point is that you and I are like waves on an ocean. God is the entire ocean, which includes the waves. Our apparent individuality is a wave, yet a wave is not separate from the ocean. It rises or extends up from the surface of the ocean and in that moment appears to gain individual definition. It then falls away back into the ocean and whatever individualisation it appeared to have is gone. Just as a flower extends or blossoms out from a plant. You can

---

2   With the use of Mind (with a capital M) I am not referring to the normal human thinking mind that most people associate this word with and typically identify with. I am referring to something much vaster than this, which will be made clear as we progress through this book.

3   God: Hmm.... Yep, the G-word — and here we have the first of many appearances of *God* within this book, and on that note I wish to make a quick aside to explain a few things. For many this word brings with it a great deal of baggage, stigma, and beliefs, and possibly disdain or rejection. For some it may even illicit repulsion, anger, and fear. Others may feel deep love, devotion, and gratitude. Whatever your story about the word "God" is, and what it may represent for you, I hereby invite you to gently gather up these views and place them somewhere to one side. Not forever — just whilst reading this book. Throughout this book you will discover more about how I define this rather nebular and ineffable *concept* called *God*. You'll notice too that I also refer to it as "The Absolute," "All-That-Is," "Infinity," and numerous other names. *God*, in my experience, is not at all like anything I hear described in any organised religion. God is not separate from you and me but is the infinite, universal, eternal totality of every*thing* and no*thing*. On that note, let's get back to the topic at hand.

say that the plant is the totality, including the flower that it has created. Yet the flower on its own (let's assume it's still attached to the plant) is not the total plant. It is something extending out from the plant. At the level of DNA, one cell in the flower has all the information within it to recreate the entire plant.

Somewhere in the scheme of things, Ego[4] created the illusion of separation from God. Separation from the Totality is not possible, and yet it is the most significant lie that creation—seen through the eyes of the ego-mind—is based upon. The illusion of separation can be brought about only by an act of perception similar to what people call *dreaming*. Ego, through a process of projection, brought about the apparent creation of the world, the human self, and its ego-mind (which is what most people identify as "me" or "I"), and this in turn created the apparent reality of separation from God—from the subtle realms right through to the physical plane of existence.

As mentioned, this all occurred in a way that is metaphorically similar to how you and I construct experiential realities in our dreams at night. The reason it is not possible to create actual separation from God is that this would go against what Is—namely God I Am. Which is to say that I AM an extension of God and hence at One with The Creator. The only way "I" can create something that contradicts this Truth is to dream it up. There is nothing wrong with doing that. It was and still is (here in our time and space) an act of creation. So, whilst the *dream* may seem very real and tangible to our human senses, it does not change *That* which *I Am*. The *Dreamer* is unchanged by the dream—except that the *Dreamer*'s awareness shifts and expands in accordance with that which is being dreamed, which in turn unfolds in accordance with a force called *intent*[5].

I wish to make it quite clear that, contrary to what many religions and dogmas would like humanity to believe, you and I have not "fallen from heaven" and lost our way, and we do not require saving or rescuing. The Ego dreaming the experience of duality, multiplicity, and separation is not some kind of cosmic error or glitch in "God's great

---

4 In the succeeding chapters we will be taking a fairly detailed look at the ego and Ego, and what I am referring to with my utilisation of these terms. It will soon become clear that in many ways my perspectives on the ego/Ego differ greatly from the prevailing thoughts on this topic.

5 We will take an in-depth look at the nature of *intent* in a later chapter.

plan." There are no mistakes, and everything we experience plays an important part in the evolution of awareness. Humanity is the living expression of the *unknowable* fluxing into the *unknown*, which in turn is incorporated into the *known*.

AN ISSUE OF MISTAKEN IDENTITY

The human experience of the ego is the product or the sum total of our mistaken identity. It is neither "good" nor "bad"; there is nothing inherently "wrong" with the ego. It simply is what it is. So long as this world has meaning and value for you then I would suggest that the ego has purpose and should be given its due consideration, or at least not be ignored or squashed. As you know, you require your physical body to be here in the physical plane of existence. It serves a purpose and it is neutral in this service, in that the body simply is as it is. Your body requires food and to deny this requirement is denying the body its due considerations. This denial would cause it to get weak, diseased, and eventually to pass away. In this way so too does the ego have a purpose and a function, and its own due considerations.

The ego is part of the vehicle that got you into this dream and hence it is also part of the vehicle that will get you out, one way or another. I do not mean to imply that your ego will co-operate in your *escape*, but rather that by your using it intelligently—by infusing it with Awareness—you will use it to unravel its false world until you again find yourself in a face-to-face confrontation with That which is Real. A wounded ego (which is what most people have inherited from their culture) remains wounded whether you deny it or not. Walking a Path of Freedom, "I"—as the Warrior—cannot afford the luxury of holding onto wounds and grievances. Wounded warriors are not fit to face the challenge of battle, and even less so the challenge of recognising their own Divinity. A wounded ego all too often leads to a deflated state of self-pity and/or inflated self-importance.

The challenge most people presently face within their ego is a challenge of mistaken identity. That is all. To make it anything more or anything less is to perpetuate that issue (getting entangled in further lies) and prolong your journey of Dreaming without the lucidity of Awareness necessary to wake-up to reality and unveil the Truth within you. Before such an awakening takes place, the ego will be experienced in a very limited form. After such an awakening one discovers that his prior experience of the ego was simply an immature and partial perception of the cosmic "I" deep within Creation itself.

This universe has been dreamed up by the Dreamer within us. Our perception of the universe—which for us primarily concerns our immediate reality—is filtered and colored by our human ego. Yes, reality as we know it is a vast and grand illusion—a Divine dance playing on our Mind. I am still experientially working my way through this *dream* and until I do that is about all I can say on the matter.

"What is God? In a way, there is no God. Our perception of God usually leads to a misunderstanding that seriously undermines our spiritual development. God is not what we think It is. God is not a thing, a being, a noun. It does not exist, as existence is defined, for It takes up no space and is not bound by time. Jewish mystics often refer to It as Ein Sof, which means Endlessness."

Rabbi David A. Cooper
from his book, God Is A Verb

THE LIGHT OF GOD IS IN ALL THINGS

Something I find rather beautiful about the *dream* is that it requires the Light of to illuminate it. I will use a metaphor that might explain this in a clearer way. In this metaphor please feel free to substitute my use of the word *God* with any word that for you best represents the Supreme Source or Infinity.

I would like you to imagine a film projector. God created the projector. The projector is the Mind of You and I as the One and only "Son/Daughter of God"—that which extended out from God[6]. We are That

---

6   Another aside…. Okay, so now I am using not only the word God, but also a number of symbols most of us recognise as "Judaic" and "Christian." I wish to point out that for the purpose of illustrating some of the points I am making, there are times when I will utilise language and symbols that may come across as fairly traditional Judeo-Christian terminology. I am not a Christian, yet I find it helpful to borrow words from these bodies of thought from time to time to convey key understandings to you. I am aware that for some people "it gets right up their nose" to see this sort of language, or at least makes them pull back, because in many people's experience, Christianity (and perhaps every commonly known

which God created, through a process of extension. The film running through the projector is the story of the Ego—the Cosmic "I" on all its many levels of manifestation from the source through to the basic human ego experience by the average person. Don't ask me how in God's name—no pun intended—it got there, but I will share that with you when it is experientially revealed to me. For now I don't think it matters. The image on the screen—the screen of your Mind—is everything you can perceive, everything you do perceive, and everything you will perceive. Whether that be all the details of normal daily human existence or more unusual things like UFO's, spiritual entities and dimension, people channelling all sorts of spiritual information, heaven and hell, other dimensions and planes of existence, time and space...you name it, it's all a projection on the *screen* of your *Mind*.

Now, the significant point illustrated by this metaphor of the projector is that there has to be a source of light. The film itself has no light and has no power and cannot produce any image. Contained within the film are the many stories that make up your *dream*. It is the Light that passes through the projector that is then qualified by the multitude of vibrations (colors) on the cellulose film, which then produces the appearance of various moving images on the screen (within your Mind).

Awareness, which is an extension of God, is the Light necessary for this projector to function. It is also what ultimately perceives the images in your Mind, although you will not know this until you've stopped identifying with the ego-mind (the central character in the filmstrip) and started again identifying with the projector, and ultimately with God—the Creator of the projector.

So why do I say this is significant?

I say it is significant because it means that no matter what you are

---

religion) has given God and Spirituality a rather poor reputation. If you are one of those "quit all this Judeo-Christian crap" people, then please consider trying to get past it and realise that what you are reading has nothing to do with any religion, nor does it have anything to do with previous experiences and memories through which you may be filtering this material. I am simply using a relatively familiar set of symbols (in a fairly loose sort of way) to convey a message in my communication with you. I invite you to see the symbols for what they represent as opposed to any preconceptions your mind may bring to your experience of these symbols. This is an act that will help set you free and reclaim your Mastery over the Dream.

seeing in terms of the *dream*, it is always infused by the Light of God. Do you get what I mean? The image on the screen of your Mind is everything you have ever perceived in your life, and that image has been made possible because there is a source of Light going through a "filmstrip"—your ego consciousness—and projecting out onto the "screen."

It is also significant because no matter what that Light shines through on the film—no matter how the ego qualifies it—it is not affected by it. The source of the Light remains untouched, luminous, radiant, and just as it was originally created. When you go to the cinema and watch a movie, what you see on the screen is not influenced by the film they were showing the week before, or by the hundreds (possibly thousands) of films the cinema may have previously shown with that projector. If the projectionist were to remove the film, unqualified white light would appear on the screen, even after having run millions of images through that projector in the past.

This illustrates that if the *dream* is perceived in a particular way—one that is in accordance with Reality—it is possible to use the *dream* to untangle yourself and set your Mind free from it all. It is possible to disfranchise the ego-mind by dissolving the images (the stories) on the film. Alternatively, one can leave a film running through the projector but doing so without identifying with the resulting picture. In this way one can be fully present with it and watch the film with total Awareness.

I am not encouraging a vain attempt to "escape" the apparent realities of Life here in the *dream*, but rather to attain some degree of conscious mastery within it. The mastery I am referring to is that of consciously aligning your self with the *purpose* and *intention* of the *dreamer*. In the ancient Toltec tradition this has been referred to as being a *Dream Master*. In numerous other traditions it has been called Enlightenment, Moksha, Liberation, Salvation, Christ Consciousness, Buddhahood, and Spiritual Freedom. I do not wish to imply that each of the traditions defining and seeking these states of being would consider them all to be identical in nature—rather that there is an essential element to them all that is the same throughout. Spiritual freedom goes by many names, and there are many paths one can walk (or fly!) to get there.

Approaching the *dream* in the particular way I am describing will also result in the living discovery that every*thing* you see around you is profoundly symbolic of Truth and Love—or put another way, is symbolic of That which is shining through the filmstrip. The whole shebang we call "life on earth" is an incredible metaphor for Love. Freedom, happiness, even bliss, is an inherent quality of who and what you are. This, of course, includes the freedom to experience limitation, pain, and suffering. What will you choose right now?

It is accurate to say it is possible to "see the gap between one frame of the *dream* and the next"—like the small blank strip of cellulose between each frame on a film roll. When our attention is given to that gap, one sees/experiences the pure Light of God...the Pure Light of That which I AM. With appropriate discipline and *intention* you will be able to focus your attention on the Light within your Awareness and follow it back out of the *dream*. Again, not as some kind of elaborate escape, but rather that you may then spend your remaining *time* within the *dream* consciously creating that which is beautiful, exquisite, joyful, loving—that which most accurately reflects your true nature as a Divine Being. One way or another you play your part in the evolution of Awareness, so why not do so peacefully as opposed to painfully? I am sure you haven't failed to notice that presently the human collective still struggles to find a way to exist that isn't highly destructive and life-taking. Yet you, right now, contain what is necessary to create *heaven on Earth*.

THE WARRIOR AS AN ARCHETYPE

> *"The real accomplishment in life is the art of being a warrior, which is the only way to balance the terror of being a [hu]man with the wonder of being a [hu]man."*
>
> Carlos Castaneda

Throughout this book and much of my other writing, you will see reference to the archetype of the *warrior*. I am aware that my use of this term is not without some personal hesitation. My hesitancy is essentially because I feel this is an archetype some people may misunderstand within the context of this writing—namely the exploration of *The Path of Freedom*. I wish to ensure we have a common understanding and appreciation of why I choose to use this archetype and from what perspectives I do so. My use of this archetype is nothing unique, for many paths have referred to it before now. As far as I know, the controversial work of Carlos Castaneda was what really put this archetype into public awareness concerning the Path of Freedom. We shall now look at what the *warrior* represents when referred to here in *Peace, Power, and Presence* and my work in general.

The *warrior* recognises that the human being is a cosmic *being* representing a great mystery, with as of yet unrealised levels of *power* and potential that are unimaginable to the average person. It is the re-cognition of this untapped and unfathomable potential, and the decision (by way of an impulse of *intention* from the *dreamer*) to act on this cognition, that distinguishes the *warrior* from the non-warrior. The archetype of the *warrior* is indicative of a person's approach to *life* as opposed to being a definition of what that person is. Here in this world, as man or woman, we are all human. Yet as humans, we can approach the mystery we call *life* in myriad ways. In his folly, the average person approaches life as if it were not a mystery at all. Such a person easily ends up losing power in the assumption that they understand what is going on, when in fact they do not. To truly understand something we must first allegorically *stand under* it. For you see, I cannot understand that which I feel I am above, superior to, or better than. Only in humility—in this case that humility of accepting my state of not-knowing—can I kneel down and get beneath what I wish to understand. Once down in that place I may stand up with the object of my understanding resting on my shoulders. If I have the necessary power in that moment—which requires having the necessary capacity or flexibility of perception—I will in fact manage to stand up. In doing so, I elevate what I wish to understand to a *place* in my world where I have the clarity of mind and heart to truly see it for what it is—eye-to-eye, so to speak. This is what it truly means to *appreciate* something.

The approach of the warrior is unique especially in the way he strives for *freedom* above all else. Obviously an ongoing challenge for the warrior is to define what freedom actually means for him at this stage in his journey. As the warrior's awareness deepens and evolves, her definition of freedom may deepen and evolve. This does not make the prior definition wrong or invalid. It simply means that the warrior's perception has altered, affording her more power, and thus affording her greater clarity and inclusivity within her awareness.

The Warrior's approach to *Life* is not better than or superior to other approaches one may take, for every approach will ultimately lead to the unveiling of our true nature, our freedom, and the fulfillment of our purpose, the one purpose of *Life*. From one perspective—that of an average person—approaching Life through the archetype of the warrior appears to be a choice, and an oftentimes-idealised choice at that. Yet anyone truly walking this path will soon discover that your predilection for the Warrior's approach is some*thing* that is mysteriously *choosing the person* on such a path. Not the other way around.

The warrior is not interested in ego-satisfaction—except perhaps to experience and observe it for greater understanding of herself and her fellow man. Nor is she interested in doing battle with the ego by way of ego-denial and suppression, for she knows all too well (from personal experience) that the ego as experienced through the common limitations of human perception is a figment of the *dream*, existing only in her imagination, and that the ego can be used to her advantage in the battle for *power*. The human ego is recognised by the warrior as having its own unique purpose, one that will only be fulfilled when it is embraced and allowed to blossom like everything else. That blossom will bear fruit, and that fruit will bear a seed. This seed has a purpose like everything else. This seed is a seed born from the Cosmic "I," the "I" of Infinity. We will explore the specifics of that later in this book and even more fully in Volume IV.

A significant point I wish to make clear concerns gender and the archetype of the *warrior*. Many people, I am sure, would tend to say that the *warrior* is a male archetype and would therefore question the applicability of this archetype to women reading this book and my work. My response to this is that the *warrior* is a **masculine** archetype rather than a purely **male** one. Both man and woman embody and function within the two gender polarities of awareness, namely masculine and feminine awareness. Every man and woman is an expression of these two polarities of awareness within themselves on the Path of Freedom.

A woman is the embodiment of the feminine principle whilst a man is the embodiment of the masculine—yet like all apparent polarities and dualities within this world, we are only ever dealing with points along a relative scale, as opposed to forces that are distinct, separate, and in opposition to each other. A woman therefore embodies a quality of awareness that is more feminine relative to that which a man embodies, and vice versa, but neither of these polarities is mutually exclusive. The approach of the *warrior* serves the masculine within women just as much as it serves the masculine within men. I trust this point is clear. We will explore this more fully in Volume III.

THE WARRIOR'S CHALLENGE

"The basic difference between an ordinary person and a warrior is that a warrior takes everything as a challenge while an ordinary person takes everything as a blessing or a curse."

Carlos Castaneda

The *warrior* approaches life, the world, everything in her *known,* as well as everything stirring within the *unknown,* as a challenge.

A challenge by and for what?

A challenge by and for *Power.*

The *warrior* knows that every*thing* she experiences is exactly what her *Dreamer* intended for the purpose of awakening within the *dream* — to *dream* lucidly or with fully en-light-ened and all-inclusive awareness. The *warrior's* challenge therefore is seldom if ever about trying to make life turn out a certain way or conform to certain wishes and desires. Rather it is about being present to the way *life* manifests itself from moment to moment and to the consequence of the various choices available to her in any given moment. The choices that will appear to be available to the warrior in any given moment are influenced primarily by the *power* she embodies in that moment, which is directly determined by her perception.

The *warrior's* challenge is the challenge from Infinity to reconcile the paradox of being the totality of all-things and no-thing, whilst also simply *being*—*being* human, *being* in the world, *being* confined to the limits of perception, or (in the author's case) being "Jonathan Evatt."

Essentially, it is this challenge we shall explore from many different angles through the course of this book and the books to follow — oftentimes even from angles that at first seem to contradict each other.

The Dreamer's Purpose

Whilst it is not my intention to go into an in-depth description of the meaning and purpose of *Life*, I feel it will be of value to touch on this briefly. Before doing so I wish to qualify what I mean with my use of the word *Life*. *Life* is often mistaken for being the stuff of this world, the happenings, and events in our daily affairs. I recognise, however, that that is an expression of *Life*, and Life itself all the while remains a mystery to most people—a mystery deeply hidden behind the veil of "stuff" that we see dancing before our mind through our faculties of perception.

I see *Life* as the profound and incomprehensible affair of Infinity dancing with itself through the vast array of manifestations we typically refer to as "life." *Life* is not something we can ever really come to know whilst our attention is firmly fixated on the manifestations of *life* (an unavoidable consequence of being bound by human perception) yet it is something we can each come to appreciate with our intuition and with our feelings.

In the simplest terms, the purpose of *life* and therefore the purpose of the *Dreamer*—as an extension of *life*—is the expansion and evolution of awareness. I am sure that to some people this proposition will sound like a rather dull affair, if read at face value. Remember, words are limited at best and have no capacity to convey the truth of something in their own right. Words rely greatly on the recipient to actively explore what they illuminate or point to within their own feeling world. Those who have experienced within themselves the nature and significance of awareness will feel the true and deeper implications of this.

Emanating through the *Dreamer* to you—the *dreamed*—is a force that is known as intention. We will explore the nature of intention later in this work.

✦ ✦ ✦

I invite you to pause, take some conscious breaths. This is your story you are reading. At the end of the proverbial day, everything you are reading here within my story means something to you only to the degree that you can find some point of reference and/or re-cognition within your own story—consciously or unconsciously. So, give yourself the space to feel it and re-view it objectively—as it is and without your own commentary. How do you feel? Does what you have read seem to make sense somewhere inside you? Is what you have read so far in alignment with your own feelings about life—when you put aside all that you have learned and all that has been conditioned into you? Do you feel a sense of "Aha…oh yes, this is what I have somehow known all along"?

The fact that you are reading this book, that it has come to be here now in your hands—in your *dream*—suggests to me that what is contained within these pages is not entirely unfamiliar to you. Somewhere within your interiority, you already know these things. Perhaps you have already noticed that. Perhaps you are just noticing it now. It is possible that as you open these words you will start to notice it, now.

"It is because we don't know Who we are, because we are unaware that the Kingdom of Heaven is within us, that we behave in the generally silly, the often insane, the sometimes criminal ways that are so characteristically human. We are saved, we are liberated and enlightened, by perceiving the hitherto unperceived good that is already within us, by returning to our eternal Ground and remaining where, without knowing it, we have always been."

Aldus Huxley (1894-1963)
The Perennial Philosophy

Empowering Principles & Perspectives

- Words and language ultimately obscure Reality. Read them with Awareness and use your feelings to guide you to what is real behind the words.
- You, your essential Self, are the dreamer of a dream.
- You can dream of hell on Earth, and you can dream of Heaven on Earth.
- It's a choice—an act of Self definition.
- Everything you perceive within the dream is an illusion—an erroneous perception of Reality. No*thing* is how it appears to be.
- The ego and the ego-mind as ordinary man relates to it is an issue of mistaken identity. It has no power. Don't get caught up feeding it or fighting it. It has a purpose.
- Everything in the dream is illuminated (given Life) by the Light of God, the Source. That Light is not influenced by the images in the dream.
- You contain the seed that will blossom into the creation of Heaven on Earth.
- The warrior recognises that the human being is a great mystery, of which we know very little that is accurate.
- The warrior approaches all experience as a challenge—whether it the experience is easy or difficult, joyful or painful.
- The challenge the warrior is facing at all times is that of mastering his or her perception, and being impeccable with the Power such perception produces.
- The Dreamer's purpose is fulfilling a fundamental role in the evolution of Awareness—both the seemingly personal awareness of the Self and the impersonal Awareness of All-that-is.

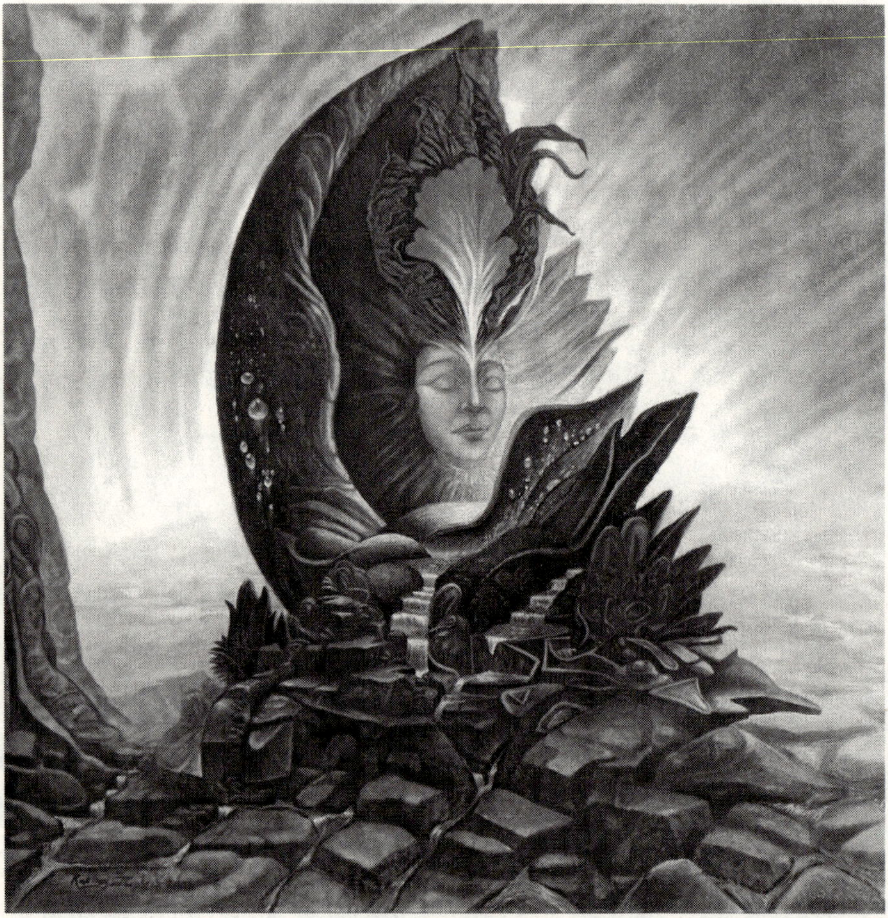

Chapter Two

THE LAYING OF NEW FOUNDATIONS

"The significant problems we face cannot be solved by the same level of thinking that created them."
Albert Einstein

When a human being *recognises* that life on Earth is a dream — an apparition within the consciousness of That which is perceiving life of Earth — many existing beliefs and assumptions about life will no longer seem so real or significant. The stories you tell yourself about reality and the perceptions you have about the-way-things-are have all been based on the assumption that you and the rest of humanity have an accurate and objective perception of life, the universe, and every*thing*. As soon as one knows this assumption is based on an illusion — an erroneous perception of reality — it immediately becomes apparent that most, if not all, of what you have told yourself is so is, in fact, not so. This knowledge can be extremely unsettling to the average ego, and often leads to the ego — and those identified with it — fighting for what seems like their grip on life itself.

In truth this fight is a futile battle. The pain of its futility is calling us — every human being aware of this call — to evolve to a new level of understanding, a new way of approaching life. One principle that becomes apparent once reality is tasted and understood — humbly stood-under and lifted up in appreciation — is that "I can only lose that which is not real." This also means that "Only that which is not real is vulnerable to being threatened." One implication of this is that my perception of reality can only be threatened if it is not true. Likewise, my perception of self and who I am can only be threatened if it is not true—only those aspects of myself that are not true can be endangered of being lost or destroyed. Once I have an accurate perception of reality, it can never be taken away. No argument can ever change it, for reality simply is as it is. Reality requires no beliefs, nor does it require (or in fact allow) "I" to maintain a particular fixed and limited position relative to reality. That which I Am is the totality; therefore it is not possible to maintain or lose my position relative to reality. As I said—and I think it's worth repeating—the ego-self's fight for its life and for its perception of reality is futile as far as that ego-self is concerned, and yet it serves to further shed light on the ways in which we are now being called to awaken.

Let's take a look at some of the many mis-perceptions that fall away once reality is seen for what it is. It's important to do this—in fact it is what much of life will revolve around for anyone who intending to awaken to the *dream*—because if you and I have been previously seeing everything erroneously, then just about every view, perspective, and belief we have about life will also contain some measure of error. I call recognition of this **the healing of perception**. It takes us to a place of True Perception. Not "true" because I or someone else says it's true—but rather "True" because we feel and experience it within us, at a level of re-cognition rather than its being just assumption and belief. Of course, any thing I share with you that does not resonate as being true for you should be put aside and perhaps revisited at a later time. It should go without saying that what happens to be true for me doesn't make one iota of difference to your life except perhaps in the degree to which it evokes a feeling of "Aha" deep within your Being.

"What lies behind us and what lies before us are small matters to what lies within us."

Ralph Waldo Emerson

Time

"Time is an illusion. Lunchtime doubly so."

Douglas Adams
The Hitchhiker's Guide to the Galaxy

There are many things that can be said about the *dream*. For instance, our linear experience of **time** is part of the *dream*—so the linear continuum of time that you have accepted as true actually does not exist beyond the human mind. It too is a product—or projection—of the ego-mind. It is constructed within the brain as a convenient way of dealing with the vastness of Now and All-That-Is. The implication of this is that everything you perceive to have happened within the *dream* over the course of time has in fact all taken place simultaneously in one Now moment. From some perspectives it is even more accurate to say that in fact no*thing* ever "happened" at all. Just like the dreams you have at night—they seem oh so real when you are experiencing them, but when you wake up in the morning, you also wake up to the fact that "none of it happened" and where you thought you were was in fact nowhere but in your mind—which could be put as "now-here in-your-mind." Again, read this a few times and allow yourself to open up to feeling what is being communicated.

It should be pointed out that I am not suggesting time does not exist, only that the way in which most people perceive time is somewhat limited. The way in which our nervous system and consciousness handle time, as a linear continuum, is a necessary part of this world—in fact it is fundamental to the entire way in which we presently experience ourselves. Yet because it is all a product of the mind, it is possible to change what has apparently happened to us in the past, and to alter what will unfold in the apparent future. It is also possible to have experiences that transcend time, and even space, that open us up to new possibilities if we intentionally decide to work with such possibilities. You may have had experiences whilst asleep of dreaming about an event or person only to later experience that event or meet up with that person unexpectedly in circumstances that mimic those in your dream. These sorts of experiences illustrate, to a limited extent, the potential flexibility of time under certain circumstances.

It is actually quite convenient that time is experienced in a linear fashion—it gets pretty intense without this convenience. I remember once when I was in the south of England, in Totness staying with a friend. One afternoon I was taking a walk in a field behind my friend's house and property when quite unexpectedly my experience of time collapsed in on itself, and in that moment I witnessed a vast array of people and events that appeared to have taken place over the course of what felt like thousands of years. My impression afterward was that thousands of years of "time" (I can't say exactly how long) were all squashed down into one long and yet relatively brief moment that lasted perhaps for only 20 seconds or so of "normal time." I reached a point with the distinct feeling that my brain, mind, and nervous system were not able to take it anymore and were rapidly getting overloaded. I did not feel adequately equipped to be processing thousands of years of history in just a few seconds, and with that realisation the experience stopped. The feeling induced by this experience could be felt intensely for the rest of the afternoon, and noticeably for a few days after.

On a different occasion (prior to this time-compression episode) I had another experience that illustrates the plasticity of time and space. I was in the Swiss Alps in a meditation retreat when partway into the retreat the participants were asked to imagine and inwardly inquire what it would mean (to our search for enlightenment) if we were no longer "waiting." For whatever reason, this seemed to be just the ticket to my completely dissolving into an experience of nothing but pure consciousness. I am unable to explain how that ensued from this request to consider not waiting—the key point is that this is the state I slipped into in that moment, sitting in that location, on that day.

The following day I was sitting on the other side of the meditation hall relative to where I was when the "not waiting" experience took place the day before. During this next sitting I inwardly went through a similar process of inquiry and subsequent realisations and again I dissolved into what I afterward described as "the absolute totality some call God." When I came out of this state and opened my eyes, I found (although at first did not realise it) that my view of the hall and the teacher, et cetera, was that from where I was sitting the day before. After some moments I realised that my view of the room was not the way it "should be," and that it differed from how it was when I last shut my eyes an hour or so earlier (I realised this is not where I was most recently sitting). I shut my eyes again and reflected on what had just happened, and I realised that yes indeed, what I just saw was "not how it should be." Upon opening my eyes again everything had returned to what my mind expected—I was again viewing the scene around me from the correct location, and not from the location I was in the day before.

As far as I can ascertain, I slipped into a particular state or dimension of consciousness—completely beyond the normal framework of what we perceive as time and space—on two occasions on two consecutive days. When I came out of this state the second time my awareness assembled itself in the exact place it was assembled the moment I went in and out of that state the day before. After that I knew clearly that time and space are in fact an illusion—a mere construct within the human field of perception.

I invite you to allow yourself to engage your feelings with what you have just read, as opposed to just hearing it recited mentally in your mind. Also allow it to sink into your feelings that your own experience of time and space is created within your own mind, and is therefore able to be modified by your own mind—perhaps not at your current level of self-experience—but is possible nonetheless.

SEPARATION

Separation is also a significant component of the *dream*, which we will look at now. It is, in fact, the most significant factor allowing this entire experience of our world and creation to unfold. Separation was the first act of creation by the "I" that extended out from the *void*. First and foremost this relates to our apparent separation from the *void* and from God—from the Totality—"apparent" because separation is not true. Beyond this we have the apparent separation between you and all other people and things on this planet. Then there is the separation between this planet and the other dozen or so in our solar system. Separation is a major facet of the *dream* and again, it simply is not how things are. One other significant aspect of separation that we will look at in this book is the division that took place within what we experience as the *self*—for instance the separation between mind, heart, body, feelings, thoughts, higher self, "our future enlightened self," et cetera.

Perhaps the most significant thing that arises through the belief in separation is what the renowned mystic and spiritual healer Joel

Goldsmith referred to as "the belief in more than one power." What I mean by this is that in our relative world—this world we are the dreamers of—God is not the only power active in our experience. We believe that disease has power. People have power. Countries have power. Money has power. Medicine has power. Laws and institutions have power, et cetera. The Truth is this: **Only One power exists** and **That Power is God.** If you could but grasp full ramifications of this Truth, your whole world would change in every regard, in an instant. This is the principle through which miracles occur. It was through the living application of this principle that the historical/mythical figure Jesus Christ healed the bodies and minds of so many who came to see him. More recently, it is the means by which Joel Goldsmith brought about healing in many people who sought him for help—whether it was in medical or financial matters, or matters pertaining to life and relationships. Many experienced a restoration of harmony, health, and balance.

Obviously there are many rather interesting ramifications of what I have just shared with you—of this "Christ Principle." It pretty much undoes all of what our culture considers to be true and real. I will point out that what you specifically attach to and identify with inside the *dream* will determine the particular quality of Awareness you embody as you step into the wisdom conveyed by this principle. My personal challenges and so-called *issues* within the dream all play a key role in determining my empowered or enlightened qualities as I awaken to the dream and illuminate my Being.

ILLUSION

"Matter is derived from mind or consciousness, and not mind or consciousness from matter."

Tibetan Book of the Great Liberation

In Chapter One I referred to creation as we know it as "an illusion." By referring to creation as we know it as "an illusion," I am not denying its existence; therefore taking this awareness on board should not result in an attempt to deny the existence of Life—in fact quite the opposite should result from understanding the nature of the *dream*. By referring to the world and creation as we know it as "an illusion,"

The Laying of New Foundations   57

I am simply denying that it exists *in the way we typically and humanly perceive it*. Put another way, I am stating that reality is not confined to the way that we—the collective and singular human self—have typically believed.

To give an example at a fairly tangible and relatively understandable level—for the collective ego-self it is not possible to be in a body in two places at one time, yet for those who have mastered certain spiritual disciplines, this is entirely possible and does in fact take place. There are numerous accounts of such phenomena, many of which are well documented and recorded in governmental, religious, and military records. Likewise, with the world as perceived by the human ego-self, it is not possible to teletransport one's body from one location to another, yet from the perspective of a skilled Shaman or mystic it is entirely possible and achievable. A well-documented example is that of the monk Padre Pio. I understand that during the Second World War the Allied air forces made many attempts to bomb the small town of San Giovanni Rotondo. This is where Padre Pio resided at his monastery and, according to military intelligence data held by the Allied forces at the time, it was the location of a German munitions store. Strangely, none of the Allied planes managed to bomb this town. The official story from many of the pilots is that they saw a monk in the sky waving them to leave. They dropped their bombs in nearby fields and returned to their base. This is apparently on official British and American military records of the events that took place during those flights. There are also eyewitness accounts of Padre Pio's ability to bilocate—to be physically in two locations simultaneously.

One such account is of a visit he paid to the Pope in Rome. There would be nothing unusual about such a visit except for the fact that Padre had not left the monastery where he resided and was still seen there during the time he was also in Rome.

So here we have an example of "reality" appearing to be one way for one group of people (perhaps most of the people alive today) with certain laws defining what is and isn't possible, yet for another smaller group of people there are entirely different "laws" that make all sorts of things possible that the bulk of the human collective would consider pure fantasy.

Now to me this is actually an example (just one of many) of the *dream* taking on very different forms depending on the ego-self through which it is being projected and perceived. It does not illustrate the overall nature of the *dream*—only that we can all have very different and even contradictory experiences of so-called "reality." Reality is not the concrete and immutable phenomena we learn about in schools and from society in general.

What you see around you does exist, and yet it doesn't. Rather odd, isn't it? Now, I'm pretty sure your mind is going to dislike reading that statement but it is simply the way it is. What we see around us does not exist in the way we perceive it, yet it does have apparent existence in the Mind of That which I AM. God created the I AM (or the "Son," as used in Judeo-Christian terminology[1]) in the likeness of Itself and as an extension of Itself. The I AM was therefore bestowed a power to Create equal to God's power to create, yet that which extended out from the Creator can never create anything that makes God's Creation obsolete or contradicts God. If this were not the case then the whole of creation would have unravelled itself before it even began.

"I want to know how God created this world. I am not interested in this or that phenomenon, in the spectrum of this or that element. I want to know His thoughts; the rest are details."

Albert Einstein

According to the metaphor of the film projector we already explored, God created Light through a process of extension. That Light is what is beamed through the metaphorical "film projector." That Light does "exist" and is "real." Yet as the Light passes through the film of the ego-mind, it is qualified in such a way that images appear on the screen (on the screen we experience as the human mind). The images themselves are not real. They do not exist beyond the one perceiving them. In that sense, the whole of physical and metaphysical creation does not exist in the tangible objective way we think it does. It is just a figment of some vast imagination. It's a lot easier to take life less gravely and less person-

---

1   Before Judeo-Christian theology personified what is now called the "Son of God," it was referred to as the "Sun of God" (the one you see in the sky during the day) or simply the Sun. I won't go into this in detail here, yet it is something to give some thought to. What we today refer to as sun-worshiping cultures and religions are actually based on the same thought-form Christianity has arisen from and modified.

ally when this perspective is deeply felt, appreciated, and understood.

If you are seeing an image of a cat on a screen and you remove the filmstrip, there is no longer a cat on the screen. Yet there is still Light—now in its pure form—projecting out onto the screen, and we can be aware of that Light. It is this Light that is *real* whereas the image (of the cat) that we make it take on is not "real." The image of Love is as close as we get to creating a real image through the ego-self, but it is still nothing relative to the Love of God that exists within us and is available to us through a direct experience of God—through directly experiencing the totality of All-That-Is. Of course, I am attempting to put into words that which is beyond words.

HEALTHY DENIAL

What I would like to emphasize is that we are not here to deny what we see around us. There is no point in running away from the so-called "world." Rather I wish to suggest there may be a distinct benefit in denying the *way* in which our ego-self is currently seeing reality and interpreting it. Denial ultimately has no purpose, yet denial when used appropriately and consciously can assist you in unraveling your apparent entanglement of false identification within the *dream*— or in the false interpretation of what you are experiencing. I am not referring to a "rigid" kind of denial that we all know is possible for the mind to get into about things it doesn't want to deal with. Rather I am talking about a "soft," "kind," and "open" sort of denial, similar to the way in which the heart so often hears the rational ramblings of the mind, whilst it denies that the mind has grasped the big picture.

Imagine for a moment you are looking at a dog (the common four-legged variety that goes "woof") and your friend—who happens to be mentally deranged and is undergoing treatment for such—says, "Hey, look at this lovely little kitty cat" (and he really sticks to the notion that it's a cat, as in the one that makes the sound "meow")—at some level you will gently deny this is a cat, whilst still being inclusive toward what your friend is choosing to perceive. This is a very different experience from the sort of denial that might rigidly say, "I never get angry," when all the while underneath the apparent calmness you are suppressing a whole lot of aggressive emotion; or that says, "I don't have any harsh feelings or judgments toward other people, and I only feel love and kindness," when in fact you quietly judge people every moment of your waking day. To this I would say that your power to love and create is equal to, and in fact (within this world) relies upon, your innate power to hate and destroy. Yes, you are perfect—this is not, however, the sort of perfection the ego, in its current state, will have you believing in. It is by your Perfection that shadow, darkness, evil, and so-called negativity can play out in this *dream* and yet have no impact on the glory of That which you Are in Truth.

I hope this makes sense. I will say I found it rather tricky trying to put this into words because my own mind actually has no idea what I am referring to or talking about! It only has memories of it that come about through an experiential awareness of what I am referring to. It is the experiential part that is real. The explanation of human reality being unreal or less real is only symbolic and indicative—yet it may allow you to release your ego's tight grip on reality just enough to allow into your experience some of what I have talked about.

Holy Ground

This world you experience is Holy Ground. The Body-mind-emotions you experience are Holy Ground—for they are all infused by the Light of God through Your I AM Presence, which is an extension of That which I am referring to as God. Therefore I invite you to treat this *dream* with the same degree of respect and gratitude you would bring to that which you consider most Sacred. Also, because that which is Sacred always has an element of the Unknown running through it, I invite you to bring to your experience of this *dream* a degree of awe, wonderment, and innocence that a child would bring to any of the great mysteries of life. This wonderment will help prevent you from experiencing rigidity and limitation in your Awareness. The gratitude and respect will allow you to open further to God's Vision of You and the Vision of Heaven on Earth.

All that you choose to experience, both in the form of "light" and "dark," has a purpose. It simply is not the purpose most people ascribe to it. The One purpose of everything in your experience (judged by you as "good," "bad," or otherwise) is to return you back to yourself, your true nature, your liberation from false perception—in full lucid awareness.

Therefore, reject no-thing.
Love everything.
Judge not. Love what is.
Allow and release.

Reading this book is going to take you on a journey—one that may lead you through unfamiliar territory. Essentially it is a journey into *my* world—into the world as I experience and perceive it. This is, however, a world I share with many of our ancient ancestors, with the Toltec, with many of the Shamanic traditions, with many thousands of mystics, yogis and spiritually realised beings, and with many of the native cultures my European ancestors made a mad attempt to wipe out in recent centuries. It has taken me my whole life so far to get to this point where I can walk along this path with you. It also has taken you your entire life so far to get to this point where you can walk along this path with me.

Establishing Our Common Ground

It is important that we walk on common ground. Much of what we will explore may be new for you, in the state of awareness you currently allow yourself to experience. Language, as you know, is nothing but symbols, symbols used—with consensus—to convey meaning and experience from one mind to another.

Because my vision and experience of the world and life may differ from yours, it is likely that I will be using symbols (language and words) in a way that is new and unfamiliar to you. Let's take a quick look at some of the key symbols you are going to come across along our shared path.

THE DREAM – Here I am referring to life, the universe, and everything as commonly perceived through the human mind. We will look at this term in more detail shortly.

GOD – Here we have a symbol that brings with it a lot of baggage, connotations, history, and collective and individualised stories. You have already come across my considerable use of this word or symbol throughout the previous few pages. When I use this symbol

I wish it to be quite clear in your mind that I am not referring to the image of God that is depicted in most common religions. I am simply referring to That which created all that is, and thus That which is the All. This God has no judgment, for It has no comprehension of human inventions such as "right" and "wrong." It has no interest or even knowledge of what you get up to in this world. It is completely impartial and detached from your perception of yourself. This God I refer to is not separate from "I"—the "I" That is in you and the "I" that is in me. We are all the same Thing. As the historical figure Jesus is reported to have said, "The Father and I are one." He was not referring to the "I" a person, named Jesus, but rather the One "I" that is the central Awareness of all Beings.

The abstraction that my use of the word "God" is referring to has been called by many names across many different cultures, religions, and cosmologies. Some of the names I use are Infinity, The Absolute, God, the Tao. I am not referring here to an entity or Deity. I am not referring to something that has any image, personality, or identity separate from the totality of All That Is. In my early twenties, after having a lot of experience of the Allness of things, I used to refer to this thing as the Absolute. I've chosen, however, the word "God" in preference to the "Absolute" because I feel it is important that people relinquish their limited perceptions of what has been referred to as God by our priests, our religions, and our society in order to embrace a much vaster and ineffable concept of what God is, and more importantly what God wants.

Why I place importance on the transformation of our perception of what God wants is precisely because God does not want anything. Wanting implies not having. Not having implies a finite thing apart from and in possession of, or not in possession of, other finite things. This implies separation, and with this implication we are no longer dealing with the vast one totality of All That Is—thus we are no longer referring to what I am choosing to call God, and also call the Absolute.

LIFE-GIVING AND LIFE-TAKING – These are terms I use throughout this book rather than terms one might more readily anticipate like good, bad, right, and wrong. Understanding of what the terms life-giving and life-taking imply and relate to is important if it is your intention to be free within this dream. The knowledge of this, like all true wisdom, is already within you. That which is life-giving is simply that which supports the purpose and fulfillment of Life—the evolution of Awareness. That which is life-taking works in opposition to this fulfillment. Because of the importance of this particular topic, we shall explore it more fully in Chapter Nine which is called "Beyond Duality." For now it is enough to recognise that on the Path of Freedom there is no "right" and "wrong" as such. There is no "good" and "bad." Not in the usual sense that most people[2] use these words.

THE STORY – This symbol or term refers to the way in which people create and repetitively talk—inwardly and outwardly—about experiences within their own individualised world (their dream). Most people have stories about nearly everything in their world, including (and usually most importantly) themselves. You may not have considered this until now, yet I am sure you will find that you, like all the people you know, are a most excellent story teller. It is a great skill we use for or against the fulfillment of our purpose. We shall explore this in more detail in Chapter Six, "The Stories We Tell."

THE EGO AND THE EGO-SELF – The ego (which I spell with a small "e") is the limited yet evolving sense of self or "I" we have whilst still engaged in the dream. The ego, as we presently experience it, is in fact the misidentification of our True Divine Self as something less than that—a limited self cut off from Divinity. I shall often refer to this limited experience of self as the ego-self. It is that limited sense of self that most people think is real and normal. It is that which fears, hates, separates, defends, attacks, judges, evaluates, uses the five senses, evolves, learns, struggles, fights, resists, denies,

---

2 It should be noted that when I refer to "most people" I am typically referring to people in my culture, in which I include the entire European and English-speaking world, and quite likely those people of Anglo-Saxon and European decent. I can't directly include people from cultures outside these particular ones because I am not familiar enough with their specific cultural qualities.

and attacks. None of that is You. Within this book I will convey an understanding of the ego that is different from the one maintained by most of the spiritual texts and teachers I am familiar with. We will explore this in more detail in Chapter Three, "The Dreamer and the Dreamed…Who Am I?"

BELIEF – There is a principle in Huna[3] that states, "Belief is necessary only for that which is not true. That which is real can be re-cognised, and it works—reliably and flawlessly." Belief is a means through which we construct our false perception and experience of reality. Awareness not only doesn't require belief, but is invariably hindered by it.

THE DREAMER – The Dreamer is the essential awareness of "I" that we each have within the core of our Being. This is what our limited sense of ego-self must eventually incorporate and surrender into as the evolution of awareness unfolds and our purpose is fulfilled. The Dreamer could be referred to as your True Self beyond this reality you find yourself in now. Ordinary reality is unfolding within the dreaming awareness of your True Self. The Dreamer could also be referred to as the Ego, in the highest meaning of that word. The word Ego (as I use it, with a capital E) is taken directly from the Latin word Ego which simply means "I." This is the deepest sense of "I" existing within the Spirit and Mind of Man and Woman. That "I" is also the Dreamer—that still, observant Self in which the dream, this world, and all phenomena of which I Am aware is arising within and through. To avoid

---

3 **Huna** is an ancient cosmology and system of perception that was prevalent in ancient Hawaii for many thousands of years. We will explore some elements of Huna—those that are most familiar to me—in more detail in various parts of this book. To quote my dear friends Lono and Lani, "Ho'ala Huna is a sacred collection of universal and timeless perspectives centered in a profound understanding of the true nature of our world. It is many thousands of years old, yet one of the clearest paths to personal enlightenment that exists. For those who embrace its wisdom, Ho'ala Huna has unsurpassed power to heal lives and set souls free. It illuminates the path of self-realisation—our inner source of light, love, peace and joy. It empowers and liberates, banishes fear, dispels gloom, and heals pain. Understanding Ho'ala Huna means understanding your connection to the magic and mystery of the universe. It also means living an empowered and sovereign life from a place of unshakable wisdom." See Appendix for further information.

confusion I will refer to this Ego as the Dreamer, and keep all other use of the word ego limited to the meaning of the word most people have already come to appreciate—namely the limited and separate-from-all-that-is sense of self as defined above. In the next chapter we will explore a deeper understanding of the nature of ego. One can also relate to the Dreamer as our Divine Self, at one with All That Is.

LIFE, BIRTH, AND DEATH – Contrary to popular opinion, life and death are not opposites. Rather, birth and death are opposites. Life has no opposite. Life is That almighty expression of All That Is in all its many manifestations and non-manifest potential. Death is simply the transition point, from a human perspective, at which "I" resume the experience and awareness of Self beyond the confines of the human body, beyond the ego, and beyond the triune self (a concept we'll be exploring in Chapter Three). Birth is naturally the opposite of death—namely that point of transition into the dream and the confined, separate, and limited sense of self (the ego-self) that arises therein. What I refer to as Life is not what most people commonly refer to as life. What we normally refer to as life is merely the many expressions and manifestations of Life—what could be called *the form side of Life*. Life is not simply the form it expresses. Rather it incorporates the formless Infinity existing within, around, and beyond all form.

MIND – I would like to make sure you have a clear impression of what I am referring to with this word "Mind" with a capital "M." I am not referring to the mental chatterbox most people would say they have in their heads. With my use of the word "Mind" I am referring to a vast field of awareness or a sea of consciousness within which the mystery we call "perception" comes into being. This Mind incorporates the human body, thoughts, emotions, feelings, soul, and spirit, and much more. Mind is like the substrate within which the dream unfolds. Mind is akin to the quantum field talked about in quantum physics. It could of course be called by many names, and Mind is simply the name I choose because in the English language I don't know of any word that refers to what I am using the word Mind for. You will note as we explore the triune self in

Chapter Three that these three aspects of the human self are various manifestations of Mind (what I refer to as Spirit-mind, Attentive-mind, and Body-mind). This is my intention and exactly what I mean to suggest.

FEELINGS – in my world feelings and emotions are not the same *thing*. I use the word emotions to refer to what most people commonly refer to as emotions—various internal states of energy such as anger, joy, passion, fear, sadness, et cetera. Feelings, on the other hand, are more subtle than these gross emotions. It is feeling that connects us to the impulse of life and intention from the Dreamer. Feeling is a faculty we all have as humans that for the most part is undeveloped and even ignored completely within a large majority of people. It is, however, the key to walking a true path of freedom. It is the key to humanity waking up to the reality of who and what we are. Feeling is both a doorway into the *unknown* and the means to truly embrace the *known* in a way that is life-giving and cooperative with the totality. As individualised units of awareness it is feeling that enables us to know and experience the totality. If you were a drop of water taken from a vast ocean, your connection and oneness with the ocean would be experienced through a feeling or what might also be described as a felt-sense. This felt-sense arises within the framework of the Body-mind.

A PATH WITH HEART – here I am referring to a specific path, or more specifically an approach to reality, that incorporates the nature and essence of what is best referred to as *heart*. The energy of the heart is inclusive by nature. The experience of Life on Earth—as it plays out through the many forms of life—is intrinsically connected to the Path with Heart. You may have noticed that only one letter in the word Earth has to change position in order to give us the word Heart. This is a large topic that would justify a whole book to explore. It will suffice to say that the Path with Heart is also The Path of Freedom, or perhaps more precisely, the Path of Freedom is a Path with Heart.

DREAM CONFIGURATION – we will explore this in more detail elsewhere in this book. For now simply understand that the term *dream* *configuration* refers to the entire array of all that you personally perceive here in this human world. Your relationships and what each means to you; your circumstances and what each means to you; your emotions; your thoughts; your beliefs; your sense of self. These are all part of your personal dream configuration. I also refer to the collective dream configuration. This is akin to the Collective Consciousness referred to in Jungian psychology, among other things.

AWARENESS – nothing less than an unfathomable mystery. From the human perspective it is impossible to intellectually fathom exactly what awareness is. We are only able to experience the nature of awareness by feeling into the many manifestations arising as awareness evolves through the dance of Life taking place within the dream, and as a felt-sense within the Self whilst engaged in the act of perceiving that dream. In a very limited sense, however, it is what remains when the "I" within you has dissociated from the human body, mind, and emotions, and drawn your attention to the still, quiet, and all-knowing *feeling* within the interiority of your essential being. Awareness is best tasted within the profundity of Life devoid of all identification with and fixation upon the superficial forms of life we perceive within and around us.

TRUTH AND REALITY – these two terms are not synonymous in their meanings. People have their own particular and individualized truth about life and whatever it is they give their attention to. This truth is based on their particular perception of Reality—the actual nature of what they are experiencing—which is determined by their particular perspective or point-of-view. Because each person has a different perspective on Reality, they each have their own particular bias on seeing Reality a particular way. Also people filter their experience of reality through their own particular and oftentimes peculiar set of beliefs. Beliefs are never in accordance with Reality and therefore produce a perception of Reality that is false. These beliefs form a significant part of what we will explore later with regards to what I call our personal Lore.

As we increasingly awaken to the Reality of our Divine nature and thus increasingly perceive Reality from the perspective this affords us, our truth will come into greater and greater accordance with Reality. What I share in this book is simply that which is presently true for me, and I do so because I have seen the effect these truths have in a person's life when they resonate with it and apply the knowledge contained herein.

On the above note, another point I invite you to remember whilst walking this path with me is that nothing in this book is *true* unless for you it is true. I ask you not to believe anything I say. I ask you not to walk along this path blindly. Use your feelings to explore my words and stalk or discern that which is true for you. Be mindful not to take what you read herein and turn it into more beliefs and especially not into a new dogma for yourself. My purpose, in your world, is in fact to assist you in releasing yourself from unnecessary beliefs. It is, therefore, not my wish to give you more to believe.

May it also be agreed and understood by you that I am sharing *some* of what I know and understand in order to assist you, the reader, at this time and through this medium, and that my *knowing* and *understanding* are evolving in every moment. There is much I have not put into the pages of this book. There is much I simply cannot put into words and especially not into words within the relatively limited medium of the written word. There is much I have put here that I may choose to change or state differently sometime in the future, or even right now were we exploring the topics at hand face to face and in person. Nothing is fixed, so it should not be internalised as being fixed.

I ask you to assume the quality of water so you may flow into the vessel created by the language and words on these pages—allowing your mind to flow into that vessel in order to gain a feeling for it. This as opposed to taking my words as a rigid construction you either allow into your mind or block out. The construct itself—the vessel—is not what is of importance here as I convey to you the knowledge within this book. The only purpose this construct (the language, words, and ideas within this book) has is that of providing you and the felt-sense of awareness—the "I"—within you some *thing* into which you can flow and experience much like water can flow down a river, into a pond, into an ocean, or even into a glass and then down the throat of a human being as he drinks from that glass.

The essential nature of the water is not changed by these things, nor do these things enter into the water. Rather the essential nature of the water takes on different qualities of self-expression, or more importantly, self-experience. Water in a glass, water within a river, water within a human body is still water yet in each of these *vessels* the water experiences itself in different ways. Similarly, by allowing yourself to flow into the form or vessel that arises through the words on these pages, you too will experience your essential self in a way that I trust will differ from the ordinary—taking you into the extraordinary and the profound.

If I state something as being *so*, then I am simply saying that it is *so* in my experience of the topic at hand. It may not be *so* for you in your experience. It is up to you, as a self-responsible and sovereign Being, to make conscious choices to decide how much of your world view you are willing to surrender in this moment, and how much of mine you are willing to flow into. Remembering, of course, that by flowing into some*thing* you always have the option of flowing out by the same means you entered, and no*thing* about you will have changed except your awareness. I am here—and these words are shared—to provoke and inspire the Divinity within you to come forth and establish itself in your human experience, within your awareness.

As we make our way through this book, it is my intention to share with you various perspectives and principles that will, if understood and applied, assist you in stepping more fully into your Power and experiencing more deeply your Inner Peace—and in this way you will experience greater Presence to Life. What I am doing in this book is simply telling a story. This is a story about how I experience the world, a story about what I remember from beyond this life, and a story about how I arrived at a place of deep inner peace and contentment. I am telling this story because like all good stories, you may be able to reflect on it and you might re-cognise within it your Path of Freedom.

> *"To know that we know what we know, and to know that we do not know what we do not know, that is true knowledge."*
>
> Copernicus
> *The first astronomer to formulate a scientifically based heliocentric cosmology that displaced the Earth from the center of the universe*

Empowering Principles & Perspectives

- You can only lose that which is not real.

- The experience of linear time is a construct within the human mind. Therefore, the experience of beginnings and endings, and of linear progression, cause and effect, and linear consequence is also a construct within the human mind.

- The human perception of separation is a misrepresentation of reality.

- There is only one Power active in Reality. Some people refer to that Power as God. You may call it what you like.

- All things are an illusion. This does not imply that they do not exist, but simply that they do not exist in the way we perceive them to.

- Typically denial is a dysfunction in our capacity to perceive what is. Yet because the average human ego is already in complete denial of Reality, you may find it beneficial to gently deny the notion that your current perception of Reality is true and accurate.

- The form side of Life—what we typically refer to as life and the world—is holy ground. Approach it with respect.

- Assume the quality of water as you read this book. In this way you may flow into the words and what they describe in order to experience a feeling of the subjects at hand.

"Everything you see has its roots in the unseen world. The forms may change, yet the essence remains the same. Every wonderful sight will vanish, every sweet word will fade, but do not be disheartened; the source they come from is eternal, growing, branching out, giving new life and new joy. Why do you weep? The source is within you and this whole world is springing up from it."

Jelaluddin Rumi

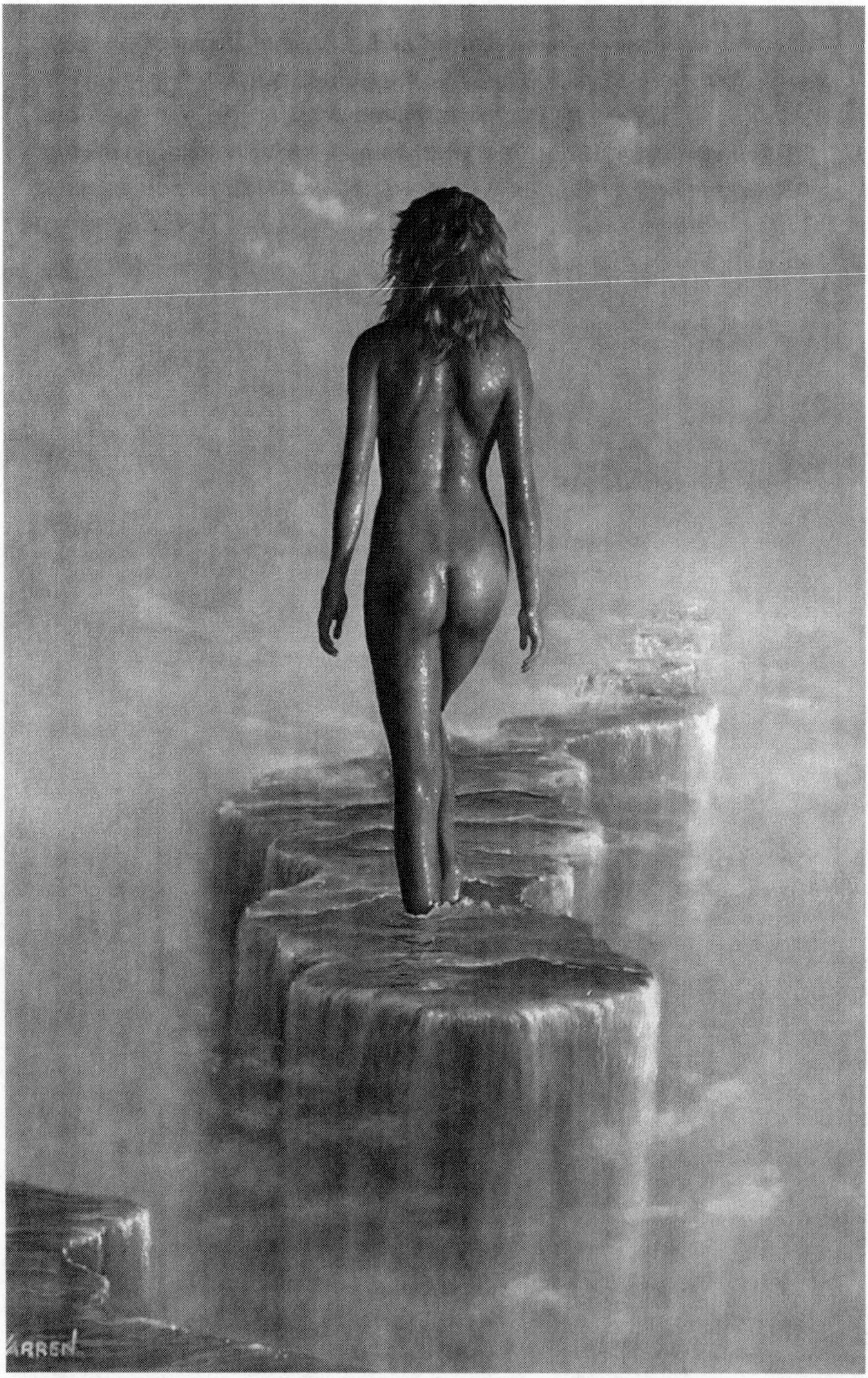

Chapter Three

THE DREAMER AND THE DREAMED... WHO AM I?

"Enquiring within 'Who is the seer?' I saw the seer disappear leaving That alone which stands forever."
Sri Ramana Maharishi

Who are you? Who are you before your physical body is born, and who are you after this body dies and returns to the Earth? Who is the one asking this within your mind as you ponder these words right now; who is the one aware of the questioning; and what about the one aware of the questioner?

What answer do you arrive at when you ask yourself "Who am I?" What if you ask this question persistently, taking it ever deeper into the recesses of your Mind and Awareness? "Who Am I? Who Am I? Who Am I...?"

In order to get the most out of this moment and what you are reading here and now, I invite you to take a few minutes—say 4 minutes at the least—to experience the following journey within yourself. You may find it easier to read this right through to familiarise yourself with it, and then actually do it whilst rereading or from memory.

You may have done this simple exercise before, in which case I invite you to do it again—but do it again as a beginner, completely new to this moment and without expectation as to the experience or the outcome. This is a process of self-enquiry that was taught extensively by the spiritual master Sri Ramana Maharshi, a man who's teachings I enjoy greatly and which I highly recommend exploring.

- Sit comfortably, in a chair or cross-legged on the floor, whatever allows you to relax without feeling sleepy. Have a clock within easy view (preferably one that does not tick loudly).

- Read over all of the following guidelines, effortlessly allowing yourself to commit them to memory. Then continue with the following simple process of self-enquiry.

- Be aware of the activity of breathing taking place in your body

- Observe your breathing as it is, without changing it. Observe and pay attention to each inhalation, then the moment of transition to exhaling, and now the exhalation itself. Again the transition to inhaling, and now the next inhalation.

- After half a minute or more of simply observing, take a number of long, full breaths. Allow your pelvis, abdomen, ribs and chest to expand, in that order, with each breath.

- Now, internally ask your-self "Who Am I?" Give particular emphasis to the word "I" and the *feeling* within you of what "I" actually represents. Remember, all words are symbols. What does "I" symbolise for you in this moment? And each time you ask this question, dive deeper into the feeling it holds for you. Pay attention to the felt-sense of "I" within the body, to the awareness of "I."

- Allow whatever answer comes up to come, and again, feeling into an awareness of "Who Am I?"

- The answer may come as feelings, thoughts, ideas, images, et cetera. In whatever form it comes, simply be aware of it, don't actively engage with it, and move continuously with your attention back to the enquiry of "Who Am I?"

- Continue like this for as long as you wish. If you want to make the most of it, I suggest you continue for as long as you can without straining. Your attention must not fixate on a mental answer to this question, nor should it fixate on a mental repetition of the question itself. In fact, after the first few mental repetitions there is no need to mentally repeat "Who am I?" at all. The key is the awareness, or the felt-sense, that arises within you.

The above exercise is a simple form of self-enquiry that can, under the appropriate circumstances, bring about a subtle yet profound transformation within one's awareness. You may find it a useful meditation practice done for a longer period of time, such as 11 to 45 minutes. You may find it beneficial and more fruitful to practice this simple meditation daily for a period of 7, 11, or even 40 days, or some other length of time that feels right for you.

THE COLLECTIVE DREAM CONFIGURATION

Before we attempt to define the Dreamer (your essential and Authentic Self) we'll first take a look at defining the dream configuration common to most human beings. This is what I call the Collective Dream Configuration (CDC). We touched on this briefly at the end of Chapter Two, and will now take a deeper look at this.

This is the aspect of a human being's dream configuration common to all humans, and not specific to any one particular person. For instance, we all have a physical body whether suffering, at Peace, enlightened, or completely comatose. We don't, however, all have a Ph.D. in advanced cognitive science, which would be considered part of one's Personal Dream Configuration. The existence of such a thing as a "Ph.D. in advanced cognitive science" is, however, part of the Collective Dream Configuration within certain cultures and societies, though obviously not all of them.

We're going to first take a look at what we—on a collective level—are **not**. The perspectives below undo some of the lies and misconceptions many of us have believed about who and what we are. Lies that most of us go on believing for the duration of our time here in the world, on and *in* the Earth. All of our lies are disempowering in nature, so it's important to be familiar with the most common and significant ones. We'll look at these from the perspective of the true "I" within the Awareness of all beings—that way when you read these it will be in the first person for the "I" within you.

I am not a body. I am not the mind with which I read these words. I am not my past lives. I am not my karma. I am not the emotions I experience from moment to moment. I am not my human sense of self. I am not the things I have experienced. I am not my memories nor am I my history. I am not my future aspirations. I am not my fears, nor am I fear. I am not the beliefs, values, judgments, and opinions I might have. I am not a personality. I am not my physical appearance. I am not what I wear in the form of clothing, hairstyle, make-up, shoes, et cetera. I am not my desires. I am not the activity of my mind, the chatter that seems to be in my head. I am not the stories I maintain about myself and my life. I am not the person other people perceive me to be and enter into relationship with. I am none of these things, and yet That which I Am gives rise to all this and more.

I am sure you are aware that at one time or another you (the chatter in your mind) thought or believed you are all or at least some of these *things* I have mentioned here. None of these *things*, however, is a true representation of *That* which you are. Believing otherwise is a lie, or at the very least a misconception, that most of humanity has bought into—quite literally buying into it with its life-force and Power—often resulting in the experience of disempowerment, pain, and suffering, and a consequent loss of joy, Peace, and the exquisite experience of true Love. To mis-conceive is quite literally to conceive in error. To conceive in error is to abort that which is true and give birth to that which is the extension of a lie.

The perspective afforded to us from this place of misconception leaves little room for feeling and experiencing the inherent nature of Life and our purpose and relationship with Life. Most people, for the most part, have forgotten entirely that the mystery we call *life* is manifesting as we perceive it for the purpose of evolving awareness. Many of us have forgotten that in order for the evolution of awareness to occur, the *unknown* must be constantly incorporated into the *known* and that we each have a role to play in this dance on the borderlands between these two *realms* or manifestations of Life—the unknown and the known. Right now is the opportunity we have each been looking for to wake up to our extraordinary circumstances, the deep mystery of Life, and the magnificent true nature of who and what we are right now, each day, moment to moment, awake, alert, and aware.

There is nothing "wrong" with the *things* I have said you are not (your body, mind, emotions, self-image, desires, et cetera), and there is nothing inherently *bad* about them. They are simply elements of the human dream that we can, to some extent, do what we like with. The habitual and rigid identification with and attachment to these things are what get most of us into some kind of suffering and difficulty — quite literally the *cult* or *culture* being at a difference with reality. That in itself is also not "bad" per se; it just isn't much fun and is not the sort of thing one would want to be addicted to — habitually repeating the experience — and yet most people are.

Of course, it's one thing for me to state what you are **not** and something entirely different for you to actually experience the Truth of this within your own self. This book you are holding and the others in the series (*Wisdom for a Life of Freedom*) will provide you with clear, simple, effective guidelines for remembering your true identity and divesting yourself of the various lies and assumptions you may have bought into — the lies regarding who and what you really are.

This journey of remembering is the Path of Freedom — freedom from lies, beliefs, self-deception, ignorance, and misunderstanding, and freedom from suffering. The Path of Freedom involves evolving your Mind and Spirit beyond limitation and misidentification. Not because there is anything inherently "wrong" with or "bad" about those experiences, but simply because this shift in consciousness is the next natural and inevitable step unfolding within the human dance. This next natural step does not take place through the exclusion of that which we at first experience as limited and misidentified, but rather through the inclusion of the limitless — of Infinity — and our true identity as That.

YOUR TRI-PART SELF WITHIN THE DREAM

Staying on the topic of our Collective Dream Configuration, we shall take a look at some deeper elements of how the human self is configured — knowledge of which makes it much easier to live in an empowered and liberating way.

Throughout my work you are seeing numerous terms that may be new for you such as *The Dreamer*, the *ego-self*, the *Body-mind*, et cetera, which I began defining in Chapter Two. In just a moment we'll take a deeper look at these terms and what they refer to — they are simply names I have either created or in some cases borrowed and modified from elsewhere in order to explain my experience of Self within and beyond the dream. I am aware that throughout human history these aspects of Self have been identified and defined one way or another in various philosophical, psychological, religious, occult, and mystical traditions, so you may already be familiar with them by one name or another.

The names I have selected employ a very specific use of words, in English, that have the potential to most accurately convey a true sense of what each of these terms refers to. There is little, if anything, I can convey To you with regard to the human self that is not already covered in great detail elsewhere in the vast field of human knowledge, culture, and spirituality. Yet often I find that contemporary writers and teachers (in English) on topics such as this borrow words from other languages such as Hindi, Sanskrit, Native American, Maori, Hawaiian et cetera, as if English were somehow deficient when it comes to describing the subtler aspects of reality. My experience, however, is that English, being a synthesis of words and word structure from a vast array of ancient and relatively more recent languages, is actually quite rich with meaning and depth—far more so than most people in my experience give it credit for. Perhaps the difference, in this regard, between English and something like Sanskrit is that the cultures that know and utilise Sanskrit have not forgotten the deeper meaning embodied in that language. Whereas English-speaking cultures, being more evolved at the level of materialism (and thus innately more superficial), have tended to forget the gems hidden within our words.

So, whilst many of the words of a spiritual inclination we borrowed from these other languages carry a very pure and clear signature of that which they refer to, this deeper meaning is all too often lost on the English-speaking psyche, and thus always requires deeper explanation before these foreign words can convey their meaning. If we are going to embark on such an exploration, then let's do it in English if that is the language the message in this book is being conveyed in.

What I have been able to discern up to now is that from one (particularly useful) perceptual point-of-view, the human self can be viewed and experienced as a tri-part being, as a triune self. I will use both of these terms in reference to this concept throughout the book. There are, of course, other perceptional points-of-view from which our human and spiritual make-up looks quite different. For instance we have a seven-part nature that we'll touch on soon, and then there are still other ways in which we are configured—yet it all depends on the *point-of-view* from which the perception is taking place. In Toltec terms this is referred to as one's assemblage point, or the assemblage point of one's awareness. This may seem new to you, but the fact is there is not one fixed reality here within our perception of the dream, and therefore not one fixed way of describing the composition of a human being, or anything else for that matter. Our point-of-view changes every*thing*. Here in this book I refer to those perspectives I feel are most relevant for now in the development of wisdom necessary to unveil Peace, Power, and Presence within your experience of life. Furthermore, there are many other significant aspects to Self, yet these go beyond our immediate human experience so they will not be elaborated on here. It is far better each person discover the deeper aspects of themselves through direct experience, as they deepen into greater degrees of self-awareness.

An important point to consider is that this reduction of the totality of the human self—which we are already dividing apart from the totality of Life itself—into a definition of its triune nature is in all regards an arbitrary exercise. It has the potential to be a very useful approach to understanding ourselves at a human level—it most certainly has practical value and significance—yet it also has the potential to become a limiting factor if taken out of context. To ensure it is not taken out of context, we'll take a quick look at what that context is.

The context in which I invite you to approach the understanding of the human as a triune being is this: No *thing* is separate from any and every other *thing*. There is in fact only one *thing*, which is arising from no*thing*. No aspect of the triune self is separate and apart from the other aspects. We are dealing with a wholeness or a totality, and not a number of separate *things*. A helpful example is that of the physical human body as understood in modern science.

If you were to study physiology and anatomy you would most certainly learn about various *systems* modern science has identified within the human body. The cardiovascular system; the respiratory/pulmonary system; the nervous system; the digestive system; and so on. What most people, in the contemporary study of the human body, fail to recognise is that these systems are an arbitrary way of viewing the human body that arises through the philosophy of reductionism. None of these so-called systems actually has an independent existence or truly an independent function within the body. Rather they are simply an arbitrary way of our trying to understand how the body works by reducing its complexity into a number of less-complex components. These components are selected by what we consider to be the *function* of certain collective parts of the body, and this is an important point. We define and perceive separate *things* by their function independent of everything else. In identifying one verb (an action or function) as different and apart from another verb, we create nouns. Our reduction and identification of many parts within the universe are a matter of linguistic convenience, with no basis in reality. When looking at a face, for instance, where do you draw the line that says this is a nose and this is not the nose? A nose is identified by its function, which differs from what we call the mouth and the function the mouth performs.

The reality is, however, that the so-called respiratory system is not separate from the nervous system, or any of the other so-called systems within the body. They all *function* as one collective totality. Even the function of these so-called systems is not limited to the cells within that particular system. Every individual cell has the equivalent of a respiratory process within it. Each individual cell has a process of perception taking place on its surface (the equivalent of a brain). Each individual cell has the equivalent of a cardiovascular system, and so on.

When all these cells come together as a community it gives rise to the organism as a whole. Human reason is able to approach that whole—that totality we identify as the organism—in a reductionist way and determine these so-called systems by superficially identifying what looks like a reasonable assessment of cells cooperating toward the fulfillment of common functions within the totality. As I said, this is an arbitrary deduction that has certain practical benefits when accepted as such. We have only to look at the benefits of modern medicine for some examples. This arbitrary deduction is also the source of many potential problems when taken out of the context that the human body is a totality that will never be truly understood by analysing its many apparent parts. It is this that has also become the downfall of modern medicine.

Furthermore, our culture typically perceives the human to be separate from every*thing* beyond the confines of its exterior skin. The human therefore has a particular function that we perceive to be separate from, say, that of a tree. In reality the tree and the human—and every*thing* else in existence—have the same unified function or purpose. Namely, the evolution of Awareness. It is only within the rational mind we separate *things* into parts and then lose sight of the unified purpose of Life—the Intention that brings all-that-is into Being.

So, when exploring the understanding of the human being as a triune self, please do so within the context given above. The true nature of the hu-man is vast, infinite, and ineffable. Even to identify a human as something separate and apart from all other things is (as mentioned) at one level a miss-take on reality. Yet we all know that this perception of human as something different from cat, or dog, or tree, or planet Earth, has its advantages—it has its own specific purpose in the grand scheme of *Life*. Equally, it has its disadvantages when taken out of the greater context of Oneness and the unified totality of Life. With that in mind, let us begin…

❂   ❂   ❂

First we shall look at "mind" itself. For the following to be clear and understood, it is important that we begin with a similar understanding of the way in which I am going to be using the word *mind*. Each of the triune parts we'll explore is labelled as a quality of *mind*. What is this *mind* I am referring to?

When I ask people what the mind is the answer is often one that refers to thinking. Some people also mention the conscious mind and the unconscious mind. Some people believe that the mind is purely a phenomenon limited to the brain, something that takes place within the human head. All of this is correct, and yet there is more to it than this. With the word *mind* I will be referring to something that incorporates a great deal more than these more limited interpretations of this word. Mind, as I use it here, is referring to something akin to an intelligent field in which the mystery we call perception arises and unfurls itself. It is not simply our thinking rationality most people might identify as *the mind*. If you prefer the word *self* to the word *mind*, please take the liberty of using that term. What I wish to convey with my use of the word *mind* is something quite subtle that I fully accept not everyone will resonate with at first.

Where I see clear parallels between these aspects of self and that which is described within other traditions—such as modern psychology, Hawaiian Huna, and esoteric science—I will point this out. This way if you are already familiar with some of these other perspectives, you can start putting together in your awareness a greater sense of the topic at hand. The knowledge you create in this way is always more significant than that which is taken purely from this book.

From the point-of-view I am presenting here the human self is made up of what I call:

- the Body-mind,
- the Attentive-mind, and
- the Spirit-mind

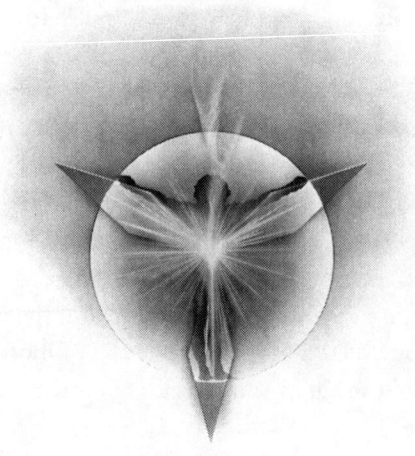

THE BODY-MIND

In some Huna traditions, what I call the Body-mind goes by the name Basic Self or lower self. I have avoided using the words lower and higher because for many people they tend to carry connotations of *better* and *worse* or some kind of hierarchy of value or worth, which simply does not exist. All such hierarchies are lies that undermine the expression of our Divinity—lies we can all do without. In the Huna tradition first written about by Max Freeman Long, it is called unihipili[1].

The Body-mind is made up of what in occult science is called the physical and etheric bodies, and also much of the astral body through which we experience our emotions. An aspect of the Body-mind is also referred to as the pranic body in some traditions. It connects us to the mana (or life-force and power) of the Earth and the intelligence inherent in the form side of Life. What I refer to as the Body-mind

---

1 Max Freedom Long,73 *Introduction to Huna* (Esoteric Publications, 1945)

also incorporates what Jungian psychology typically refers to as the *unconscious* or the *subconscious*. This last point is a key one to remember and contemplate, for it is through the Body-mind we gain access to what is otherwise beyond the reach of our conscious experience. It is through our relationship with the physical body that the unconscious (the unknown; or that which is beyond the conscious) can be mapped out and incorporated into our awareness.

The Body-mind controls all involuntary aspects of the physical body and does everything within its power to maintain homeostasis (balance within the body). The Body-mind (when functioning correctly) is intent on your survival, safety, pleasure, and physical well-being. It is also where many of our desires, passions, and instincts arise from, including the instinct to have sex and procreate, and to eat and be comfortable.

The Body-mind communicates through symbols and also feelings and emotions. The most direct form of communication within the Body-mind is through a *felt-sense* that one can experience within the physical body. For the Attentive-mind, the symbols of the Body-mind are more obscure or abstract than its own language, and can appear to be a few degrees further removed from what is being symbolised than are the word-based symbols it uses. However, one could argue that it's the other way around—that words are further removed from the described reality than the felt-sense of reality within our Body-mind.

It is within the Body-mind that our memory is accessed. I am not simply referring to the rational memory or mental images that one might assume constitute our memory. The Body-mind has what some schools of thought refer to as "cellular memory." Cellular memory is a form of memory that links us to our own history at the level of Body-mind. This is history of one's present life and what some choose to call *past* lives, as well as history of our ancestors and the entire memory of the human collective unconscious. Exactly how this functions is beyond the scope of this book, and it's up to you to feel into whether this is something you recognise as true for you or not. Various aspects of this are sometimes also referred to as Karmic Cellular Memory, Pain Tapes (when referring to painful memories), the Pain Body (as described in Eckhart Tolle's work in *The Power of Now*), cellular residue, and many other names.

I have seen that some skeptics state cellular memory is not real because *"cells don't have the capacity to remember things."* I invite such people to explore more deeply the nature of cognitive memory (what most people relate to as normal garden-variety "memory") and also the process of thinking. A great deal of relatively recent research indicates that the process of thinking is not restricted to the grey matter between our ears, and that all cells have the capacity to "think" at a biochemical level. People involved in physical disciplines such as martial arts, dance, acrobatics, and sports all rely on a basic (physically orientated) form of cellular memory to perform their tasks without having to think about or even be consciously aware of what they are doing. Anyone who can drive a car or ride a bike is also familiar with this experience.

Dr. Candace Pert[2] in her pioneering work described in the book *Molecules of Emotion: The Science Behind Mind-Body Medicine*, says, "Memories are stored not only in the brain, but in a psychosomatic network extending into the body...all the way out along pathways to internal organs and the very surface of our skin." There is a multitude of cases studied where people receiving major organ transplants take on memories and attributes of their donor[3]. Much of this research has so far been focused primarily, often exclusively, on the physical (biochemical) aspect of this whole body memory phenomena.

My experience, however, is that the physical aspect of the body is only part of the Body-mind I refer to, and in fact the information that we say is stored as memories is not recorded in the cells and chemicals of the body. Rather the cells and chemicals in the cells—in particular the receptors on the surface of the cells—attune the cell to the vaster energy field in which the body exists. It is this field combined with the physical form that is encompassed by what I refer to as the Body-mind. The pioneering work of Dr. Bruce Lipton is now confirming exactly this. His discoveries clearly show the inseparability of the body and the *mind*, with each cell being attuned to and responsive to the Self (including one's thoughts, perceptions, and beliefs) even when that cell is removed from the body and kept alive in a culture dish[4].

Of course there are many traditions in the world (dating back thou-

---

2   Refer to Appendix for information on Dr. Candice Pert's work.

3   Refer to *The Heart's Code* by Dr Paul Pearsall; also, *The Living Energy Universe* by Gary Schwartz, PhD, and Linda Russek, PhD.

4   See *The Biology of Belief* by Dr Bruce Lipton. Refer to Appendix.

sands of years) that recognise the physical body is not only permeated by consciousness but actually arises from consciousness itself. Any person who intends to awaken from the painful dream in which Humanity is presently living must now wake up to the fact that the physical body is not in the slightest bit separate and apart from every-*thing* else you identify with as self (mind, emotions, soul, spirit, and so on). Religion has done a fantastic job at promoting this lie, and it is now time for you and me to do an even better job at seeing through it and reclaiming the power we lost through past belief in this lie.

So, as far as I can ascertain, memory is a non-local phenomena that has a local biochemical (and hence cellular) element to it, yet we can't specifically deduce that a memory is *stored* within a brain cell. There is a holographic, non-local, and multidimensional aspect to memory that goes beyond the simplicity of cells and biochemical reactions. Therefore the same way that memories may manifest through and influence the biochemistry and physical structure of brain cells, the same happens within all cells of the body. Therefore I think it is safe to say that all cells have memory in the same way brain cells are conventionally considered to have memory.

It is also important to note that the Body-mind is a primary provider of the energy (Chi, Prana, Mana, Ki, Life-force, vitality, vital essence) we use not only to live and thrive, but also to bring into manifestation the Intent of the Dreamer. The Spirit-mind impregnates or inspires the Dreamer's intent into the physical world—into the Body-mind. The Body-mind then provides the energy and physical "stuff" to bring that concept-ion into being, through the applied will of the Attentive-mind (through the appropriate use of one's attention).

The Body-mind is intelligent and self-organising. This incredible intelligence can break down or get a bit stupid when there is a loss of vitality in any one or more of its vital centers (also referred to as Chakras in Hinduism and Yogic traditions) and their corresponding organ systems. Many forms of healing and also herbal and nutritional medicine can help restore this intelligence by literally re-minding the Body-mind of what it knows to be true.

The Body-mind has awareness and faculties of perception. Every cell in the body has faculties of perception[5]. Much of what some

---

5   Refer to *Biology of Belief* by Dr. Lipton for further exploration of this point.

approaches to psychology consider to be sub-conscious is incorporated by what I call the Body-mind. The Body-mind is also deeply connected to the Earth, for its matter is in fact the Earth. Earth and body are one and the same at a rudimentary level. For this reason, deep within the Body-mind is the living experience—the tangible living reality—of your unity with all the many forms of Life. All is inseparable. All is one. The Body-mind not only knows this, it also provides that direct felt-sense of this reality to any person willing to pay attention to it. Let us now look at that aspect of self that can do exactly that.

The Attentive-mind / Attention

The Attentive-mind, which incorporates what we describe as one's attention, is perhaps the aspect of self the majority of people are most familiar with. The Attentive-mind incorporates our rationality or our ability to reason and to *think*. We employ this aspect of self to make sense of and to *map out* the unknown as it arises within our perception. The Attentive-mind is not limited to our rationality, otherwise it might just as easily be called the Rational-Mind, but this name would not accurately and completely represent what I am referring to. I consider the Attentive-mind to be very similar to what is described by the word *manas* in Sanskrit. "Manas came to be understood as that aspect of the mind that synthesizes perceptual forms derived from the six modes of perceptual awareness (sight, hearing, taste, smell, touch, and mental awareness) into conceptual images. It perceives the alaya-vijnana (store consciousness) that underlies it [aka the Body-mind], but mistakenly apprehends this as a personal self (atman) and hence is the location of that false belief."[6] That last point is important, for it relates to the exploration of *ego* and our false or limited sense of identity, which we will explore shortly.

The Attentive-mind is the equivalent of what I understand in some Huna teachings is referred to as the Middle Self, and in more traditional Huna has been called Uhane[7] (as the inner expression) and Lono (as the outer expression). It is also incorporates what Jung referred to as the *conscious mind*.

---

6 Manas. Answers.com. A Dictionary of Buddhism, Oxford University Press, 2003, 2004. http://www.answers.com/topic/manas-3
7 Max Freedom Long, *Introduction to Huna* (Esoteric Publications, 1945)

The Attentive-mind relates intimately to one's attention. The origins of the word *attention* imply stretching toward some*thing* with our mind, or perhaps more accurately with our awareness. Our attention stretches toward the object of one's perception. If I asked you to pay attention to some*thing*, it is that aspect of your human psyche I call the Attentive-mind that would consciously hear this request and would then extend toward the object I specified. Even if you elected not to pay attention, to some degree the Attentive-mind would have already stretched toward the object I specified in order to determine if that is a desired course of action, so it is not always entirely under one's conscious control. When we speak of paying attention and being attentive we are referring directly to this aspect of self I call the Attentive-mind.

One way to relate to the Attentive-mind is as our command center. It is from here that we can consciously choose to engage with the Body-mind and the Spirit-mind, to develop a conscious relationship with these other aspects of self, and to engage these aspects of self in the fulfillment of Intention or the carrying out of a particular task.

It is from within the Attentive-mind that most people in the "Western world" derive their primary sense of self-hood at this stage in our collective human evolution. This sense of self gives rise to what I refer to as the ego-mind. The way I see it, for most people the ego-mind arises within the collective field of the Body-mind and Attentive-mind. The ego-mind gives rise to the ego-self, or what many people simply call the ego. We will take a deeper look at the nature of ego shortly.

It is from the level of Attentive-mind that you are able to direct your will, focus your attention, make decisions, rationalise, reason with an idea or situation, and generally go about your day at the level of cognition and re-cognition. The ego-self arising within Attentive-mind, however, does not have the capacity to truly discern—especially the discernment between truth and falsity—at least not beyond what is within your known. This becomes an issue with regard to discerning what is Real and what is not. Truth—if it is to be in accordance with Reality—must incorporate and prove itself consistent with the known and the unknown—potentially even giving clues or indications of the deeper Reality of the unknowable. Discerning truth without taking both the known and the unknown into consideration is going to produce incomplete and distorted results. The human heart center is better equipped for discerning truth from falsity than the head center.

The reason for this, in simple terms, is that the heart center has within it the capacity to be truly inclusive toward all Life at both the known and unknown level. The heart center is best accessed through the Body-mind by simply bringing one's attention there in an open and soft way (which is carried out with the direction of the Attentive-mind).

The so-called "western world" is a culture based on the exploration, realisation, and oftentimes the glorification of the ego-self. Prior to this we were more strongly centered in the Body-mind, its level of activity, and its particular sensitivities. The Attentive-mind was less developed than it is now, although I suspect it may not have always been this way. At present an increasing number of people are making the transition within their awareness toward incorporating more of the Attentive-mind and Spirit-mind into their perception of reality.

This transition is nothing new in the human experience. Mystics, yogis, and innumerable spiritual aspirants have been leading the way in this endeavour for many thousands of years. What is perhaps *new* is the vast numbers of people presently making this transition. One must be mindful, however, not to pursue the Spirit-mind at the expense of leaving the Body-mind and the developing ego-self behind, the same way those of us in the Western cultures must sooner rather than later cease our practice of pursuing the developing ego-self at the expense of the Body-mind and Spirit-mind. Initially it may prove okay, but ultimately it is the full integration of self that brings about the fulfillment of the Dreamer and his or her purpose.

As mentioned above, some spiritual paths promote squashing the ego and getting rid of it. Yet the ego is not the issue—not in the way many people commonly perceive it to be—and in fact it plays a very significant role in the integration of spirit into matter (spirit—father, matter—mother). Identification with the *developing* ego-self is where the trouble begins. With a healthy, whole, and functional ego-self we acquire a clear and complete vessel for incarnating the Dreamer's intent into physical reality. As will be seen in our exploration throughout this book, there is a much deeper mystery to this notorious ego, this sense of "I" within each of us. A deep and power-filled mystery, which we only estrange ourselves from when we insanely attempt to break away from the ego. It is, after-all, only our own ego—the "I" within us—that is trying to breakaway from what we identify as the ego and all the challenges it presents us with.

THE SPIRIT-MIND

The third key component in this model of the human self is what I call the Spirit-mind. For the purpose of this book I will say that the Spirit-mind is made up of what some traditions call the causal body, the higher mental body, and the human spirit (higher Ego)—which in some traditions is referred to as the *I Am Presence*. This is an extension of the vast One Mind that some call God, the Tao, Infinity, et cetera.

The I Am Presence is the tangible inner sense of **I Am** that arises within our awareness above the head. The I Am goes beyond the human dream. This is what Huna calls the higher self, as do many New Age belief systems. Jung called this the *super conscious*. The human spirit or I Am Presence is the seemingly individualised aspect of this element of Mind, whilst the One Mind or the infinite quantum field of information and possibility—both every*thing* and no*thing* simultaneously—is the impersonal and non-individualised aspect. The Spirit-mind is made up of the higher mental body and beyond.

In the Huna tradition as I understand it, the Spirit-mind is recognised as not having a direct connection with the Attentive-mind. It may rain down life-force and perhaps even certain impressions upon the Attentive-mind directly, but for the most part its connection with and influence upon the Attentive-mind is through the Body-mind. I can say that within my own experience it was and is through my connection to my body and the felt-sense that arises within my Body-mind that I have throughout my life maintained a relatively clear and definite sense of connection with my Spirit-mind and my purpose.

The Spirit-mind orchestrates our dream configuration in order to manifest and support the fulfillment of our purpose—both collectively and individually. It does this through intention. The Body-mind provides the form, substance, and prana or life-force to bring or literally in*spire* this dream—this intention—into manifestation.

There is a lot more that could be said about these aspects of our tri-part nature, yet I have put this in relatively simple terms whilst still keeping it accurate enough to be useful. If you wish to learn more about this, then I recommend studying any of the following: esoteric science, occult science, Anthroposophy, Theosophical science, and mysticism.

"'Well then,' I said to myself, 'this body is dead. It will be carried stiff to the burning ground and there burn and reduce to ashes. But with the death of the body, am I dead? Is the body I? It is silent and inert, but I feel the full force of my personality and even the voice of I within me, apart from it. So I am the Spirit transcending the body. The body dies but the spirit transcending it cannot be touched by death. That means I am the deathless Spirit."
Sri Ramana Maharishi

THE MUCH-TALKED-ABOUT EGO

Here we will explore an important topic[8]. A topic that in my experience is too often riddled with misconceptions, duality, and distortion. Rarely have I seen this subject explored in a way that does not perpetuate suffering and confusion. Let us get it straight now—for your sake, for my sake, and for the sake of all our relations. Let us explore the ego from a perspective you, like me, may also recognise as more accurate than the one most commonly discussed.

First a few esoteric technicalities! In my experience of the human sense of ego it has its center of activity in the Attentive-mind—it is most clearly perceived in the Attentive-mind. I understand that people experience their ego most strongly here. The forces giving rise to the average human ego also emerge in part from the Body-mind and the Spirit-mind. There are subconscious aspects to the ego that arise from the Body-mind. There are super-conscious aspects that arise from the Spirit-mind. We could refer to these collectively as simply the beyond-conscious aspects of the mind. It is my wish that our exploration of these should clear up any confusion about the ego once and for all.

The undeveloped ego is what most people derive their sense of self or "I" from (or within) and it is primarily, perhaps exclusively, experienced as a thought process—and a reactivity of thought/emotion—

---

8 I wish to point out that I will be covering this topic only to a degree and depth I feel is appropriate to fulfilling the intention within my writing this particular book. There is, however, a lot more to be said and understood with regard to the true nature of the personal and impersonal (or universal/cosmic) "I" manifesting through each human being. Therefore this topic will be explored more fully and deeply in the subsequent books in this series, particularly within Volume Four.

within the Attentive-mind. It is this thought process that most people identify with as "me," or at least as a major part of me, along with the body. For this reason I consider the Attentive-mind to be the primary *location* or sphere of activity and influence of the egoic sense of self or one's persona. The persona is quite literally the *mask* through which I approach the world around me. That is the root meaning of this word[9].

I typically refer to the field of energy from which the ego is most directly composed of as *ego-mind*. The actual experience—the personal perception of the ego and its activity—we'll look at in a moment, and that I refer to as the ego-self. My reason for using these terms is that the word ego has taken on certain meanings and connotations within the collective human psyche that is misleading at best, and utterly distorted at worst. Undoing these distortions in the collective psyche is a difficult yet important task, so in order to differentiate my use of the word ego here in my sharing with you, I will typically use the terms ego-mind and ego-self. The other reason for ego-mind/self as opposed to just ego is that the ego for many people seems to have taken on a sense of somehow being a separate kind of some*thing* that resides within them some*where* and relentlessly plagues them, gets the better of them, obstructs them, drives them forward in their desires, limits their spiritual development, torments them, deludes them, and creates all manner of other difficulties. It's as if we are, with the word ego, referring to an independent entity within the human being. The word ego-mind/self, however, like Body-mind and Spirit-mind, draws our attention to a sphere or field of a particular quality, nature, and purpose within the individual's mind, the collective human mind, and even the Universal Mind or what these days might be referred to as the Quantum field.

Each person has a felt-sense and more particularly a thought-form, experience, or perception of *self* that arises within the ego-mind. In my particular case this would include the perception that I am Jonathan

---

9   Per- means through or by which, -sono or –sonus/sona, relates to sound or noise or the making of noise. The persona was literally the mask ancient Greek actors wore whilst on the stage. This mask represented their role, purpose, and character in the play. Similarly our persona or persona-lity represents our role or purpose in the great play or dance of Life. My persona is not "I," it is simply a *re-presentation* of "I" in order to fulfil my role and purpose.

Evatt, with my own particular history, my own collection of memories, my own particular beliefs, thoughts and emotions, and even a particular life I am living through **my** particular body. You may have noticed this sense of self is bound up within a relatively superficial perception of what constitutes the self. This sense of self that many people have—within humanity's present degree of awareness—is relatively limited (vastly so), only incorporating a tiny fraction of the totality of the true "I" that is simultaneously the "I" of *God* or *Infinity*. I refer to this limited sense of "I"—this limited sense of self or ego—as the ego-self or simply the ego.

The ego-mind is the sphere of energy or consciousness in which our sense of "I" arises. The ego-self is one's actual felt-sense or experience of the "I" within this field. It is that aspect of the ego-mind one is paying attention to when engaged in self-reflection, such as when searching for the answer to the question "who am I?" The ego-self is the aspect of importance here, so it is not necessary to try and remember the difference between that and the ego-mind. Unless you are very technically minded, simply take a felt-sense of these terms with you from here, and leave the rest behind. Words are only words after all. I've only broken it up into this level of detail for the sake of those people pursuing study in metaphysics and esoteric science.

Speaking of words: Linguistically the term *ego-self* may appear somewhat redundant. By some definitions *ego* and *self* mean the same thing, namely "Your consciousness of your own identity." Yet their root meanings differ, and the root of a word takes us to the root of the matter about which it pertains. *Self* refers to one's own person or persona (which, as mentioned in the last footnote, is our mask and not the essential "I"; not the wearer of the mask). Self also refers to sameness. My hand has a sameness or likeness to the rest of my body that apparently differs from your body, so I consider my hand *a part* of myself, and not *a part* of yourself. The word self has deeper roots attributed to "separate" and "apart." In the dance of words[10] even in my describing the sameness of my hand and thus the fact I incorporate it into my sense of self, I had to use the term "a part." Thus, in

---

10 I find that words and language have an incredible level of complexity, symbology, and subtle meaning perhaps not originally intended—at least not at the conscious human level we used to define them.

identifying the sameness of my parts, as separate from your parts, we end up perceiving ourselves to be *apart* from one another. As I just mentioned, the word *self* has connection to base words meaning *separate* and *apart*.

We've also already touched on the fact that the ego is directly derived from the same Latin word meaning "I." Humanity in its present state of awareness has a relatively limited perception of what the "I" encompasses. In reality the Supreme Source ('Atma' in Sanskrit) and I ('Aham' in Sanskrit) are one and the same. Yet within human perception as most people presently experience it, "I" becomes identified (id-entified / id-entity / i-entity[11]) solely with the form side of Life (the tangible world of form), and many people are therefore ignorant of the oneness of all that is and the vast formless side of Infinity (of Atma; the Supreme Source; Infinity; God). So ego-self, in my books (figuratively and literally) refers to "a sense or consciousness of 'I' experienced as a-part/separate from the totality that is thusly experienced as not 'I'."

This sense or consciousness of ego-self within the ego-mind arises through the attention of one's Attentive-mind. The Attentive-mind is, at a conscious level, the birth place—and eventual death-bed—of our most basic and perhaps superficial experience of "I," the human individual, different and apart from the "other" *out there* (beyond the boundaries of what that ego-self i(d)entifies as self). The ego-self can become quite complicated and tends to be filled with all sorts of complexes, social conditioning, superstitions, beliefs, and thought-forms[12] all arising from the basic assumption that I am separate from all that I assume is not I.

Most people, when asked to describe who they are, will describe the conscious attributes of the ego-self as experienced within and through their Attentive-mind. In general, they describe their persona—the mask the essential "I" took on in order to fulfil a role in the dance of Life. This description will typically also incorporate some of the more superficially obvious aspects of the Body-mind such as one's appearance, body shape and weight, eye-color, state of health, and the like. In most schools of thought, this sense of self most people identify with is

---

11 The word *entity* relates to the is-ness of some*thing*, to "that which is," and to "be."

12 We'll be exploring what I call "thought-forms" elsewhere in this book.

simply called the **ego**. Yet, as mentioned, I find this use of the word **ego** to be altogether misleading and cause for much confusion, and I will explain why in a moment. Repeating a point made earlier, the English word "ego" has been directly taken from *ego* in Latin, which refers to our sense of "I" or "self." The ego-self therefore is that developing aspect of our triune self most people identify as "I" or "me." It is not in fact who and what we are, but rather and quite simply our identity (or i-entity) within the dream.

If you have explored spirituality through any of the major or less common spiritual traditions, you will surely be familiar with the idea that suggests *the ego is bad and must be overcome*—in one form or another. Some spiritual paths speak of "transcending the ego," whilst others talk about out-right destroying it. I have heard there are even religions that completely forbid the use of this tiny little word "I." The ego is portrayed as some sort of separate entity that has attached itself to the individual, and as the cause of much suffering and even evil in the world.

I would like to suggest, to the contrary, that the ego is a facet of the dream we cannot *destroy* or *transcend*. That all attempts to somehow overcome the so-called ego are futile, and only lead to further ignorance of one's essential nature. You see, it is only our egoic sense of self that even maintains the perception that the ego has an independent existence in the grand scheme of things, and has any real power. Hence any attempt to squash and rid oneself of the ego is nothing more than the ego fighting with itself—an ego-trip, one might say. It's like trying to cut off both your hands; you'll get stuck half way through—with one hand removed—only to discover it was a futile act to engage in, and a waste of a perfectly useful hand.

Simply put, the implication of this is that attempting to **do** anything at all to the ego is in itself an act of the ego-self. The human ego-self has no power and has no existence beyond the dream. It is constructed within human consciousness to serve a function, just as we construct our perception and subsequent experience of time and space to serve various functions, when in fact at a quantum or metaphysical level, time and space do not exist in the way we assume them to. Whilst it was necessary and in fact entirely inevitable for human beings to awaken to a sense of individual self—a sense of 'I' or the limited ego-self—our adherence to a pluralist perception of the ego as a separate entity must now be transcended for people to awaken to Inner Peace and for the evolution of Awareness to continue. It is not the ego that spiritual seekers must transcend, but rather our limited perception of what the ego—our sense of "I"—actually incorporates.

> *"You realise beyond all trace of doubt that the world is in you, and not you in the world."*
>
> Sri Nisargadatta Maharaj
> A *contemporary Indian spiritual teacher describing his own awakening*

GREATER INCORPORATION THROUGH THE HEART

On the Path of Freedom, the Warrior's goal is not to squelch the ego-self into oblivion or submission, but rather to incorporate more and more of the *known* (the world he perceives around him) into what one perceives as *self*. Once the greater part of my known is incorporated into my sense of ego-self, I will have a much easier and more empowering relationship to the unknown as it extends and manifests into the known—because I will cease being in a state of conflict with the world. What's more, I will naturally incorporate the manifesting unknown into my sense or perception of self. The illusion of *self* and *other* dissolves.

As mentioned before, it is the heart within man and woman that is capable of being inclusive toward all Life and its many manifestations we refer to as life. A lot of people don't pay much attention to their heart, preferring to focus on life primarily through more rational forms of perception. As our attention expands to include more of the heart, we simultaneous expand our awareness to incorporate more of Life. The limited sense of ego-self or "I" (Aham) that we live with expands until eventually it is inclusive of the One "I" that is God (Atma). The drop of water returns to the ocean, and in fact discovers it never left.

This unfurling of our limited sense of "I" into the vast and infinite "I" of God is nothing akin to the ego aggrandisement so common in today's world. It is vital to distinguish clearly between the two, for each has an entirely different consequence. Ego aggrandisement is akin to blowing up a balloon making it bigger and bigger in appearance without it ever actually increasing in substance. It's just filled up with air, and will eventually pop and deflate back to its original substance and size, although usually it gets blown to pieces in the process! Using the same metaphor, the process of incorporation and inclusivity is akin to increasing the actual material the balloon is made from. Imagine a floor covered in small partially inflated balloons. Now imagine one balloon merging with another one next to it. Then this double balloon merges with another, and another, and another. The original balloon is getting larger and larger but not through a process of independent self-inflation. The other scenario is one where one balloon simply takes on more and more air, getting bigger and bigger in appearance but its substance (the rubber) is getting thinner and thinner, stretching under greater and greater tension. Aside from the self-aggrandisement taking place here, the other major issue is that typically the inflating balloon acquires this additional air by taking it from the other balloons surrounding it, deflating them in the process!

A more literal example of this process of expanding one's sense of self is seen in the following examples—the first a collective one and the second that of an individual. Again imagine a floor or perhaps a vast field. Standing in this field are one hundred people. They are all going about their business, whatever that might be, quite independent from each other. Now see that two of these people notice each other and decide to hold hands. As a unit they are now bigger than anyone else on that field. Their intelligence, their Power, and their creativity will also have increased beyond that of most of the individual people on that field. Now these two people join hands with a third person. These three join hands with another, and another, and another. Eventually there is one huge circle of people on the field. The collective intelligence, creativity, and energy of this community are now much greater than that of the one hundred separate people who were there before. You might also like to note that the expression of this collective intelligence will be expressed most fully and magnificently when each of these individuals has a healthy sense of I, a healthy sense of self-esteem.

At an individual level the following example may help. Initially, as a baby, I have no sense of self. As I get older a sense of self develops. Soon I start believing and perceiving myself as separate from everyone else around me. Now, if I "fall in love" with someone, I will have the perception that there is an individual me in love with another individual self known as my lover. If this person does something nice to me, this act has been done to me by an-other. If my lover does something horrible to me, this act has been done to me by an-other. Yet as my awareness of what constitutes the self expands and becomes increasingly inclusive toward all of Life, I shift into the perception that the "I" within this person who I love is the same "I" within me. Their kind or unkind deeds are no longer things done *to me*, but rather deeds taking place *within me*, *for me*, and *created by me* (a much vaster "me" or "I" than what ordinary man perceives himself to be). The more this inclusivity unfolds, the greater my capacity to receive each and every apparent individual as Self. This inclusivity is of course not somehow limited toward other human beings. It will also extend to include all the many forms of life—the Earth, animals, the plants, the wind, the Sun, et cetera. Ultimately one's awareness expands to such an extent that one realises the Supreme Source and "I" are one. Just as the historic figure of Jesus is reported to have said, "The Father and I are one."

In this approach—the one found within a Path of Freedom—the "I" (the ego-self) has not been squashed, pushed aside, or destroyed. It has simply been opened up to all of Life. The prior approach is futile, whilst the latter is inevitable. The ego-self, therefore, is nothing more or less than a kind of vessel manifesting in this world that will increasingly provide a vehicle for the essential Self—ultimately the Supreme Source—to evolve awareness. A wounded and/or squashed ego is in the long term about as useless for the evolution of awareness as a car put through a crusher is for you or me to drive somewhere.

THE DEEPER 'I' OF LIFE

In exploring the interrelationship of the Attentive-mind, ego-mind, and ego-self, we have already touched on much to do with the so-called ego. For the sake of an even broader understanding[13], let's take a look more deeply at what I will here refer to as Ego (capital "E") as opposed to the ego or ego-self. I will use the word Ego to refer to the essential "I" that exists not just within the human being but also within

---

13 The reader is advised to skip over this section if it does not feel of interest or comes across as too technical or "heady." Yet, if you find it innately interesting, then by all means read and consider what is covered here.

the totality of Life itself—the "I" referred to in the decree "I Am that I Am." Within esoteric science[14], and most specifically my appreciation of Anthroposophy (as taught by the late Rudolf Steiner), it is understood from one particular perspective that a human being is made up of different *bodies*. At the grossest level is the physical body. Moving into the increasingly subtle realms there is the etheric body, the astral (emotional) body, the mental body, and the spirit body (higher mental); there is also the Ego running through all of these. In some cosmologies the Ego and Spirit are synonymous. The Ego, rather than being a layer of the overall human form (the physical and metaphysical form), is more like a beam of light penetrating its way right through all these other layers, and exists with or without these denser layers.

Each of these "bodies," or layers of manifest life, imbibes specific energies or levels of consciousness. A rock, for instance, has at an individualised level only a *physical body* and a relatively subtle etheric one—one that moves very slowly and with minimal amount of life-force expressing through it. For a rock, all the other *bodies* remain in what one could refer to as an organised, intelligent, collective *soup*. It's not that there isn't an etheric or subtle dimension to a piece of rock; rather it is simply that nothing beyond the physical dimension and basic etheric level is in an individualised state when it comes to these (and all other) rock/crystal formations. A rock, for instance, does not require oxygen to exist in the state in which it typically exists. According to my appreciation of Anthroposophy, oxygen is the physical/material element that carries into physical existence the etheric. Without oxygen the etheric withdraws from the physical form and *dies*. Carbon is what carries into manifestation the physical aspect of life forms. Hence we live in a world that is made up of carbon-based life forms. On other planets things might manifest differently, but this is how it is on Earth according to this particular field of esoteric cosmology[15].

If we take a look at vegetative manifestations of Life—namely plants

---

[14] The exact way these are classified varies within different occult systems and the way I have classified them here is a basic look at the subject within one particular classification system.

[15] This system of understanding was brought forth in a contemporary form by Rudolph Steiner in a body of knowledge he called Anthroposophy. If you are interested in exploring this topic further, the many books of Steiner would be one place you could start.

in all their many expressions—the physical and the etheric levels are manifest in what one could call an individualised expression. Plants, therefore, have a distinct relationship with oxygen as well as carbon. In fact, plants have an amazing ability to regenerate and maintain the etheric body of the planet. They have the capacity when exposed to sunlight (during the normal day) to draw in carbon dioxide, water, and photons, to keep the carbon in the form of glucose (ultimately returning it to the soil), and to release oxygen and water into the atmosphere. Plant life-forms have a vital role in that regard. Plants, however, do not represent a physical individualisation of the astral, mental, spiritual (higher mental) bodies, and they certainly have no individualised Ego or sense of "I."

Plants do embody the astral to some degree at one particular phase of their development. When we physically witness a plant entering into the process of bud formation and eventual blossoming, what is taking place metaphysically is that the collective astrality of the plant closes in on the developing bud, *kissing* it and leaving the matter impregnated with its energy or influence. I refer to it as "kissing" because that is how it feels to me, but we could be more technical and simply say that the astral body descends from the collective astral of that particular species of plant and impinges on the physical~etheric matrix humans call "the plant" or "the rose bush," or whatever it may be. When the astrality of the plant pushes its way into the physical~etheric matrix, it gives rise to the exquisite phenomena we call "flowering," which in special cases also brings with it a beautiful aroma—an aroma that greatly appeals to the human senses.

Many people have learnt to work with this aspect of plants in the creation of what are called flower remedies. Flower remedies are water- or alcohol-based fluids that contain the vibration of various flowers. These remedies are known to be useful in affecting the way a person feels—affecting them emotionally—when taken internally and sometimes externally. Simply put, flower remedies work with the human (and animal) astral body, affecting our emotional state. The intelligence inherent in the astrality of a particular plant is passed on to the perhaps failing intelligence in the astrality of the person receiving such a treatment.

There is a lot more we could discuss on this topic but that's not my intention here, so let's leave it at that. I will add that according to my understanding of Anthroposophy, it is nitrogen that anchors the energy of the astral body in the physical world, into physical expression. One impact of this can be seen in what manifests as the product of flowering. What do you think that might be? Well, after the plant is impregnated with the astral body of the organism, its flowers produce seeds in the form of nuts, legumes, grains, and the like. In general, seeds and nuts are one of the few forms in which you will find a high level of complex proteins in a plant. Protein is essentially a nitrogen-based molecule.

Another way we can experience the astral nature of nitrogen is to ingest one of the many nitrogen-based amine alkaloids that Western culture commonly classifies as hallucinogenic drugs. Chemicals such as LSD and psilocybin all fall into this category of consciousness-altering substances. Each of these gives the user a relatively powerful experience of the astral realm (among other things). Amines are organic compounds and a type of functional group that contains nitrogen as the key atom.

Now we come to animal life. The majority of animals are a manifestation of individualised physical, etheric, and astral energy. Hence the flesh of an animal contains a high level of complete or complex proteins. Protein is made up of amino acids, which again are nitrogen-based molecules. Animals, like humans, have a distinct and individualised experience of pain and other emotive expressions. Animals, in the wild[16], do not have a physically manifested individualised mental body, spiritual body, and Ego. I am keeping this quite simple because it could consume an entire book, and that is not my intention here.

Humans differ from most animals. We represent the incarnation (the stepping-into-flesh) of physical, etheric, emotional, mental, and potentially higher mental and spiritual "bodies" or aspects of Selfhood. Penetrating through all of this is Ego. Now this is where I wish to elaborate further on the vaster ramifications of the Ego or what one might call the Cosmic Ego.

The Ego that I am referring to here (spelt with a capital E, for the sake of clarity) is not what I refer to as the ego-self and what most people

---

16 I suspect that the domestication of animals may in fact induce the early stages of individualised mental body processes within such animals, often resulting in very distinct and individualised personalities.

and spiritual literature refer to as the ego (this troublesome thing that some believe we must rid ourselves of, et cetera). The Ego that I am referring to here is simply the Awareness of "I" or "I AM" that exists within the consciousness of a human being. The felt conscious sense of I-ness. The "I" within you that is aware you are aware, right now, of reading this book for instance. Any human being can, with an appropriate focus of their attention (which may or may not be something they inherently do), derive a distinct felt-sense of the I-ness within their consciousness. This I-ness I am referring to is devoid of all the many elaborations their ordinary human self holds onto and uses to identify itself with as separate and apart from the perceived other. This I-ness or felt sense of the *I Am* is free of all history, human thought-forms, and accumulated ego-centered machinations we come to know as our persona/personality.

From an Anthroposophical perspective, the form of Ego we are exploring here is carried into expression by the element hydrogen. It is interesting to note that scientists have determined that hydrogen was the first element to manifest. According to contemporary science, hydrogen is the most abundant element in the universe, making up 75% of normal matter by mass and over 90% by number of atoms. This element is found in great abundance in stars and gas giant planets. It is, however, very rare in the Earth's atmosphere (1 part per million by volume). Its scarcity is due to the fact that hydrogen is the lightest gas, allowing it to escape Earth's gravity. When compounds are included in our analysis, though, hydrogen is the tenth most abundant element on Earth. The most common source for this element on Earth is water, which as you likely know is composed of two parts hydrogen to one part oxygen (H_2O). Hydrogen forms a vast array of compounds with carbon (the anchor for the physical realm). Because of their association with living things, these compounds are called organic compounds.

At a symbolic level we see the nature of how our collective spiritual awakening requires expanding our awareness of Self to incorporate that which is beyond the influence of the Earth and *its strong gravitational pull*. This awakening is not to the exclusion of the Earth and what she represents, but rather toward the inclusion of that which is beyond the Earth—the vastness of Infinity in which the Earth is manifest. From another perspective, what I am referring to is not so much *beyond* the Earth as it is around the Earth. The Earth is manifesting within a greater field of consciousness that is only recognised when we take our attention away from being entirely fixated on matter.

We also see illustrated here the fact that it is only through the combination of hydrogen (Spirit or the Cosmic Ego) with the physical (carbon) that we get physical life. The "organic chemicals" that are the basis of living things result from the marriage of matter (C) and Ego (H). Throw some astral (nitrogen) and etheric/pranic (oxygen) into the mix and we have the wide diversity of life forms we find on this planet. This is, in biochemical terms, the Ego, or the cosmic I AM, creating or dreaming the dream we experience ourselves existing within in our day-to-day lives.

In Judeo-Christian terminology, what we have here is the "Son of God" (hydrogen) extending out from the Void of infinite potential. The "Son" extended out from his heavenly Father. I think this Son being referred to is in fact a personification of the Sun (with 92% of its volume thought to be hydrogen) in the center of our solar system, which was the primary focus of much devotion in most, if not all, Pagan (non-Christian) religions. If you take a closer look at most traditional churches you will notice that behind the image of Jesus there is also the image of the Sun with its rays shining out through the clouds. On the back wall of the famous Sistine Chapel the image of Jesus (the Son) has been omitted entirely. Instead there is the former pagan image of a huge golden Sun. The "Son of God" is quite literally and figuratively the Sun given to us by God as the source of all physical light and most life here on Earth. The light that dispels darkness each morning when the sun rises. The light that dies on the constellation of the Southern Cross in the midwinter night sky (for those in the Northern Hemisphere), when the nights reach their longest number of hours. The light whose resurrection is celebrated on the Spring Equinox (Easter) when the number of hours in the day once again outweighs the dark hours of the night.

Hydrogen manifested into the physical dimension from out of the non-manifest totality or the void. The remaining 10% of atoms in the universe are what the "Son" Dreamed up as the play of consciousness unfolding, creating all the many thought-forms and resultant life-forms we see in the universe today.

Ego or "I" in this sense is that primordial and profound sense of "I" that is within all things. The "I" of you and the "I" of me are in fact one and the same, and are also the same "I" of That which we call God. Again, I am expressing this with a minimum of detail simply to impart a general understanding of this topic because I see so much confusion and dualistic thinking when it comes to the notion of ego.

Now...back to the ego-mind.

As you have probably noticed, what I am calling the "ego-mind" is some*thing* different from the Ego we have just looked at. The ego-mind arises within the human psyche through a misidentification of "I" with the *stuff* of the Dream. It is a mere shadow or seed of the true Ego, arising in consciousness as the light of Infinity turns around to look at itself. Looking at it chemically we could say that hydrogen, once combined with other elements (primarily carbon, oxygen, and nitrogen), loses its clear sense or awareness of its original "self" (pure hydrogen). One thing I would like to point out is that for most people the true and highest sense of "I" does not incarnate into the human on Earth at this stage in our evolutionary unfolding. I suspect the spiritual (or higher mental) body also remains dormant and dis-incarnated throughout the life of many people. It is something humanity in its present state of evolutionary unfolding is still in the early stages of. There was a time when the mental *body* went unnoticed also, and didn't incarnate in the life of the average human being—at which time humanity did not have the faculty of cognition and logic we have now. Likewise, many more thousands of years ago the human astral *body* was also much less incarnated than it is today. At that time humans did not perceive color in the way we do now, and people had a range of emotional experiences more limited than that of today.

THE UNFOLDING OF SELF OVER TIME

Each of these subtle *bodies* incarnates (comes into flesh) in stages during a person's life. The average baby is primarily a physical, etheric, and partially astral expression of Life and the Life-Stream[17] or Soul associated with the child. Babies have some of their astral body

---

17 The Life-stream is a term referring to the flow of conscious Awareness that is *streaming* in from what spatially appears to be far above the head and makes its way at least into the body, and for many extends down into the Earth. It is sometimes inwardly perceived as a tube of fiery Light that surrounds the body at a distance similar to where you reach with outstretched arms and hands.

in place, although rather little compared to what is available. This is a major reason for babies sleeping so much, because when the higher astral *body*, mental *body*, and Ego are not present, you end up (in simple terms) with something more akin to a plant—alive, but without the full presence of consciousness afforded to the mature human being. The same goes for all human beings whilst in a sleeping state.

I have a hypothesis that roughly in cycles of seven years, each subtle layer or *body* of the human being unfolds more fully into flesh (incarnates)—one subtle layer or *body* every seven years. There are exceptions, where partial or even full incarnations of these other *bodies* happen very early in a human being's development. In the East when a person is born with all of their Self in the flesh (or relatively soon after birth) they are referred to as an Avatar. "Avatar" derives from the Sanskrit word *avatāra* which means "descent" and essentially implies a deliberate descent of supreme consciousness ("God" if you like) into mortal realms for special purposes (usually to directly assist the evolution of human consciousness from within the human Body-mind matrix or morphogenetic field[18]). An Avatar is someone who has full conscious self-awareness from birth or at least within the first seven-year cycle. I have spoken to many people who feel and think they experience seven-year cyclic patterns in their lives. I think that potentially the reason incarnation and life experience may take place in a pattern of seven-year cycles is related to the seven primary energy centers (or Chakras) in our Body-mind anatomy.

Although I am yet to explore this hypothesis in more depth, I suspect that as our body (which is situated on the Earth) spins around a full orbit of the Sun (a huge mass of hydrogen), it has a particular impact or effect on the activity of Ego (the I AM) within our chakras or energy centers. My suspicion is that our first rotation around the Sun independent of our mother's body (from birth until our 1st birthday) a

---

18 Morphogenetic fields are defined by Sheldrake as the subset of morphic fields which influence, and are influenced by living things.
"The term [morphic fields] is more general in its meaning than morphogenetic fields, and includes other kinds of organizing fields in addition to those of morphogenesis; the organizing fields of animal and human behaviour, of social and cultural systems, and of mental activity can all be regarded as morphic fields which contain an inherent memory."
—Sheldrake, *The Presence of the Past* (Chapter 6, page 112)

degree of Ego is focused on the 7th chakra. On the second rotation this makes it way into the 6th chakra the following year, and so on until this activity (whatever that is) has reached the base chakra and thus fully incarnated. This is round one of a seven-year cycle. Many people I have spoken to about this seven-year cycle have confirmed that in their experience there is a seven-year (or very close to it) pattern that plays out in their lives—with similar *themes* playing out in each cycle but expressed in a different way each time. That's all I will say on this for now as it's still just a theory I am yet to explore within myself. I've mentioned it here for the sake of those readers who have also noticed the cyclic seven-yearly nature of their unfolding on Earth.

For the sake of simplicity within this book, and to avoid confusion, I am going to refer to Ego (the highest expression of "I" that I mentioned in this chapter) as the True Self or as The Dreamer. When I use the word ego or ego-mind I am going to be referring to the limited sense of self that people experience until they wake up to *the* Dreamer.

MALU, ENTITIES, AND NON-SELF

As mentioned in a footnote in Chapter Two, there is an ancient cosmology that was prevalent in Hawaii and other Pacific island cultures dating back many thousands of years. In recent times this perceptual system and its body of knowledge has been called *Huna*. In the Huna tradition I am most familiar with, reference is made to malu, which in English means "life-taking spirits." In some Toltec traditions, another ancient system of perception, reference is made to a type of *parasite* or *parasitic entity* that infects our mind and robs us of our life-force. I get the impression that these parasites and what Huna refer to as malu are the same thing.

Malu take away the personal life energy their host is not willing to embody and own as *self*. This causes the *host* to experience pain until such time as he reclaims these misplaced or disowned parts of his Life-Stream, resulting in the evolution of Awareness and an awakening to his Divine nature. The experience of pain is the consequence of the life-taking choices we will make and the false perceptions we adhere to and invest our energy into when we are asleep to Reality. Contrary to what many people assume, this is not a form of punishment. It is, in fact, a failsafe feedback *mechanism* here within the Dream that ensures we will all eventually choose to wake-up to our true Divine nature and see things as they really are. This feedback is an essential mechanism in the evolution of Awareness and ensures the fulfillment of such. We will explore malu in more detail as our journey through this book unfolds.

A person's contracted or limited sense of self, as mentioned, comes about through a misidentification of Self with the stuff and stories within the Dream. Because the Life-Stream of human beings carries the potential for the Ego or True Self to incarnate, until this actually happens there is a flow of energy that remains unqualified and unused by the individual, remaining firmly within the realm of the unknown. It then expresses itself and is experienced by the individual in a very limited way, just as a 1-year-old child can only express herself in a very limited way relative to how she will potentially express herself when she is 40. Somewhere in the human story—in the Collective human drama or Dream—the vegetative and animal nature of Man~Woman was cut off from the Spirit-mind (higher mental body) and the true sense of "I" or the I AM Presence. Some would say this is the work of Lucifer, Satan, or some other dark force, and within the collective Dream that would certainly appear to be the case. Through the work of Dr. William Baldwin, and others also working in the field of Spirit Releasement Therapy and possession by entities, we have tens of thousands of case studies of people under hypnotic trance describing the influence and existence of these Luciferic forces. Dr. Baldwin says the descriptions given are highly consistent from case to case.

What I have observed myself is that when I don't actively utilise parts of my Life-Stream (that flow of Intelligent Life Force that is manifesting my body and awareness here within the Dream) this energy gets taken up by the aforementioned malu ("Life-taking spirits"). We could also call these "entities." These malu are in fact our allies here in the Dream. It is through their life-taking activity and the painful consequence of such activity that you and I can re-cognise where, how, and why we are forgetting our true nature. Pain is the consequence of life-taking choices, and it provides an excellent psychological feedback mechanism to tell me where I am not utilising the full extent of my Life-Stream (my Soul, or my power) and thus are doing things unconsciously and in a way that is life-taking. Put another way, malu show me where I am making choices that do not accurately and fully represent my true nature as a Divine Being. In the grander and more impersonal scheme of Life this whole process establishes the ongoing evolution of Awareness through the human experience. It also represents an aspect of the challenge we all must face in claiming and incorporating our Power.

"Malu is a Hawai'ian word that refers to a "life-taking spirit." Like all things that are Real, these spirits are a part of the ALL THAT IS that is God. They play a very important role because it is their job is to take our power away wherever we are unconscious. They do this by giving us thoughts and feelings that we confuse as ours. When we give these thoughts and feelings power, we make choices that bring us pain."

Lono Ho'ala, Kahuna Kupua A'o[19]

THE DREAMER

Since my late teens, I have often asked myself, "If reality is just a Dream, then who and what is doing the dreaming—who is the Dreamer?"

In my experience the Dreamer is what some spiritual traditions call the Essential Self. The Dreamer is a Divine Being. You are first and foremost a Divine Being. What this means is that you are of Divinity and no*thing* else. Anything else you might have thought, perceived, or believed yourself to be is a lie, a fiction Dreamed up for an experience of one sort or another—in accordance with the evolution of Awareness as made manifest through the intention of the Dreamer. What you have Dreamed to the contrary of Truth is neither *right* nor *wrong* and has no inherent value or even an existence in the Mind of God (or *the Source*). What you have Dreamed is an act of self-definition and that is all.

The Dreamer is the original Awareness of "I" that first extended out of the potent void within the Mind of God. That "I" continued to extend out into no-thing-ness creating the stuff of what we today call reality. This primordial "I" is the deepest Awareness of "I" that a human being can endeavour to realise for it is the "I" of that which

19 Refer to Appendix for further information.

we call God. Extending from this earliest of stuff arose the "I Am," which was the original unqualified "I" taking on the earliest and most subtle expressions of form or qualification. Here we have the most original and most subtle manifestation of information—literally in-form-ation or the activity of informing or bringing the formless into form. The word inform is derived from the Latin word *informare* which means "to shape, form, instruct…," and this is derived from *in-* "into" + *forma* "form." This gives rise to the phenomena and experience of I AM THAT.

I want you to know that as a Divine Being, as the Dreamer, you and I have never diverged from how we were first created. We have never left God, so to speak. We have never done anything *wrong*, nor can we. Actually at this level of Creation there is no "we" per se, there is simply the Creator (God) and the Creation (the Christ in the Judeo-Christian symbols most of us are familiar with). That original creation—which came about through extension, like your hand extending out from your body when you reach toward the sky—is eternal in nature and shall never change. It is perfectly *informed* by the Source always (*in all-ways*). The "I" (the creation), which is Awareness, continued to extend—Awareness continued to expand. From out of this extension arose the "I Am."

Now, there is much here that I simply cannot put into words. It is difficult or even impossible to do so at the present time. I can't accurately describe in words what was before "I Am" because it is absolutely and fundamentally devoid of any-*thing* you and I can rationalise and conceive. It was beyond and before the conception of things that ever occurred. I will say that this in my view was the moment within time and space that scientists call The Big Bang.

This was the Immaculate Conception of the I Am or The Christ (which Christianity got a tad confused about by taking early Biblical stories too literally). Again I can't put into words how the Big Bang arose—not that I am entirely sure anyway—because it's not possible to use that which is a product of the Big Bang (our rational mind, words, symbols, language, perception, and concepts) to describe that which is not the Big Bang. It would not be right to say "that which preceded the Big Bang" because in a paradoxical sort of way The Source did not precede the apparent outcome, for The Source and the apparent outcome always are and always will be the same. You may like to keep in mind that in relative terms the present size and scope of the known Universe (all that arose from the Big Bang) came about extraordinarily quickly as far as the measurements of *time* and *space* are concerned.

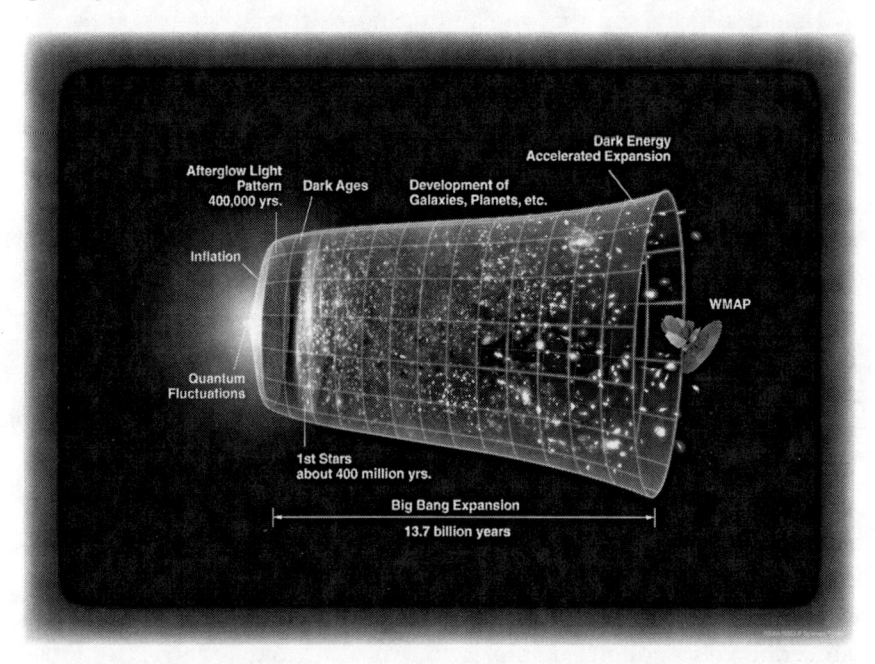

I quote the following from NASA as reported on their web site on 16 March 2006, "*Scientists peering back to the oldest light in the universe have evidence to support the concept of inflation, which poses that the universe expanded many trillion times its size faster than a snap of the fingers at the outset of the big bang.*

Image above: *Time Line of the Universe — The expansion of the universe over most of its history has been relatively gradual. The notion that a rapid period "inflation" preceded the Big Bang expansion was first put forth 25 years ago. The new WMAP observations favour specific inflation scenarios over other long-held ideas.*[20]

We're talking about when the universe was less than a trillionth of a trillionth of a second old. In that crucial split second, changes occurred that allowed for the creation of stars and galaxies hundreds of millions of years later.

It's admittedly mind-boggling. Inflation poses that the universe expanded far faster than the speed of light and grew from a subatomic size to golf-ball

---

20 NASA is the source of this image. It is from the public domain.

size almost instantaneously. This concept, however, was a mere product of calculations done with pencil and paper around 1980. The idea stands on much firmer ground today."

I shall simply say that the unfolding of this Divine *in-formation* continued through extension via the *I Am* and more of the *stuff* of this Universe was brought into manifestation—the advent of "I Am That."

Skipping a few eons, "I" created something that contradicted the eternal reality made manifest by and within God—namely "I Am that which I Am not," and voila, the Dreamer dreaming *that* which is not intrinsically real…the birth of the Dream as we presently perceive it. This is the moment in cosmic evolution that some people call The Fall. At this point the perception of duality arose. Awareness split into two polarities that can be identified as Masculine and Feminine awareness, which has by some accounts been metaphorically referred to as Adam and Eve.

I'll not continue this part of the story further, as it is too long for us to explore here. The essential point I invite you to impress upon your mind is that you are perfect, whole, complete, and free from all guilt, sin, or defilement. Yet, you're reading this book here in this Dream of all dreams because, for a reason of your own making, you have to some degree forgotten that this is so. Welcome to the Matrix (for those who have seen the movie by that name).

"Reality is not only stranger than we suppose but stranger than we can suppose."

J.B.S. Haldane
(the British geneticist who was one of the founders of population genetics)

THE EGO AND THE DREAMER

Let's take a point-by-point recap of the Dreamer and the ego:
The Dreamer (your essential and True Self):

- Is a Divine Being. This Truth can never change
- Has no needs, except one. In your Divinity you need only a mirror—the purpose of which is the Expansion of Awareness
- Is at One with All things, and with God / Infinity / The Tao / The Light (call it what you like)
- Is Perfect, whole, and complete
- Needs no healing, no completion, no evolution, and has nothing to *learn* (only Awareness to be re-cognised)
- Simply Is as It Is

The ego of the ordinary person maintains the following about your nature:

- You are a *fallen* being that has faltered from inception (i.e., it carries what some call *original sin*)
- You have a vast multiplicity of needs and desires. The one thing the ego does not need or want is a mirror
- You are in opposition to all things; are separate from Infinity / God / The Source / The Light
- You are imperfect, inflicted with "original sin," are fragmented and incomplete. Are carrying the burden of Karma and past wrongdoings
- You are under the illusion that you need healing, are seeking completion, are evolving and are here in the Dream to *learn* (of course the ego doesn't relate to this world as a Dream; rather it sees this dream as reality)
- You can never simply be at peace with being as you are

Of course I could elaborate on these lists, but perhaps you would like to take the time to do that? I invite you to spend some time looking at the following questions:

- What stories do I hold onto with regard to who I am?
- What limitations do I tell myself I have?
- What is it I am trying to do and achieve in the world?
- What beliefs do I have with regards to what God / Spirit wants me to do and be and how I am to behave?

IN HONOUR OF SRI RAMANA MAHARISHI

"At that very moment [of Sri Maharishi's death], in many places all over India, there were independent reports of seeing a bright light rising into the sky[21]."
Henri Cartier-Bresson, the French photographer, who had been staying at the ashram for a fortnight prior to Sri Ramana's passing, recounted the event to S. S. Cohen:
"It is a most astonishing experience," he said. "I was in the open space in front of my house, when my friends drew my attention to the sky, where I saw a vividly-luminous shooting star with a luminous tail, unlike any shooting star I had before seen, coming from the South, moving slowly across the sky and, reaching the top of Arunachala, disappeared behind it. Because of its singularity we all guessed its import and immediately looked at our watches – it was 8.47 – and then raced to the Ashram only to find that our premonition had been only too sadly true: the Master had passed into mahanirvana at that very minute."[22]

---

21 Sri Ramana Leela, Chapter 43
22 Memoirs and Notes, S. S. Cohen

EMPOWERING PRINCIPLES & PERSPECTIVES

- The Collective Dream Configuration is the aspect of human perception common to all human beings.

- A useful perspective on the nature of the human being is that we each consist of three qualities of Mind or consciousness. I call these the Body-mind, Attentive-mind, and the Spirit-mind.

- The Body-mind is primarily the physical body and what most people think of as the subconscious or unconscious mind. It is one with all at the seen level of form. It is like the hull, ruder, and keel of the human ship.

- The Attentive-mind is that aspect of you that can rationalise, think, and comprehend, and which you experience as your attention.

- Metaphorically it is like the captain of the human ship—which, among other things, must have his or her hand on the ruder!

- The Spirit-mind is that aspect of self typically referred to as the higher-self or the spirit. It is one with all at the unseen level of form. It is like the wind blowing in the sails of the human ship; this includes the quality of that wind and the direction it is blowing.

- The human ego is a seed of the Ego—the Cosmic "I." It has a Divine purpose. Approached with wisdom it will develop into a tree bridging heaven and earth, providing fine fruit to eat from. Approached with ignorance it will either die or spread out across your realm like a noxious vine.

- Malu is an Hawaiian Huna term that refers to life-taking spirits. Malu are an aspect of Infinity intended to awaken human beings to the ways in which we forget our Divinity and negate our Power.

- When we are ignorant of our Divine nature we make unconscious choices and behave in ways that do not accurately re-present our Divinity in the world of form.

- Such ignorance primarily arises through our misidentification of Self with the stuff and stories within our Dream.

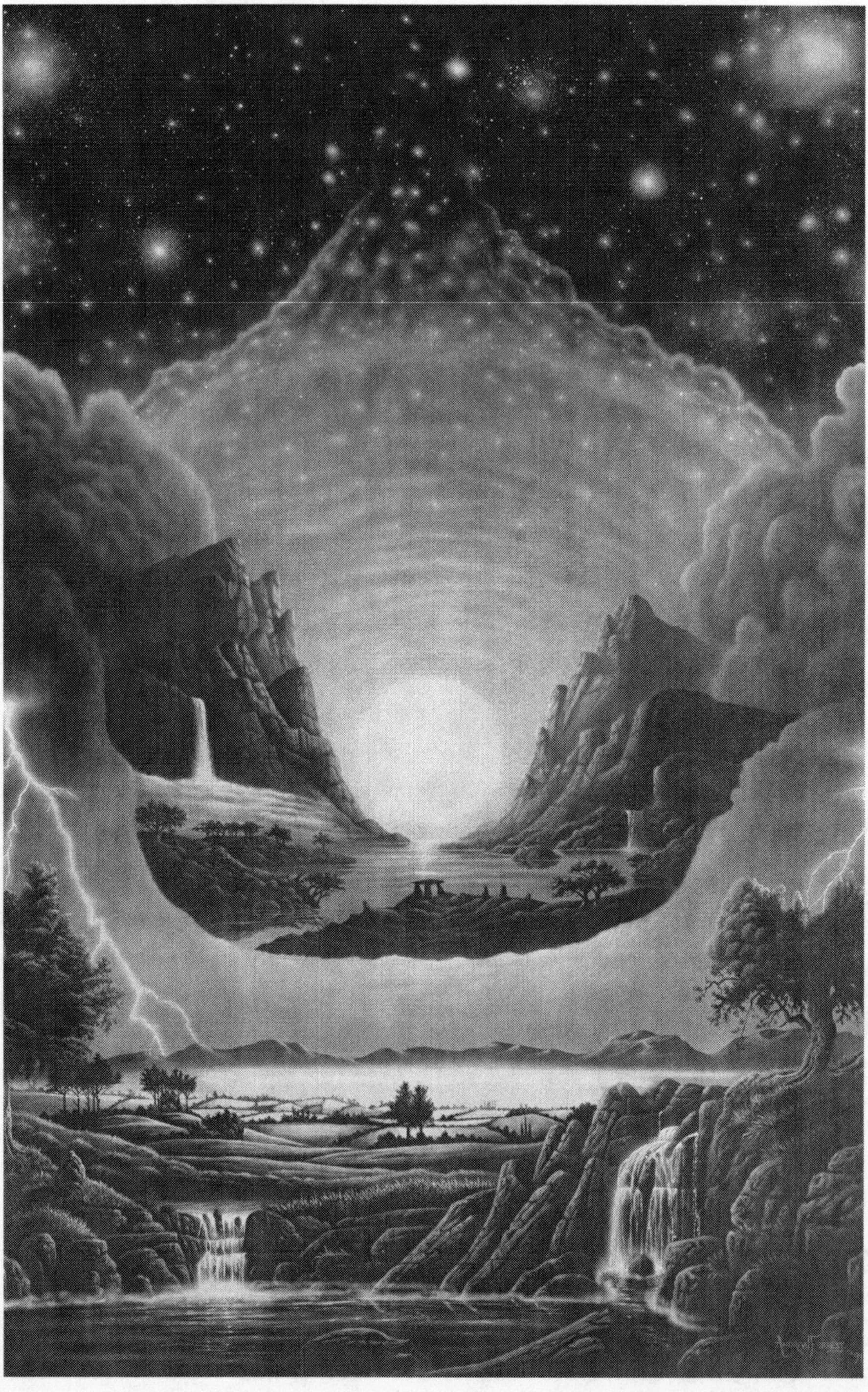

Chapter Four

Your Dream Configuration

"All that we see or seem is but a dream within a dream."
Edgar Alan Poe

Are you ready now to enter into a clear understanding of your particular Dream Configuration? Are you willing to take responsibility for the power that is afforded to those who are aware of how their Dream is woven together? Come with me now as we step into that possibility…

I shall first explore this with you in short form prose
During which I invite you to pause and feel at the end of every line
Intuiting what it is you have in that moment just read.

The "Dream" is that which you experience from day to day.
It is that which you experience from moment to moment,
As you go about your life.
The Dream is the ordinary perception of reality
You and the people around you collectively agree is so.
Within which we appear to live at all times.
The Dream as humanity knows it,
Commences with birth, and ends with death,
For it is not life and death that are opposites as some say,
For life has no opposition.
Birth and death are two moments within the dream on the infinite

spectrum of life.
Your Dream is your particular, even peculiar, and most certainly
unique and subjective experience of the Dream Configuration.
Both that of the collective, and that you might call "my own."

Your particular Dream Configuration
Is the unique way in which Infinity
Is expressed and experienced
Through that which you identify as "I" or "me" —
The person sitting here right now,
Reading these words, on this page.

Imagine a beautiful Persian rug
Of finely woven patterns and pictograms.
The rug is made up of perhaps millions of threads
Of many different colours.
These threads are strands of energy, strands of consciousness,
And their convergence brings the mystery of perception into being,
And through this, and more, Awareness evolves.

Seen as a whole — in its totality — it is undoubtedly a rug,
And that rug clearly has some particular order to it,
An order that creates a particular image.
To the naked eye and the uninformed mind,
To look at this rug is to look at the splendid picture on its surface.
This is akin to the more superficial aspects
Of that which we each refer to as "myself."

If you look at this rug in more detail, you will see
It is made up of a complex configuration of threads.
There is the backing or structural foundation.
This backing is relatively course,
The nature of the backing common to all rugs
In terms of a rug's basic structure.
The backing of one rug might differ from the next
In the exact number of threads and the material used,
Yet the essential structure and configuration are the same.
We can liken this to the basic configuration

Of how the collective ego-mind perceives reality
And the "world" as we collectively have come to know it.
This is the collective dream configuration.
The backing of a rug is a matrix of perfectly aligned threads
That holds the rest of the rug materials in place.

People of different cultural ancestry have distinct differences
In how they perceive the world, life, reality,
and the cosmos as a whole.
This would equate to slight variations in the backing of their rug, so to speak.
Yet the fundamental way a rug is constructed is still the same
no matter what the final rug looks like.
Hence whilst the Aboriginals of Australia had a completely different way of perceiving reality —
For instance, before people from another land and way interfered,
They had no concept of ownership,
And no perception of time as we know it, except,
"The Dreamtime," the "first day," and "now" —
And yet, like all the people in the place we call New York,
The Australian Aboriginals experience the fundamentals of a body, a mind, emotions, the need to eat,
The need to drink, the warmth of the sunlight on their skin, and so on.
A rug is a rug at the end of the day.
Humans are humans.
Again, this is the collective human dream configuration.
Yet each human lives in his own individual and collective world.

Woven into this backing are thousands,
Perhaps millions,
Of multi-coloured threads.
These are woven into the backing according to the design set forth for that particular rug.
That design represents the intention of the designer,
Creatively expressed or extended from Her mind onto paper.
The Bible states,
"First there was the Word."

That Word is this design.
An intention.
The first.
Akin to a vibration or a harmonic tone, hence it was once likened to the "Word."

The person who actually sits there at the loom and makes a rug
Is seldom the person who created the design.
They simply agree, through their own intention, to use and follow the particular design they're working with.
Thus the intent of the Designer—the Creator as such—is fulfilled
Through the intent of the weaver.
Your true nature,
That which you really are beyond this body,
Beyond this self you call "me" or "I,"
Beyond this self that has a birth date, a name, a history,
And all sorts of likes and dislikes,
Your true nature is the weaver of the rug
That you experience as this self called "me."

The likes and dislikes, the wants, desires, and aversions,
The particular way you react and respond to life,
All this is determined by what is woven into this great rug.
This is your personal dream configuration.

At the most basic and primary level some of it is also determined
By the backing of the rug.
The fact, for instance, that you need to eat, breathe, and drink in order to survive
Is not unique to you and is not particular to you.
These are facts of human life,
Determined by the backing common to all rugs,
Or the fundamentals common to all human beings.
So, You in Your true form, are the weaver of the rug.

You in your dream form,
The "you" that appears to be here within this illusion,
This play, this dance, this enticing affair with Life,

Called "Life on earth,"
Is the equivalent of the overall rug and the way it appears.

The true You is the dreamer of a dream.
The true You is the dreamer of a dream.
The weaver on a loom.

The limited "you" that you are perhaps more familiar with
Is but that which is being dreamed.
A rug can be altered. It can wear and tear.
And can be unwoven and rewoven.
It can be marked and stained.
It can come in many different colours, shapes, and sizes.
Yet none of this has any bearing on the weaver.
The weaver is unchanged by what happens to the rug.
All that varies is His experience of weaving,
And perceiving,
The rug.
Weaving and perceiving a super-fine silk-on-silk rug,
Imagine if you will,
Such a rug feels different, tangibly different,
From weaving a courser wool-on-wool rug.
The weaver, however, remains the same.

Even less so does any of this have any bearing
On the Creator of the design,
From which the rug was first envisioned, or imagined.
The relationship among the rug and the weaver and the Designer
Is this illusive force called "Intent" or "Intention."
Intention also spells In-tention or in-tension.
The whole universe is held together and maintained by a subtle "tension,"
By a force that maintains coherency and integrity of the whole.
Even the structure of an atom,
With all its many components,
Is held together by the forces of tension between these various components.
Let us say that (in)tension and (in)tention are interchangeable words

in this text.
The particular way a particular atom is maintained
Is reflective of the "in-tention"
Through which this atom comes into manifestation.
The particular way a rug appears to be
Is also maintained by the tension holding the whole thing together.
That tension is provided by the backing of the rug,
Which took it on from the (in)tention of the loom,
On which it was strung.

Without this tension it is nothing more than a pile of threads
With no semblance to a rug,
None whatsoever.
So the way a rug appears is the result of the tension
That exists within the rug.
That tension is created by the pull between two polarities,
The two ends of the rug that are pulled apart and held in-tension
On the loom.

The way a rug appears is the result
Of the in-tention behind the design of that rug
And the in-tention of the weaver.
The weaver, I shall add, is an extension of the Designer as far as rug making goes.
Ponder on this point for a moment and consider what that implies beyond this story and its metaphor.

Thus the rug is reflective of the intention of the Creator / Designer
And it is also reflective of the intention of the weaver,
Who for the purpose of rug making,
Is an extension of the Designer.
Her role, as weaver, is to fulfil the intent of the Designer.
Therefore their Will and Intent are One.

Your subjective experience of the rug,
Is what I refer to as your particular *dream*.
The exact configuration of your rug,
The way in which it goes together,

Is what I refer to as your "Dream Configuration."
Apparent flaws in the rug
Such as holes, tears, and fraying around the edges,
Are not flaws in the weaver,
Nor are they flaws in the Designer.

They are simply areas of the rug that are no longer congruent
Or in harmony with,
Or no longer in atonement with (or at-one-ment with),
Or are out of integrity with (we can put this many ways),
The design set forth by the Designer of the plan
From which this rug was woven.

It is important to point out that the Designer
Does not see these apparent flaws,
For She looks only at the design that is in Her mind,
In Her large room of dusty scrolls and manuscripts,
Full of maps or plans for beautiful, and perfect, rugs.
It is only the weaver who actually sits with the rug and sees the way it appears
In that particular manifest form.
Thus in the eyes of the Designer—may we call Her or Him "the Creator"—the rug is perfect,
For that is what His design indicates at all times.
For eternity, in fact.

The manifest rug and your experience of it—the dream—is a co-creation of
The weaver and the Designer.
Thus it is reflective of the creative intent of the weaver and the Designer.
Apparent flaws in the rug,
Which we may liken to those issues you feel the need to heal within yourself,
Are reflective of where the rug is out of integrity
With the intent behind its creation.

There is nothing right or wrong about this

For it is only a matter of perception.
The design, in the eyes of the Designer, is always whole and in
all-ways complete.
The weaver, in the eyes of the Designer, is also always whole and in
all-ways complete,
For He is an extension of the Designer.

So, putting this metaphor aside,
Let us consider your "Dream Configuration."
By now, I trust, you have gained some feeling
For what is referred to by this term.

Yes?

You are not the rug.
You are not the stuff you call "my life."

You are not your dream configuration.
Your dream configuration—the rug so to speak—is the result
Of consciousness unfolding
According to the intention set forth by the Creator of the design
And thus carried out by the weaver of the design.
That aspect of You, in Truth,
That you could most accurately (in relative terms)
Consider to be "unique" and "individual,"
Is in fact the weaver, or the Dreamer of the Dream.

The deeper truth is that the "I" within You is in fact the same "I"
That is the Creator of the design,
The same "I" within me, the writer of these words.
The writer and the reader are,
In Truth,
One and the Same.
For there is in fact only one "I."

Although for now it is enough to say that
You, in truth, are the dreamer of a dream,
And your particular dream configuration is what

You have,
Here in this world,
To work and play with, to heal and to explore.
Your task, in Truth, is to bring your dream configuration into accord
With the intent of You, the weaver, and with the Intent of the Creator.
Actually the Will of Thy Self and God are one and the same,
Although this is not so in the perception
Of the ego~self. As it is now.

The secret is that in Truth, it is easier done than said.
Easier done than said.
Yet the ego makes it appear that it's the other way around.

Ponder this for a moment.

Your Personal Dream Configuration

Your personal dream configuration is from one perspective a subset of the collective dream configuration. Whilst it may include some elements that are in fact unique to you (as one incarnate unit of awareness) it is, for the most part, made up almost entirely of dream elements that are completely impersonal. Your particular way of perceiving and positioning that material may be specific and unique to you, but again, this is a tiny fraction of who and what you (as a personality) consider yourself to be.

Your personal dream configuration includes everything you see around you, everything you think, feel, and emote, and everything you are able to consciously and unconsciously remember and reference internally, and all your beliefs and thought-forms. It is essentially what most people refer to as "my life" and "who I am," although it typically runs deeper than what most people care to consider as a part of "my life and who I am."

When people—such as many who adhere to New Age beliefs—state "you create your own reality," this is both true, and not true. It really depends on what the word "you" is being used to refer to. As already mentioned, the "you" or "I" that most people think they are is in fact just the product of identification with and within their dream configuration. Creation does not take place at this level—for this is the level of the ever-changing *created*. If, on the other hand, what one is referring to as "you" is in fact the Dreamer, then yes, it could be said that "you create your own reality." How much conscious communion most human beings have over this creative aspect of Self is, however, rather minimal.

So, it's really not worth getting too hard on yourself over the fact that what you see around you—your so-called "life"—doesn't always match up with your expectations. What most of us experience as "self" or "I" within the dream is fickle and unstable at best, and commonly completely fragmented and neurotic. We won't even bother looking at the worst-case scenario, but I am sure you can imagine.

Those who believe that "I create my own reality" (only ever knowing "I" as something within the dream) often take the next logical step and also believe "I can therefore create it any way I like." Again, this is only partly true, and highly dependant on how much one is willing to surrender and transcend the false human sense of self we inevitably inherit from our family and culture, and incorporate into our experience the direct awareness of the dreamer. That's all I'll say on this for now.

The Personal and Collective Dream Configuration

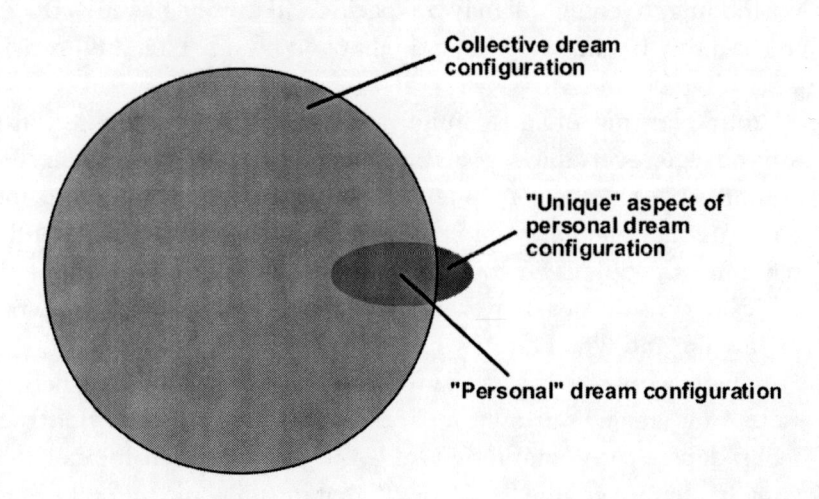

Collective dream configuration

"Unique" aspect of personal dream configuration

"Personal" dream configuration

EMPOWERING PRINCIPLES & PERSPECTIVES

- At the most fundamental level your Dream (your human existence) is defined by the collective dream configuration (those elements of perception common to all human beings).

- Impregnating the collective dream configuration is your personal dream configuration. This incorporates those beliefs and perceptions common to your tribe, society, religion, and community, right through to those that are relatively unique to you.

- Identification with your dream configuration brings about a loss of awareness of the Dreamer. We identify with the manifest form of Life and in so doing lose awareness of Life itself, which is not the form it takes.

- Your dream configuration is simply one way of describing all the many things, events, circumstances, and people—and the relationships between all these—that exist within your world. This is what you might otherwise refer to as "my life."

"He felt that his whole life was some kind of dream and he sometimes wondered whose it was and whether they were enjoying it."

Douglas Adams
The Hitchhiker's Guide to the Galaxy

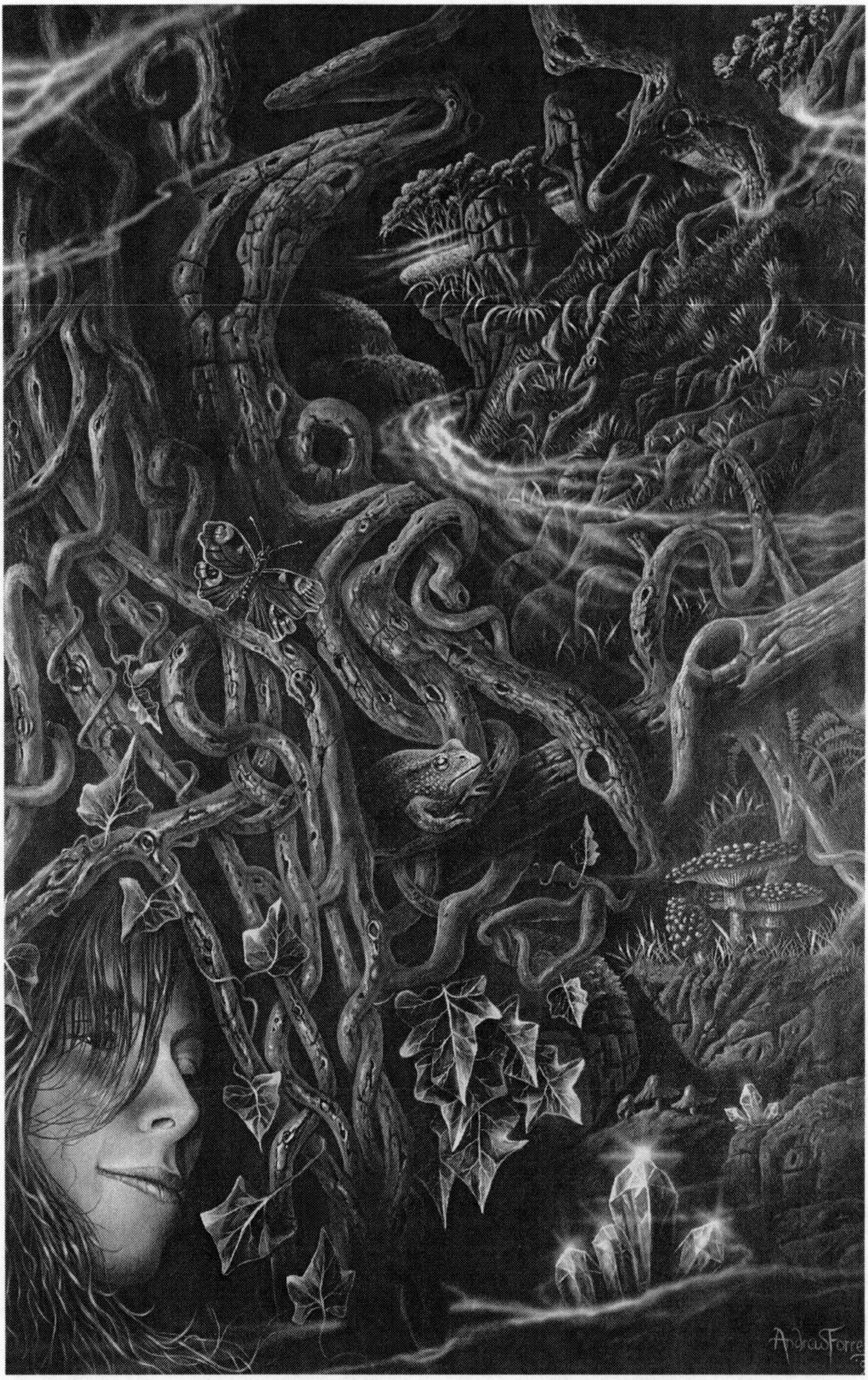

Chapter Five

Your Personal L.O.R.E.

"I know nothing except the fact of my ignorance."
Socrates

Lore is a body of knowledge pertaining to a particular subject or view on reality. Here's the meaning of the word "lore" as defined in various dictionaries:

Lore
1. That which is or may be learned or known; the knowledge gained from tradition, books, or experience; often, the whole body of knowledge possessed by a people or class of people, or pertaining to a particular subject, as, the lore of the Egyptians, priestly lore, legal lore, folklore
2. Acquired knowledge or traditional beliefs
3. All the facts and traditions about a particular subject that have been accumulated over time through education or experience
4. The whole body of knowledge on a particular subject, especially the kind of knowledge that has been enhanced by legends, anecdotes, traditional beliefs, et cetera

I particularly emphasize the last definition, namely that lore is "the kind of knowledge that has been enhanced by legends, anecdotes, traditional beliefs, et cetera." This is very much what we will be looking at in this exploration of what I call our *personal lore*.

Most human beings maintain their particular perception of life and the world by telling *stories*. It is the developing ego-self within that does this. These stories are usually configured in such a way that they enable us to maintain a certain position relative to the world, other people, our life, and all-that-is. Some of these stories are elaborate, whilst others are relatively simple. Some of them we inherit from the collective ego-self of humanity and some from our local "tribe" and family, and others are more personal stories that we have created or imagined into being.

Most people utilise these stories to maintain and uphold an experience of that which is **not** real. Until we wake up within the dream and begin to dream lucidly (with full Awareness of That which Is Real, of the Dreamer), these stories make up the bulk of our day-to-day experience and apparent existence. It is through these stories that we interpret our world, our relationship to the world (and other people), and what we experience. It is even more accurate to say it is through these stories that we create our experience of our world and relationships. Many of the stories we tell are stories that have been handed down to us by our ancestors, and over to us by the society in which we exist. We'll explore the nature of our storytelling more fully in Chapter Six.

As human beings we also maintain a list of *rules* that we use to regulate our world and to keep our world in accordance with our stories. Because the limited ego-self is based on the folly of mistaken identity and a perception of life that only accounts for the most superficial level of reality—namely the form side of Life only—our List Of Rules about Everything is erroneous. Simply put, our *List Of Rules* is all erroneous. They deviate from the Truth. Hence they are lies or errors. To create a useful acronym, I call this a person's *List Of Rules in Error*. This List Of Rules in Error becomes our personal *L.O.R.E.*—the personal body of knowledge we each have that replaces Truth with error and helps the ego (our false perception of self) maintain a dream that contradicts Reality.

Our personal *Lore* is the ego-self's *List Of Rules in Error*. We could also call it our *List Of Rules about Everything*, because ordinarily we quite literally only allow into our perception (and therefore our experience) that which we have a Rule set up to regulate and through which we then relate to and interpret that experience.

Recognising Your Lore

On the Path of Freedom it is essential we each re-cognise our personal Lore and eventually transcend the folly of applying it to the world if it does not have a life-giving consequence. If my Lore does not create the experience of a world (a dream) that accurately reflects the true nature of That which I Am, then it is likely to have a relatively life-taking consequence. It also won't be much fun. I found that most importantly I had to stop using this Lore in the relationship I have with myself. Much of the moment-to-moment chatter about self that goes on in my rationalising Attentive-mind is simply the repetition of the contents of my personal Lore—or statements that reaffirm my personal Lore. I discovered that my ego-self was then asserting these affirmations upon my experience of life. It is this constant reassertion of our personal Lore that prevents most of us from seldom—if ever—directly experiencing the present moment, as it is, right Now.

Most human beings have established rules in their minds about pretty much everything. During the course of this lifetime I have observed within my own personal Lore rules about how I must look and dress in order to fit in; how I must behave to be accepted; what would happen if I were not accepted; what sort of things I can say that are "appropriate" and acceptable; the sort of things I can't say because they are inappropriate or *"rude"* and not acceptable; the sort of questions it is okay to ask people, and the ones that are rude to ask people; how much love and kindness I can extend to people I meet and know; how much money I can or can't charge for work I perform; what foods I can and can't eat; how long I must be inside my partner during love-making before I feel it is okay to orgasm even when my body is telling me something else; how much love and kindness I can express to people who consider me to be a complete stranger; and, a whole host of other rules. Of course, all of these rules come down to one basic assumption—a belief in what I assume to be "right" and what I assume to be "wrong" with regards to how I behave and conduct myself in the world. This issue of "right" and "wrong" is the bulk of what our personal Lore relates to.

I also observed that I inherited these rules from sources outside myself, and that none of these rules had any basis in Reality. They were all fiction and fantasy. They were all *"the kind of knowledge that has been enhanced by legends, anecdotes, and traditional beliefs."* That doesn't make them "wrong." It also doesn't make a person "wrong" for having such a personal Lore. It just is how it is. We all go through this experience of creating a personal Lore as part of incarnating into the dream. It serves a crucial purpose as "I" incarnate more fully into the form side of Life.

In my own life, I found that to experience Inner Peace and to live in my Power I had to go through identifying and releasing my personal Lore. I am sure this is something everyone must do eventually. It is a natural part of maturation, much like a child having to release his childish perceptions as he grows into adulthood. One key to this path is that once I stopped relating to myself through these rules, I started discovering and accepting all my inherent Virtues and I discovered I am overflowing with such virtues. I also discovered that everyone around me was overflowing with virtuous qualities. So I think that as we release our rules, our virtues come forth. We progressively stop living according to Lore and start living according to the expression and realisation of our virtues. Virtuous qualities are those qualities that are life-giving and are the human expression or extension of Love. It is LOVE that must replace our personal LORE.

From Lore to Love

When I live according to my virtues—the life-giving qualities inherent within the Reality of That which I AM—I no longer need rules to regulate how I conduct myself, my world, and my relationships to other people and to the events that take place in my dream. This is the shift from maintaining one's personal Lore to instead unfolding one's personal and unique expression of Love. The result is we each blossom into self-governing and sovereign expressions of Life, conscious and aware of the interrelatedness of all things, every*thing* and no*thing*.

As touched on above, one of the many beautiful consequences of living in adherence to Love is that I soon discovered that within the world and all the people I meet there is in fact Lots Of Virtues Everywhere. The whole world is in fact filled with virtuous qualities, with life-giving qualities. I know you too will find the whole world becomes a mirror of the Love you are allowing to blossom within you. We simply need the eyes to see it—eyes that are looking through Love and not our personal Lore—and the open heart to feel it.

Much of what people here in the dream think and feel is "love" is actually just a particular kind of experience of one's personal Lore that we consider favourable. Simply put, when everything inside me and my outer world—particularly a person "out there" whom I consider myself to be in love with or in an intimate relationship with—all conforms (albeit momentarily) with my personal Lore then I will have a very moving and self-affirming emotional experience. Many of us erroneously call this *love*. Of course, my internal human state is always changing, the internal human state in my partner or lover is always changing, and the configuration of my dream (the world) is also constantly changing. It is inevitable that these three things collectively or individually change in such a way that at least one of them no longer conforms to my personal Lore. One result is that I will no longer feel so "in love" anymore.

I have found that the reality of Love is that it is always here—it does not come and go, and it is not present in some situations and not in others. It is the very glue that binds the quantum "stuff" of this universe together. My father once asked me as a child, "What is the most powerful thing in the universe?" and my response was "Love, dad." At the level of human experience, however, we have this notion of falling "in" and "out" of love. I think we're actually just falling in and out of experiencing conformity between our world and our Lore.

The first step to breaking free of your Lore is to start identifying what it is. The next step is to pay more attention to noticing the stories your ego-self is creating and/or repeating during your day-to-day existence. Remember, we repeat these stories to maintain the illusion that our Lore is accurate by constantly reinstating them in our minds. You are likely to notice these stories are particularly obvious in your relationships with other people. The closer or more intimate you consider the relationship to be, the deeper the stories you will have playing out. This is why relationships can be so challenging and such an intense source of pain and confusion in life. It is also why relationships are potentially so healing, so fulfilling and joyous, and why they can be used so effectively as a guiding light to wholeness and waking up.

Once you develop a clear sense of what your stories are, and what the rules woven into these stories are, you will start to let them go. It is essentially only a matter of becoming aware—aware of what they are and aware of how the affect you, and of the pain these rules are causing you. Later in this book we will take a look at how to unravel these stories and how to let these rules go.

Inner Peace and Inner War

Many people fail to experience Inner Peace—even though it is their natural state of Being—simply because their Lore is in conflict with reality. From another perspective, the person's perceived reality and his experience of that reality are in conflict with his Lore. It is the limited human ego-self that maintains this chaos as part of the journey of learning to dream in a way that is lucid and aware, and inclusive toward all Life. **Experiencing the pain of this conflict is intended to be our cue to reassess our current perception and to make new choices that are more inclusive to a greater expression of Life**.

I have found in my own life that pain is invariably my cue to pause where I am and take an honest look at where I am being called to move away from a choice which is relatively life-taking, and step into one which is life-giving—to move into a more life-affirming and creative way of being with a more inclusive approach to reality. This *movement* is always an internal one, and very often also extends out into my world as an outer shift in my relationship to the circumstances of my life. When I am humble, open, and willing to see (to shift my perception and thus reconfigure my relationship to and configuration of Power) I without fail find that under my every experience of pain is an awakening waiting to emerge. The *unknown*, in that moment, has something to *say*, something to push forth into my known world, something I have more than likely been resisting and unwilling to re-cognise—which is why it has resulted in pain. Many of the Buddhist teachings I am familiar with say that life is suffering and that this is an unavoidable fact of reality. Yet I simply have to disagree with this—what I can only classify as a life-negating—perspective.

In my experience it is not necessary to suffer through the pain that might arise within me. When taking the Warrior's approach to Life, much of the time it is not even necessary for this pain to be anything more than a subtle shift from feeling deeply at peace in one moment, and a little less at peace in the next. That subtle shift is at the starting point of even the most intensely painful experiences. I will add, it has taken me many years to come to this state where my baseline experience is one of deep peace. Yet what got me there was applying and living exactly what I am describing here, and throughout this book. You see, the Warrior's approach does not afford us the folly of wallowing around in pain, nor the indulgence of getting self-inflated over our moments of jubilance. The Warrior accepts both as they are, and consciously approaches both with an equal degree of awareness and open-heartedness. Should I choose to ignore these subtle shifts—from my baseline state to a less harmonious state—then the experience will invariably escalate into greater and greater degrees of pain. This is true, but only so long as I ignore the feeling that is there within my body, and fail to stop and reassess my situation.

With regard to the above-mentioned *baseline state*, what I am referring to is the state of one's interiority—your inner feeling world—when no*thing* in particular is moving your state toward pain or pleasure. I realise that for many people it is common to be almost always swinging one way or the other, seldom resting in the middle—happy one moment, less happy the next, miserable the next, and just feeling okay after that, and so on. Yet, I trust that all beings know—even if it has been only a glimpse—what it means to simply feel at peace now. The prerequisite of this feeling at peace is discovering and residing in one's center. Deep within the Body-mind we have a psycho-energetic center—our core—and it is here that the experience of peace resides. It is from here that suffering ends, and with this pain is transformed into a gift—a message from the unknown that we can act on—moving us closer to the fulfillment of our purpose.

You may be sitting there thinking "I hardly ever feel totally at peace; what's he on about, and I certainly don't like feeling pain; pain *is* suffering and it ain't nice whichever way you look at it." This, or something like it, may be true for you, and if it is, I invite you to remain open to the possibility that something more in accordance with feeling at peace and with pain being a source of life-changing empowerment can be experienced now. It is because the principles and perspectives in this book work, without fail, that I have made the effort to share them with you now through the words on these pages.

Typically it is our personal Lore that creates the thin veil of maya between our painful experience of Life and an empowering and jubilant one. A basic understanding in Toltec wisdom is that in any given moment I always have the power necessary to fight my way forward—to take the next step toward empowerment—no matter how low or poor my current situation appears to be. If I am still here in this world perceiving my life, then that perception affords me a certain degree of power. Power is the product of perception. So even if what I am perceiving looks like I must have sunk down into hell with nowhere to go, this perception brings with it a measure of power, and that power is all I require to take the next step… to fight my way forward through the challenge I am facing, and to reach *higher ground*.

Humankind will cease destroying each other and this Earth we live on (or within!) only when this internal transition from Inner War to Inner Peace has been made. In my own life this required transcending the many ways in which I perceptually create and experience separation and segregation in the world and within myself. It was my personal Lore—my list of rules in error—that brought about this separation. These rules are nothing but lies that distort and twist our perception, such that an ordinary man or woman becomes a destructive force in the world. Thankfully we have a way to unravel this Lore—setting our mind and heart free—and to transform this immense destructivity into a force that is life-affirming, creative, and profoundly beautiful.

Are you willing to face that challenge now?

Empowering
Principles & Perspectives

- What I am referring to as your personal lore is the sum total of your beliefs and judgments. These are the rules you maintain at a subconscious level about life, the universe, and everything.

- By paying attention to your stories about the world and about life, it becomes much easier to identify your personal lore.

- Rigid beliefs and judgments about life—and any aspect of our life—will result in a lock-down of our perception.

- Power is a product of perception.

- When our perception loses its fluidity/flexibility, our access to Authentic Power is diminished.

- The less we rely on our personal lore as a source of security in the world, the more we will see and experience the world through love.

- Perceiving the world through love provides us with the most accurate representation of Reality. Love, therefore, provides us with the greatest access to Power.

- Pain and suffering are not synonymous. It is not necessary to suffer through the pain we experience. Rather we can intelligently use pain to awaken us into a more accurate experience and expression of our Divine nature.

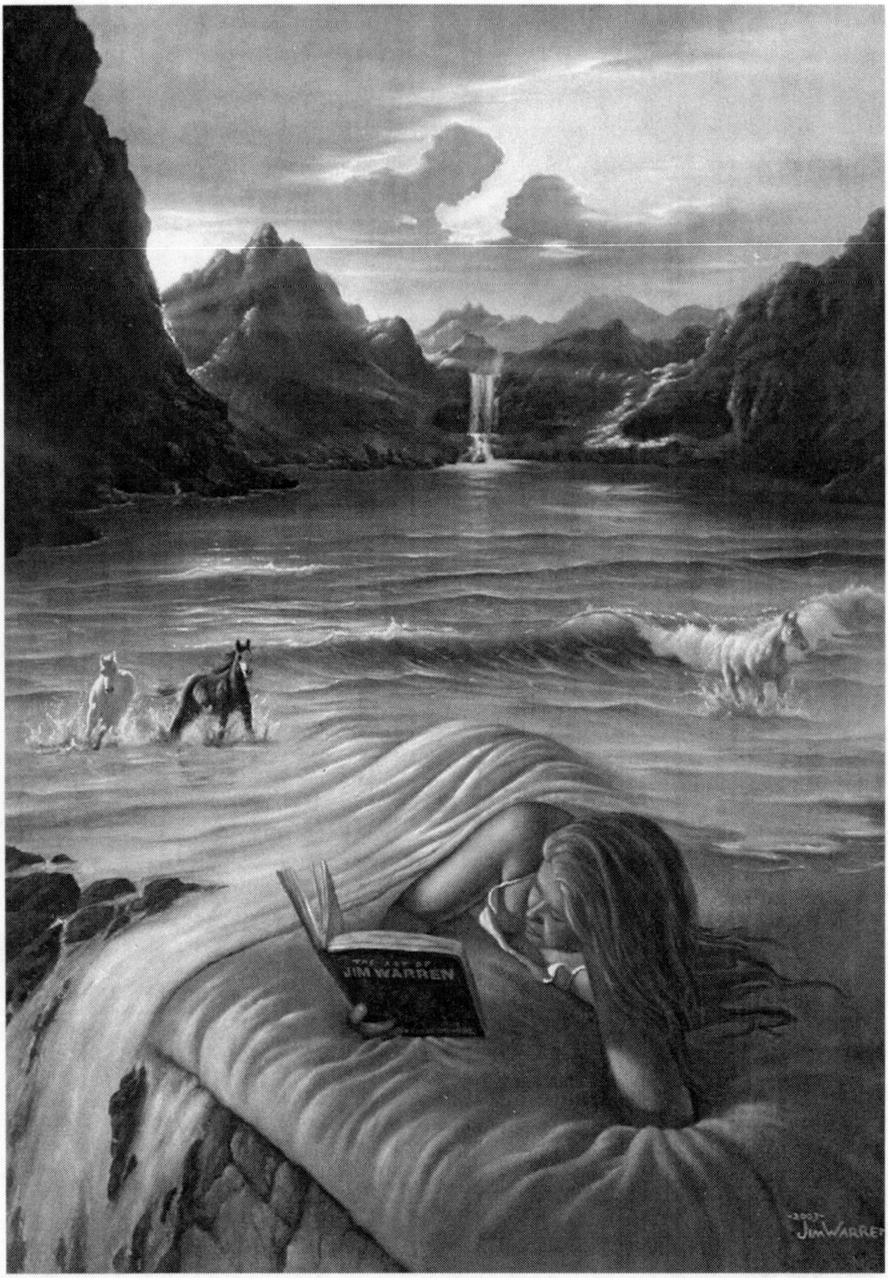
JIM WARREN

Chapter Six

The Stories We Tell

"Every man's world picture is and always remains a construct of his mind, and cannot be proved to have any other existence."
Erwin Schrödinger[1]

Contrary to popular perception, the deeper meaning and purpose of life as a human being has relatively little to do with the apparent events and circumstances we experience. The ego-self within the ordinary person attempts to believe the opposite—that my experience of all these *things* taking place in my world constitute absolute reality, and my purpose within reality is about manipulating, accumulating, and possessing these many things in some particular way. For the ordinary human there is also the perception that the seemingly external world creates the internal sense of reality, when in fact the external world is a construct and projection of Man's interiority. Yet all of this—the seemingly *external* world of form—is simply the dream.

How I approach this dream—the form side of Life—and the meaning I bring to it are what matters. In what way is the known side of my life impacting my power? In what way is my relationship to power being determined by my experience of the form side of Life? These two rather important questions rarely get asked, for the ordinary person

---

[1] (1887 to 1961) Austrian - Irish physicist famous for his contributions to quantum mechanics. Received a Nobel Price in 1933 for the development of the Schrödinger equation which, in simple terms, in is an equation that describes how the quantum state of a physical system varies

favours indulging in a never-ending game of storytelling. I could put these questions another way, in order to clarify what they mean.

1. How does my known world (the world I experience through my senses) impact how impeccably I live my life?

2. In what ways is my perception of life been affected by my relationship to the world around me?

In my late teens I started to realise my interpretation of the events and circumstances in my world creates an internal story. I became increasingly aware of this as time went by and with ongoing consideration. I realised I am constantly telling stories. Most everyone I meet is constantly telling stories too. Most of the people I discuss this with eventually realise and confirm they are in fact creating stories, although they may not have seen it that way prior to my enquiry. Typically we just think we are thinking about the way things *are*—without realising that it is our *thinking* that is creating our experience of the way things are. The whole world seems to be constantly telling stories, and we can see the most tangible form of this in the media, movies, gossip, history books, music, wars, et cetera, that go on, and on, and on—at least until we decide to get off.

This storytelling plays out in many ways. It plays out in many obvious day-to-day ways and also in subtle ways within each person not yet experiencing True Freedom. It is this storytelling that creates the script for the dream we find ourselves in. It is this storytelling that provides (or is) the script or tape running through the movie projector called the *human mind*.

Receiving the Gift of the Present

The other day I was at the supermarket with my brother, who met up with someone he knew, and they began to talk. They didn't plan to meet up, and it was obvious they hadn't talked to each other for quite some time. While I waited, I listened to what this man was saying. He talked about his story. It was a story about something that was apparently troubling him at work that week. It was not about the here and now, but was rather the story he was replaying within himself that *"certain people were not doing their jobs properly and this meant this and that and the other thing, and what can I do when they don't do this and that properly, et cetera."* This had nothing to do with what was peacefully here and now as they met and conversed together. It was simply a story from the past superimposed upon the present in order to avoid engaging with reality. Reality is only occurring in the *present*. This *present* is a *gift* most people refuse receiving without even knowing it. Perhaps this man felt uncomfortable meeting my brother and me in that moment. Perhaps he felt he needed to avoid being truly present for some reason. I won't know without making assumptions, so I can only guess what was going on for him.

How often do you simply relive stories? Stories that you've been playing over and over for quite some time now? How often do you fail to meet the present moment—say a chance meeting with an old friend or acquaintance—because you instead get caught up in telling an old story? These stories blot most, if not all, of the present out of our immediate experience. In my experience, this man did not truly *meet* my brother and me in that moment. He was not present to our meeting. Rather, he met with his story (his ego projection) and used the situation to perpetuate his story/ego. I am using these words "ego" and "story" together in this way because for most people the ego-self is in many regards simply an agglomeration of all the stories we each tell ourselves and the world about who and what we are.

It is my experience that each and every moment brings a gift. That gift is the gift of perception. Because *power* is the product of perception, each moment is also bringing to me a gift of power. I can, however, receive this gift only when I am myself *present* to the here and now in each moment of perception. It is no mistake that the words *present* and *gift* can be interchanged quite happily. The flip-side of this is when I am fully present to the situation at hand, here and now, That which I Am fulfils its role as a gift to the world and all my relations. The gift of the present is a two-way phenomenon. The degree to which I approach the present moment through the stories and beliefs of my past is the degree to which I shall miss the gift of power each moment naturally and willingly affords me. When I am present, I receive the gift of the present.

It's worth mentioning that whilst I have referred to "*each* moment," I don't mean to imply that there are lots of separate moments. As far as I can tell, there is only one moment, which we call now. The word moment comes from the Latin word *momentum* which means movement or moving power. It is movement of some kind—which I won't go into here—that brings about our perception of time. If all movement, all unfolding, ceased, then time stops too. One leaves time and enters the timeless. For the ego-self this is a rather unsettling experience because all history vanishes, from as far back as you can remember right up to a fraction of a second ago. Without your personal history the ego-self dies to its current state, and that's the scary part. In this regard *freedom* has no history. Oddly, if one then steps back into time—if perception of time resumes—there is no memory (not in the usual sense) of having been out of time. One might remember leaving time and returning to time, but the bit in between only lingers as an intuitive feeling that one was outside of time. Also in this regard, freedom has no history—freedom from time has no history, just as someone free from time loses and has no personal history.

Coming back to this observation of people living in past stories, I find this is something I see all going on constantly. When people gossip and chatter about stuff, they are, in my viewpoint, simply sharing stories from within their world and the worlds of other people. Gossiping is also storytelling. It has nothing to do with Reality, and nothing to do with the beauty and eloquence of Now. These are not true stories that people tell. They are all fiction. There's nothing "right" or "wrong" about this. It just is how it is, so I feel it's best we be honest about what is taking place. Only with absolute honesty about how I am, right now, can I ever possibly shift my perception and therefore shift my relationship to power, and through that, increase the power I embody.

THE SILENT STORIES WITHIN

The other way in which this storytelling game plays out is within each person—in our interiority. I have observed within myself that when I am coming from a place of a limited sense of ego-self, I will immediately start telling stories about the world I perceive around me. If someone comes up and says: "*Jonathan, you're an asshole and I hate you,*" I might tell a story that goes something like this: "*Oh, this person is so mean and horrible; how dare he say this about me. I am not an asshole.*

No, I certainly am not. Oh, I feel so hurt...so angry he would say such a thing. What a horrible thing to say. He has hurt and offended me. How could he? He can piss off and not ever come into my world again."

Underneath this, at a deeper level of the ego-mind, another story might be playing out such as: "*Oh, gosh, am I really an asshole? What have I done wrong? Am I really such a bad guy? I know I am quite silly sometimes, and do stupid things—my father always used to tell me that too. How stupid of me. Oh, and now this person hates me... it is understandable really....*"

This is all storytelling. It's all fiction. It's all a lie actually. It's all part of my personal Lore.

This person shared his story with me. That was all. Nothing more. The story he told me was that he hated me and that in his experience I am what he has eloquently referred to as "an asshole." He told me this fictional story. He shared with me an element of his dream. From a place of my limited ego-self I then started to tell my own story about this. It's as if he gave me a chapter of a book (the life-long story) and then I provided the next chapter as a continuation of his chapter. I maintained the continuity of the story. His dream and my dream merged for a while. I chose to let his dream merge with mine.

If I were not hearing him through the eyes and ears of my limited sense of ego-self, I would have heard a very different story and hence told a very different one. This man in his world would have said what he said, yet what I would have heard might have been something like this: "Jonathan, I am in pain and I am calling out for love, for I am blind to the Love that I AM. In my pain I am projecting out at you the way I feel about and judge myself in this dream."

"I have given everything I see... all the meaning it has for me."

A Course In Miracles

THE LOVE STORY

In truly listening to what is said, rather than telling a sad and pain-filled story around the challenging events in my world, I will instead tell a story of Love, for that is naturally what the next *chapter* would look like, when it is written by one's Divinity. I liken it to a movie: One scene leads into the next and there is a continuity of theme running through them, otherwise the movie would be all jittery, jumping from one unrelated image to the next. For some people this is how much of their dream is, jittery and jumping randomly from one picture to the next within their minds. Perhaps you're aware of how your mind jumps around from one thing to the next.

If I truly hear and feel humanity's call for love, the only story I will tell will be a loving one. Likewise, if I hear a story of attack and hatred, in the next scene in the movie (the scene where I now step into the role of lead actor) I will tell a story of attack and hatred. Most likely it will be a story of attack and hatred toward myself, and that might then lead to the next scene where I tell a story of attack and hatred toward this man as an act of revenge. About now, a fight might break out and we go to war with each other. In truth it is only our egos that are at war, and it is only our malu that are engaging with each other.

On the other hand, when I hear and recognise nothing but *a call for love* I will immediately find myself within *a love story*. Love stories begin and end with love—even the ones we perceive to have *sad endings* are in fact part of the mysterious perfection of love. As each moment is the Alpha and Omega (the beginning and the end) unto itself, this story will be wholly (holy) loving. I will hear this man's story, "Jonathan, I am in pain and I am calling out to you for love," and I will then continue this love story by extending the Love That I Am into his dream, in whatever way is appropriate—which may depend on what he is ready for.

You see, in the first and typical scenario I was hearing this man's projection and matching it up with the Rules in my personal Lore. When I find elements of my Lore that state I am less than perfect and beautiful, I will align this with what this man has just projected into my dream. What he has said will polarize with my own dream pertaining to myself—with some of my personal Lore. This will then give rise to emotional energy that I am in this moment being challenged to feel, embody, and master. Because I have not yet learnt to master this energy, there is bound to be one or more malu associated or aligned with it. These malu will go into relationship with this man in my dream. As it was only his malu that called me an asshole in the first place, my malu are in fact going into relationship with his malu. A large proportion of relationship dynamics going on in the world are of this kind—malu relating to malu. The people involved (the hosts) have often checked out or are just standing back watching from a distance internally and perhaps feeling totally or partially out of control.

As mentioned earlier, when I put my List Of Rules in Error aside, I end the folly of relating to my dream through these rules and start to experience the world through my virtues—my life-giving qualities. I then experience this man and his projection of self-abuse with Love, not with my personal Lore.

How centered I Am within God's Vision of the world will determine the exact story I tell. If I am centered in God's Vision of this man, then the story I tell might go something like this: "God[2] is the only power. God is all there is. God is love and God knows only Love, and knows nothing of pain or suffering. I am an extension of God; therefore I am Love and I know nothing of pain. I am wholly Love and this world is an extension of My Mind. The man I see here is an extension of That Mind. I share My Mind with God and hence this man is Love and knows nothing of pain or suffering. For I AM wholly Love within this man and he is 'I' also."

Now, that's a rather long story and it can be told in just two words, if I have a clear relationship and experience of my true nature as a Divine Being. That whole story could be condensed down to *"God Is"* or *"God is, and That I Am"* with the deep feeling that what I see before me is, in fact, my Self. It can even be told without any words at all. That's when the story becomes a blissful silent state of prayer or meditation—silent communion with Reality. Here is simply, yet profoundly and truthfully, the feeling of Truth, the Truth being that this man and I AM one and I AM an extension of God; I am Love. The key here is held within our capacity to feel because our deep intuitive feelings have their source not in this known world, but in the unknown.

As you can see, these are examples of two very different stories I can tell. This apparent situation with this apparent man (actually just a figment of my dream) *has happened for me and not to me*. It has happened for me so that I may set myself free—both within this apparent man before me and within my apparent self. In setting my Self free I set the world free too. The first example was a story about fear and hatred, but

---

2 Feel free to replace my use of the word *God* here (and throughout this book) with another word of your choice which refers to the Supreme Source of all-that-is.

it can only be told if there are ears to hear it and a mind to conceive it. If I don't have the ears to hear it, it doesn't exist—for I experience only that which I conceive within my imagination, then impregnate into my energy system (my physical and non-physical body), and birth into my world through Dreaming. Ponder that for a moment.

The other story was a beautiful love story with a happy ending—one where everyone is acknowledged as That which they truly are. Again, this love story can only be told and heard if I have the Vision to see it. This is the Vision of the human heart. It is not something familiar to our current state of ego identity. If the limited ego does appear to be telling a loving story, then it's just a fairy tale that it's telling me in order to try to avoid its story being seen for what it really is—a story of pain, fear and separation.

THE NEVER-ENDING STORY

What I wish to impress upon your mind—to re-mind you of—is that unless you have already broken this habit, you are constantly telling stories. Most of these stories are pure fiction. Occasionally some wondrous inspiration—something true—will make its way through the noise of all these stories, and it's important to have enough lucidity of mind to be alert to when it does. Some stories get pretty far out—science fiction perhaps! Most of these stories are lies. They have no basis of Reality in them. I know if you really recognise what I am saying here, you will start to see you are literally telling thousands of stories all the time—and not just about what you think you are experiencing in this moment but also about nearly everything that has ever happened to you. This is called "my personal history." Right now, take a moment to think about someone in your past whom you really don't like and have had trouble getting along with. Immediately, I am sure, you will be facing your story about them. That story plays again and again in your mind whether you give your attention to it or not.

Yes, all these stories are being told over and over all the time in every moment. It's no wonder the mind can seem so busy and noisy most, if not all, of the time. This noise is all these stories playing like stuck records going round in a loop. It's also no wonder most people find they hardly have enough energy to do the things they believe they "have to" do (like working, shopping, eating, et cetera), let alone the many dreams they have of what they would like to do. All the energy that is given to them each day to conceive and birth the various inspirations they have into their dream, ends up being consumed with maintaining all their stories and dealing with the many dramas that come up around those stories.

I know this is how it is because this is what I have seen in myself and in my part within this dream. As I Am you, in Truth, it must be the same for you in one way or another—that too is why you are reading this book. We might appear to tell ourselves different stories, yet even that is an illusion. I have found there are only two basic themes to every story humans seem to tell. I either tell a horror story—one of fear, lack, separation, and attack—or a Love story—a story of Love and Acceptance and Truth. All the billions (trillions) of stories that appear to be possible all come back to a variation on these two themes in one form or another. Such is the simplicity and complicity of it All. Of course, you will have to make up your own mind about what of this is true for you.

REPLACING THE STORY – AN EXPERIMENT

A story can only be told if there is someone there to listen to it. Just as human beings are great storytellers, we are also our greatest fan and audience. The ego-mind listens very attentively to everything it has to say. We basically talk to ourselves. We are at once both the narrator and the audience.

It is possible to replace your stories with a new and very simple one. For the next week or more I invite you to conduct the following experiment.

Every time you catch yourself judging your situation or thinking up a story about your immediate world, immediately replace that thought with another—with something simple like "beautiful," or "I love you," or something along these lines. For instance, walking into the kitchen you may notice there's someone else's mess on the bench and this may be something that typically annoys you. Rather than engaging in the story that "this bench is a mess…who has left all these pots here…am I the only one who thinks about cleaning up after myself…" (or whatever your story may be), instead immediately replace this thought with the word "beautiful." Just drop the story, and replace it.

Similarly, if you see a person and you notice your mind immediately creating judgments such as "that guy looks like a real slacker... look at his messy clothes" (or whatever), again replace the story with something more life-giving such as "I love you" or "beautiful."

It is important to note in this thought substitution exercise that this is not about suppressing the feelings that are coming up in response to your perception of the world around you. Rather this is about generating a new feeling and thus a new perception. So for this to work effectively you must not fixate your attention on the words in your mind, or fixate on the replacement word or words. Your attention should instead be engaged with a felt-sense within the Body-mind. First a felt-sense of what had come up in the way of a judgment or criticism, and again with the felt-sense of what you are replacing this judgment with. If you do not experience a transformation of this felt-sense from disharmony to Inner Peace, then this suggests there is deeper work to be done than this simple thought substitution exercise.

In a situation where you are more intensely engaged with a person or circumstance and it is bringing up a lot of destructive emotional energy for you, try asking Infinity to reveal its true nature to you. "Infinite Source, where are you in this situation? Show me now," or "Infinity is the only reality here, let me see this here, now." Again, use whatever statement works for you. The key here is to replace all the life-taking garbage thoughts that relentlessly repeat in your mind with something more life-giving and in alignment with reality. You've got nothing to lose right? It's just a weary old story you're giving up (and for just a few weeks, right?). So give it a go and discover something new.

Elsewhere in this book we will look at how to unravel your stories and judgments as a means of gaining deeper awareness into your limiting beliefs and perceptions. When exploring that path, this one of replacing them with a new word can be carried out afterwards—once you have become cognisant of what your original story consists of.

So I invite you to play with this self-experiment. Observe how you feel and what happens to your energy levels when you drop all the relentless stories your Attentive-mind has been paying so much attention to. Be aware that at first it will take rather a lot of discipline to make the most of this experience. Yet you will most certainly find after a few weeks and months of this the mind will start to quite naturally either remain peacefully aware and silent, or will bring a loving and life-giving affirmation to the many details of your life.

STORIES WITHIN THE TRI-PART SELF

I have found that this process of story-telling plays out in different ways within the three aspects of self we explored in the model of the Triune or Tri-part self.

Stories play out in the Body-mind at an emotional level (where they are felt as emotional energy moving and changing) and also at the physical level. It is at this physical level that life-taking stories bring about tension, dis-ease, ill health, stagnation and degeneration. All of these degenerate physical manifestations are an attempt from the Body-mind to restore and maintain balance. It takes a fair amount of life-force to maintain stories from the past here in the present. One could liken it to swimming up a stream as opposed to flowing with the stream. The Now is the flow of the stream, and when I am psychologically not living in the Now I go against the stream and it is rather enervating. Imagine if right now whilst still going about your business you had to verbally, out loud, repeat a story constantly in a loop, for the next 10 minutes. Now imagine doing it for an entire day? Add to this, if you will, that it is not just one story you are telling for a whole day but in fact 5 stories simultaneously. It is tiring just thinking about it, let alone doing it. Yet at a conscious and subconscious level this is exactly what most people are doing. Not just for one day, and not just 5 stories, but every day (and night) and many stories all at once.

This life-force has to come from somewhere and what I and many others have observed is that sooner or later it is drawn from the physical body. Prior to this it may find its source of energy in the mental and emotional bodies, but eventually as they collapse down (depression) into the physical form this energy is sourced at this level. It is at this stage that sickness and enervation set in. When our life-force is caught up in maintaining our stories it is unavailable for health, vitality, inspiration, creativity, and genius—making the fulfillment of our purpose difficult, if not impossible.

At the level of the ego-self our storytelling manifests as slanted and distorted perception, fixation on particular points-of-view, constant mental dialogue and monologue, limiting beliefs and possible fanaticism around those beliefs. Denial is also likely to set in, be that denial of one's current state of being or denial of the true nature of reality in the grander scheme of Life.

In the Spirit-mind these dynamics play out as karmic tendencies, a deeply unconscious and rigid perception of reality, unconscious and relatively contracted personal agendas that result in a tendency to try and manipulate reality, situations, people, and even perception itself in order to maintain a particular deep-seated perspective on "the way things are."

We could explore all of this in greater detail, yet I feel that this is all that is required for now, as my intention is to simply illustrate the interconnected nature of how something such as storytelling plays out within the triune self.

I invite and encourage you to give attention each day to becoming aware of the stories you tell about the world. You will notice yourself telling them to other people. You will notice you repeat them to yourself through the mental chatter in your mind. Take note. Be aware, and know that these stories are not based on Reality. Such awareness will set you free.

Empowering Principles & Perspectives

- The external world is a construct and projection of my interiority.

- How I approach this dream—the form side of Life—and the meaning I bring to it are what matters.

- My interpretation of the events and circumstances in my world creates an internal story.

- My thinking is creating my experience of the way things are.

- Reality is only occurring in the present. This present is a gift most people refuse receiving without even knowing it.

- My human ego-identity is an agglomeration of the stories I tell myself and the world about who and what I am.

- Freedom has no history; there is no history to one's freedom.

- Gossiping—inwardly and outwardly—is also storytelling. It has nothing to do with Reality, and nothing to do with the beauty and eloquence of Now.

- If I truly hear and feel humanity's call for love in every person and human event, the only story I will tell will be a loving one.

- My deep intuitive feelings have their source in the unknown.

- In setting myself free I set the world free.

- I experience only that which I conceive of in my imagination.

- A love story will be told if I have the vision to see it. This is the vision of the Heart.

- Telling false stories about Life consumes our life-force, making it unavailable for health, vitality, inspiration, creativity, and genius.

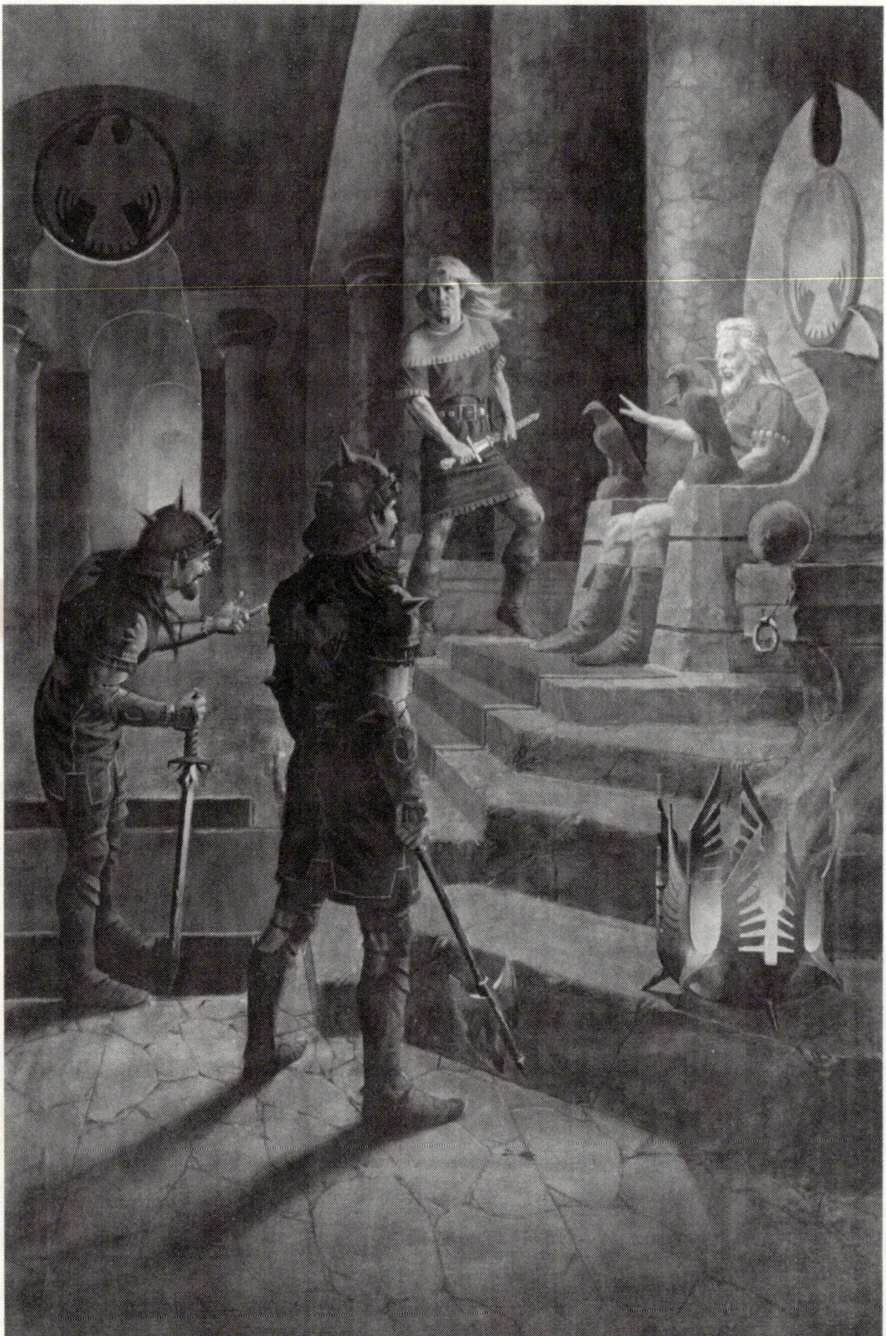

Chapter Seven

Your Realm and the King Who Fell

"They that can give up essential liberty to obtain a little temporary safety deserve neither liberty nor safety."
Benjamin Franklin

I want us to go on a little journey together. I would like you and me to take a look at a once mighty King, a King who falls from his Kingship and no longer knows of his power and might, or his rulership of the world he sees around him. First, we will take a look at some aspects of the world, perception, knowledge, and objective reality.

The World and the Earth

Pause for a moment now.

Ask yourself, "Is there any difference between what I call the world and that which I call the earth?" Feel into the answer, your own inner answer, to this question. Give it some time and space to unfold from within you. Hold that thought.

Now ask yourself, "Is there just one world, or are there in fact many worlds, and just where in reality does the world exist anyway? What's more, how can I know the answers to these questions about the world, if I myself am in the world I perceive and have nothing with which to compare it one way or the other?" Again, allow some time and space for your answers to come forth.

I am going to share with you now an element of my experience of the Earth and what we collectively and individually refer to as the "world." There is nothing new about this story of the Earth and the world that I am about to share, yet it is my wish that my sharing may serve as a reminder to people who have forgotten this particular story about the way things are.

In my experience, and according to this story, there is one so-called "Earth"—the mass of intelligently organised quantum and physical *stuff* spinning at great velocity through space and around what we call the Sun. She—the Earth—is her own Being with her own experience of evolution or self unfolding through time and space, and beyond time and space. The Earth is intelligent and conscious, yet she doesn't embody awareness in the same way that human beings do. The Earth, in her own right, embodies a different quality of awareness to that of human beings. Just as the awareness embodied by different people and especially races and cultures varies even among what we collectively call "humanity." Likewise, the awareness that a plant could be said to have most certainly differs from that of a human being. The Earth does also *embody* human awareness, in the way we collectively do, in cooperation with the Spirit of humankind—our bodies, after all, are the Earth!

So there is one Earth, and then we have what most people call "the world." The world is quite different from the Earth. Imagine this if you will, and imagine how this might be…

You see, the world is something within our consciousness that we superimpose onto our experience of the Earth. It's not actually accurate to say "the world," for there are in fact many billions of worlds. Actually there are in fact as many worlds as there are people to perceive them. Each contains elements of the Earth and her evolution and consciousness, to a lesser or greater degree, and each contains other factors that come from our individual and collective Dream. Your world may contain many elements that appear to be in accordance with and consistent with the world of people you meet and relate to from day to day. According to this particular story of the world it is also said that many human beings—the spirit within these people—bring with them perceptual tendencies and predispositions from other planets and places in our universe, although we won't go into that for now, except to say that this has created an even greater diversity in the many worlds here on Earth. This has had a significant effect on the course of human evolution.

Perception

Now imagine your world is the result of a great mystery called perception, and each human being has a truly unique point of view—a unique perception. Yet how does this perception operate and how does a world come into being in the mind of humankind? Imagine, if you will now, vast empty space. Dark. Empty. Yet aware and alive—it is like a vast womb, empty, yet teeming with the potential of Life. Imagine one strand of something akin to a spider web. Thin, shiny, and luminous—it's as if a bright light is illuminating this thin strand from within, and it is stretching out further than your mind can see. Now picture more of these strands, and even more now. Imagine there are millions, trillions, in fact an infinite number of these strands spread throughout the vast empty womb-like space. Now you notice an area where these strands coalesce into what looks like one of those pictures you may have seen of a hurricane photographed from outer space. A tight twirl in the midst of all these strands, pulling a large number of strands tighter and tighter together to a point at the center of this twirl. It is here at the center of this spiral that a world is born, in the mind of Man. Now consider this: each person on Earth shares a very similar set of these strands—giving rise to perception—yet each has a slightly different set and arrangement from the next person—giving rise to a perception unique to him or her alone.

Collective World Views

When we refer to any given collective of people as a culture or society, we are simply referring to a group of people (perhaps hundreds of millions or more) that collectively agree on and adhere to similar basic sets of elements of how they go about constructing or perceiving their worlds. This is, in part, represented by what we call a culture's predominant world-view, a religion's theology, a metaphysician's cosmology, or a society's beliefs and philosophical perspectives. If a member of a society deviates from the society's world-view too dramatically, this person may be labelled as eccentric at best, and possibly as mad or insane—they are classified as de-ranged, literally meaning they have gone outside the range of perception that society considers normal or acceptable. If an individual deviates only in particular areas of their reality—whilst remaining relatively "normal" in most regards (usually social ones)—such as believing in and promoting the healing power of using herbs as opposed to drugs for health and healing, he may be labelled as a quack or a natural health freak, but still be accepted within the society.

The world we, as humanity, collectively experience was created by Man and Woman. In reality—or so this story goes—there is only one Man and one Woman, or more precisely, there is one Divine Masculine Principle and one Divine Feminine Principle, each representing a particular quality of Awareness. They are like two sides of one coin—they are inseparable, they are one, yet each side of that coin has a very different view on the space around it. It is said that the Feminine side of the coin faces the vast Unknown, whilst the other side, the Masculine of course, faces into the Known.

Hand in Hand

I have noticed that many intelligent thinking people believe the present state of the world has been predominantly influenced by the Masculine Principle as expressed (primarily) through Man—oftentimes unconsciously, haphazardly, and destructively. Going along with this line of thought, one must also suppose the Masculine principle within Woman followed the lead of her male counterpart, although it would appear she's started to wisen up more recently. I've even heard it said that men throughout history seem to be so destructive, and that women are not like this and have played no part in this destruction. I don't disagree with the above mentioned observation, yet it does seem somewhat incomplete. You see, according to the story I am recounting to you now, the Feminine principle, as expressed (primarily) through Woman, has not been a victim to Man and his destructive gallivanting in the world. Contrary to what many proactive and passive feminists would like the world to believe, Woman, in her unconsciousness state (like Man), has supported this haphazard and imbalanced co-creation in one way or another. The Masculine and Feminine principles of creation are neither mutually exclusive nor independent of one another. As I said, they are like two sides of the same coin. They may at times be antagonistic yet never entirely separate. The antagonism that plays out between the Masculine and the Feminine is part of the fulfillment of the Universal Intention for expanding and furthering Awareness. Collectively Man and Woman—as expressions of the Divine Masculine and Feminine sides of Awareness—have created the world as it now stands.

Each of us, until we wake up to our true Identity—our true and essential I-entity—will at some level feel trapped within, or at least confined and limited to, our particular experience of "the world." Far from being something intrinsic that is out there and happening to us, the world you and I experience is actually the projection of the perceptual constructs within one's mind. We literally co-create the world from these mental constructs or thought-forms. Using the terminology just given, the degree to which my thought-forms or mental constructs coincide and correlate with yours is the degree to which we appear to be living in the same so-called "world." In simple terms, this is how the collective Dream configuration—the configuration of those strands of Awareness you imagined—is woven together.

Objective Reality? Perhaps Not...

In the Toltec and other mystic traditions, it would be said that the way in which humans assemble their perception of reality conforms to a particular range of what is possible, or what is perceivable. At a metaphysical level, the form side of Life was identified by the Toltec as many strands of light—the ones we explored a few pages ago. The phenomenon of perception is one whereby the Intent working through a human being causes certain of these strands to coalesce into a bright spot of light when seen within the human energy field. This spot is referred to as the assemblage point. Again, a culture is made up of people who subconsciously agree to keep their assemblage point within a certain restricted range of movement or locality. Once outside that range, a person is said to be de-ranged. A very quick way to change the position of the assemblage point is the use of psychoactive substances, where one immediately experiences a new and at times unexplainable perception of the world, the Earth, and Life itself.

Slower, yet perhaps more sustainable and less haphazard methods, involve certain spiritual practices, visualisations, an initiations.

Despite the fact that many empirical skeptics would like to deny it, contemporary—or shall we say "leading edge"—science is presently slipping over the proverbial edge of historic reason and discovering that the nature of reality cannot be separated from the mind that perceives it. Quantum scientists began to discover that the quantum particles they were trying to observe and empirically define would in fact change their state based on the expectation of the scientist. This made it rather tricky to draw any fixed conclusions about the definitive nature of these quantum particles. In the field of psychology there is a well-established perception that after quite early in our childhood much of what our brain conjures up in the way of images and experiences is in fact pieced together at a level of re-cognition. It is understood that as adults we typically take in (through our senses) just a small percentage of what is "out there," cognise that small percentage and then re-cognise the rest of our experience from memory via a complex process of association. So without even taking on board the modern theories of the quantum universe, the empirical world-view does to some degree assert that we are "co-creating our own perception of reality."

I Know Nothing

In order to break free from our apparent bondage and the suffering in this world—this collective Dream configuration—we will each, sooner or later, open ourselves and surrender to the realisation that "I have no idea what is going on here in the world." Humbly accepting this lack of real knowing might just afford us the psychological and spiritual space and flexibility to breathe in something entirely new that will inspire us toward love and away from our collective fixation on fear. Most people falsely believe that they have a reasonable understanding of how the world operates, whether that understanding be consistent with the established world-view of the materialists and empirical skeptics, or the increasingly popular world-view of the contemporary spiritualist and those who identify with the so-called New Age movement—either way much of it is only true at the level of consciousness through which it arises, and represents a relatively slow and convoluted journey to freedom that will one day be transcended. In my own experience, I've been observing and studying the nature of reality and the world both inside me and around me since I was in my early teens. Now, nearly two decades later, I can safely say I know less and less every day, simply because with each discovery I make, the playing field increases in scope. I can see now, that this field of perception has no end to it—it's Infinite.

THERE'S LIFE, JIM, BUT NOT AS WE KNOW IT

"If real is what you can feel, smell, taste and see, then 'real' is simply electrical signals interpreted by your brain."

Morpheus
in The Matrix (movie)

Since childhood I have observed that many of the people I have met and seen (personally or vicariously) essentially have no idea how reality comes into being nor (more importantly) what exactly is playing out on this planet. A lot of people have hardly a clue as to what really goes on in the world with regard to global politics; global economics; global banking and finance; the disastrous effects of American foreign policy (which, using the US Government's own definition for the term, can be technically classified as terrorism); the nature, impact and true motivation of economic globalisation; the real-life impact of organisations like the World Bank and World Trade Organisation; the extent of environmental destruction taking place; the illusions and lies regarding the post 9/11 threat from "the Axis of Evil" and "the wide-spread global terrorist threat" we hear so much about in the post-9/11 media; the true motivation behind the many "wars" the USA and other countries have declared such as "the war on cancer," "the war on drugs," "the war on terrorism," "the war on communism," (et cetera), and the actual outcome of these "wars"; and a whole array of other issues that humanity is facing the effects of every day—knowingly or not.

My point is that there is a great deal more going on in the world than ever meets most eyes and ears—things that would both shock the unsuspecting masses, and things that would amaze, enlighten, and inspire them. In my life it was my inherent awareness of these many other "things" that allowed me to be content and happy with not inwardly conforming to the collective mindset. I agreed in many ways with the analogy I once read that said something like this: Humanity is like a family in a high speed car, heading toward a large and solid wall; there's a brick on the accelerator, we haven't figured out how to steer it, and we have no idea how to hit the brakes. Yet we sit there in this car, watching the world whiz by at an ever-increasing pace, thinking we are making some kind of desirable progress. The good news is that it's all a Dream. The good news is that it is not "humanity" that is in control of Life and the perfect fulfillment of Universal Intention. Nonetheless, it is humanity that will have to awaken, change its ways, and step beyond our complete fixation on fear and separation.

CORRUPTION AND DENIAL

The world of human affairs is heavily corrupt and distorted in more ways than most people would care or dare to imagine. The ego-self that created this world will rigorously defend against this contention. It will come up with all sorts of arguments to refute what I've just stated here. Ordinary Man—those people not yet embodying Peace, Power, and Presence—derive many aspects of their sense of security, their sense of existence, their sense of purpose, and their sense of stability and survival from their false perception of the world. Hence, what I have just said about the world being so heavily corrupt and manipulated is something most will try to deny.

Many of the people I have met, even those who consider themselves to be "spiritually aware," seem to choose to remain ignorant of just how distorted the human world has become. I don't point this out as something "wrong," it is merely an observation for the sake of understanding where we are and how things are. I have observed that within this state of ignorance a lot of people choose to continue going about an ego-centered approach to life under the illusion that this is how things will continue to unfold forever. The folly in this is that nothing could be further from the truth. Paradoxically the present state of human affairs is exactly what had to unfold in order for Awareness—for Life—to evolve in the way it does.

Let's take a quick trip back into my childhood. Come and join me there for a moment as you step into the story now…

"Truth is stranger than fiction, but it is because fiction is obliged to stick to possibilities; Truth isn't."

Mark Twain

HUMANITY'S OLD MENTAL BLOCKS

When Jonathan was 8 or 9 years of age, there was a national political election taking place in New Zealand. The country was deciding on who the next government and Prime Minister would be. These happen every three years in the country where he lives. Radio, television, and billboards were all awash with information and advertising related to the elections. Signs with words and photos on them were on every major corner and intersection promoting one politician or political party over another. One couldn't help but notice all this going on, and Jonathan was no exception. He looked at all this fuss and felt it was all a bit mad and seemed to have no real purpose. He also felt like much of the time the people were being lied to, and this did not feel "good" to him.

One day, whilst driving home with his mother from somewhere they'd been to visit that day — there may have been some election-related material playing on the radio — he made the following comment:

"Mum, why do people vote each time an election happens? What do they think it is going to achieve?"

It was explained that this is how a democratic political system works, along with other related information, long since forgotten by Jonathan now.

Jonathan considered all this for a while, and then replied:

"But the whole system is a mess, it is not going to improve this way, and voting won't make any difference." He paused as if taking a moment to imagine something, and continued, "It's like we have a whole lot of building blocks to construct our society with. These blocks are all damaged and crumbling on the inside. Many of them might look okay on the surface, yet they are rotten inside and falling apart, or close to it. Society and the systems we have are made out of these blocks. Each time there is an election we are voting on how we want to rearrange the blocks into a new configuration so that we seem to have a new construction. The people in the society are never all happy with the outcome. Most of them seem to always be complaining about something in the society. They always want various things to be different and they vote for a new government with the idea that this will improve things because each political party promotes just how its way of combining the blocks is better than the other party's way. But because all the blocks are faulty inside, it really doesn't matter how we arrange them. Whatever structure we build with such blocks is also going to be faulty and will one day collapse."

His mother inquired as to what he thought the alternative was.

"Mum, I don't know, but it's like somehow we just have to create completely new building blocks and start constructing things with these. I don't know how we'll manage to do that, but nothing else will work. You can't build a house with bad building materials and expect the house to be stronger than what it is made of. We have to do things — everything — in in a whole new and different way." Jonathan had no idea in that moment just how such a feat could be pulled off, yet he felt strongly that something as major as this would be required if his vision of the potential of the world was ever to be made manifest.

I remember that conversation well. Of course, I don't recall the exact words used at the time so I have told the story based on what I remember and partly how I would tell it now. The gist of what I saw at that time, and up to this day, is that the "system" in which we live is fundamentally flawed through and through. A great architect friend of my brother once said to him, when he was expressing his distress over the ego- and greed-driven politics within the architectural and construction industry; "Justin, I've looked at a lot of different things on this planet, and I tell you the world is rotten to the core. It's rotten to the core."[1]

Remember, the so-called "world" is a construct in our consciousness. Therefore it makes no real difference how we piece together the various "parts" or elements of this system. The end result will also always be flawed or rotten through and through if our perception of reality is flawed and in error. We have to do away with the existing "building blocks" — human thought-forms — and create entirely new ones based on completely different sets of principles and inner wisdom. This is taking place right now, and it is not easy as it necessitates the death of

---

1   Not a verbatim account, but it was something to this effect.

our ego (as it currently stands) and its obsolete reality, whilst simultaneously experiencing the birth of a new perceptual paradigm into collective consciousness. We must shed this obsolete perception of Life in the same way a snake sheds its skin, or a butterfly does away with the caterpillar. There was nothing "wrong" with the old skin, nor with the caterpillar; it's just that their purpose has been served.

Since that time, all those years ago, I have come to realise the "building blocks" — as I called them back then — are in fact within you and me. The people, and the constructs within the minds of the people, are the building blocks I was referring to — although I didn't quite see that back then. The worldly objects and concepts we constantly reshuffle around in order to make things more comfortable are a projection of these building blocks — these thoughts forms — into the world. The building blocks of this world are all contained within our Mind. Healing the world, or reconstructing the world into a place more aligned with our Divinity, will take place through healing our Mind and reconstructing our thought-forms. I am not the first to say this, nor am I the only one. Once we open our eyes it becomes apparent that many have said this in the past and many are saying it right now, all around the Earth.

The fundamental change I was talking about is something that must — and will — take place within the human Mind... within the Spirit of all my Relations. Only then will the so-called outer world take on a new form and appearance. Only then will the Dream change. Sooner or later, we literally must revise (re-vision) the in-form-ation we have at hand, and conceive of a new way of being that accurately reflects our awesome power and magnificence as Divine beings... the Divine made manifest in consciousness and in form. We must use our imagination to start dreaming up a world wholly different from what we have dreamed so far. Everything you see in the human world had its seed in the imagination of Man, so at one level it is only a matter of using our imagination in a new way in order to bring about the change that is required for Humankind to create a future not filled with the collective pain we are experiencing now.

So how did the global state of affairs get this way? Is this man in the sky called "God" punishing us? Is this retribution for eating that forbidden apple Adam and Eve got on the wrong side of God with? Did we fall from Grace, from Eden, and what was that place anyway?

I have another story to tell. Will you join me now?

Let me introduce you to the King and Queen. The master and ruler of the world—your world, and mine.

THE KING AND HIS REALM

Once upon a time, before time began, there existed a beautiful world, and in that world a mystical land. This land stretches as far as the eyes can see. To the North, there are magnificent mountains ascending into the clouds. They are higher than anyone known to this land has explored, and have never been crossed as far as people can remember. To the South is a beautiful ocean, stretching out into the distance. There are lush forests and crystal-blue lakes, with lively rivers flowing into them from a source high in the mountains.

In the middle of this land is a vast Kingdom. The Kingdom extends as far as your eyes can see in all directions. You can see what appears to be a golden line around the full perimeter of the Kingdom, and you realise this defines its boundaries. Guards sit in towers along the golden line, ensuring that only those who come in a way that is "life-giving" cross this line and make entry into the Kingdom—which like any true Kingdom in its height of glory, has an air of mystique and fortune about it.

Right in the middle of this Kingdom is a majestic castle that stands tall and silently, yet radiantly, proud. It appears to be made of gold, although you consider that perhaps these walls are made of large, solid earthen bricks only painted in gold. It's hard to tell, although it's an inspiration for your mind to see and a joy to behold. Rising from slightly north of center, approximately in the middle of the castle, is a high tower—high enough that from this vantage point one can look out and see the entire Kingdom and all its land. This tower is higher than one might imagine a castle would have, with a view surpassed by no other, except perhaps that from the top of the mountains in the North.

I am sure, by now, you can say who it is that would be looking out from this vantage point, right? Yes, there is a King there in the tower, and outside with earth on her hands, the Queen is working with her abundant gardens. From these locations they can see each other easily, and of course they meet within the castle at times throughout the day; they make love within the royal bedroom at night. This love that they make, or "create," pours out into the surrounding land and kingdom, although not in a way that your naked eye would see. It is a golden ball of soft yet warming light that radiates out from the castle by day and by night. The King and the Queen live in a way that is harmonious, innately understanding, and they live by the principles of intelligent or life-giving co-operation. They have always known that love in this world is best expressed by co-operating in a way that is life-giving for all concerned—in a way that is intelligent and wise. They have never had to think about the way they interact, for it has always been as it is—the epitome of intelligent co-operation.

Taking your attention back to the mountains in the far North, you can see that there is one particular river, with a steady and strong flow, carving a channel down from the high peaks, making its way right through the Kingdom and eventually out to sea. This river differs from the rest in that it has the appearance of what might best be described as liquid light, glistening like a torrent of diamonds. The castle, perhaps strangely to a mind none the wiser, was built over the top of this river. At the front and rear of this compound is a channel into which the river flows—controlled, in fact "focused," for just a brief period on its winding path—before it pours out the other side, continuing toward the sea. Here in the depths of the castle the King has a large waterwheel in place. The flow of water through this channel provides the much-needed energy for this castle to operate and be maintained. Water is also drawn off at this point and used in the Castle and its surrounding gardens through a system of channels.

The High Priest of the Kingdom also comes to the river here beneath the castle in order to draw mana (life-force) from it. "And what of the magicians and shamans in the area?" you might ask. Well their tale is for another story entirely, but let it be known that they draw their mana from the river further upstream and from the trees in the forests.

You can now recognise that this flow of water and all the vital energies within it are crucial to the health and wellbeing of the Kingdom.

✵ ✵ ✵

This story of the realm we have briefly explored is akin to what some mythologies call "The Garden of Eden." The King and Queen are what these same mythologies call Adam and Eve. The archetypes of Adam and Eve exist within each of us, be we man or woman. Woman embodies more the energy or archetype of Eve (the Divine feminine principle or the feminine polarity of Awareness), whilst Adam (the Divine masculine principle or the masculine polarity of Awareness) is there too, although he stands in the background. Man embodies primarily the energy of Adam, yet Eve is not far beneath the surface. The King in our fable represents the fully realised earthly potential of the creative masculine principle within each of us. The Queen is representative of the fully realised earthly potential of the supportive, nurturing, sustaining, and ultimately enlightening feminine principle. Neither can function without the other if life is to unfold in a balanced and life-giving way—for they are like two sides of the same coin.

We each live in our own realm and symbolically it is like the one I have described—although even more incredible, albeit incomprehensible. At the level of our Divine nature we are each the master or sovereign of our realm—the King and Queen of our world. We are each the master and creator of our world within our own field of perception—within the Mind and within consciousness. Humanity, however, has taken a fall somewhere along the way, and subsequently slipped into the school of hard knocks. The pain and suffering that is now a common aspect of the human experience has come about to ensure we each wake up one day to the reality of who and what we truly are—Divine Beings dreaming the human experience for the purpose of evolving Awareness[2].

THE FALL

Bringing your mind, now, back to our story, back to that time before time, back to the mystical Kingdom....

Much has changed since you were here last, much more than you ever might have expected. As you stand here surveying, it's apparent that life in this Kingdom is now a very different state of affairs. A cloud of dark-

---

[2] The nature of Man and Women, the masculine and feminine principles of creation, and the relationship between these two complementary (yet often antagonistic) polarities is explored fully in Volume III of this series, which focuses on how human beings can co-create conscious loving relationships. Refer to the Appendix for full details on this upcoming book and how to obtain it once in print.

ness has fallen over the Kingdom. The golden boundary marker has all but faded away in most parts. You also see the remains of walls not far out from the castle, which have broken down due to lack of maintenance. There is a great number and variety of people—mostly bandits and thieves—and wild animals coming and going as they please. Observing this grim scene spread out before you, you see that the primary and once glistening central river hardly flows down to the ocean at all. Just a small trickle remains, although you also discover there are now numerous small creeks flowing to the ocean from various winding trails along the barren land. "How could this be? What happened here?" you think to yourself. Looking North toward the mountains, along what was once the grand and lively river, you see that most of these small streams and creeks start way up beyond the castle, in the foothills somewhere. On closer observation it is apparent to you that there is a dam in the river. Actually, more than just one dam, you can see many dams, creating a wide array of small and stagnant lakes. The small streams and creeks you followed up to here are where water has broken out around the sides of the dams, or made its way over the top, and trickled down the hill—in its vigilant attempt to merge with the ocean.

As you visually follow these creeks down, it becomes apparent that most of them circumnavigate the castle, often at a great distance. There is a small creak of slow-flowing water making its way through the channel beneath this now-derelict relic of the grand Castle that once was. The waterwheel inside barely moves—yet it turns just enough to dimly illuminate the few lights remaining in various parts of the building.

Only now does the obvious question dawn on your mind, "Where is the King, and what of the Queen?"

Stumbling your way through the many dark and dimly lit rooms you find no sign of either King or Queen. They are not here—nobody is. Apart from the eerie silence and stagnant air, this place seems strangely devoid of life. The feeling here is not a good one. You pull back to your bird's-eye view of this realm and take it all in from a distance. From this vantage point you see what were once the gardens now overgrown in wild plants, with cracked pathways and dry thirsty earth. In the South garden there is a Pagoda overgrown in vines. At its entrance, fallen from its now broken post, is a sign. With paint cracked and peeled, the sign still reads, "Here lies the Queen of this Realm. May she rest in peace and one day return." It feels anything but peaceful here. Haunted perhaps, but not peaceful, you think to yourself.

The memory you had of the golden castle and... and the river...and... well...it's fading rapidly from your mind, as if this dark cloud has affected you in the same way it tainted the realm. Your increasingly vague memory of what once was leaves you with just the remnants of a now forgotten myth, and a feeling of compulsion to move on and away — to try and forget it all even existed.

The feeling to be anywhere but back there blindly pushes you forward as you set off down a disused path winding its way into the forest ....

✦ ✦ ✦

Oh yes, although you didn't know it, that is precisely what the King felt compelled to do some years prior to your return. The path wasn't as overgrown as it is today, and it looked like a relatively attractive means out of this dark and foreboding place — inspiring a little hope and a faint desire that there might be a better world elsewhere. Yet the King, like yourself, underestimated the vastness of this forest, and really had no idea what lurked in these unknown parts of his realm — here in the deep belly of Nature where he had until now not ventured.

✦ ✦ ✦

The King, not long after entering the black forest, unknowingly strayed from the path in some particularly dark region, and wandered off into confusing and disorientating territory. Hungry, he ate from a tree with delicious-looking fruit — not knowing of the powerful hallucinogens they contained. By the time he satisfied his appetite with this fruit, he could no longer remember who he was, where he had come from, or where he was heading. His mind, now de-ranged and delusional, was hallucinating whilst awake and dreaming restlessly whilst asleep — he could no longer tell one state from the other. Night and day, sleeping and waking, conscious from unconscious — all merged into being one long dark night of his soul.

✦ ✦ ✦

With a few days of walking behind you, it is a disturbing surprise to look upon the naked, skinny old man lying in the damp leaves before you. Were it not for my description of the King's present state, you would not begin to imagine that this is he. Yet is it the King? He certainly doesn't seem to know it himself. His days of former glory are not even a faint memory for him now, made quite apparent by the drab and half-dead look in his body and face. Yes, that much is more than apparent without even the need to first speak. He looks at you through wide eyes—glary and wild. Astounded, you can do nothing but look back into his crazy gaze hoping to see some faint glimmer of the former King.

✺   ✺   ✺

The consciousness that we each identify as "self" whilst here in the dream has taken a fall such as the King depicted in this story. Once masters of our realm—masters of the dream—most human beings presently experience themselves as products of the dream rather than creators of it. Most of us contend daily with feeling (either consciously or unconsciously) victimised by people and events in life, and we are therefore either constantly in a mode of attack or defence toward the self and the world around that self. Attack and defence are in fact the same thing, and both arise out of relating to self and the world around that self (our Realm or World) through fear and separation.

Our purpose in this dream of dreams is to experience Love in all its many manifestations. For your nature is Love, and there is only That Love manifesting as consciousness unfolding, as awareness evolving. That may sound a tad corny to hear or read, and I encourage you to not relate to this as the sentimental perception of love that society generally relates to. It's easy to confuse love with the heightened emotions of ego-satisfaction and the fulfillment of the numerous other human desires we all taste from time to time.

With that, let us now enter into the next seven chapters of this journey…Your Immaculate Conception. Each moment we either birth ourselves in a cyclic repetition of "sin,"[3] missing the mark of that which is true here and now, and carrying into this moment the weight of our

---

3   The Greek word hamartia (ἁμαρτία) is often translated as sin in the New Testament; it means "to miss the mark" or "to miss the target." It also has Latin roots that came to mean "guilty," for which the root meaning would appear to be "it is true"; that is, "the charge has been proven."

past affairs; or we birth ourselves immaculately, in a state that is clear and pure. A mind impregnated with a complex web of beliefs, lies, assumptions, and misperceptions has little chance of experiencing the Now whilst in a condition such as this.

From here on, our exploration will focus on regaining or unveiling the innocence of your Mind as Immaculately Conceived by Infinity, God, or that which created All and is All. Of course let us not throw the baby out with the bath water, but be certain to assimilate the Awareness that has come about during our time of lost innocence— this Awareness when lived and applied in a life-giving way is what transforms an ordinary person into a Man or Woman who lives life with impeccability and as a bearer of true wisdom.

EMPOWERING PRINCIPLES & PERSPECTIVES

- The "world" and the Earth are not the same.

- There is one Earth, whilst there is a "world" in the mind of every man, woman, and child to ever walk this Earth.

- The world is something within our consciousness that we superimpose onto our experience of the Earth.

- We are each the ruler of our own realm. This realm is the equivalent of each person's individual world.

- Culture and society are a collective of people who agree to subconsciously maintain a certain level of basic agreements about their worlds.

- Man and Woman have played equal roles in bringing about the current state of apparent masculine/feminine imbalance in the world today.

- There is no truly objective perception of the world for one who is still perceiving through the senses that are a product of that world.

- Typically the ordinary person is completely unaware of the vast majority of what is playing out through humanity and life on Earth now and historically.

- The world will only change for the better when we change our mind for the better.

- We are each the master of our own realm or world, but not simply from the level of the typical ego with which most people identify.

- From one perspective our consciousness has taken a "fall." The choice available to you now is whether or not you co-create your resurrection.

Part Two

Your Immaculate Conception

immaculate, *adjective*
1. Impeccably clean; spotless
2. Free from stain or blemish; pure
3. Free from fault or error

conception, *noun*
2.
a. The ability to form or understand mental concepts and abstractions
b. Something conceived in the mind; a concept, plan, design, idea, or thought
3. *Archaic.* A beginning; a start

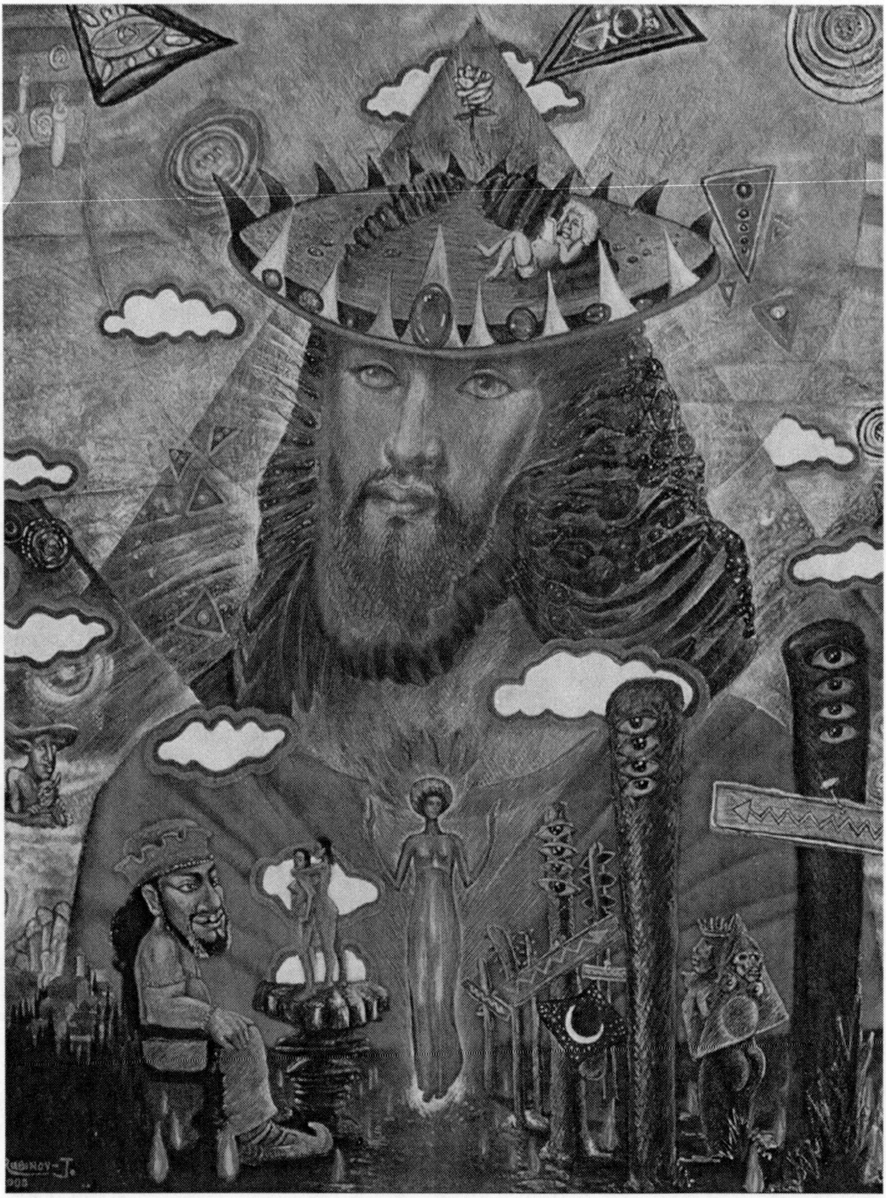

Chapter Eight

UNRAVELING THE STORIES WE TELL

"If the doors of perception were cleansed everything would appear to man as it is, infinite."
William Blake

Once I recognised that I was telling stories about everything within my experience and everything that I perceive, and that how I perceive all things—the world around me—is based on the stories I tell, the next step was to unravel these stories. Actually, it is more accurate to say that I knew it was all stories and dreams early in life, yet the requirement to unravel them was not immediately obvious to me. What I first attempted was to change my stories or tell new stories, more "enlightened" stories, and "spiritual" stories. Yet, somehow that was not the answer. Somehow that set up a situation where I was running away from my old stories, which would go further into my unconscious, and investing energy in new stories that had to make their way through the now-tainted unconscious in order to come into manifestation. Which of course they wouldn't—at least not without first taking on the shadows of what they had to pass through within the depths of the Body-mind.

A lack of Inner Peace—the experience of pain—helped remind me that I was somehow barking up the wrong proverbial tree. Trying to delete rather than transform these stories left much of my power hidden in the shadows cast behind me as I foolishly tried to run toward the light. In running toward the light, away from what I judged to be darkness, I was forgetting a very important fact. Namely, that I Am That Light, and the evolution of awareness is not through going back, but by extending forward into what appears to be darkness and void. I recently read something where the author was saying that the Great White Light many occult, spiritual, and mystical traditions refer to is just another one of the lies implanted into the collective human story. It keeps us distracted from the fact that we (in essence) are the Light, meanwhile foolishly mesmerised by this Great White Light like moths drawn to a light bulb. We spiritually head out in pursuit of this Great White Light expecting something from it, some form of illumination and even en-light-enment, when really this just moves us further and further away from the Truth of our Divine Essence. It's not the first time I've heard this proposition. Perhaps there's some truth to it?

THE MORAL OF THE STORY

Over the years I have realised that each story has a message, often a beautiful and exquisite message. A message of power; one of Love. Each story contains a message of how to go about reclaiming the Truth of That which I AM. I had been blind to the secret whisper rustling through the trees. So focused was I on the trees and the dark shadows under their overhanging branches that I missed what was dancing in the light right before my eyes in the spaces between the trees. Even in trying to chop down the trees and clear the ground, there was no end to this dark forest I was dreaming about in my ego-mind. In appreciating the space around the trees I learnt to read between the lines to receive the previously hidden messages.

Just like the moral of a story you read in a good book or a children's fairytale, the message or moral is never directly spelled out for you—you have to read into the story, feel into the story, through the story, and see the message waiting beyond the mere words on the page. Life is like this. Or like the nature of a wonderful poem—profoundly saying so much without ever actually directly stating it in the words. Every*thing* in this world is in this way like poetry. The dream is all back-to-front—everything is symbolic. Powerfully symbolic of the Truth, yet we must each fight for our true eyes and Vision to see it. This is the path of the Warrior; this is what it means, in part, to live with the clear intention and impeccability of the Warrior. This is what it means to stand with Authentic Power in relationship to the world or to your personal dream and the collective dream. We must read or penetrate into our stories and extract from them the hidden messages of power therein.

Yes, each story is telling me some*thing*, but not what it appears to be telling me, not what is there at the surface level—what we call the "face value" of something. It's like a symbolic metaphor, or like a parable. Every story I am telling and hearing (which is still me telling it) is a parable—a parable devised to show me how, where, and why I am forgetting my Divinity. If I take the stories of my life and ego literally and react to that literal interpretation, it's inevitable that I will only head off into further darkness and confusion. This is not unlike the vast destruction and confusion that has resulted from so many people fanatically taking the parables of their religious texts literally, completely missing the deeper meaning that was waiting there for them.

The fulcrum of power here is the one sitting between the literal approach to reality and a symbolic one. Learning to read and approach every*thing*—the many manifestations of Life—at a symbolic rather than literal level, is fundamental to claiming our power. It's also fundamental to finding and living in Peace.

You – The Path of Your Perfection

An astounding and mysterious secret to life is that the problems, issues, weaknesses, personal quandaries, self-defeating behaviour patterns, the addictions, and the darkness we so often try to keep hidden away is exactly where our power is waiting for us to reclaim it. Power—Universal Power—has configured our dream perfectly, to challenge us into our liberation and the full realisation of our potential. You are quite literally the *one* and *only* path of your own perfection. All it takes is being Present to what you experience within yourself and in the apparent world around you.

Unraveling your personal stories and our collective stories is the return to your Divinity. Once centered in Divinity, we start to tell and hear only Divine stories of Love. Love, here in the form-side of Life, manifests as intelligent cooperation. Imagine, if you will, a world were all your relations, where all beings, are cooperating in a way that is truly life-giving for all. Such is the blessing of unraveling the stories we tell, and such is the reason why everything is happening for you and not to you. The question I can hear curiosity silently asking between the words on this page, like a shimmer of light reflecting off the still lake in the mind, is perhaps this, "So how are these stories unravelled... what must I do?" A pertinent question indeed, for I know from my own life experience thus far that this is perhaps the one key factor that has transformed my life and world from one of struggle and pain into one predominantly Peaceful and empowering.

Regaining Objectivity

"Few people have the imagination for reality."

Johann Wolfgang von Goethe

To perceive Life as it really is—the actual Reality, or as close as we can get to it whilst our attention is fixated within a human form—we require objectivity on our experience. To be completely objective is nigh impossible, for we will always perceive Reality from our particular and typically skewed perspective—the perspective afforded to us as human beings and the way in which human perception assembles itself. As Johann Wolfgang von Goethe points out in the above quotation, it takes imagination—the capacity to assemble perception or internal images beyond the mere appearances before our senses—to perceive Reality as it really is.

With this in mind, how do we gain objectivity from our skewed perception of Life? First and foremost, I invite and encourage you to start looking at what stories you are telling. I invite you to observe and be aware of what stories you verbalise to other people. Observe and be aware of the stories you tell yourself internally. Don't buy into these stories, yet don't cut them off either. No, please don't try to do that at this stage. Don't suppress them or deny them. Rather, just continue to let these outer and inner dialogues play out but take a step back from the story being told; take a step back from the Dream. Take a step back and be aware of the story as it unfolds. Know that it is not you and has no impact on your Divinity, on who and what you are. Nothing in this Dream can touch that—nothing.

What you will be paying attention to are the judgments you hold (toward yourself and other people), the criticisms you make, the things you complain about, the people you don't like, the state of the world you disagree with. The key is to pay attention to all these things, and observe the feelings and emotions that come up, and the stories you start to tell. This requires directing your Attentive-mind toward a new level of relationship to these stories, judgments, and feelings. It is about reclaiming your attention from its previous fixations, and allowing it to attend to reality—the reality of your own human self—in a new way.

Once you become aware of the stories you are telling yourself inwardly and telling others outwardly, you will cease to experience yourself being so in the story. It is only our incessant identification with the story—being associated into it, and consistently giving it our attention—that make it all so real. With awareness and with your attention directed toward the symbolic nature of life you will see the story and you will see yourself telling the story, as opposed to simply being in the story—you will be able to dissociate from it. It is in this way that you will start to awaken to a feeling-sense of the Dreamer and detaching from the dreamed experience of "I"—the little "me" of our misidentified human ego-self.

Once you experience yourself telling the story and no longer experience yourself as the story, you will find yourself in a very different perceptual position. The assemblage point I mentioned earlier starts to change its position and becomes more able to flexibly move around. From this place you, through further and sustained awareness, will be able to look at exactly what story you are telling yourself and then you will be able to stop telling the stories that don't result in your being filled with Peace (being peace-ful). That will probably mean you give up the vast majority of all the stories you have been telling and hearing. We give them up not by suppressing them, but rather through seeing them for what they are—nothing but lies and distortions set up within the ego-mind and perpetuated by life-taking spirits until such time as you willingly step up with courage and reclaim your Power and reclaim your Spirit and the Life-Stream extending out from your I AM Presence (the Dreamer).

WE INTERNALISE THE STORIES ALREADY WITHIN US

At some stage in my life I discovered I can *hear* from the world around me only those stories that I myself am willing to tell. It has become apparent to me that I can determine what stories I am willing to tell—and most likely am telling myself inwardly—by taking a look at the stories I appear to be hearing from other people, and from the world around me. *Hearing* is not about what words reach your ears but rather what words and symbols reach your inner feeling world and invoke a felt-sense of the story which has just unfolded before you. It's about what and how you internalise from the things you hear and see in the world around you. Hearing from an ever-deeper perspective is one of being aware of the felt-sense of what is in fact arising from within me and manifesting as these words being spoken by someone "out there" in my world.

If I hear someone say "I hate you" and I then also internally emote (and perhaps inwardly dialogue) the extension of that story, something like "this person hates me and is rejecting me and attacking me," and I feel (emotional) energy arise in reaction to this story, then I have found that on some level this is one of the many stories I am repeatedly telling myself—even when I am not conscious of it. Again, all events happen for me and not to me. It is a blessing in disguise waiting to be discovered and incorporated into my perception. It doesn't matter what comes out of this other person's mouth. What I *hear* depends entirely on the story I am telling myself. Is it a love story or a hate story? Am I living in Heaven or in Hell?

The other day I had a situation arise, which may help make this even clearer for you. I will explain this is fairly superficial terms so as not to complicate the point being made. I recently met a man who has a long history of behaving very negatively. In my experience, his outlook on the world is that of a victim. It would appear, based on what he talks about, that he has given up on life and on discovering and fulfilling his purpose in the world. When he talks it is often charged with a high level of anger and negative/life-negating energy. Many people find him to be very negative when he talks about things in the world. He feels stuck, like a victim, unable to do anything about his situation and about his world. He says he only talks to people in order to be polite, or to convey practical information. Yet in my experience he talks a great deal about many worldly topics and more often than not gets into a place of victim and negativity regarding these things. I noticed that listening to this man brought up an uncomfortable feeling inside. I was aware of what was playing out through him, yet even so I was internalising some of his story. I spent some time reflecting on this, and it put me in touch with that aspect of my own story where I feel that the corruption and distortion in the human world has too much power for humanity to overcome it. I felt into that place where I also feel like a victim to the world around me and feel powerless to do anything about it, and the ways in which this prevents me from fully living out my purpose. This is an aspect of myself that I've explored over the years and reclaimed much of my power from. Yet here it was again. So I spent some time meditating with this, feeling into where in my Body-mind this is still playing out. I called my spirit back from this story—reclaimed my power by shifting my perception—and I felt much better for it. I've noticed that since this incident I have found it much easier to remain focused on my purpose-related tasks. For instance, my degree of focus on finishing this book has increased noticeably, because I have called back my power from the perception that it is a struggle to fulfil my purpose in this world.

I've only touched on the dynamics involved in the above real-life example, but I think the point is clear. Every time I feel my internal state shift into one of pain—anything less than feeling at peace and beautiful inside—I stop, and shift my attention from its fixation on the world and my story about the world, and pay attention to the message Infinity is conveying to me in that moment, in these circumstances. The result is always very empowering, liberating, and relatively effortless.

THE PROCESS OF UNRAVELING A STORY

A fictional example of this process might look might be something like this. Joe appears to come up and say, "I hate you, you're ugly, and you stink." If that is what I internally hear—and more precisely, what I feel—Joe say, then this is indicative that I am telling myself some sort of story with a similar theme—a theme that invokes or embodies a similar emotion. So it may not be that I tell myself "I stink." It's usually not about the words and their literal meaning, but instead about the theme running symbolically through every*thing* that was said. So in this instance, it may be about the story of hate and fear in general, which I may have running in my ego-mind. You see, the emotion I feel when someone speaks words of abuse to me is my energy-in-motion. It has only gone into motion—into a commotion—because what Joe projected within his dream of me polarised with and re-sonated (re-sounded) something in my dream about my self.

If this is the case, you can simply step back. Feel what you are feeling, and detach your sense of identity from it. It is not You (this is not "I"); it is the dream. The inner story might have said, "Joe hates me, he rejects me, and what's more, he thinks I stink (gosh, do I really smell that bad—I better take a shower). This bastard hates me. How dare he say these things? et cetera, et cetera."

Turn that story around.

"Somewhere in my ego-mind, do I harbour feelings of hating myself or not fully loving and accepting myself? Somewhere in my Body-mind, do I harbour feelings of ugliness and non-acceptance of who and what I am?"

How does that feel?

Go into how it feels. Allow yourself to feel how it feels, but take Joe entirely out of the picture. Forget the world out there and bring your attention to the world within. Joe, in the way you perceive him, does not exist and never did exist—he is simply part of your dream. That is the Reality. So please, **remove him completely**. Remove the perceived "other." There is only you, there is only one, and it is all-one, and therefore you are al-one in your dream. Healing will **only** truly take place when it is approached from this perspective, for healing is about coming into wholeness and only this perspective is Whole. This is the nature of Healing. Joe—the world, or "the other"—was simply part of Your story being told for you and not happening to you.... Go into those feelings. Joe, if you like, was in fact medicine that you now have the choice to self-medicate with. You will quite likely find these feelings are stories that have been playing over and over again and have been in your Dream for a long time.

Remember, Joe (the world) cannot do anything to you—for Joe does not exist in the way your mind perceives him. Joe—the apparent other as a separate self out there in the world—is an illusion. Therefore, whatever you are feeling has arisen 100% from within yourself. It was already within you. You might not have been aware of it until now, but that's why this apparent event has happened *for you*—so that you could be aware of what you're carrying around inside and constantly projecting out onto the world without realising it.

THE FOLLY OF SELF REFLECTION

The following is an important point, so please read it carefully now. The process described above could be more appropriately described as a state you invoke whilst making an internal approach to a felt-sense within you, within your Body-mind. This is not about mental dialogue, self-analysis, auto-psychotherapy, or any other form of mental enquiry. This is not about self-reflection, which is something that typically takes a person away from his power.

Self-reflection has already taken place, out there in the world around you, and therefore it is not something that can truly happen within the mind or within the framework of thought and emotion within the body. You are the Self—whole, perfect, and free—which makes internal self-reflection a complete distortion of what is, and this results in a displacement of power. Reflection requires a mirror, just as you require a mirror to see what your face looks like. The world out there is that mirror, reflecting your being or your Self. When you hold a mirror up to your face, the only thing required from you internally (in order to perceive your face) is to simply be aware of what is there before you. The same is true when you stand before the mirror called "my world." I trust it is clear in your mind that this is not a process of mentation and self-reflection. So what is it?

Because the world has already reflected your internal imagining of Self back to you, what is required is simply your awareness of what is there. Yet until a person is embracing the truth about her true nature, she will hold within herself an internal re-presentation of Self that is distorted. The mirror—your world—will reflect this back to you perfectly. Unraveling our stories is about becoming aware of this distorted re-presentation of Self by simply acknowledging (acting on the knowledge) that what I am perceiving in the mirror (the world) is bringing about pain within the framework of my Body-mind and some form of confusion within the Attentive-mind/ego-mind. This pain—anything less than Inner Peace—is where awareness must penetrate. Awareness shrouded by mental and emotional process is about as useful as a flashlight covered over with a woolen blanket when one is trying to see around a dark room. So how does one bring awareness, without the blanket of mental and emotional stuff, into this painful situation?

What is required is to simply bring your attention (your Attentive-mind) to the Body-mind—to the space within the framework of your physical body. With your attention/awareness focused within the body, all that is required is to engage with the felt-sense of what has come up within you in response to the external trigger, which in my above example was Joe telling me he hates me, et cetera. With the thinking mind to one side, and the emotional dramatisation off to the other side, you will find that the Body-mind, through your engagement with this internal felt-sense, will talk to you. It will communicate, just as it all has been doing since the day you were born. This communication will not be with words or even images. Yet, words and images may arise as this communication enters through your awareness into the Attentive-mind. Should images and words manifest, it is quite okay to be aware of them and to even explore this felt-sense with these words/images there. At this point the felt-sense may start to change and transform. The ego-mind is so addicted to mentating and/or emoting the energy that arises from the felt-sense within your Body-mind that at first it may be a challenge to not get caught up in that again, when the purpose of this exercise is one of remaining aware of the felt-sense. If you notice your attention has associated into thoughts and/or emotions, the solution is a simple one. Just gently be aware that this has occurred and bring your attention back to the felt-sense within the framework of your Body-mind.

Coming back to my earlier example…

In allowing and exploring these feelings fully—namely without holding onto the image of Joe and therefore owning that the feelings are within you and not about him—you may become aware of the moment or internal "space" where you first started choosing to tell this story and when you first started to feel this way within your Body-mind. You may become aware of the power—as a felt-sense—within you that was previously displaced by your distorted re-presentation of Self. You will see the nature of that and how pointless it is to keep telling this story here and now. This is where you can choose to forgive all the roles that revolved around this story from the Alpha (where it first started) to the Omega (the last point where it appeared to be told, with Joe). MU is between the Alpha and the Omega. It is Now, within the eternal space between the apparent beginning and end. MU sounds a lot like YOU, and this is what defines your experience of You here within the dream. The story you tell around the Alpha and the Omega will determine MU (Now, You).

The act of true forgiveness is the act of rewriting the story with how God's Vision sees things—the world when viewed through the eyes of Infinity. This is about reclaiming our attention from its fixation on the world of separation. Only then can we bring our attention to a wholly/holy different world, as seen through the eyes of God. In God's vision Joe—or any other person you care to name—does not exist separate and apart from you. In God's Vision hatred does not exist in reality—it's only something we conjure up in our mind for the sake of a new experience in order to better appreciate the realities of Life. In God's Vision none of what you perceived ever happened—not in the way you might think it did—and there is no (subject) matter around which to form an unhappy story. In God's Vision there is only Light and that Light has no opposition beyond the mind of Man. Want to change the world? Then change your mind about things. This is the essence of Changing the Dream.

The truth as I experience it is that everything I perceive, and therefore experience, is arising and passing away within the framework of the triune self (Body-mind, Attentive-mind, Spirit-mind). Every emotion arises and passes away within the framework of the Body-mind. I simply cannot feel or emote something beyond the framework of the body. Every thought I experience arises within the framework of the Body-mind.

The implication of this undeniable reality is that every feeling, emotion, and experience begins and ends *within*. There is a deep mystery to this that I encourage you to sit silently with and explore. Sure as you are willing, the answers will appear.

TWO SIDES TO THE STORY

This phenomenon of the stories we tell holding keys to our liberation doesn't only apply to stories about things we don't like—the things about ourselves we consider to be ugly. It actually applies to anything I suppress or deny within myself, which of course includes my unrealised life-giving attributes and talents. Just as I project onto the world the things about myself I don't like, I also project onto the world the magnificence I contain within yet don't accept. This again results in my suppressing and denying these aspects of myself. In an organisation I have worked with as training participant and staff member called The Mankind Project (MKP)[1] we teach men (it's an organisation supporting the empowered masculine in men) about their Gold and their Shadows. Let's take a look at what is meant by this.

In the earlier part of this chapter the focus was on a way to discover — to literally uncover — one's shadows. Shadows being those life-negating aspects of self I don't like and which are generally considered "bad." If I judge these aspects of myself as less than acceptable I will suppress and deny them. They then manifest themselves in my world as a projection of judgments and pain in the form of my stories about the world, as we have seen. This projection occurs in an attempt made by my Body-mind to restore balance and bring about healing. Yet I can also suppress and deny what in MKP would be called my Gold.

My Gold includes all the life-giving, uplifting, and creative aspects of myself. These are what most people normally think of as "good," "wholesome," and "positive." Many people have learnt, for one reason or another, to shut down the Light within them, usually in fear of rejection of one sort or another. This is poignantly touched on in this quote from Marianne Williamson in her book A Return To Love[2]:

> *"Our deepest fear is not that we are inadequate. Our deepest fear is that we are powerful beyond measure. It is our light, not our darkness that most frightens us. We ask ourselves, Who am I to be brilliant, gorgeous, talented, fabulous? Actually, who are you not to be? You are a child of God. Your playing small does not serve the world. There is nothing enlightened about shrinking so that other people won't feel insecure around you. We are all meant to shine, as children do. We*

---

1 See the Appendix for further information on The Mankind Project

2 Marianne Williamson, *A Return To Love: Reflections on the Principles of A Course in Miracles*. This quote is often incorrectly attributed to Nelson Mandela from his Inauguration Speech in 1994. These are neither his words nor are they cited within his Inauguration Speech.

were born to make manifest the glory of God that is within us. It's not just in some of us; it's in everyone. And as we let our own light shine, we unconsciously give other people permission to do the same. As we are liberated from our own fear, our presence automatically liberates others."

When we embrace our Gold and illuminate our shadows we truly are powerful beyond measure. Yet so long as I deny my Gold I will tend to project it out onto the world in the form of a story, just like the projection of my shadows. This is what takes place when people admire certain people and heroes in their lives. When I see a quality in another human being that I really like, unless I am in that moment also feeling and honouring that quality in myself, it is more than likely I am looking at something in this person that I don't currently give myself full permission to bring forth. As the saying goes, "You spot it, you got it." I can only acknowledge in the world that which I have knowledge of within myself.

So if there are people whom you greatly admire whilst also feeling incapable of what they do (either literally or symbolically) and, more importantly, how they are as people, take some time to explore the stories you have about these people, and the stories you tell yourself with regards to why you're not as able as these people. For instance:

My Guru is so enlightened, so unconditionally loving and so aware. I'll never be like her, but at least if I follow her and do what she says she might help me to start having some of these qualities myself...

That guy is such an amazing singer. Wow. I'd never have the courage to get up there on stage and sing like that. Gosh that must feel good... if only...

She really has the most amazing communication skills. The way she handled that meeting, and the antagonism from those clients, was just incredible. I'm such a klutz when it comes to words and being diplomatic. She's just great at it. I wish I were more like that...

In each of these examples it's highly likely the person is seeing in someone else a quality they in fact have but have not realised it yet. I see in other people the potential I have within myself. Every human being has immense potential, and yet when we are born this potential is completely unrealised. It is unfulfilled. It's like a seed waiting for the right conditions to grow and eventually blossom. Many people are unknowingly walking around with a big bag of fertile seeds wondering why they are always hungry (unsatisfied) and hankering after food, when all it takes is to plant these seeds into some suitable soil, tend to them as they grow, and then partake in the fruit that comes as a result. Only then is a human being satisfied, when one has eaten the fruit born from the seeds of one's own inner potential. It is the world around me that will lovingly reflect what I contain within. It is then my choice to decide whether I am willing to fight for it—to face the inner challenge of being true and authentic with who and what I am. This is the choice that determines my impeccability. Not just as Warrior but also as a human being.

The Taste of Chocolate

Consider this: When you eat a piece of chocolate, where is the taste and the feeling of that chocolate-eating experience taking place? Where does it arise? Of course it arises within the framework of the human self. Meditate on this for a while. You might even want to eat a piece of chocolate (or something else you like) and meditate on where the taste of this chocolate is arising. I also used to do this whilst eating my meals from time to time. When I smell a rose, where does this smell actually occur? When someone strokes me lovingly, where does the feeling of this occur? When someone expresses her love to me and I feel "loved" as a result, where does this feeling of love arise? Explore these questions in meditation, if you so desire, and I'm sure you'll be empowered by what you discover within.

To answer and truly consider these questions you will have to feel (with awareness) into the Body-mind, and not think or emote your way through them. Also important, as always, is an attitude of curiosity, fun, and inquisitive exploration. Enjoy.

EMPOWERING PRINCIPLES & PERSPECTIVES

- Our experience of the world around us is based on the stories we tell about it.
- There is a moral—an essential message—to every one of these stories.
- That message is designed to wake us up to our true Divine nature.
- In order to see this message we must find a balance between approaching life from a literal level and a symbolic one.
- You are the path of your own Perfection. Everything about you—be it things you consider good, bad, or otherwise—is the very basis of your liberation, your Enlightenment.
- Start looking at what your stories are telling you, rather than being overly identified with the act of telling them.
- You will cease being so in the story and thus gain perspective on the meaning of the story.
- We only internalise (emotionally react to) the stories that are already being told and maintained within us.
- Pain—from severe to even a slight deviation from Inner Peace—is our cue to give our attention to a life-taking choice we have made or are making, consciously or unconsciously.
- To get to the heart of the matter we must simply turn our stories around. Every story I tell with emotion is a story about myself.
- The only place for health self-reflection is in the world around you. Internal self-reflection is a self-defeating trap.
- We project onto the world what we do not accept about ourselves—both our unaccepted life-taking and life-giving attributes.
- We can only acknowledge in the world that which we have knowledge of within ourselves.

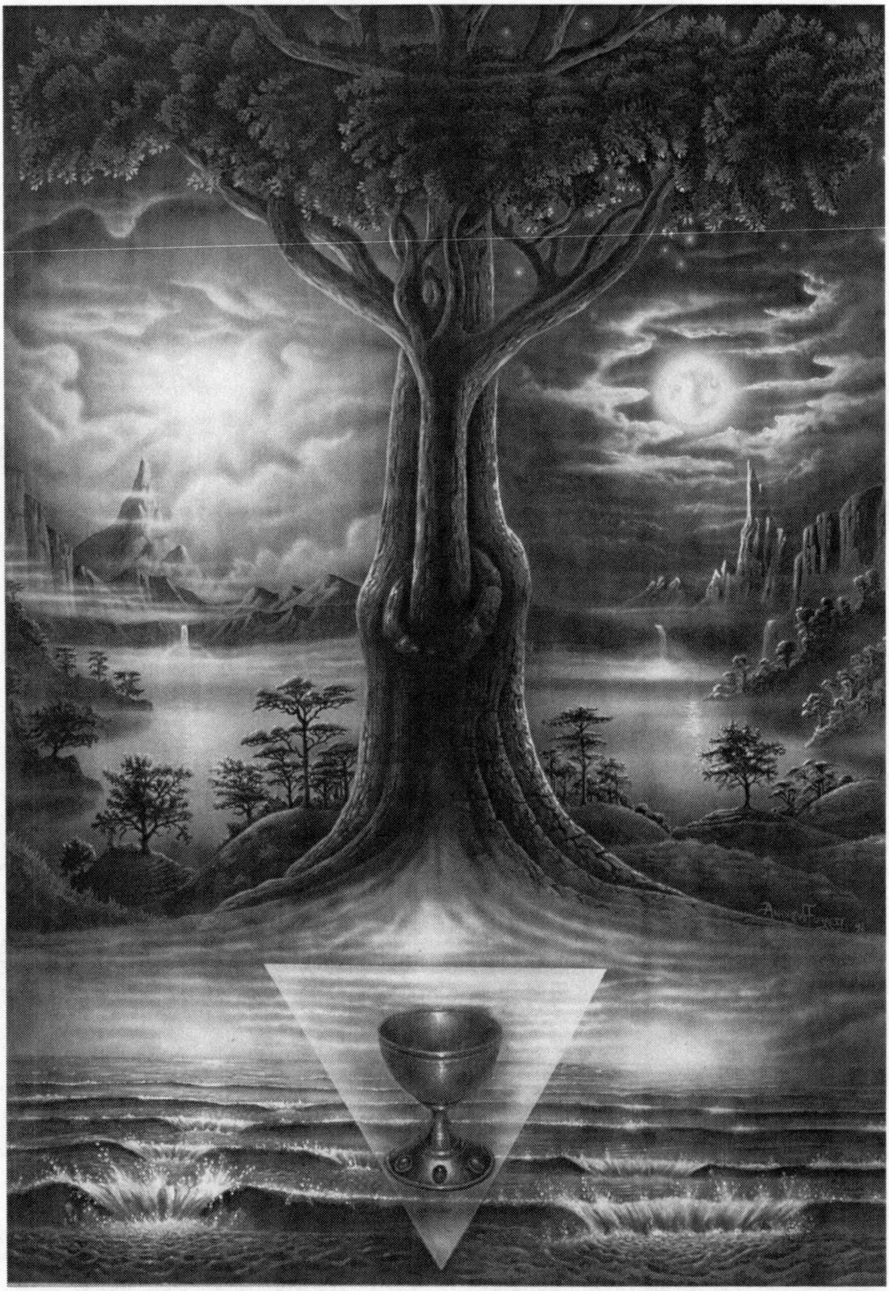

Chapter Nine

BEYOND DUALITY

"The mystical techniques for achieving immortality are revealed only to those who have dissolved all ties to the gross worldly realm of duality, conflict, and dogma. As long as your shallow worldly ambitions exist, the door will not open."
Lao Tzu (c.604 - 531 B.C.)
Chinese philosopher & mystic, founder of Taoism

The ego-self, in its current undeveloped state of limitation, maintains a rigid experience of what we may call duality. If you wish to experience Inner Peace and reclaim your Power, it is important to step beyond one essential duality, the duality of "right" and "wrong," "good" and "bad," "positive" and "negative." These are relative terms that arise within a particular symbolic re-presentation of reality that only the ego-self has any concept of. It is a moralistic re-presentation, often established by dominant religions during our human development. Your Spirit-mind does not know of this set of symbols and what they mean. Your Spirit-mind can neither work with nor communicate through this particular symbolic re-representation. Therefore it is important these symbols be seen for what they are and then dropped or internally transformed into the direct experience of what it re-presents (usually as a feeling of knowing). The apparent process of dropping or transforming it might appear to take time. That is okay.

Many ancient cultures were and many contemporary cultures are aware there is no right and wrong. All simply is as it Is. In the cosmology of the Huna from ancient Hawaii, it was recognised there is no good / bad / right / wrong. There is simply that which is "life-giving" and that which is "life-taking." That which affirms and supports Life, and that which does not.

As you are a Divine, Infinite and Eternal Being—an extension of the Supreme Source—it is in your nature to create. Creation is the unfolding of increasing Life; therefore it is in your nature to give forth and affirm Life. Thus your nature is ultimately Life-giving and Life-affirming. The degree to which you are yet to remember your True nature is the degree to which you will make choices that are life-taking in nature and is also the degree to which you will experience life-taking consequences manifesting in your experience of the world. This remembering is an act of incarnation—an act of being present and conscious to what Is.

May it be quite clear that something that is "life-taking" is not bad, nor is it wrong. It is simply some*thing* that does not accurately reflect the true nature of That which you are. Stealing, in most instances, is life-taking because it does not accurately reflect the truly abundant nature of your Being. Rather, it affirms lack, disempowerment, and fear of not having. It is not, however, right or wrong—although society will certainly judge it as being one of these. This does not imply the act of stealing doesn't serve some purpose in the grand scheme of Life. Rather it serves the purpose of Awareness evolving to incorporate that which you are, as a unit of awareness. It is through the painful experience (or, alternatively, the peaceful re-cognition) of THAT which I AM NOT that I incarnate and bring into manifest being THAT WHICH I AM.

The key here is to unravel and relinquish all the moral values you have inherited from the society in which you were raised and now live. In relinquishing these values you in effect release your Self from these constrictions—which on the one hand is about setting your self free, and on the other is about literally re-leasing your true nature. Let's take a quick look at this word "release."

To lease is, according to the dictionary, to "grant use or occupation of under a term of contract." The word "contract" means a few things. One definition of contract is agreement. The Latin source of the word *contract* is *adduco*, which is defined as follows:

adduco *-ducere, -duxi, -ductum*
1. to bring or lead to a person, place, or condition; of persons, to bring to a certain state of mind, to influence, induce.
2. to draw to oneself, pull in; hence to contract; partic. adductus -a -um, contracted, taut; of persons, strict.
Compar. adv. adductius

So one way of looking at this is that we are leasing the Self under a term of contract. Meaning that in the re-lease of the mind from what the collective unconscious has conceived within your unconscious, you draw to yourself and pull into the mind the Spirit-mind and ultimately Infinity.

Once free of these values, which have until now been infesting your Mind, you will no longer act based on such values. Does this mean that you will go out and start stealing? Well, no of course not. For me, as I suspect it is for you, it is my intention to incarnate (to bring into the flesh—into the dream) the Truth of That which I AM. Therefore I will choose not to steal. I will choose not to deceive people. I will choose not to harm others. Not because I have society in my mind—in the form of social conditioning—telling me these things are "bad," but because these activities do not accurately reflect That which I AM as a Divine and Infinite Being. These activities under ordinary circumstances are life-taking relative to That which I Am. To the unaware this may seem like a subtle and insignificant difference, yet the final consequences of each are worlds apart. It is in this way that we as humans will evolve into being self-governing and truly sovereign—as units of the Totality. This is the true nature of Man.

If I do choose to engage in these sorts of life-taking activities then I will, as a result, experience pain. We live in a truly self-governing universe. Human laws are only required because most people have no understanding of the principles you are reading about in this book. At the most, the only "laws" an enlightened society would require are those that lay down the collective understanding of what a human's rights and responsibilities are—nothing more. Even then, these are not really "laws" per se, but simply declarations of Truth.

Over the coming days and weeks—in fact for the rest of your life—I invite you to be aware (beware) of all these instances where your ego-mind jumps to the duality of right and wrong, good and bad. Notice this going on, and let it go. Bring your attention back to the stillness within you and simply feel into whether what you have observed is life-giving or life-taking. Does it affirm That which is loving, kind, beautiful, healthy, balanced, whole, at Peace, et cetera, or does it denigrate these things?

"Peace is when the heart is no longer in duality, when the struggle within has been resolved.... A voice has been calling out: "What you are looking for is within you. Your truth is within you, your peace is within you..."

Prem Rawat[1]

THE DUALITY OF THE PERSON AND HIS BEHAVIOUR

In Chapter Three we visited the topic of malu, entities, and Non-Self. We'll take another look at this because it ties into an important point about a duality that exists with regard to people and how they behave in this world.

Briefly reiterating what we touched on in Chapter Three, when I forget my true nature as a Divine Being in certain parts of (or in all of) my sense of self, this results in Life energy afforded to those "parts" of myself leaving my command, use, and control. This Life energy continues to stream down into my dream, yet it now does so in a way that is in shadow, or beyond the dominion of my awareness and control. Malu arise in these areas of my psyche and make use of this Life energy. Malu are life-taking in nature; therefore the consequence of their activity is painful. In the Huna cosmology it is recognised that any life-taking action a person performs is in fact performed by malu and not by their Divine Nature. It is only when I forget who and what I am in reality that I begin to make life-taking choices.

This means that if a person has a tendency to steal, they have a malu working through them. Someone who gets angry a lot has an angry

---

[1] Prem Rawat, known also by the honourary title Maharaji, has travelled the world for four decades, inspiring people to find peace within. To learn more about this message of peace visit his web site is at www.tprf.org.

malu living within him or through him. A person who criticises and judges a lot has a critical malu living within her or through her. These malu are in fact our allies, although this is not always immediately obvious and may take some time to appreciate. I have realised that malu are here to show me the ways in which I am forgetting my Divine or True Nature. Yet they will show me this only if I have the eyes to see with. Otherwise they simply wreak havoc and cause chaos in my life.

Relating to your self and other people in a way that does not confuse the person and the malu they are facing or displaying can be liberating and empowering for both the other person and yourself. Ordinarily most people relate to other people as a total package—their malu and the Self is all seen as the same thing. This only serves to reinforce the identity we each have with our malu—and our behaviours—as opposed to our Divinity.

The ego always tries to identify with its experience. Therefore, if I have a tendency to lie and cheat—which is simply a particular behaviour pattern—the ego will have me so convinced "this is what I am—a liar and a cheater" that I will lose all sense of That which I truly Am—a Divine Being, whole and complete in all regards. I am only lying and cheating because I feel I need to—because somewhere along the way I learnt that this behaviour pattern was necessary for my survival. I only feel I have that need because I have forgotten some aspect of my Divinity. So long as you are identified with what is not true, it will be impossible to re-cognise and experience That which is True. So long as you see the people around you as something other than a Divine Being (albeit one that is perhaps forgetting its Divinity), then you are in fact playing a part in holding them to this illusion—you are helping to maintain the lie they are living under. You will do this to the same degree that you are holding yourself to this illusion.

Another way of looking at this, particularly for people who struggle with the idea of malu, is to recognise that a person is not his behaviour. You and I are also not our behaviour. The relationship between a person and his behaviour has value only insofar as one's behaviour can indicate one's internal re-presentation of himself. The degree to which a person's behaviour does not accurately reflect his Divinity is the degree to which that person's internal re-presentation of Self is in a state of discord with reality. When someone I know is behaving out of fear and pain I can choose to react and engage at the same level they are operating on or I can choose to hold a vision of their true nature whilst they experience the darkness they are creating. To hold their light is to hold an image in my mind and heart of their true nature, of their perfection beyond the fearful story they are dreaming. In doing this I do not attempt to protect this person from the painful consequence of their behaviour, although if they ask for assistance I will of course help in what ways I can, which means helping them to see clearly.

A clear and loving understanding of how these life-taking spirits (malu in Hawaiian, but by different names in other cultures) operate is a key part of stepping beyond duality — beyond the duality of right and wrong, good and bad — and your identification with these illusions.

It's All Relative

We have looked at the notion that there is no good and bad, no right and wrong. I have stated there is only that which is life-giving and that which is life-taking. Let us now take that a step closer to the Truth.

There is in fact only That which is Life. Here within the dream, Life is impregnated into the many forms of life — the things of this world — to varying degrees. If we were to try and quantify this we could say, for instance, that the highest degree of Life that something in the dream can embody comes to 1000 units of life — this is just an arbitrary figure for the purpose of illustration. So, a choice that embodies or reflects 100 units of Life is life-taking relative to a choice that embodies 400 units of Life. The choice that was at 100 units is still an expression of Life and, relative to a third choice coming in at 50 units, it too is life-giving.

What this all means is that ultimately every*thing* is life-giving — every*thing* is an express of Life. We are simply dealing with different points on a sliding scale of relative expressions of Life. Every*thing*, including those things that we perceive to be life-taking, serve the one purpose of the All — namely the evolution of awareness and the fulfillment of the intent of the One. That which is life-taking evolves awareness toward that which is relatively more life-giving — which simply means that Life and Awareness are being expressed more completely.

"Every explicit duality is an implicit unity."
Alan Watts

No Opposition

"The created world is but a small parenthesis in eternity."

Sir Thomas Browne, English author (1605 – 1682)
Works (volume III, page 143)

In Reality there is no opposite of Life. *Life has no opposition*. Breathe that idea in for moment; feel it. *Life has no opposition*. You see, Life is All, and Life is magnificent. As noted in Chapter Four, some say there is "life and death," as if these are opposites, yet this is not accurate. *Birth and death are opposites*, and Life is expressed through and beyond both. Birth and death are simply phenomena that arise within the continuum of Life—if you were to draw Life as a line across a page, birth and death would be like two little dots on that line. Remembering that the "created world" is in fact within the mind of humanity, birth and death are like the *parentheses in eternity* referred to by Sir Thomas Browne in the above quote.

Some people think, as stated in some cosmologies and religions, that there are such things as "good" and "evil"—again like some kind of opposites that are separate. The word "evil" has been given a lot of bad connotations through history and it is often stated or implied that one must avoid evil at all costs. This has spread fear, created division, encouraged hatred, and perpetuated ignorance. I think we are ready to embrace a more conscious understanding of what "evil" really is. Picture this: if you wrote the word "evil" on a piece of paper and held it up to a mirror, what would you see? Something like this: **live**. Put together we get this:

live | evil

As you can see, it's pretty obvious "evil" is simply another expression of Life—the other side of the coin where we find on one side that which is defined by the word "live". Looking at the word "live" in a dictionary, I find the following definitions to be pertinent to me:

Verb: *live*
1. Continue to live; endure or last
2. Support oneself

3. Pursue a positive and satisfying existence

Adjective: *live (liver, livest)*
1. Exerting force or containing energy
2. Abounding with life and energy
3. Of current relevance

That which is "evil" is merely the mirror opposite of the above definitions of "live." That which is evil is simply that which is life-taking or that which is antagonistic to Life—not as something separate from Life but simply as one of the two polarities we find in the expression of Life. It is this antagonistic effect of evil—as I've just defined it here—that brings Life into greater and greater awareness. It is the disorder- or chaos-side of the cosmic order/disorder equation playing out in the universe. Ultimately every*thing* is playing a perfect and wholly intra-connected purpose in the evolution of Awareness. Obviously that which is life-giving more accurately re-presents our true nature as Divine beings, yet if we outright negate that which is life-taking we in fact negate a valid aspect of Life. Have a think about it—a coin with one side?

"A human being is a part of the whole, called by us Universe, a part limited in time and space. He experiences himself, his thoughts and feelings as something separated from the rest—a kind of optical delusion of his consciousness. This delusion is a kind of prison, restricting us to our personal desires and to affection for a few persons nearest to us. Our task must be to free from this prison by widening our circle of compassion to embrace all living creatures and the whole nature in its beauty."

Albert Einstein

EMPOWERING PRINCIPLES & PERSPECTIVES

- The experience of Peace and the fullness of your Power are found only beyond the duality of "right" and "wrong," "good" and "bad," "positive" and "negative."

- There is no "right" and "wrong," et cetera. There is simply that which is "life-giving" and that which is "life-taking." That which affirms and supports Life, and that which does not.

- For someone to step beyond duality, one key is to release all the moral values you have inherited from the society in which you were raised and now live.

- One may choose to live the same way, but it will now be entirely from a place of choice and not "because I have to."

- People are not their behaviour. They are also not their malu, which may influence their behaviour.

- "Life-giving" and "life-taking" are relative terms. That which is life-giving is so as it relates to something that is less life-giving. That which is life-taking is so as it relates to something that is more life-giving.

- Ultimately everything is life-giving because it is all an expression of Life.

- Evil is simply the flip side of what it means to "live" fully. There are no "evil" people, just people who have temporarily forgotten how to "live" in accordance with Reality.

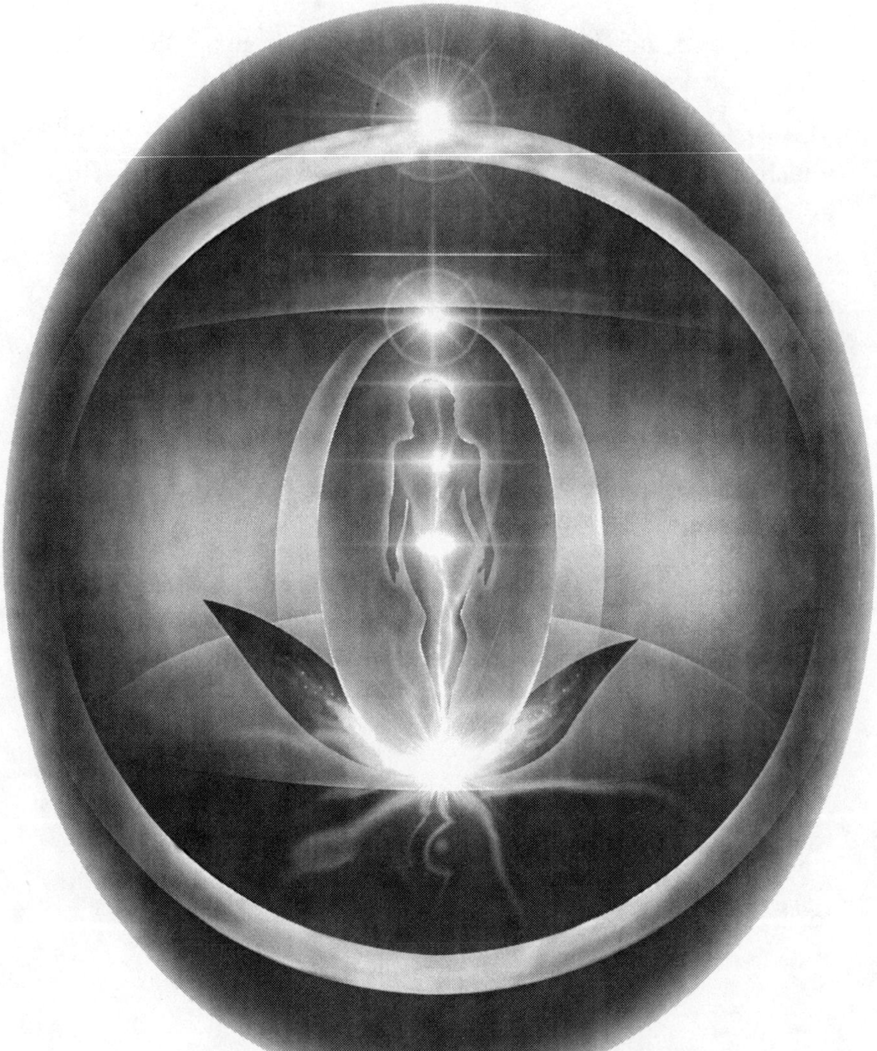

Chapter Ten

AUTHENTIC POWER

"This life is yours. Take the power to choose what you want to do and do it well. Take the power to love what you want in life and love it honestly. Take the power to walk in the forest and be a part of nature. Take the power to control your own life. No one else can do it for you. Take the power to make your life happy."

Susan Polis Schutz
American Poet

For the purpose of this communication between you and me — through the writing in this chapter of this book — I will capitalise the "P" in "Power" when I am referring to Authentic Power. I will use a lowercase "p" when referring to the kind of false power the ordinary person relates to as power.

✸ ✸ ✸

It is a misidentification of Self that gives humanity a distorted perspective on the nature of power — one that has caused us no end of suffering. Because the human ego-self at its current stage of development revolves around the illusion of separation, it inherently defines power as the ability to externally manipulate or alter the other apparently separate parts and things *out there* in its world. A simple example of this is my ability to hit a nail with a hammer in order to force the nail into a piece of wood, and equating this with power. Those other "parts" and "things" may be represented by inanimate objects, events, situations, relationships, or people. Essentially the ego-self of the ordinary person considers power to be the ability to force my will over aspects of the apparent separation I perceive. The ego-self has it that I am powerful—full of power—when I can in some way externally dictate the experience or unfolding of "things out there" in the world. This form of so-called power depends on my ability to externally force my will upon other people, situations, and events and make them change or go against their way in favour of my own.

For example, the CEO of a successful company is typically considered to have a lot of *power* relative to the janitor, who goes around and cleans up the offices when everyone has gone home (of course it's not uncommon for the "powerful" CEO to be still sitting at her desk as the janitor makes his rounds). Such a CEO is considered to be *powerful* for many reasons, the main ones being that she dictates what the company or organisation, and the people who work there, will do from day to day. She also has the *power*, afforded to her by her role, to determine the current as well as future work experience of the staff within the organisation; their careers and level of financial remuneration are seemingly in her control.

A police officer might be considered by many to have a considerable amount of *power* within his community and society. He is the arm of the law, and the law dictates how a society conducts its affairs. If people break these laws, the police officer has the *power* to arrest them and make them face the consequences of their actions. Teachers within a school are also considered to have *power*—*power* over the children. Parents might be considered to have *power* over their children because they appear to determine and control the experience of that child.

None of these examples illustrates what I would call Authentic Power, Inner Power, or even simply Power. These are all illusions of power that are in fact not Power at all. It is a lie that most people have bought into—human life force being the *currency* used to make this dubious purchase.

You may have noticed that the common element running through all of these examples is that each of these people has his or her power only because someone or something external to them has granted it to them. The CEO is granted power by the owners, board members, and perhaps shareholders of the company. The teacher is granted power by the educational institution he works for, which in turn is granted power by the parents of its students and also by the society in general and any power granted to it by law. The police officer is also granted his power by the society he serves. Parents are granted their power as a matter of circumstance and to some degree by the child custody laws of the society they are raising their child within.

Of course the people in all of these examples are free to bring Authentic Power into their job, position, or circumstance, yet this is not the power that their job, position, or circumstance grants to them. The kind of power granted to them can be taken away again, very quickly and with absolutely no say on their behalf. Authentic Power—the kind that stands silently and humbly present to the world—can never be removed from a person once he has truly embraced it. Authentic Power can be displaced within a person, but not taken away from him. Displacement occurs through a conscious and/or unconscious act of will, usually out of fear.

Imagine a person—we'll call him Joe—who owns a property on which he has built a house. Now, behind the property is a beautiful spring. When the owner moved into his new house the beautiful spring was within the boundaries of his property. At some point a neighbour came along and threatened Joe into moving his boundary. Joe went along with this, only to discover that now the spring is no longer on his property. The spring has not gone. In fact, it hasn't even moved. All the water that was pouring out from the spring is still pouring out. Yet a consequence of Joe's decision is that he no longer has access to this water and all of its benefits, such as watering his land. The neighbour cannot take this spring away, because it is where it is. So what has occurred here? The spring has not moved, yet Joe can no longer take the water from it. The only thing that changed was the configuration of the way Joe establishes the boundaries of his property (his personal field of influence). Legally the boundaries of the property have not moved, except Joe has abnegated his rights to the full extent of his realm. To regain the use of this spring, all he has to do is take possession of what is his and tell his neighbour to take a hike. He may decide to be inclusive toward the neighbour and let him have water when he wants it, but of course that is up to Joe.

True Power is Within

Gary Zukav has the following to say about Authentic Power:

"Authentic power is the experience of being fully engaged in the present moment, having what you need and being grateful for what you have. It is knowing that your life has purpose and what you are doing serves that purpose. It is also an experience of acceptance of yourself and others, of moving forward in your life with an empowered heart and without attachment to the outcome. Joy, creativity, and gratitude fill your awareness, even when what you are experiencing is difficult or painful, and you naturally strive to create harmony, cooperation, sharing, and reverence for Life—the intentions of your soul."

Visit his web site at www.zukav.com

True and Authentic Power comes from within, and that is where it stays—which is why one might also refer to it as Inner Power. Authentic Power is silent, having very little to say, although when it does have something to say it is direct, clear, authentic, and inclusive in its approach to the present moment. It does not seek attention—perhaps even avoiding it—and in fact most people don't even consciously notice it when someone in their presence embodies Authentic Power. If they do notice some*thing*, they might not be sure just what it is they are feeling or why. They might say to themselves, "Gee whiz, there was something about that guy…he was so…. Hmm…so…I don't know… interesting somehow…?"

I have noticed some people feel quite uneasy in the presence of someone embodying Authentic Power—they typically feel exposed or *seen*, and feel like there is nowhere to hide (from themselves). This only happens because some people are so heavily invested in trying to hide from themselves (from their own Power), and the Power within an empowered person silently challenges their disempowered conditioning. An empowered person will typically see right through the power games disempowered people play. She won't judge this person or his behaviour, though commonly the person feeling exposed has been judging himself all his life, and this judgment is often mirrored right back to him when face-to-face with a being of Power.

Through the laws of attraction, the sort of Power I am talking about will influence the world of your personal dream and, perhaps to a lesser extent, that of the collective dream, yet it simply extends out into your world and does not leave you. When your world is influenced by Authentic Power in a way that exceeds the apparent boundaries and parameters of what is considered *possible* within the dream, we commonly refer to it as a miracle. At the hands of some people, used in a particular way, it is also known as magic or sorcery. Most of the time Authentic Power tends to work invisibly, although it will most certainly take action when necessary (but never when not necessary). It is efficient: it is conscious of energy and conscious of how to use energy in the most life-giving and appropriate way.

Authentic Power is about your capacity to maintain a connection to the Intent of your Spirit…with the Will or Intent of that which some people refer to as "God." The more we align our human self with the intention flowing forth from the Dreamer, the more Power we typically will embody (hold within the body) and the more effortlessly the world—your realm—will align with your will.

Authentic Power is not imparted upon a person by the outside world. It is not given to us. It is not dependent on the outer world at all. In fact it has nothing to do with the so-called "apparent outside world." Nor can it ever be taken away by anything "out there" in the world. People can only appear to lose Power through using that very same Power to make a choice—consciously or unconsciously—to forget what Is or to abnegate their right to it.

Just as Authentic Power can be lost only through a choice of exercising my Power to do so, it too can be regained only by choice. The beauty in that is this—no matter how lacking in power you perceive yourself to be, there is always enough power in your command to pick up where you left off and complete the journey to claiming and mastering all Power given unto you by God (by That which is your Source and Creator—call it what you may).

※ ※ ※

False Power

"He who controls others may be powerful, but he who has mastered himself is mightier still."

Lao Tzu
Chinese Philosopher, founder of Taoism, wrote "Tao Te Ching" 600 BC-531 BC)

False power—the kind of power sought and vainly accumulated by the ego-self within ordinary Man—always comes with an element of outer strain and competition attached to it. Strain is inherent to this kind of power, therefore being unavoidable, because this sort of power is forever at odds with the world and with Reality. You have to specifically do something on the *outside* in order to obtain this form of power. You will then have to keep doing something to hold onto this power. This sets up an ongoing struggle with the world and with the content of your dream resulting in strain.

You can always tell that your sense of personal power is false when you notice it was an outer struggle to attain and/or is a struggle to maintain. Authentic Power requires no maintenance; it simply emanates and extends outward from the very core of your Being. It is self-maintaining and self-sustaining. It is incredibly simple and so beautiful how such Power unfolds. This is not to say that reclaiming our Power is not a challenge and does not involve utilising our strength and intelligence. Often it will. Because Power comes about through perception, it is only a shift in perception that will bring about an increase in one's Power. Intentionally shifting our perception is one of the greatest challenges we face as human beings, and yet it is one of the few acts truly worthy of our effort.

People who seek and/or have false power are invariably feeling deeply insecure about who and what they are in the world. Often it is their vain attempt to avoid the insecure feeling inside themselves that motivates them into busying themselves in some way that eventually leads them to accumulating and typically misusing false power. There is a saying that power corrupts and absolute power corrupts absolutely. This statement is referring to false power and the intoxicating effect it has on people who are prone to identifying with it.

The experience of false power can be extremely addictive and destructive, especially for someone feeling innately insecure about his place in the world. Sometimes it happens that the activity a person chooses with which to busy himself—as an act of avoiding how he truly feels inside—is one the society he lives in respects and values. If he has enough drive and motivation to be proficient at that busy-ness, he will start to experience a new level of ego-based power within the collective dream—granted to him by the collective ego-mind. If caught up in identifying with the dream, as many people are, then this first taste may be all it takes to set such a person on a long road of apparent success, and false power appears to be the reward for that success. Misuse of this power is typical.

Here's a simple example from my own life of what we've just looked at. I remember from my time at school there were a number of teachers who found me very difficult to have in their class. Throughout my many years at school I very rarely caused any disturbance in my classes and seldom got into any sort of trouble for my behaviour. Yet a few teachers really found me challenging and they would react in what for me seemed like bizarre and irrational ways. Although I found this somewhat inconvenient at the time—especially when one teacher tried to ban me from his class and I had to sit outside for many weeks until he agreed to have me back—I was aware that the teachers with this issue were always the ones with inferiority complexes. It was their sense of inferiority and lack of Authentic Power that caused them to abuse (misuse) their false power afforded to them by the school. Apparently my presence made them all too aware of how poorly they felt inside and they'd try to take it out on me.

✹   ✹   ✹

A Fresh Perspective on the Nature of Success

We are always successful. We are not, however, always successful at things we like, desire, or enjoy—and we call this kind of success a *failure*.

Success is simply the *succession* of one thing or event after another. Every act has a *consequence* (every act comes *with-sequence*) therefore every action is succeeded by another action or a reaction, and therefore every action and every endeavour or undertaking is *successful*. What people generally refer to as *success* is simply *desirable success* or an act/endeavour being followed (in sequence) by a desired outcome—and even what most people find desirable is the result of conditioning. So, someone whose ego-self has a predisposition to accumulate money will feel she is *successful* if her actions result in further monetary gain. If, however, such a person ends up in a position she judges to be lacking in enough money, she might conclude she failed. In reality she was successful and skillful at creating what she calls "lacking enough money."

The reality is that you are always a total success. What most people refer to as failure is only a misunderstanding of what it is you're currently being successful at, and is disagreement with whether it is in alignment with what you would like to be successful at. Put another way, does the result of what you are successful at accurately reflect how you wish to define yourself within the dream? Also, is that the limited human *you* you're referencing when pondering these thoughts, or is it the vaster Divine You that is in alignment with the greater Intention of the Universe?

Authentic Power does not depend upon worldly success. It also does not depend on your worldly actions having a particular or successful outcome in the common sense of the word *success*. A person who embodies her Power will seldom act in a way that has an outcome not in alignment with her intention. Sure, she may from time to time experience an immediate outcome that does not accurately reflect her intention, yet this will be appreciated as a step toward the intended outcome. Intuitively such a person will know (or wait until she knows) what more she must bring of her Self to the situation, or what limitations she has to release, and will then act again. Without strain, this dance will continue to unfold until the intended outcome is realised, yet without any attachment to the outcome. She may even come to see that Infinity had a slightly different Intention from her own, and that this differing outcome is the one she—as a vaster Being—was actually seeking.

At a deeper level of Power it becomes apparent that this process of succession I've described above is not a cause-and-effect phenomenon. At the level of reality, succession is not about one thing causing another, such as X causing Y. If Y is experienced after X and has a direct relationship to X (a situation where X appears to cause Y) this is not because X *caused* Y but rather because Y is the natural progression of the expression of Life that was experienced as X. Imagine slowly moving your fist out in front of you as if you are punching something. Imagine your hand is now 12 inches out in front of you. If you continue, it will eventually get to being 18 inches in front, won't it? Would you say that having your hand at 12 inches distance from where it started *caused* it to a few seconds later be 18 inches distance from where it started? No, a prior position of your hand has not *caused* it to be at the later position. What has actually happened is your intention to extend your hand fully out in front of you moved your hand through the position of 6 inches, 12 inches, 18 inches distance and so on. The intention you had to punch, in this example, is similar to the intention within Life as it expresses into the many forms of life we see around us. Intention comes from within, from the center of what can be termed Life. Therefore there is only one cause to all the many forms of Life, and that is Life itself. It is more accurate to refer to that "cause" as the "source."

THE ILLUSION OF CAUSE AND EFFECT

What you have just read is a very brief look at the non-reality of cause and effect. The belief in cause and effect is a significant one for most people, and it may take some focused self-enquiry to generate a feeling inside you of how cause and effect is an illusion. That feeling can evolve into the dis-covery (un-covering) that what appears to be cause and effect is in fact the succession of Life moving in and out of being through the power of Intention.

Let's look at one more angle on this. Quite a few people are presently discovering what some refer to as The Law of Attraction. There is, as I write this, a popular movie going around called The Secret, which explores this Law to some degree.[1] Those exploring the Law of Attraction may experience themselves going through the various motions of consciously *attracting* what they want—say they want more

---

1 Note that the author is writing an ebook that takes a much deeper and empowering look at the Law of Attraction as put forth in The Secret. This e-book is available online. See the Appendix for more information.

money—and then sometime thereafter they eventually experience themselves having the additional money. It would appear that their going through the motions of consciously attracting this money is what *caused* that money to come into their possession. The reality, however, is that what they did before getting the money was an *earlier* state or condition of the state or condition that *later* included the possession of that money.

As another example, sitting down to meditate every day for a couple of years and then one day having an enlightening experience, it may appear that all that meditating *caused* the enlightening experience. The reality is that all that meditating (and everything else going on for that person during those two years, and leading right back to the beginning of so-called time) was simply an earlier expression of that state or condition that was to later manifest as an enlightened state or condition. The meditation did not *cause* the enlightened experience, but rather it simply preceded it within the human linear perception of events through time.

If you are finding it challenging to get your head around what you've been reading then it might be useful to leave the head right out of it! I can tell you now that the logical/rational mind will find it challenging to make much sense of what could be called *progressive evolution* in place of the old and dearly loved superstition of *cause and effect*.

Power and Perception

Power is the product of perception. Just now my beloved asked me to explain what I mean by this. Rather than attempting to describe the mechanics of this directly—an impossible task—I gave a few examples that made it all quite clear for her, just as it may for you.

My beloved, Yolande, works as a healer (a cranial-sacral therapist, among other things). She is very good at what she does. Many people report all sorts of physical disorders disappearing after just one or two sessions with her. These disorders are often tissue disorders and pain that has been around for years, pain that other treatments have failed to alleviate in that time. Yolande finds that she can put her hands on a person, locate the energetic epicenter of the person's discomfort, penetrate to the source of that discomfort, then go into a relationship with it and one way or another assist it to release and dissolve. Now, it would be valid to say she has the Power to do these things. But we must also recognise that this Power is entirely dependent on her ability to perceive what is happening within the patient at this subtle level of reality within the Body-mind. Without that perception she has no Power to do these things.

Another example is this. A person who is highly intuitive could be said to have the Power of a highly developed intuition. Let us say, for example, we set up an experiment where someone pulls a playing card from a deck of cards. The intuitive person must state which playing card was pulled out (without seeing it), and she gets it right most or perhaps all of the time. This Power—call it intuitive power—can only come about because she is able to *perceive* the subtle forces present within the context of this card-pulling exercise. Without that perception she is *powerless* to accurately state which card was pulled.

Whilst the above two examples are relatively crude in relation to the vaster nature of Power and perception, they perfectly illustrate how Power is the product of perception. Without perception there is no Power. Perception brings about a particular alignment and concentration of energy—peculiar to that particular perception—and it is this alignment and subsequent concentration of energy that we equate to Power.

GAINING POWER

As mentioned above, Power is the product of perception. Power is not *gained* in the truest sense of that word. Nor is it *lost* in the truest sense of that word. Rather, your Power is either positioned within your field of influence or it is positioned beyond it. Put another way, Power is either within your field of perception or it is not. When it is, then you can make use of this Power; when it is not, you cannot make use of it. If I maintain the perception that I am an idiot when it comes to mathematics, then I will feel Powerless when it comes to dealing with complex mathematical equations. If my perception of myself changes to one where I have deep conviction of my ability with mathematics, my ability to do complex equations will greatly improve. The Power to be good at mathematics was always there within my field of human potentiality, yet it required a shift in my self-perception to bring it into my command and use.

As far as I can tell, it is the human Body-mind—our matter or mater-*mind*[2] which serves as a reminder that it's not just physical stuff. Within the physical structure, and extending slightly beyond it, there is an etheric structure. Within and beyond that structure there are other dimensions of energy that you may already be familiar with or can easily become familiar with through a wide range of books on the topic of occult anatomy, energy anatomy, and pranic healing[3]. I understand that overall, the human *body* (including its subtle structure), when *seen* spiritually/psychically, has the appearance of a luminous egg. This is certainly how I experience it and imagine it within myself, because this simply feels right. If you take a look at the images presented in the book *Hands of Light* by Barbara Ann Brennan, you will gain an impression of what this looks like to those who perceive such energy fields. From our exploration of the Body-mind in Chapter Three you will recall that I suggest the human subconscious is within the Body-mind structure. I know of a number of very successful psychotherapists who have developed and utilise body-centered psychotherapy techniques with great results. This body-centered approach to therapy for the *mind* works so well because it's the subconscious mind that is a problem for people and this is held within the body.

So, as it is our physical body that encompasses our field of influence at a physical level, the subtle dimensions of the human form constitute our field of influence at those same subtle levels. When your personal Power is located within (and free to move around) this entire structure it could be said "you are empowered"—physically empowered, emotionally empowered, mentally empowered, spiritually empowered, et cetera, depending on where the Power is situated, moving, and active. When it is displaced beyond the person's awareness—through an act of perception or mis-perception as the case may be—or beyond the field of influence, such a person is disempowered. The Power, however, does not *leave* you per se. It is not *lost*. It is simply displaced beyond immediate access to your central intelligence (to the Attentive-mind and the "I" within). To *regain* that Power it is simply (or not so

---

2 As mentioned else where in the book, matter is very similar to the word mater which is Latin for mother, origin, and source.

3 Refer to the Appendix for a list of suggested reading.

simply, as the case may be) a matter of using the Power one has now to approach the world—and Power as it is manifesting through the world—in such a way as to redistribute the energy that was previously dis-placed in an inefficient or life-taking way. Some traditions refer to this as *calling back the spirit*. Put another way, I must use the Power I have now (however small or great that may be) to bring about a shift in my perception, which will afford me more Power.

The Warrior's approach to Life is one in which every event—"good," "bad," or otherwise—is seen as a challenge from Universal Power. This impersonal and Universal Power is challenging one's personal Power. Personal Power, by the way, could be defined as "perception acquired through practical experience." Being fully present to this moment, here, now, is therefore an opportunity to take on a new level of Power. When a person has called the fragments of her spirit back into a configuration that is life-giving and thus supportive to fulfilling her purpose, she can get on with that task. A significant part of every person's purpose is connected with lucidly incarnating (bringing into bodily form) the Intent of the Dreamer.

> *"Anyone can become angry—that is easy—but to be angry with the right person at the right time, and for the right purpose and in the right way, that is not within everyone's power and that is not easy."*
>
> Aristotle
> Ancient Greek Philosopher, Scientist and Physician, 384 BC-322 BC

THE FOLLY OF POWERLESSNESS

ALL PERCEPTION GIVES RISE TO A MEASURE OF POWER GREAT ENOUGH TO TRANSFORM THAT PERCEPTION AND THE SITUATION BEING PERCEIVED INTO AN EVEN MORE EMPOWERING ONE—THUS ENSURING THE ONGOING EVOLUTION OF AWARENESS.

An important point I'd like for you to be aware of is that you always have the Power necessary to take *the next step* in your life—whatever that step might be and however insignificant it might at first appear. Some people live for years (even lifetimes) under the illusion that "I *am powerless to do anything about my situation.*" This is the archetype of the victim playing tricks with the mind, because in reality no matter how powerless I may appear to be, the simple fact that I am alive and perceiving within this realm indicates I have and embody a certain degree of Power.

The incredible fact that you are alive implies you have some measure of Power. To be conscious and present here within the dream is itself a profound albeit highly mysterious act of perception and this act must result in some measure of personal Power. That Power, no matter how small it may appear to be, is always enough for me to shift my perception in such a way that an increase in Power results. That new level of power is, again, enough for me to shift my perception in a way that further increases my personal Power, and so on, and so on.

So, if nothing else, please remember this simple point. Whatever your state or condition might appear to be, you are **never** truly Powerless. You may lose hope in your Power but even the experience of hopelessness is an act of perception and gives rise to some measure of Power—at least enough Power, if not more, to change the (mis) perception that gave rise to it in the first place.

Here's another way of looking at this: you always have at hand the resources required to facilitate your next step into even greater resourcefulness. It is only by denying, suppressing, or running away from some*thing* within the every*thing* we label "my life" that we end up *believing* we have no*thing* to enact our next step with—or at least have no*thing* of value. Yet, as pointed out already, **belief is only required** for that which is **not real**. Therefore, whatever state of no*thing*ness a hopeless person believes himself to be in, he is still in fact firmly fixated on some*thing* within the known—this, as opposed to the true no*thing*ness of the unknown. Specifically, this person is fixated on an ego-identification masquerading as no*thing*. All of this neurotic dancing around requires perception and therefore gives rise to some measure of Power. All perception gives rise to at least enough power to transform that perception into an even more empowering one. One can only smile at the illusion of powerlessness and see it for the folly that it is.

To put this back into simple terms, here's a great example of this principle in action. At the moment, my nephew Zebadee likes to collect cards that come wrapped inside certain packs of bubble-gum. At the beginning of last week he had none of these cards, nor did he have any money he was willing to spend on buying the packets of bubble-gum with the cards in them. Now, it could be said that these cards represent one particular manifestation of Power—perhaps a fairly insignificant one in the grand scheme of things, but an important one to Zebadee at that time. So for all intents and purposes, and putting stealing aside, one could say that Zebadee was powerless with regards to attaining a collection of these cards. He, however, had another way of approaching things.

On Monday Zebadee was given one card by his friend. To attract this act of kindness was in itself an act of Power. He then found someone with an excess of duplicate cards who did not have his particular card. He traded his card for a number of this person's cards in return. Continuing this process, by the end of the week Zebadee proudly showed me a significant stack of cards. "Uncle Jonathan," he exclaimed, "I had no cards on Monday, and now at the end of the week look how many I have!" He had quite a handful!

This simple situation provides a powerful example of the principle we have just explored, namely...

The Warrior is a being who at all times recognises he always has available to him the Power (the resources) to enact the next natural step on his path—which for him is a Path of Freedom. Therefore he is never truly stuck, never truely unable to move forward. However small or large his next step might be, it is a step he is able to take. Revisiting this principle in terms of perception we have the following aphorism as cited above:

> *All perception gives rise to a measure of Power great enough to transform that perception into an even more empowering one—thus ensuring the ongoing evolution of awareness.*

Losing Power

As mentioned above, a loss of Power is really a displacement of energy—brought about by an act of perception—within your luminous egg (the field of Life in and around your human form) to a location that is beyond your reach, or beyond your ability to utilize it intelligently (in a way that is life-giving).

Some people believe that other people can take or steal their Power and energy. Similarly, some people believe it is possible to give their Power away to another person, to an event, or to a situation. This is not my experience and is therefore not something I go along with, although it's not entirely inaccurate. They way I see it is this: when I appear to be giving my Power away to a person, event, or situation, what I am in fact doing is investing my energy into a perception of that person, event, or situation—a perception that is an inaccurate assessment of reality, and one that is relatively life-taking. This perception redistributes my Power in such a way that I experience an apparent *loss of energy* (as defined above). Where someone appears to be *stealing* my Power I am again investing my energy into a particular perception of myself and/or that other person—a perception I may have accepted from that person or someone else in my life. As humans we usually accept these disempowering perceptions of ourselves unconsciously. Sometimes we do it willingly, under the illusion it will result in obtaining something we *need*.

> *As a Divine Being I have only one need. That of a mirror. Any other need I think or believe I have is the result of a misperception of the reality pertaining to my Divinity*

The effects of *losing* Power in this way are manyfold. The first thing I notice is a diminishing of Inner Peace. This is experienced as a felt-sense within the body and may also be experienced emotionally and mentally as agitation, judgment, incessant thinking, life-taking self-talk, harsh emotions, et cetera. I find that any divergence from feeling somewhat blissful within the Body-mind and lucid within the

Attentive-mind is indicative that I am negotiating my Power in some way that is less empowering than what I was experiencing before this shift. There is nothing *wrong* with this. It is simply a sign that something—known or unknown—is calling for my attention.

I've heard some people say they don't know when they are *losing* Power, to which my response is that the effect of losing Power cannot be missed if one is present to the feelings within the framework of the Body-mind. Many people are so engaged in the habit and sensation of being out-of-body (having a partial out-of-body-experience) that they are not aware of the felt-sense of *losing* Power when it occurs. It's possible to go on for days, weeks, months, years, and even lifetimes perpetuating the same Power loss simply because one has shut off from feeling the body.

If I am not aware of a life-taking redistribution of my Power when it takes place—and consequently do not *call* that Power back through a shift in perception—its effects will transform into an experience that is increasingly painful until I do eventually notice it. The effects of this are felt initially as increasingly painful emotions and mental patterns, and eventually as a breakdown of the physical body. This breakdown of the physical body is what we more commonly refer to as physical dis-ease. The emotional/mental breakdown is commonly referred to as psychological dis-ease. Insanity might be referred to as a state of mind where one's perception has left the normal range of human awareness in such a way that one no longer has the Power to fixate his attention on that bandwidth or range of reality common to the human experience. Hence the person becomes mentally deranged.

Power and Disease

From the above perspective, disease is not some form of duress inflicted upon us from the outside (from bacteria, viruses, toxins, emotional abuse, a less-than-ideal childhood, et cetera) but rather the internal duress of our own unconsciousness or lack of awareness. Duress, by the way, is defined in the dictionary as a "compulsory force or threat." Similarly one can also experience a break-down or deterioration of outer circumstances. Because it is the Body-mind that provides the energy or mana necessary to maintain a balanced state of affairs in one's world, when it loses power one's state of affairs may degrade into something we experience as painful. Like internal disease this outer degeneration is not some form of duress inflicted upon us from the outside, but rather the result of our inner conflict extending out into our world.

Looking at this a little deeper, it can be said that my mismanagement of Power (my life-force) sets up a compulsory force that is a *threat* to the overall wellbeing or health of the triune human self and the world it is creating/experiencing. The human self, in its great intelligence and wisdom, sets up an opposing force that we then experience as disease. The purpose of this dis-ease is to awaken the unconscious aspects of the organism (me) to the life-taking way in which I am conducting my perception of reality — how I am managing (or mismanaging) my Power. Put another way, the purpose of dis-ease is to awaken the unconscious aspects of the organism to an increasingly life-giving way of managing its energy.

Please refrain from investing your energy in the idea that disease is a form of punishment or even a consequence of doing something bad or wrong. Everything that manifests within human perception is the result of *an impersonal force in motion* with the sole (or soul) intent of evolving awareness. What we may experience as dis-ease does at one level appear to be a personal consequence of some form of dysfunction, yet we can just as easily approach it as the manifestation of a call to embrace more Power. Note also that most common forms of disease are collective phenomena — arising from within the human collective unconscious — as opposed to something personal to the individual. We each have to deal with these collective thought-forms of disease until such time as we drop the energy chords/alignments that hook us into the collective's way of perceiving life and the world.

Collective Disease

Disease of this collective sort is a response within the human to the Universal intention for the Self to come into its sovereignty, into its full individuated expression. The degree to which people have their energy or Power invested in the collective perception of reality is the degree to which they will appear to be personally challenged when their purpose (as a unit of the Totality, of God) necessitates transcending those perceptions and incorporating into one's perception a more life-giving way of approaching reality.

An example of this that will help make this point clear is this: If I have my money invested in the financial systems of the collective—that of the share markets, banks, corporations and the like—when that system enters a state of dis-ease (a financial crash) my money (my energy) will *crash* with it. In the 1987 stock market crash, here in New Zealand, those people who had invested their money (their financial power) into that collective system or thought-form woke up one morning to find they were suddenly financially *powerless*. The few people who were in no way invested in that collective system of financial power were not directly affected by it at all. An example would be people who have established themselves on free-hold land with a self-sufficient lifestyle. Of course, it is rare for a member of a society to be completely apart from the financial power system of that society, so some indirect effect may have still been experienced. The way this works with finances is also exactly the way it works with our other forms of energy or Power.

A Challenge from Infinity

The form of disease I have outlined above is, simply put, the consequence of the way in which a person is unconsciously managing his Power, and ultimately a call to go about it another way. There is another way in which disease can arise that differs slightly from the above. When Universal Power (Infinity, God, call it what you may) intends to incarnate a greater degree of Power through the organism (a human being in this case), it can result in a form of *pressure* that imposes itself upon the luminous egg of the person. This pressure is also a form of duress that sets a force in motion to redistribute that person's existing configuration of Power within the luminous egg. Keeping in mind that Power is the product of perception, another way of putting this is that this duress sets in motion a force that will change the person's perception—resulting in a life-giving redistribution of Power.

The Body-mind and Attentive-mind of the average human being typically relates to this *pressure* to change its perception as a threat—a threat to my current state that I identify with as self or "me." The redistribution that takes place necessitates old limiting perceptions and energy configurations to release and dis-solve. It is this release and dis-solution (the undoing of my old *solutions* to handling Life's challenges) that one might experience as a manifestation of disease. There is nothing particularly personal about this. Much like a seed freshly planted in a garden, at some point the hydroscopic pressure of the enduring moisture in the surrounding soil—indicating the time of year is right for growth—will set a force in motion around and then within that seed.

So long as the seed has what it takes to *go along* with this force, it will release its hard shell and dissolve its inbuilt enzyme inhibitors—its solution to handling brief spells of rain or moisture during seasons not fit for growing. The seed has released its old way of being and before we know it, that little seed is changing its form into a higher state of energy or Power. Eventually we end up with a mature and fruitful plant. If, let us say, the seed had an ego (a sense of "I"), it would have experienced the dropping away of its shell and its enzyme inhibitors as a state of dis-ease; as a death of what was—a disturbance in its *known* world. It is this death of what was *known* that makes way for the birth of what is to be—that which was until now *unknown*. All is in the perfection.

One final point I shall make with regard to the mechanisms of disease is this: the resolution of disease—answering the call to Power a disease re-presents—is not always about the symptoms of disease going away or about the physical organism surviving. It is quite common a person will heal—reconfiguring the management of their personal Power—and yet the physical body dies and passes away. *Healing* and *curing* do not necessarily go hand-in-hand, although they can and often they do.

I would define healing as a return to greater wholeness in some way, shape, form or formlessness, whereas curing is the elimination of the signs and symptoms of a disease. A person's return to wholeness—a return to greater Power—within the context of experiencing cancer, for instance, may also bring about the curing of that cancer and its symptoms and allow the life of this organism to endure (the person lives on). Yet, it may also mean that the organism gives way to the disease and passes away, whilst the indwelling spirit continues to the next step on its journey into greater Power—its journey of forever expanding awareness in liberation.

> *"He is most powerful who has power over himself."*
>
> Seneca the Younger
> Roman philosopher, statesman, dramatist (4 BC – AD 65)

POWER WITHIN THE TRI-PART SELF

Power will manifest in different ways depending on where in our being we embody and embrace it. Let's take a look at this now, as I think it will help you become aware of when you are, or are not, embracing your Power in particular areas of your self. This list represents only a very brief overview of this subject. We could go into far greater detail, but I will leave that exploration for another time, in another book.

POWER AT THE LEVEL OF THE SPIRIT-MIND MAY MANIFEST AS:

- *Fluidity of perception*
  The ability to shift your perception in the moment, such as stepping into another person's way of seeing the world; taking on new perceptions/knowings that completely contradict what you thought was real and true; appreciating other cultural perspectives on life; et cetera

- *Alignment with Intention and Purpose*
  This is the experience of feeling aligned with and empowered by the intention of your Spirit and your purpose for being alive in any given moment

- *Awareness*
  The capacity to remain aware and alert to the present moment; how you are managing your Power in this moment; noticing when you are being challenged by Power to receive and incorporate some*thing* from the unknown into your known, et cetera. Also the awareness you are not what you perceive through your senses, which includes your body, emotions, thoughts, feelings, or even your higher-self.

Power at the level of Attentive-mind may manifest as:

- *A state of sobriety and lucidity*
  An awake, alert, and clear mind with a non-attachment to time and minimal identification with the world of form.

- *Knowing*
  Here I am referring to our capacity to simply know things, accurately, as and when required. This differs from learnt knowledge and even from *seeing* things clairvoyantly and the like.

Power at the level of the Body-mind may manifest as:

- *Physical vitality*
  The body will have an abundance of chi / prana / mana / vitality. The immune system is typically strong and healthy. The muscles and tendons will also typically be strong, flexible, and supple. The bones are typically strong and able to support you.

- *Clear feelings*
  Here I am referring to our capacity to clearly feel subtle energy and intuitive in-form-ation within the Body-mind without grosser emotions and thoughts obscuring this perception.

There is Only One Power

There is much I could elaborate in the above exploration of Power, health, and disease. In fact a few books could be expended on this topic alone. I have, however, covered quite enough to give you a taste of how these dynamics play out. That taste will, perhaps, spur you on to dis-covering even more of whatever aspects of this knowledge are of use to you, from within the core of your being—that is my wish. All this knowledge, and more, is awaiting your attention right there within your interiority much like that seed I spoke of, awaiting the presence of water—the flow of life—within the fertile soil in which it patiently waits.

As we awaken within the dream there is some*thing* about Power that becomes apparent. When I am no longer relating to the world through my personal Lore—rather I am relating to it through Love and thus through the Heart—a deep secret is revealed. Of course, it was not always a secret. It only entered the realm of secrecy—veiled by our ignorance—when we fell asleep with the deception of ego-identification. This secret is as follows:

"THERE IS ONLY ONE POWER. GOD IS THAT POWER. GOD AND I AM ONE. THEREFORE THERE IS ONLY ONE POWER ACTIVE HERE IN MY WORLD."

The deep realisation of this secret will quickly unravel the illusion that there is Power inherent to the dream and the hold it has over your vision of Life. Yet, in accordance with the nature of Authentic Power, it will typically do so silently, invisibly, and in a way that is direct and efficient. Very often the things of most significance unfold in the most humble and simplistic ways. The trick is to remain open and inclusive toward Life as it arises from the unknown into your known. The trick to that is to remain unattached to your known so that Power can rearrange your known as the unknown is incorporated into it.

In Reality this One Power is always at work anyway and in every way—silently and invisibly—we simply don't have the eyes to *see* it until we awaken our Mind to the Law of One Power.

Remember…There is only Love.

You are that Love.

Love is the most *powerful* force in the Universe.

"Power does not corrupt.
Fear corrupts… perhaps the fear of a loss of power."

John Steinbeck
American Novelist and Writer
Awarded Nobel Prize for Literature for 1962

Empowering Principles & Perspectives

- It is a misidentification of Self that gives humanity a distorted perspective on the nature of power.

- The ordinary person is under the illusion that power means to have control over something external to themselves—an externality.

- True Power is within us and remains within us. It determines our ability to direct our attention and affect and control our Will.

- Success is inevitable and unavoidable. You are always successful. The pertinent question is not "Am I successful," but rather "What am I being successful at right now?"

- Cause and effect as seen through the eyes of the average person is an illusion. In Reality there is only one cause and one effect. That effect is experience as a linear progression due to the nature of human perception when our attention is fixated on time and space.

- Power is the product of perception. A shift in perception creates a redistribution of power.

- Power is not gained and lost as such, although it can be convenient to talk about it in that way. Our power is simply displaced—it moves in and out of our conscious domain.

- We are never truly powerless. The perception necessary to have the experience we are having—whatever that may be—always affords us enough power to take the next most life-giving/empowering action.

- As a Divine Being you have only one need. That of a mirror. Any other need you think or believe you have is the result of a misperception of the reality pertaining to your Divinity.

- Disease arises from within. The healing of a disease does not necessarily imply the curing of its symptoms.

- Sometimes disease is purely the result of a push from our Spirit for us to embody a greater degree of power.

"Life is perpetually creative because it contains in itself that surplus which ever overflows the boundaries of the immediate time and space, restlessly pursuing its adventure of expression in the varied forms of self-realization."

Rabindranath Tagore
Indian Poet, Playwright and Essayist, 1861-1941

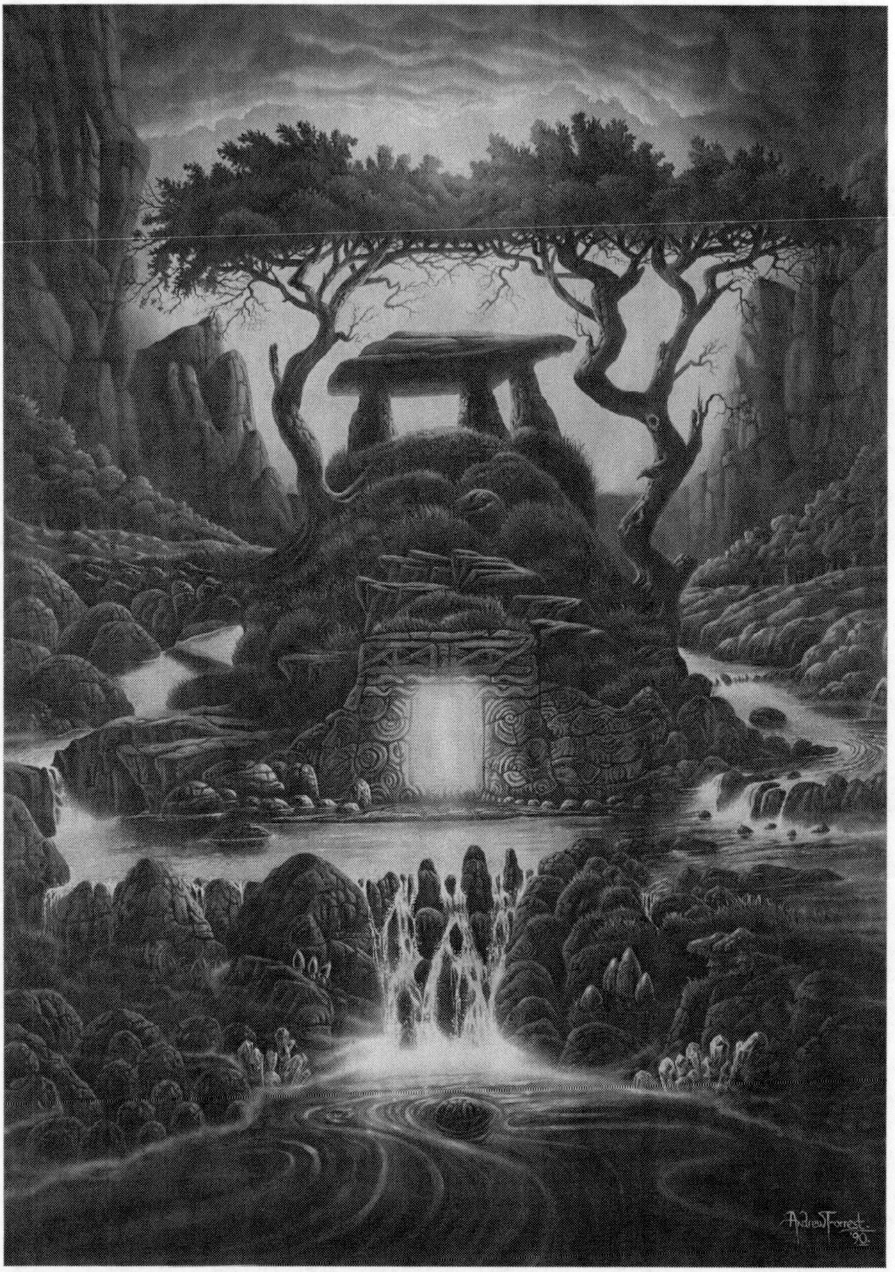
Andrew Forrest
'90

Chapter Eleven

INNER PEACE

"There is no peace in the Himalayas, and there is no noise in the world; everything is within you. If you are at peace with yourself, you can find peace anywhere in the world, and if you are not at peace with yourself, you will never find peace in isolation in the mountains."

Swami Niranjanananda Saraswati
from his book Yoga Sadhana Panorama, 1997

What is Inner Peace? Do you have a feeling for what "Inner Peace" is in your experience? Do you currently experience Inner Peace or recall a time when you have?

Most of the people in this world are in a Dream of Inner War.
This is reflected in the number of casualties they experience each day.
The ego-self, and here I am referring to the ego-self in the condition the ordinary person experiences it, is constantly under attack.
The ego-self is constantly defending its position,
Hanging on to what it thinks it has,
Fighting for more of what it wants
And what it thinks it needs,
Whilst denying what is true,
Hating and judging any other ego-self that gets in its way,
And running and hiding from that which it fears.

Every time you experience pain and suffering,

You are a casualty to this war the ego is engaged in.
Your Light goes out — even seems to die — in that moment.
If these moments happen so consistently as to be like the individual images on a film,
Or like the images in one of those little books that we, as children, would quickly flick through
In order to create the illusion of the figures in the book appearing animated,
If your Light appears to go out often enough,
And rapidly enough,
Then in each moment, looking at your dream, your personal movie,
It will appear to tell a sad story.
One of death.
One of pain and darkness

This is not Inner Peace.

Inner Peace is being at ease, calm, and still,
Yet fully Present and Aware,
Even whilst highly active and involved in the joys
And challenges
Of Life and Living.

Inner Peace is feeling joy, equanimity, and deep Love
At all times,
Even whilst faced with what some might call
An "adverse situation."

Inner Peace is uniting the separate parts
That for most of your life have conflicted,
Argued with, sabotaged, and undermined your Divinity.
Inner Peace, once realised, is being able to walk into any situation
And remain exactly as you are,
Loving, calm, centered and enjoying (in-joy-in) yourself.
The idea that there are "good" and "bad" situations
Will fall away from your world,
For Inner Peace meets all situations in the same way,
As I Am.

THE SEED OF DISCONTENT

"Yearning is a part of the beginning of anybody's practice. You have to yearn to grow. You can't want it one day, but not the next, and expect to make any real progress. You have to begin with some steady, inner hunger."

Swami Chetanananda
in The Breath Of God

Inner Peace is the *thing*, the one and only thing alongside Power, that human beings are looking for within this world and through what we call *life*. We are knowingly or unknowingly seeking to reinstate our innate Power—the Power that is inherent in the Dreamer and which we all have some recollection of, even if only deep within our subconscious. Reinstating the Power of the I AM is akin to reinstating Inner Peace. Finding Inner Peace within is akin to finding our Authentic Power. To reinstate Peace and Power we must be Present to Life as it is now.

When I was a child I had the overwhelming feeling that people are somehow not free in their present condition of who and what they perceive themselves to be. So many masks, so many rules, so many beliefs, so much conflict, so much ignorance of what is taking place in this world, and so much war inwardly and outwardly. I used to write about these feelings and observations, silently in the special books I had set aside for such things. Yet I couldn't at that time remember what the answer was. I too had forgotten what it was I was looking for and this made me feel sad deep inside. Many people thought I was such a joyful and contented child, such a confident and self-possessed teenager, yet underneath it I was far from content and constantly plagued by sadness or what I now look back on and see as phases of depression.

I once wrote how it seemed to me that everything people around me were doing—everything they said, did, and even thought—was all arising in reaction to their own discontentment. There may have been some accuracy in that observation but I can't know that for sure without asking everyone in the world if it's true for them. Yet I know now that my feeling so strongly about these things was really just my own dream. It was a projection of my dream about myself, and how discontent I was feeling with the world as maintained by the stories within my ego-mind, the dramas and energy games played out by the malu I was in cahoots with, and the struggles sustained through viewing the world through my personal Lore. I knew none of it was real; I knew there was something else I could feel within me but didn't yet experience as fully as I was destined to. Actually what I felt in my youth was that I had a glass ceiling above my head. I could see the Heavens beyond that glass ceiling, but the ceiling was blocking my ascent into fully experiencing those Heavens. I can see now it would have been more accurate to say that Heaven—the experience of Heaven on Earth—was not able to incarnate into my world due to that ceiling.

The ceiling was in fact made up of *glass* bricks—I could see through them but felt unable to move through them. Each of these bricks was a lie the malu in my mind were maintaining about reality. This reminds me of something my mother used to say. When I was a child she would say it was important I not tell lies to her. She said that each time I told a lie it was like putting a brick down between us, that these bricks would eventually form a wall, and when that wall got big enough we would be cut off from one another and unable to truly connect and love each other. I can relate to that story my mother told, and I can see how each lie I believe within my ego-mind about reality and life is also like a brick. These are lies I tell myself; therefore these bricks create a wall between me (here in the dream) and That which I AM, that Dreamer of the dream. They also cut me off from the Life Force I Am beyond the Dreamer, beyond all *things*, out (or within!) the vast unknowable void—teeming with Life and possibility.

In the time since then I have discovered that the discontentment that I, and the people I observed around me, were experiencing was in fact a substitute for the Inner Peace inherent in our True Self. The discontentment, when acknowledged and felt without judgment or denial, was there to motivate (move) me into seeking the truth and finding that which is Real—that which I experience now as Inner Peace. At some point a snake feels discontent with the skin on its body (I imagine it gets dry and uncomfortable), and this motivates it to make the effort of shedding that skin so its new one can come through.

There is a seed of discontentment within most, if not all, human beings. That seed is the antithesis of our inherent Inner Peace. Personally, it drove me to act and to explore. It is only through action (including the act of non-action) that I brought into being and into experience the con-sequence of my actions. Being present to this sequence of events, I became aware of what motivated me to act in the first place. As that motivation became clearer it embodied a greater degree of Power from the Dreamer's intent. This seed is one aspect of what ultimately awakens a person to reality. Please be aware that I've talked here about consequence as though there were such a phenomenon as cause and effect in this world, yet as I've said previously there is only one cause, and this world is its effect. That cause is beyond comprehension. Some call it God. Call it what you wish.

There is a simplicity and innocence to Inner Peace. There is something all pervading about it. In Reality this state called Inner Peace is with each of us all the time. It is a deep calm undercurrent beneath the many crisscrossing energies that form the fabric or matrix of our dream configuration. It is close to us, yet to many people it seems far away. Actually the secret of Inner Peace is closer than many dare to imagine. It is, in fact, as close as the breath passing in and out of our bodies. Yes—that close—and even closer.

Minding the Gap

Have you ever stopped to notice the transition from one breath to the next? Have you paused and noticed the transition that takes place after an inhalation, before the next exhalation begins? Or after an exhalation, before the next inhalation begins? If I were sitting with you right now and asked you, ever so gently, to observe your breath, it is likely you would observe the incoming and outgoing breath. It is likely you would not notice the transition between each half of the breathing cycle, not because you are incapable, but rather because the ego-mind is fixated on the form aspect of the Dream, and the pause or transition between two breaths is formless. Any form this pause might appear to have is only due to the exhalation and inhalation on either side of it.

Why not try it now? Read these instructions and then try it out. Sit quietly and observe your breathing. Don't change it. Just observe, as it is. Sweetly. Gently. Peacefully. I also invite you to attend to your breathing in such a way that you begin each breath cycle with an exhalation and complete each breath cycle with an inhalation. You might notice that you've always approached the breath with the feeling that you start with an inhalation and end on the exhalation. Switching this around in your mind and in your feeling world is likely to help deepen your awareness of the breath and the stillness between each breath.

Now, allow your attention to gently notice the transition between each inhalation and exhalation. Even if there is no immediately obvious pause, there is a transition that takes place—much like the transition after the high or low tide, the water going neither in nor out. Or when the moon has waxed fully and to the eye it seems that it is now full for a day or so, or when it has waned fully and the moon seems to disappear. Neither waxing nor waning.

Notice this transition. Just observe it at first, and then after a few breaths (perhaps 7 for now), start to prolong the transition point a little by pausing for a few moments after each exhalation and inhalation. In the subways in London are signs posted everywhere, and announcements on speaker systems, saying "Mind the Gap." This is what we are doing here: minding the gap, or being mindful of the gap—the gap between the pulses of Life as experienced in your body through breathing.

If not immediately, then certainly after some practice you will discover peacefulness in this space between each breath. It's like coming across the most delicious flower—one that was always there despite your lack of noticing it—blossoming in the midst of an overgrown garden, perhaps a wild rose courageously holding to its intention to bloom its sweet fragrance into the world of chaos and form because that is simply what it does. It's not hard work for a rose bush to blossom, just as it is not hard work to pause and bend ever so slightly and take in the sensual gift such a rose offers openly and freely to those who care to notice. The gap between each breath is like this also, for those who care to pause and simply take notice—to simply be aware.

I have also found, and you too may also discover this (if you have not already), that when I dissolve my attention into *minding the gap*, it becomes apparent the stillness experienced *in* one gap is in fact connected to the stillness experienced *in* the next gap. Like trees growing closely together in a forest. At ground level they appear to be separate, one tree standing apart from the next. Yet she who innocently looks up, perhaps to notice the dance of a passing butterfly, will notice that in the canopy the trees are all joined. Burrowing down into the soil we also find their roots are all interlinked as well, and the roots from one species of tree produce substances utilised by the roots of another neighbouring species of tree, and vice versa. In noticing the dance of the butterfly, or the flittering of the small forest birds, she was minding the gap between the trees.

By following this gap up or down, we find it revealed that the trees are connected. So too is the stillness and Inner Peace between two breaths interconnected, like a perfect continuum. Simply follow the breath up and down in the body, noticing the dance of life within. This is where the exquisite perfection of Now is found. Not "out there" somewhere, but right here, Now, within your Body-mind, in the gap between two breaths.

As mentioned already, this stillness is a deep calm undercurrent beneath the many crisscrossing energies that form the fabric or matrix of our individual dream configurations. This stillness is accessed by minding the gap—the gap between two breaths, the gap between two thoughts, the gap between two *frames* within your dream—yet this is only an access point. What you may discover is that Inner Peace is right here, beneath every breath, underlying every thought, permeating the entire movie called your dream, your life.

> *"Never be in a hurry; do everything quietly and in a calm spirit. Do not lose your inner peace for anything whatsoever, even if your whole world seems upset."*
>
> St. Francis de Sales
> French Roman Catholic bishop of Geneva, active in the struggle against Calvinism, 1567-1622

TWO SIDES TO INNER PEACE

One way I look at Inner Peace is that it has two sides to it. Both are important and mutually supportive of the other. There is what I would call the passive side, and there is the active side.

The passive side to Inner Peace is that of surrender. This is the Peace that results from surrendering my stories, judgments, beliefs, past hurts, victimisation issues, and all related emotional states. The Warrior's approach to Life is forever alert and aware to his projections, judgments, and pain-filled stories. He is always alert to how much energy / Power he is investing in these historical figments of the imagination. As Eckhart Tolle points out, all these things are excuses as to why I can't be happy right now. Excuses are excuses—letting them go is the only useful thing to do with them.

The active side to Inner Peace is the Warrior's predilection to stalk the Truth and that which is real, to courageously push her way into the unknown, incorporating into her known all that is discovered and has proven itself to be empowering. The active side is that of facing, even pursuing, the ongoing challenge of grasping the Power available to her from within her shadow side—all that she blocks, rejects, judges, suppresses, and denies within the self.

Such is the nature of any true battle. A battle approached purely from the active side eventually degenerates into a painful and bloody mess—a spar between two limited ego-selves lost in their own arrogance and their fixed positions and approaches to reality. Clear vision and a lucid and sober mind—a state the Warrior is always mindful to cultivate and maintain when possible—is afforded only through introspection and the recreation (re-creation) introspection provides. Hence when engaged in the active side of Inner Peace the Warrior must also know how to put down his sword of truth and simply feel with awareness where he currently stands. Likewise, a battle approached entirely from the passive side is much like a hunter trying to hunt his pray by sitting in a hut contemplating how his last hunt was conducted, releasing any life-taking stories and judgments he was harbouring about it, yet not setting foot in the wild and unknown territory in which his prey—his next meal—freely roams.

Above I refer to introspection of the sort where one is present to the feeling-sense arising within the self as it extends its Power into the world, as opposed to the obsessive self-reflective form of introspection many people waste so much of their energy on. As mentioned previously, introspection of the self-reflective kind is an illusion set up within a mind engrossed with ego-identification, for the simple reason that the Self can never reflect upon itself. The Self is self-radiant and extends from the center out into infinity. It is the world of our dream that provides us with self-reflection, which is utilised effectively only by stalking one's Power within the symbols that the dream world presents to the Self. If you wish to know what your face looks like, it is not possible to do this from within the mind—rather you must look in a mirror, out there in the world.

Revisiting the Projector

Recall now the metaphor we explored regarding the Mind of the I AM as a projector and the stories of the ego-self as the roll of film, et cetera. You will recall that we looked at how the Light of Infinity is what shines through the film. We touched on how, because of this, when we slow down the film and perceive the gap between each frame on the cellulose filmstrip, we see only unqualified Light on the screen of the Mind. Within that metaphor this is akin to minding the gap. This Light is our Inner Peace. This Light is what in every moment is "given by God." Such is the perfection of Life, that even in our mad Dreaming of war, and suffering, and killing, and loss, and death, and all the other insanities in this world, this Light is there at all times.

I just mentioned slowing down the film. I should point out that this slowing of the film happens through a quickening of the Mind—a quickening of your consciousness. Careful now. Be on the lookout, as the ego-self may have a Rule that says it is difficult and is a struggle to quicken one's consciousness. This is a lie. Yes, it may appear to take time, but only as long a time as it takes you to let go of your stories, to release your many rules about life, and to allow your virtues to come through. Letting go may take some time here in the Dream, yet it doesn't need to be a struggle. It just takes some patience and a clear intention; that is all.

The reward…is Inner Peace. The reward is contentment no matter what your Dream configuration—your world—might look like in any given moment—and swiftly returning to that contentment in the event that you momentarily lose sight of it. The reward is feeling deep stillness within even when on the outside (in your worldly affairs) you are dreaming up a lot of business (busy-ness) and things you must attend to as you deal with your life and make manifest your inspirations.

If nothing else, remember just this:

Inner Peace is as close to your mind and heart as your breathing is close to your body—and then even closer

---

Empowering Principles & Perspectives

- Humanity's perennial discontent is a seed intended to motivate us toward an ever greater and more inclusive perception of that which is Real.

- Between one breath and the next is a gap. Meditate on this and you may eventually discover the stillness in one gap is connected to the stillness within the next gap. In this way the stillness within you is a continuum and it only requires your constant attention for you to experience it continuously.

- There is an active side and passive side to our Inner Peace. The passive side is that of surrender. The active side is that of stalking, stalking one's own Power.

- When I am in my Power I am quite naturally at Peace. When I am at Peace I am quite naturally in my Power. Either way I am in a natural state of ease and authenticity.

*"I am now speaking and eating through so many mouths.
I am the Soul of all individual souls.
I have infinite mouths, infinite heads, infinite hands and feet.
My pure form is spiritual.
It is absolute Existence, Intelligence,
and Bliss condensed, as it were.
It has neither birth nor death,
neither sorrow, disease, nor suffering.
It is immortal and perfect.
I see the indivisible Absolute Brahman within me
as well as all around me.
You are all like my own parts.
The Infinite Brahman is manifesting Itself
through so many human forms.
Human bodies are like pillowcases of different shapes and various
colours, but the cotton wool of the internal Spirit is one."*

Sri Ramakrishna
The Gospel of Ramakrishna

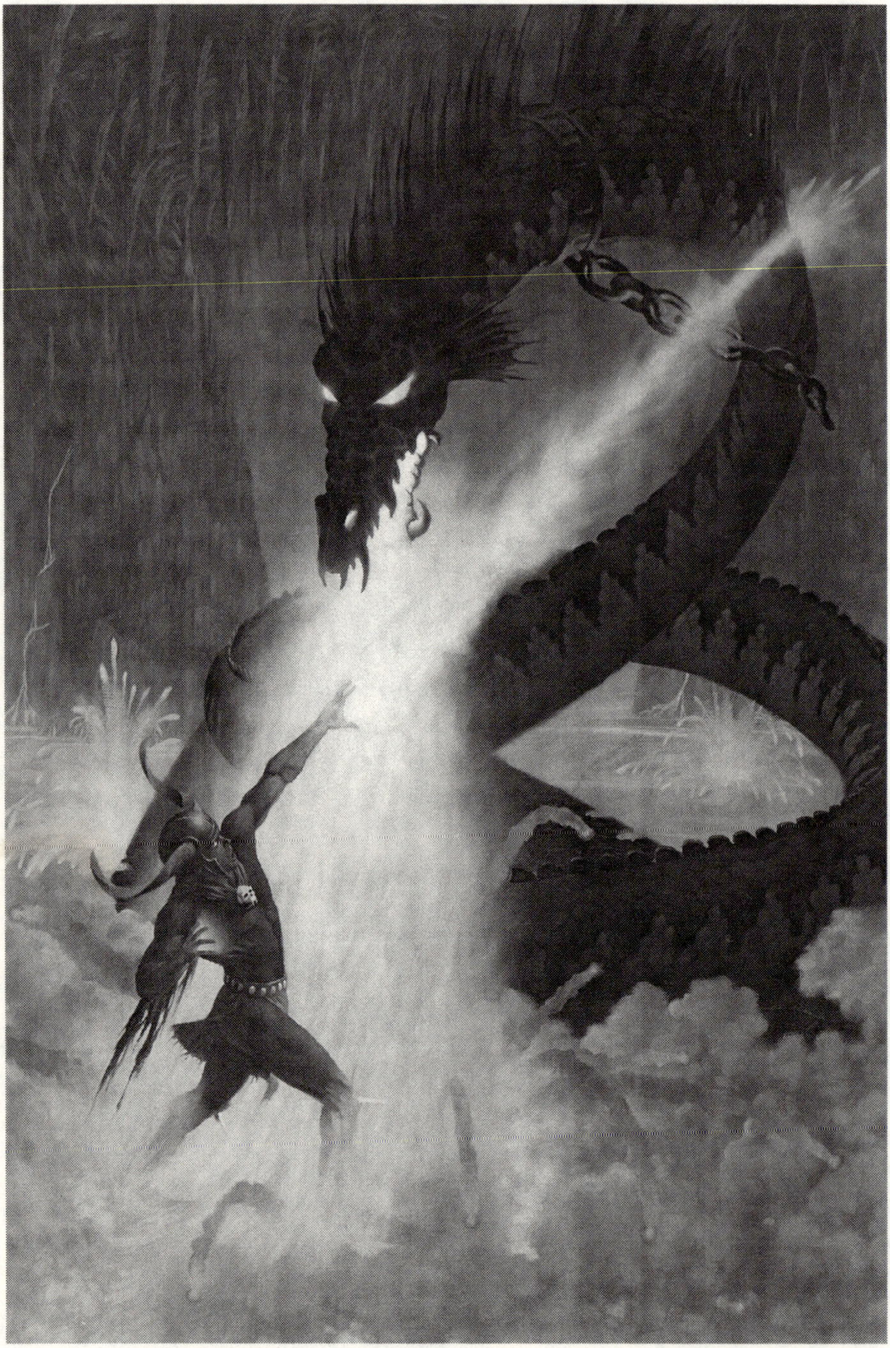

Chapter Twelve

RECLAIMING YOUR ATTENTION

"The surest way to corrupt a youth is to instruct him to hold in higher esteem those who think alike than those who think differently."
Friedrich Nietzsche

Here we are going to explore attention and intention in simple terms. By keeping this simple it will be much easier for readers to follow.

In my experience **attention** and **intention** are two important aspects of how the dream unfolds and how the Dreamer impregnates the dream with its image (imagination). We are going to look at how these forces might be operating in your life so that you may gain greater mastery over your relationship to the dream and to your Self. This material obviously has direct relevance to better understanding what I have defined as the Attentive-mind. Because the Attentive-mind is like our control center, it is important to learn how it operates.

To put it very simply, *attention* is the application or focus of awareness. You experience this as an act of directing your Attentive-mind. Intention is the Universal guiding *force* that intelligently directs attention or awareness to where it will fulfil the purpose of Intent in any given moment. Ordinary people are not typically aware of this force and where it emanates from, yet they will certainly notice the effects of this force at play in their world. There is another way of defining attention as understood within the Toltec tradition. The following is a quote from an article Mark Edwards wrote entitled "The Toltec Art of Dreaming":

1. The First Attention: I have seen this described as the full potential of that which may be termed rational, or normal awareness. It incorporates culture, the social order of things in the world, language, and reason. This is the world of the known.

2. The Second Attention: Here we transcend the limitations of the known entirely, entering the realm of the unknown, the irrational, and what might be termed non-ordinary awareness. This is the realm of astral and out-of-body travel, dreaming, sorcery, visions, and the sort of awareness that can be induced with numerous psychoactive/entheogenic plants and substances. This realm is beyond the understanding of average men and women.

3. The Third Attention: To quote Theun Mares[1], "The Third Attention is a form of awareness which transcends the Second Attention, and which is not accessible to any other than those trained upon the Path of Freedom," and "To try to explain the Third Attention in just a few words is well-nigh impossible, but let it suffice for now to say that the Third Attention is that point in the manifested universe, that level of awareness, where the awareness of both the unmanifest and the manifest is assembled in a mutual and fully intelligent act of co-operation. In this respect it is the ultimate paradox, but a paradox which grants access to the blueprint of the universe." The Third Attention is beyond the parameters of language and therefore cannot aptly be put into words.

Where you focus your awareness—the object of your awareness in this moment—is where you are holding your attention. One way I experience attention is as an act of awareness being compressed or condensed into a particular aspect or aspects of the intelligent field in

---

1 Mares, Theun. Preface to Volume Four, *Shadows of Wolf Fire*

which the dream (and this world) is constructed.

As human beings we can focus our awareness into the *known* (1st attention), into what constitutes the *unknown* (2nd attention), and ultimately into the *unknowable* (3rd attention). Most people, however, keep their attention (and hence their awareness) firmly and consistently fixated on their *known*, and what's more on an extraordinarily limited spectrum of the *known* available to them at any moment in time. What we focus our attention upon and into determines what we are aware of in that moment—it defines what we are able to perceive. As Power is a product of perception, our attention plays a crucial part in determining the Power we have available to us. Ordinary people directly experience the unknown, for the most part, only within the realm of their nocturnal dreams. People exploring the use of psycho-active substances also experience the unknown and the realm of the Second Attention during such journeys.

If most people are operating within the realm of the First Attention, it is important we look at what this constitutes. In simple terms, most people have inherited their First Attention from their immediate physical and metaphysical environment. Typically for a child this environment includes (in brief) the parents, extended family, the tribe/culture the family lives within, and the religion the family subscribes to. We start acquiring this inheritance much sooner than most people realise—it has been determined[2] and scientifically observed that these influences go back to at least two months before conception. Already at this stage of preconception the egg is ripening within the mother for release two months hence. Right back at that time in those early moments of development the environment (physical and metaphysical) in which that egg developed started influencing the outcome—namely You.

It has been shown that a fetus that develops in a harsh environment—say one where the mother is consistently experiencing abuse, stress, and adversity—will tend toward developing greater physical brawn and a brain wired up for excellent physical survival instincts (at the expense of higher intelligence). A fetus that develops in a mother who is in a loving, safe, and nurturing environment will tend toward less physical brawn and greater development of the upper parts of the

---

2 See the work of Dr Bruce Lipton, *The Biology of Perception*

brain (which gives rise to higher intelligence). It could be said that the imprint of your First Attention began at this stage.

Further to this, the first six or seven years of a child's development are spent in a hypnogogic state where the brain is for the most part functioning at theta and delta brainwave levels. This is the trance state to where a hypnotist will take a patient before giving him therapeutic/remedial suggestions because it is the level at which the subconscious mind (the Body-mind) will most readily take on knowledge without the interference (filtering) of the conscious mind (the ego-self and its personal Lore).

THE WHO, WHERE, WHAT, AND WHY OF THINGS

I have noticed that the majority of people I know focus a lot of their attention on the *why* of things. "Why did he say that?" "Why did I not get what I wanted?" "Why did you do that?" "Why did this have to happen to me?"

Usually running alongside this train of mental aberration is the question that asks about the *what* of things. Either one might precede the other, and if you see one, you're bound to see the other. "What exactly happened here?" "What exactly do you mean by that?" "What exactly did that make me feel?" I consider the *what* enquiry to be a little less superficial to the seeking out the *why* of things.

Deeper still is the enquiry into *where*. Because most people have their attention firmly fixated on the material aspect of reality, the question *where* tends to be thought of as self-explanatory so people seldom explore it. If Joe came into the room and verbally abused me, the mind of an ordinary person will conclude that it happened here in this room and will look no further into it than that. Yes, if one really explores the *where* enquiry, it soon becomes apparent that there is far more to it than just the physical locality of what unfolded. One will notice, for a start, that the feelings (my reaction) to Joe abusing me arose entirely within the framework of my body. The benefit of recognising this is significant, for I can no longer blame Joe for how I am feeling. Why not? Because I'm the one inside and in command of my body, not Joe.

Moving along now.... The point I wish to make here is that asking WHAT and WHERE takes one's attention deeper than we'll ever get with asking WHY. Moving our attention (as far as enquiry is concerned) from the superficial to the profound takes us from an enquiry of asking *why* into exploring *where*, into dis-covering *what* and ultimately directly experiencing *who*. Who is again something we seldom ask, because at the apparent level the answer seems obvious, and this is an interesting point. What seems most obvious through to what seems least obvious at the apparent level is in fact completely reversed in terms of significance when we take our attention deeper to the non-apparent level. *Who* seems so obvious we barely consider it. Yet a sincere enquiry into the *who* behind things has the potential to truly set a person free from whatever it is that might be challenging him.

Ordinary man typically fixates his attention on the *why* of things. Self-reflection is often about analysing the *why* of the ego-self and its various reactions, conditions, and beliefs. It is a process that takes one's attention away from the profundity of That which is real and deep within the Self, into the superficiality of our stories about the world and further identification with those stories and the ego-self that perpetuates them (and is perpetuated by them). Enquiry into *who* has the opposite effect, and is the basis of Ramana Maharishi's[3] spiritual practice of meditating on the question "Who am I?" This question has the potential to reengage the enquirer with her Divine nature, transcending the illusion of "me" and one or more other people or things. With that illusion transcended, forgiveness becomes infinitely easier — in fact it will usually take place spontaneously. Once I realise there is only One cosmic "I" in all *things*, who is there left to do me wrong or do me an injustice, let alone forgive?

On with the topic at hand — attention.

THE NATURE OF ATTENTION

I think of attention as being the alignment or movement of awareness, guided by intention. I can align myself with an intention, yet I must then align my attention to the formative forces, actions, and non-

---

3 See the Appendix for references to books about Maharishi's teachings if you are interested in learning more about them

actions that will ultimately bring the fulfillment[4] or maturation of that intention into my awareness and direct experience. Put another way, I may have the intention to build a house, but this will only come into being when I align my attention to those *things* within the known and the unknown (if house building is not entirely familiar to me) of my world pertaining to house building. Things such as creating or obtaining plans, securing a suitable piece of land, procuring suitable building materials, et cetera. With each of these steps I must align my attention and take action in the most appropriate way.

Our attention—our Attentive-mind, which began taking shape before we even entered the womb—is what we as human beings have used to take on everything we know about this world. It is what directed our perception to the various *things* we end up believing are *real*. Again, as Power is a product of perception, it is your attention that has determined what Power is available to you.

The ego-self will pay attention at its worst to that which is not real and at its best to that which is superficial to the real. The ego-self of ordinary Man and Woman always pays attention to that which is transitory and passing, yet it has an uncanny ability to thereafter relate to that transitory *thing* as if it were permanent and ever-lasting. The ego-self therefore pays attention to the superficial element of reality— to the shallow appearance of things on the surface level of what "I" perceive and experience. Your true Presence naturally pays attention to that which is eternal and that which is at the level of the profound. By definition it is therefore paying attention to that which is at the non-apparent level of reality…that which is at the very depth of things— even the no*thing* from which all things arise.

For example…

Let's take a look at a situation most of us deal with each day, food and eating:

Within the confined context of "food" and "eating," the ego-self of an ordinary person may pay exclusive attention (at the cost of paying attention to what's on the next list) to the following elements:

---

4 I am not using the word "fulfillment" in the common sense of the word, for that typically implies the illusion of cause and effect. What I am referring to is more akin to the way an apple arises on an apple tree. The tree does not *cause* the apple, rather that apple is part of the natural unfolding of *the flow of intent* we at first identify as a seed, then a tree, and eventually flowers and fruit.

- The taste of the food from the perspective of its effect at a sensory level
- The effect the food has on my emotions (how it makes me feel)
- How quickly and cheaply the food can be grown whilst maintaining a socially desirable appearance
- How quickly and cheaply the meal can be obtained or prepared

I am sure many other things could be listed here but this is enough to make my point.

The ego-self will pay attention to the above-mentioned factors at the cost of paying attention to the following:

- The quality and quantify of the life-force within the food
- The organising intelligence that is embodied and therefore imparted by the food to my body and mind
- Production of the food in such a way that its life-force and organising intelligence are optimised and enriched
- The impact this food will have on my state of well-being within this human form
- God/Infinity/Life as the true source of the food and, in particular, the sustenance the food provides
- …. and many other factors too numerous to list

Relatively speaking, the first list is of things that are all transitory and short-lived in nature. Once I've finished drinking that can of cola and have satisfied my sensory craving for sugar (something sweet) and caffeine, the satisfaction passes almost immediately. It's gone. That which I (a limited sense of ego-self) gave my attention to has come and gone. A hidden outcome is the average ego-self will often put substances into its body that are life-taking in nature, paying attention to short-lived oral satisfaction (such as the craving for something sweet) rather than the overall whole body impact. The soft drink does not support life in the long term and in fact is typically a detriment to one's health. The effect of this on one's health is much longer lasting. It too is impermanent, yet relatively speaking, it is far more permanent than what the misdirected ego-self was interested in—a sugar fix.

The second list is something quite different from the first, with attention being on longer-lasting factors such as the life-force within the food I eat. The life-force is an organising, living, intelligent force that is not destroyed within the body after I have eaten it, for it is incorporated into the Body-mind and *lives* on in that form. When I bring that life-force into my Body-mind, it is assimilated and becomes a small yet important element of my being here in this world, as that being is an extension of the Presence that I AM (beyond this world). The life-force from an apple, for instance, will also in some small way be assimilated into my awareness and beyond. An organically grown apple—free from artificial chemicals and grown in an environment that has some degree of natural balance within it—will have a different quality of life-force from an apple that has perhaps been grown in a commercial orchard that uses toxic chemical sprays and grows the trees in a relatively sterile environment of bare sprayed earth and very little resemblance to what nature intended.

The impact of life-giving food on my state of well-being is always enduring, for life-giving food has elements that do not pass away. It becomes an integral part of that which I AM as expressed through the physical and metaphysical extension of the Self (a human body).

I've tried to keep the above point as simple as possible although I realise it may not seem that way. A quick reread may help with understanding it if it seems a tad complicated to you. A lot more could be said and many questions may come to your attention after reading the above example. It is my wish that this example be explored within the small-scale context that I've placed it. Please keep in mind that my intention here is not to illustrate the effects of different foods, but rather to illustrate how the ego-self of ordinary Man and Woman and the True Self will each give attention to quite different aspects of whatever it is we are relating to in this world. Leading on from this is the important consideration that the ego-self of ordinary man must sooner or later incorporate into its sphere of perception, a greater perception of the true nature of the "I" both personally and cosmically. It is in this way that our limited and often-times wounded sense of ego-self can heal and eventually bring into manifestation the unified cosmic "I" that knows no separation. This is what Christ Consciousness is about. We'll explore this more in a later book in this series.

So the point here is *the average ego-self and the Spirit-mind will focus on or give attention to quite different elements of your day-to-day experience.*

I invite you to start exploring just what you are giving your attention to in each event, experience, object, or phenomena that you encounter. Your state of Awareness will determine just what you discover in this sort of exploration. The good news is that no matter where you are within your perspective, this sort of exploration will lead to greater and greater Awareness. Once you become aware that you are going with the ego's take on reality (which is always *life-taking* in nature) you will have the option to make a different choice and go with the Soul's take on reality (which is always *life-giving* and supporting).

Whilst you are being alert to what you give your attention to, it would pay to ask, "What is my intention in this moment, choice, or act?" This is an important question to ask—or feel into—as often as possible, but especially at critical junctures in your relationship, and especially with regard to definitive choices you make from day to day. If you are not clear on what the intention is behind any given act, then are you acting responsibly in taking that action? Reclaiming your Inner Peace and Power depends greatly on putting our willy-nilly behaviours aside and instead living (making choices) from a place of clear intention. Of course, this must be done with heart because when pursued solely with the rational mind, it can become another form of rigidity, which will surely lead to pain. When done with heart, one is able to remain water-like and flow more freely and gently into *feeling* the nature of one's intention in each moment. Eventually it becomes an ongoing state of feeling or being, ever present in one's awareness.

The only other point I wish to make here is that switching from the First Attention (that of an ego-self misidentified with the tangible world) over to the Second Attention (that of the Spirit-mind and an ego-self inclusive of that which is intangible) does not mean that the object of the First Attention becomes obsolete. In coming back to the above example of food and eating, just because I start to pay attention to the non-apparent level of the food I choose to eat does not mean I will now ignore the apparent level of the food (i.e., whether it actually tastes good and I enjoy it). Both elements are important within the human experience. The key is simply that I will no longer give my attention solely to the taste and exclude an awareness of the more profound factors involved (such as the few I have mentioned here).

"Who looks outside, dreams; who looks inside, awakes."
Carl Gustav Jung

ATTENTION AND ENERGY

Whilst on the topic of attention I would like to share some additional wisdom regarding this, again passed on by the Huna knowledge of ancient Hawaii. There is a principle from Huna that goes as follows—

> Energy flows where your attention goes /
> Life flows where your attention goes.

What this recognises is that wherever I place my attention is where my Life energy will flow in my world. It could also be said, "Where your energy goes, things grow." The implications of this are many. One common example, for instance, is the situation of having a lack of money. If you give your attention to the apparent lack of money, then this is where your Life energy will flow—and will more than likely continue to create an apparent lack of money, because Life energy is a creative force. It doesn't care that you think having too little money stinks. If you're giving your attention to it, then it'll go there and dutifully boost that reality even more. On the flipside, if you give your attention to having more money, then your Life energy will flow there and give that a boost in your world. Another example is that of health and disease. If I am experiencing a disease, focusing my attention on that disease and its symptoms is not going to aid my recovery. Far more conducive to healing would be to pay attention to how I can restore health in this part of myself, and even to pay attention to the vision—the image—of health in this area that appears diseased. By giving my attention to this image I will in fact give it my energy and thus it will—putting all other possible circumstances aside for the sake of simplicity—grow into being.

This also applies to the vision you hold of the world and the people around you. In a previous chapter we looked briefly at the possibility of differentiating between a person as a Divine Being and the malu (life-taking spirits) that are acting through him. Put another way, this means differentiating between a person and his behaviours. A key part of this is that if you identify yourself and the people around you with the malu they are dealing with, then this is where your Life energy will flow—creating a greater propensity for these malu to continue their tricks and to also invite malu into your sphere of being—such as the make-wrong malu that judges and criticises others. If, however, in your mind you do not see yourself and your relations *as* the malu but rather at all times see and acknowledge the Divinity, then this is where your Life energy will flow and this is what will grow.

These are simple concepts (although perhaps unfamiliar to you until now) with deep and far-reaching repercussions when embraced, understood, and lived.

There is a great deal we could explore with regard to Intention—its nature, how it operates, how it influences your life, how you can attune to and align yourself with Universal Intention (or *The Will of God* if you are partial to Biblical terminology), and more. I'll leave that topic for another time in another book.

Reclamation

Reclaiming our attention is essentially (and at the early stages) about looking at everything you have made assumptions about; every belief you have; your every judgment about the world; your every opinion about yourself and other people; and what you seek when in relationship with others (this list could go on). In looking at these things one is able to do so with a degree of sobriety that was simply not there from the age of preconception through to six years of age or so. During that time a vast array of what determines the way in which you perceive life made its way into your human self with little or no conscious human choice on your part[5]. Whether what you let into your mind was stuff that would cause you to suffer and struggle later in life or stuff that would help you to rapidly excel and succeed in business, or to be a great artist or a fantastic doctor, was pretty much a hit and miss affair—as far as your conscious thinking human self was concerned.

In revisiting all these *programs* within the Body-mind we are able to

---

5 I say "conscious human choice" because at a more profound level it was the unfolding of who and what you are that brought that particular conception and childhood into being. I will leave that line of exploration at that for now.

start letting go of the ones that really don't serve us in feeling at Peace and in our Power. This book and the other books in this series provide some of the tools and understandings I have found invaluable in order to successfully undertake that journey of reclaiming my attention.

As soon as a person drops his fixation on and identification with the known (the subject matter of his First Attention) the unknown will start to become increasingly apparent. The presence of the unknown will no longer invoke feelings of fear and denial—rather it will elicit a feeling of curiosity, adventure, and enquiry. The unknown is constantly pushing its way into our known—collectively as humanity, and individually as one person. We see the effect of this every day when things don't go as planned, when "accidents" occur, when our health starts to break down, when we are challenged by the many mysteries of trying to relate intimately with a partner or loved one, and so on.

When a person is willing to bring the Power of the Second Attention into her engagement with these *things*, a level of knowledge, growth, and Power suddenly and almost miraculously becomes available. At the most basic level the following example may help illustrate this point.

For someone caught up in her First Attention, the experience of "catching" a flu or cold every year might seem quite normal. I know many people who don't give it a second thought. I even know of someone who carries antibiotics around in her handbag as a matter of course so she can knock the regular appearance of a cold out, before the cold knocks her out. She also has pain-killers on hand at all times in case a headache or some other ache crops up. Someone who is open to the unknown and is therefore eliciting her second attention would never see things in this way. Rather she would stop to pay greater attention to what her body is communicating to her via this cold or flu. Rather than seeing the cold (I'll stick with just the cold for now) as something going *wrong* with the *known* she would perceive it as something arising from the *unknown* and impressing itself on her *known*. She may discover, for example, that she is consistently eating foods that don't support her body adequately, that she is not getting enough sleep, that she is overworking herself in her career, or perhaps something else that is proving to be life-taking for her wellbeing.

The key here is that letting go of our attachment to the *known* and to the perceptions we developed in our First Attention makes *room* for the *unknown* to reveal rather significant and important *things* to us. These *things* will invariably benefit and increase our Power and aid us in both discovering and fulfilling our purpose. Your purpose quite literally arises from the *unknown* into the *known*, which happens most effectively when you are fully Present to Life and the world.

Self Reflection

We started exploring self-reflection in Chapter Eight. We touched on it again in the last chapter. It's an important topic so we'll take another look at it here, with regard to reclaiming your attention.

Recently a friend lent me a book called *The Active Side of Infinity*, the last book written by the late Carlos Castaneda. Whilst there are some things in this particular book that I don't go along with, there was something near the end of this book that I thought was particularly important and relevant to many people. Don Juan consistently tells Castaneda that *self-reflection* is one of the major problems the ordinary modern human faces with regard to losing his or her power. Because he's not around for me to talk to, I can't be certain exactly what Don Juan is referring to with his use of the term "self-reflection," yet it led me to explore this topic more deeply within my Self. I'll share a little of this exploration with you now because I think it's an important aspect of reclaiming our attention.

When I read Castaneda's passages on self-reflection to my partner, she asked me what self-reflection is. Don Juan made it pretty clear that self-reflection is a dangerous thing to get caught up in. Yet what exactly is this self-reflection? It feels to me that self-reflection is that process of internal self analysis many people make a consistent habit of. I've noticed that it can be a very convoluted process that seldom leads any-where productive. Often it revolves around an internal dialogue pertaining to the question "why…?" Usually, after some time, the ego-self tires of it and lets it drop, until we pick the process up again, often quite soon thereafter. For most people a great deal of their internal self-dialogue is self-reflective in nature. "Why did I do that? Perhaps I shouldn't have done it that way. There must be some reason why I did that; I mean was it just stupidity or what? I always do stupid things like that. Just not thinking properly and then I have to deal with the consequences. Perhaps I…" and so on.

Rather than my trying to describe self-reflection in great detail, I invite you to pause for a moment and feel into your Body-mind with the question/intention of "what is self-reflection?" Feel into this and be with what comes up. You can also refer back to the material in Chapter Eight on self-reflection for further insight. Simply allow yourself to remember those times you may have been self-reflecting and recall how it was for you. How did you feel? What took place?

I would like to point out that self-reflection is different from self-awareness and going within—such as in meditation. It is also different from inner contemplation. Self-reflection typically involves a lot of mental dialogue, often trying to figure out why the self is a particular way in some given moment or situation. It typically takes the ego-self round and round in an endless convoluted spin.

The fallacy of self-reflection is this: You, in your essence and wholeness, are the Self, so how can you bring about reflection within that same whole Self? It is not possible, within the ego-mind, to truly *self-reflect*. What we are doing when we self-reflect is actually the ego-self getting all tangled within its own illusions, neuroses, and fragmentation. One fragment reflecting upon another fragment.

This madness displaces an incredible amount of our energy into the false sense of self the human ego-self is presently based upon. It also tends to lend a person toward self-centeredness, which is another great energy diverter we'll explore shortly. Your dream—the world you perceive around you—is where true self-reflection is taking place. The majority of people have learnt that it is by placing their attention on their internal ego-self that they will gain insight and growth beyond the ego-self. Remember, energy flows where the attention goes, and where your energy flows things grow. In this case it is one's distorted sense of ego-self that enlarges. Reclaiming your attention from this self-reflective process typically takes time and discipline. We often become addicted to the energy configuration that self-reflection creates within us. A key to stepping out of self-reflection is to remain present to your dream—the phenomenal world unfolding around you—and to simultaneously remain aware of the felt-sense arising within the framework of your Body-mind as you relate to the dream.

The Cosmic Mystery of One

It is common to assume that the felt-sense I am having internally is a reaction or response to what I am experiencing *out there* in the world. Consider, for a moment, that what is arising out there is in fact the stuff of the Universe reflecting or responding to the nature of what exists at the profoundest level of where or what that felt-sense arose from deep within your Beingness. By being present to this unfolding—to the story it tells at a symbolic level—and how we feel about it we remain in alignment to our Path of awakening.

In my experience there is a deeper truth in this that you may have a feeling for now or may have some time soon. Namely, the world "out there" is not in fact responding to your interiority, nor is your interiority responding to the world out there. In reality *out there* and *in here* are different aspects or perspectives of the same force arising from the unknown into the known—the formless side of Life arising into the form side of Life. The whole experience of out-there and in here—the interior self and the exterior world—is an illusion arising from the way human perception is presently configured at this point in our collective journey.

Empowering
Principles & Perspectives

- Attention and intention are two important aspects of how the dream unfolds and how the Dreamer impregnates the dream with its image (imagination).

- The are three levels of attention. The first attention is made up of the known. The second attention is made up of the unknown. The third attention can be described as a paradox that grants us access to the blueprint of the universe.

- The ordinary person lives a life made up entirely of the First Attention. Some people, although rare, start engaging with the Second Attention during their lifetime. Only those deeply established on a Path of Freedom ever engage in the Third Attention.

- We lose energy when our attention is fixated on trying to understand the "why" behind events and phenomena.

- When our Attentive-mind is caught up in the superficial aspects of life, we completely lose sight of the unknown.

- When we open our Attentive-mind to the profundity of life our attention gains access to the unknown.

- Any and every increase in power comes to us through the unknown.

- Energy flows where our attention goes. Life follows attention.

- Recognizing people not as their malu (or their behaviour) but as Divine beings will strengthen your experience of their Divinity. It will help heal them in your world.

- That which you perceive to be out there and in here (within you) are one and the same. There is only one.

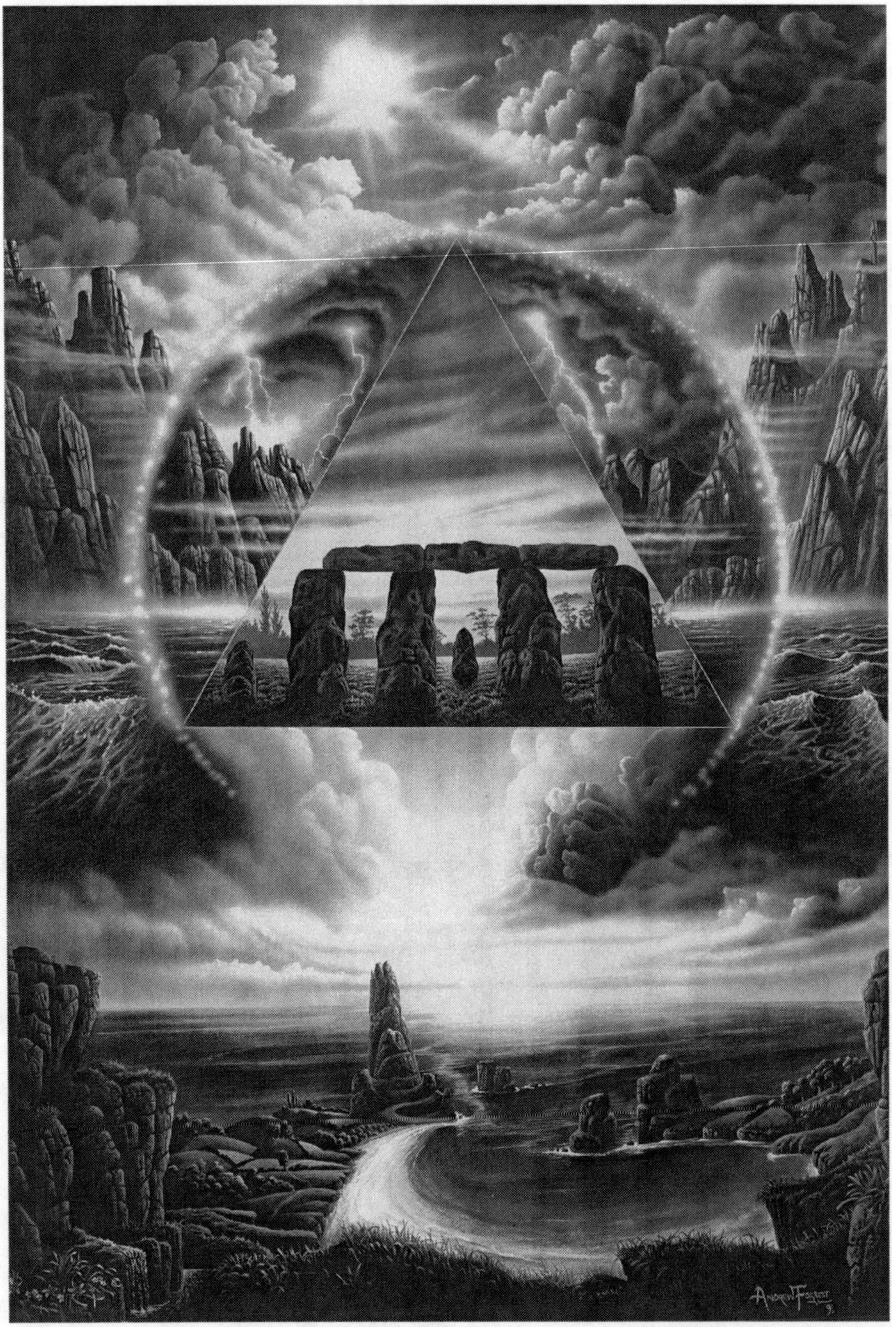

Chapter Thirteen

LIFE AS MEDICINE

*"Life will give you whatever experience is most helpful for the evolution of your consciousness.
How do you know this is the experience you need?
Because this is the experience you are having at this moment."*
Eckhart Tolle
A New Earth: Awakening to Your Life's Purpose

The recognition of *Life as medicine* is something that has been stirring within my awareness for many years now, and I'd like to share what I understand in this regard. It's really quite magnificent...transforming the world into an experience that is kind, supporting, loving, and intelligent.

So, what do I mean by "Life as medicine"?

The meaning of "Life as medicine" goes back to something else we have already explored, that "Every*thing* is happening *for* you and not *to* you."

Everything that is happening for you has one particular and essential purpose—it is *medicine* intended to restore wholeness, to dispel illusions, and expand awareness. I've just taken a look at what a dictionary has to say about the word "medicine" and have been pleasantly surprised—it actually makes reference to the Native American use of the word, which is the one most akin to the way I am using it here.

Let's take a look at what the word medicine means and how this applies to life. Your life, my life, and Life itself.

Medicine, *noun*
1. **Something that serves as a remedy or corrective**: medicine for rebuilding the economy; measures that are harsh medicine.
2. Shamanistic practices or beliefs, especially among Native Americans.
3. Something, such as a ritual practice or sacred object, believed to control natural or supernatural powers or serve as a preventive or remedy.
4. Among the Native Americans, any object supposed to give control over natural or magical forces, to act as a protective charm, or **to cause healing**; also, magical power itself; the potency that a charm, token, or rite is supposed to exert.
5. *The North American Indian boy usually took as his medicine the first animal of which he dreamed during the long and solitary fast that he observed at puberty.* F. H. Giddings.

The words in bold indicate the defining points I find particularly applicable. The meaning I am associating with the word "medicine" is "something that brings about healing or provides remedy to dis-ease." I don't limit the word dis-ease to physical ailment, but rather I see that it includes all the ways in which a person can be or become not-at-ease. Not at ease with herself, with her life, with her body, her circumstances, et cetera.

What I wish to remind you of is that everything in life is happening *for* you and comes to you as medicine to remedy dis-ease or an absence of health and wholeness. Health, as defined in most dictionaries, is "the wholeness or soundness of body, mind, and soul." All things in our world are here to bring about healing and wholeness, one way or another.

People, family members, events, situations, accidents, coincidences, pain, joy, struggles, friends, et cetera, are all a form of medicine perfectly orchestrated into your life to remedy that which is in a place of un-wholeness, disparity, and dis-ease. Life is really one vast conspiracy working not *against* us and the other manifestations of Life, but rather is working powerfully *for* the wellbeing of all that is. Conspiracy literally means *to breath together*. The origins of the word breath also mean spirit. The word conspiracy can also be interpreted from an etymological point of view as *to come together in spirit* or *together as one in spirit*. The Universe is one in spirit working toward the wellbeing of all the many manifestations of life—and that includes you and me.

LETTING THE VICTIM GO NOW

To really get into the feeling of what I've just said, it is necessary, I think, to absolutely let go of being a victim. As far as I can ascertain, *victimitis* is a dangerous psychosomatic plague that has passed through the contemporary human collective consciousness, and is presently a global pandemic. Forget about scares of bird flu and the global hoax named "terrorism," victimitis is far more prevalent and is a far greater threat to the wellbeing of humankind and this planet. In fact, much of the world as we know it is the product of and is heavily dependent upon this state of dis-ease I refer to as *victimitis*. I have not met many people who are not engaged in a victim mentality at some level. Over my lifetime I have, and still do, watch how a victim mentality crops up within myself, and I've found that it gets more and more subtle and slippery the deeper I delve into it.

There is, of course, a gift of *power* waiting patiently within this pandemic dis-ease. That gift is the re-cognition, the re-membering, that "I" am one hundred percent re-sponsible for my experience of reality. The *Dreamer* and the flow of intention moving through and from the *Dreamer* are entirely responsible for what "I" experience, therefore "I" too must assume that degree of responsibility. Only then will "I" truly experience its divine nature within the dream. One of the greatest steps a person can take on the path of freedom is to reclaim his or her power from the false perception that "I am a victim" to the things and events happening around me.

To ground this theory in a level of practical benefit, I'd like to suggest that for the next week or two each morning and several times throughout the day you set the intention to remember to pass through the following steps in some form when struggles and challenges arise in your world. This might be a challenge with your circumstances or with particular people. You may want to bookmark these pages to come back to this practice when you find yourself experiencing a conflict. Here are your steps:

First a note about breath and the deeper significance of breath. In my experience breathing fully is crucial for engaging with deep feelings. Each conscious inspiration literally inspires the Body-mind with the spirit and matter. It is our conscious use of breath that engages our attention back into the conspiracy of Life working together as One Power, for the benefit of all. I will point out that spirit or *the heavens* is representative of the masculine principle, or the masculine side of Awareness. *Matter*, which may be derived from the Latin word *mater* meaning "origin, source, mother," represents the feminine principle, or the feminine side of Awareness. Every conscious expiration literally allows that which has *expired* or come to an end within your Body-mind to pass back to spirit and the Earth.

So, the first step is to breathe. Breathe deeply and fully, intending your breath through the whole body, whilst physically engaging the pelvic diaphragm (the pelvic muscles), abdominal muscles, thoracic diaphragm, and finally the clavicle. Engaging the lower part of the body in this way stimulates and activates the first three energy centers and neural plexuses within the Body-mind. This is important because if they remain dormant it is very difficult to get to the truth of the *matter* (the truth within the body).

Step back from the internal reaction that has come up. Being familiar with meditation and 'the witness' may be a prerequisite to consciously knowing just what this entails, although I feel that an awareness of 'the witness' within one's consciousness can be felt and experienced with a minimal amount of effort. The key really is to recognise it, as it is always there. This is one of the many benefits of cultivating meditative awareness, and it's an important element of The Path of Freedom, and something we will explore in the second volume in this series of books[1]. If you are not familiar with meditation I invite you to do your best with inwardly stepping back from the situation you are feeling challenged by. Typically this will mean pulling back from the emotions and thoughts that have been stirred up—which does not mean suppressing or denying these emotions and thoughts.

Remove all notions of "the other," the "other" being anything or anyone external to yourself. Hence if a person has done something

---

1 The second volume is entitled *The Seven Empowerments*. See the Appendix for further information.

that annoys you, it is necessary to remove that person from your reaction, and from your story about the event. Stay with the reaction but drop the association that has been automatically made between the emotions you are experiencing (your reaction) and the person "out there" who seemed to cause that reaction or emotional response.

If you find it difficult to disassociate the outside world from what you are feeling, simply ask yourself this one question, "Where do I feel this emotion?" It will be immediately apparent that you feel the emotion (the energy that is stirring in response/reaction to the challenging circumstances) within the framework of your own body. You do not feel the emotions out there somewhere. You do not feel them in other people. This energy—this emotion—is within the framework of *your* body and therefore it is entirely, absolutely, and undeniably, one hundred percent your responsibility. Is this point clear? Remember he who bears the consequence holds the responsibility. The consequence of my destructive emotions is first and foremost experienced by me, so I am the person first and foremost responsible for what I am feeling.

With the "other" removed, that leaves only you or "I" (in the first person, from within you). Now that there is only YOU/I in your relationship to these emotions, bring your awareness (within your feeling world) to the notion that "This is happening for me. I am an Infinite Being and out of that infinity this is what I am co-creating for myself in order to actualise the full magnificence of all That I Am into this world…into the dream."

It is also now important to release all judgment and opinion around what has happened and around the emotions that have come up. This requires deep trust. To not judge rape or abuse, for instance, as "good" or "bad" requires deep trust, for the ego wants things like this "bad" and "wrong." If you approach this energy (the emotion you are feeling) from a perspective of right and wrong when you try to explore the notion that it is happening for you and not to you, the victim is going to jump up and start sabotaging your efforts to stay present with what is unfolding.

From this place of no judgment and oneness (there is only YOU and no other) the next steps are going to have to arise from within you. Stay with your feelings. Stay with the emotions. Stay with the thoughts. Continue to breathe. Feel the pause between two breaths after each exhalation for about 2-6 seconds. Stay with that which is within you.

When your awareness/attention projects out to some distraction or thought, gently bring it back to the feeling that is within you. Bring your attention down to your belly and breathe.

I suspect you will find that the medicine will make itself known one way or another when you go through a process something akin to the one I have just outlined.

An Agent of Healing

Oh, and before we move on, there is one further important point I wish to make.

Medicine is an agent that induces or supports healing. I've said that trust is required for this process to take effect, yet there is something else required, something even more important than trust—Humility. In the Huna and Toltec traditions I am familiar with, it is said that it takes humility to heal.

Humility requires understanding—literally to mentally, emotionally, and spiritually stand-under the situation you perceive and elevate it into a place of high esteem. This is one application of the affirmation "I am the resurrection and the Life" (also "…and the light") Jesus Christ is reported to have said on occasion. To resurrect something is to revive it from disuse or lifelessness. It is through our humility that the I Am within us resurrects the content of our dream into the Life and Light of our Divine Presence.

Healing is the resurrection of our discordant beliefs, memories, and self-image into the fullness of Life, into the Light of the Dreamer.

Energy and Issues

Yes, life is medicine—an agent of healing, growth, and expanding awareness—and yes, there is much to be gained by owning what I experience in reaction to the apparent *other* people out there in the world. Yes, it is useful to dissociate the *other* from my reaction so that I may face the challenge that has arisen and claim the gift of Power that awaited my attention. There is, however, an important point that would be folly to ignore once I have claimed that Power.

As human beings our internal reaction to the world beyond our body is denoted by a shift in our internal energy state, by a shift in our emotions. Once I have owned and transformed my relationship to this energy I may or may not continue to have an issue with the situation that stimulated my reaction. For example, let us say that someone I know behaved in a particular way to which I reacted with a feeling of anger. The energy manifesting as anger is my own—this much has thus far been made clear. Yet what about the original issue I had with this person's behaviour?

I often find that once I face my inner challenge, reclaim my Power, and come to a place of clarity and Presence on a situation, the issue disappears on its own accord—it's simply no longer an issue for me. While I believe a situation to be a problem, I am making the situation into a problem through what I internally bring to it. Sometimes, however, there continues to be an issue, a basic pragmatic reality that is in discordance in some way, and this is what we'll look at now.

Taking an example from my own life, I found I had an issue with the incredible talent my partner had for leaving her things around our living space. In my experience she was constantly leaving things unfinished, not cleaning up after herself, and just generally leaving what I considered to be a trail of chaos and clutter behind her in just about every room of our house from bathroom to bedroom. After a while I noticed this was really starting to piss me off. I would feel so frustrated and annoyed each time I walked into a room and her things were spread around on the floor. Rather than blaming her for how I was feeling, I owned those feelings and worked with them in a way similar to what I've described in this chapter and elsewhere in this book. Knowing that *this is happening for me and not to me and is ultimately created through me*, I gave my attention not to my partner but rather to shedding light on what this challenge was presenting me with.

I discovered all sorts of things that I then healed and brought into a place of balance within myself. In this particular situation I discovered old emotions I was carrying from the way I had reacted to and taken on board my mother's predilection for tidiness (she was a Virgo who liked things very tidy)[2]. After clearing the story I was carrying from

---

2 The issue went deeper than this. My mother was not the *cause* of my feeling this way. Some*thing* within myself was the cause of both my mother playing the role she played in my world in this regard, and now my partner playing the role she was so good at—that of triggering awareness of this causative force within me, a force that no longer serves my purpose in this world.

that experience, I found that her talent for making what I considered to be a mess no longer brought up energy for me. (Well, sometimes it does, but only rarely and minimally, at which times I explore the challenge further and gain even more insight into my own healing). There was, however, still a basic pragmatic issue I wanted to discuss with her. You see, owning and honouring that there is only One, that we are all that One, does not mean that the individual aspects (or units of awareness) within that one cease communicating with each other. Just like cells in a body that constitute an organism, it is vital that the cells remain in communication (communion) and share that which is ultimately life-giving to the wellbeing of the whole organism.

In this instance I was aware that my partner was also frustrated by the behaviour patterns that resulted in her leaving things unfinished and untidy. She was forever losing things, misplacing things, and feeling overwhelmed by the amount of tidying up she felt she had to do to stay *on top of things* (on top of her mess). I happened to know this through living with her and talking to her over the course of our relationship. Of course, we don't always know what is going on for the other people in our world—the people whom we feel challenged by—and it is not necessary to as far as what we're exploring here is concerned.

So I still had an issue with an aspect of how my friend was behaving. Once I had dealt with my energy surrounding this issue, the issue remained. So I talked with my friend about this issue. At first she was a little defensive, but because I was not sitting on energy around the topic at hand, I was able to remain peaceful, loving, and present to her and to her own story about this matter. Had I come to her with a whole lot of unresolved energy, it is quite likely her defensiveness would have triggered a reaction in me and we'd end up battling over each other's energy. I am sure you know as well as I do that this sort of interaction only results in pain and conflict.

So I explained to my friend that I didn't enjoy living in a house with her things all over the place, that for me it was not conducive to the level of clarity and energetic flow that most accurately represents who I am. I explained that I really enjoy clear spaces, that I honour the chaos that is a necessary part of creativity and living creatively, and that I also honour and enjoy completion and order emerging from the chaos. She understood what I was on about and also re-cognised that for as long as she could remember people had been on to her about "her untidiness" and that she too felt frustrated by it. I was able to remain present with her and play what part I could in helping her gain a clearer understanding of her own inner and outer situation.

By communicating without energy about what was a genuine issue for me, I was able to quite naturally play a part in reflecting to this friend what was for her an ongoing challenge with her own power. For many years she had felt disempowered by the unconscious beliefs and stories that resulted in her untidiness, and yet in the past people had typically reflected their reaction to this only in a way that was condemning and filled with the energy they didn't wish to own within themselves. Conflict would typically arise, which was reflective of both her conflict (with this particular behaviour pattern and some aspect of her self-image) and reflective of the conflict the other people had within themselves. We've all been along that path, and I am sure you know as well as I do that it's not a Path of Freedom but rather one of pain and misery.

My challenge to you is to own and embrace the energy that is aroused by your challenges with people around you and then to honour the gift of sharing the issues you have with those people in a loving and constructive way, if you still discern there is a genuine issue there. This requires no thought; you'll simply know. Either there is something I can lovingly share that may be of benefit to this person, or there is not. A simple question you can ask yourself is "What would love do now?" You can also ask yourself what your intention is in sharing this issue with this person. Do I want to change him? Am I trying to improve or fix him? Or am I simply and genuinely expressing from the heart what my experience of his behaviour is—from one unit of awareness to another? Another simple question I ask myself before choosing to communicate to another person about issues I might have with their behaviour is this: "Is this a path with heart?" Is my sharing this an act taken with heart, or with something else such as anger, self-righteousness, self-centeredness, a desire to change people, and so on? The heart, as mentioned, is an inclusive force within man.

The simple principle behind what we have just explored is this: Always deal with the energy before dealing with the issue.

Essentially this is a question of prioritisation. The most important battle for my power is the battle I face within my own being. Only after I have fought this battle successfully (i.e., in a way that produces a life-giving outcome) am I ready to share what has been revealed with an-other, so that they too might have the opportunity to face whatever challenge is presenting itself to them, within.

In this way life is medicine through all my relations.

EMPOWERING PRINCIPLES & PERSPECTIVES

- Life as medicine is what you will discover as you embrace and embody the principle that everything is happening for you and not to you.

- Medicine is that which serves as an agent for healing.

- There are no victims. The sooner we step out of pretending we are a victim to life the sooner we will step back into our Power.

- When one steps back from identifying with his or her reaction to life and feels what has come up within the Body-mind, healing is not only likely, it is inevitable.

- There is a difference between the issues you face in the world around you and the energy that comes up in reaction to those issues.

- That energy is yours, and within it is a doorway to more Power. Neither suppress it or express it out of habit. Rather remain aware and feel what is there. You will know what to do next.

- In dealing with issues always deal with your own energy first. Then, if the issue remains, deal with the issue as an act of intelligent cooperation with whatever or whomever you have the issue.

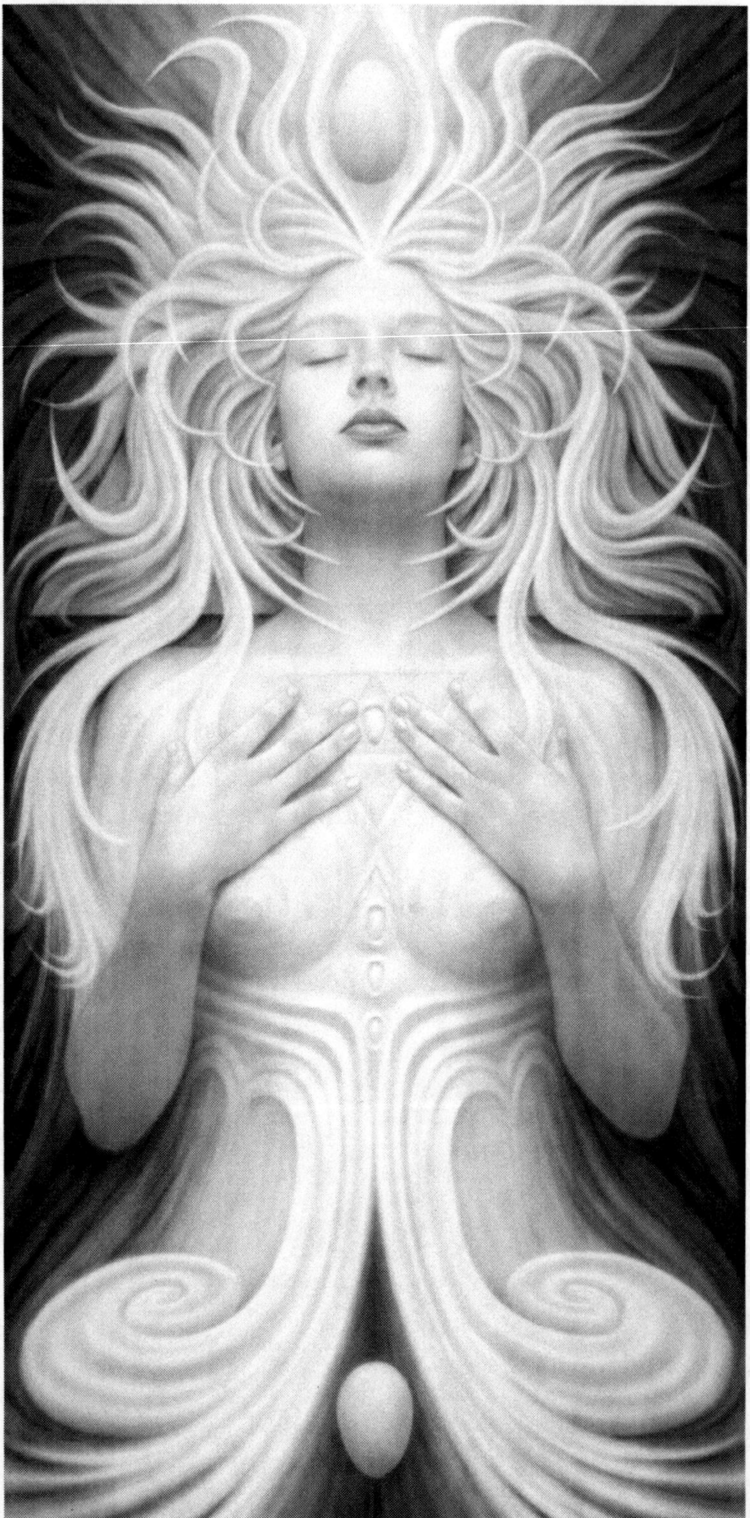

Chapter Fourteen

HEALING YOUR BELIEFS AND PERCEPTION

"You are not a human being in search of a spiritual experience. You are a spiritual being immersed in a human experience."
Pierre Teilhard de Chardin
20th century philosopher, mystic, and Jesuit priest

In my experience the cause of all suffering arises through identification with a small fragment of the Mind (the Self) that is engaged in the act of perception. Beliefs, and the concepts on which you base your beliefs, shape and mold your perception. Therefore healing—of any authentic kind—is about the healing of our beliefs and the breakdown of disempowering concepts and their associated perceptions. You will always perceive that which affirms and supports your beliefs. You will believe that which has been confirmed through your experience of what you perceive. Breaking out of this cyclic trap of belief and perception requires a radical leap within one's consciousness. As explored in Chapter Five, *personal Lore* is a term I use for referring to the sum total of a person's beliefs. Your personal Lore is the total sum of all your beliefs—your particular and personal take on reality, and thus it is akin to your personal truth.

"Belief is necessary only for that which is not real. That which is real can be recognised, and it works reliably and flawlessly."
A timeless Huna principle (quoted from Lono Ho'ala)

Invariably when people live according to the beliefs and rules that make up their personal Lore, their life-stream will become fragmented and some, if not most, of their energy will become dispersed and dissipated instead of becoming focused clearly throughout the Body-mind before it extends out into the world. Within Huna wisdom it is recognised this dissipated life force typically attracts or gives rise to malu within a person's life. From one perspective, malu are parasitic in nature—existing off the life force that we fail to manage and utilise effectively and in accordance with our Divine Nature. Yet from another perspective—a more complete and holistic one—malu are in fact personal allies and play an important part in awakening us to our purpose and how we manage or mismanage our Power. Understanding each of the following principles will help you in understanding the particular gifts of awareness various manifestations of malu are offering you if and when they arise.

✸ ✸ ✸

Victims and Blame

The ego-self of the average Man and Woman is commonly engaged in the illusion of victimisation (the "victimitis" discussed in Chapter Thirteen)—the false assertion that I am under attack from the world around me. Such a person typically finds himself at war with the world, with other people, and invariably with his own state of being. At a human collective level this manifests in the multiple and perennial state of war that has played out in the world from as far back as our history books allow us to recall through to the present day. I recall reading somewhere that for the past two thousand years there has been on average something like 100 wars taking place at any one time within the world. Whether I've remembered these numbers with complete accuracy or not, I think it is highly apparent this human world is a world at war with itself.

I wish to make it clear that you are completely invulnerable. You are a powerful, infinite, and eternal Being. In truth there is only One consciousness unfolding through all Life. Thus there is nothing "out there"—separate and apart from your true essence—that can do you

Healing Your Beliefs and Perception 269

harm. Nor is there anything "out there" that can inflict something upon you and your world that You have not agreed[1] to experience. Of everything I have imparted in this book, this one point is the one I feel will potentially bring up the most fear and rejection in those who read these pages. The ego is typically very afraid of discovering that "I Am" not a victim to anything in or of this world.

The other point to consider is that every time you blame someone or something else for what you have experienced, you are relinquishing your power to that person or thing. Think about this for a moment.

Every time you blame anything or anyone for what you experience, you relinquish—you give away—your power to that thing—that person, that circumstance, that object. Someone who is living with a lucid awareness of his true nature—awake to the Dream and his own Authentic Power—will never accept responsibility for power that another person tries to hand over to him, so when you attempt to hand your power (through blame) to one living lucidly, you will in effect be handing your power over to the malu or entity associated with this aspect of your unconscious behaviour.

A key principle that has a deep impact on the Victim malu is this: with any given act, responsibility sits with the bearer of the consequence. As you feel into and ponder this principle and whether it resonates as true for you or not, keep in mind the inclusive nature of the heart in its approach to reality. I shall explore this principle, and many others, more deeply with readers in a subsequent book in this series.

✺   ✺   ✺

---

1 With my use of the word "agreed" I am not referring to the ordinary human act of *agreement* most people are familiar with, namely the act of consciously and independently (with the ego-self) agreeing upon something with someone else. The form of agreement I am referring to is much less personal than this. It is more akin to saying a particular seed agreed to give rise to a particular species and quality of tree. Yet it is the essential substance (in this case DNA) within this seed that will bring about the particular species of tree it will grow into. This essential substance—equivalent to an expression and manifestation of *intention*—is not separate and independent from the vast web of life in which it came to be. Thus it could be said the totality of Life as manifest through this seed *agreed* to give rise to a particular type of tree.

For You and Not To You

It is rather easy, and in fact "normal," within this world for people to maintain the idea that "things are happening to them." Much of life is experienced as some form of attack or abuse or hardship, et cetera, that happens *to* them. This ties in very closely with the victim mentality—and its associated emotionality—we have just explored above. Metaphysically speaking, that perception is an incorrect assessment of the events of life—a misperception created by our limited sense of ego-self. This perception is one that maintains the illusion of separation and upholds the belief in the victim mentality from which we all must one day break free if freedom is what we seek.

To give an example, if the average Man walks down the road to the shops and he gets hit by a car, his ego will attempt to create and maintain the idea that this event happened "*to me.*" Similarly, for the average Woman, if her husband runs off with another woman, her ego will maintain that this has happened *to me*—that I am somehow a victim to these events. It's likely she will also get into an internal quandary to do with trying to determine what is wrong with her and "why was I not good enough for him?" So long as I maintain the illusion that it has happened *to* me, I will maintain separation within my experience of that event and hence perpetuate pain and suffering within my world. I will prevent myself from ever really recognising and receiving the gift of Love and awakening that is constantly being handed to me in every moment and through every circumstance I experience.

What I know to be true—contrary to what the average ego believes to be true—is that every*thing* is in fact happening *for me*. What this means is that every*thing* is happening *for* you and nothing is happening *to* you. It is all—the totality of Life itself—unfolding in service to You (an expression of the totality of Life). It is all in service to one purpose—namely reflecting to you your true nature and how/why/where you have forgotten your divinity. This is not some form of punishment or retribution for forgetting your true nature, rather it is the natural order of Life in the evolution of Awareness.

I know this is something the collective and individualised ego will find rather hard to comprehend. I have seen how the average ego fights this idea to the very end—and that's just it, the end of rigidly holding onto the illusion of separation is when this fight will stop. This reality completely undermines the ego of the average person in its attempt to maintain a belief in a world of attack from which it must separate and defend itself. All that I perceive as an attack is in fact a challenge to transcend the illusions of separation and to evolve my awareness. All forms of attack, on whatever scale they might appear to be taking place, are inflicted by the ego upon itself.

In a world based on the perception that things are happening *"to me"* it is easy for the ego-self to maintain its innately aggressive (and/or passive-aggressive) stance toward the world. Even *"playing the victim role"* is an aggressive position, for it never plays out alone. It always involves a perceived *aggressor* and very often turns the tables upon the aggressor making him the victim. In a world where things are happening *"to me,"* it is easy for people to maintain the illusion that there is no all-pervading intelligence, that "God" does not exist or—and more importantly from the limited ego-self's point of view—the idea that God is a vengeful God and God is vengeful toward me because I have done something wrong or bad. This sort of madness is, in part, how we maintain the delusion that "I am guilty of sin or doing wrong, and that the undesirable things happening *to* me are retribution for my wrongdoings." That belief maintains the illusion that "I must therefore be separate from God (from the rest of Life and the Universe), for God is perfect and I am imperfect." This implies that God and I are separate from one another. This madness goes on and on and on. Sooner or later—or even right now if you like—this madness must come to an end.

I would like to suggest that as you go through your day facing the events unfolding in your life, you make a point of reminding yourself that "This is happening *for me,* not *to me.*" If something you perceive as adverse comes up in your world, then just as soon as possible during the course of reflecting on this event, remind yourself that "This has happened for me and not to me."

Ask yourself, "What am I showing myself through this event or circumstance?"

"How have I forgotten my Divinity in this situation?"

"In what way am I losing/negating/giving away/et cetera my power in this moment?"

I have found I can most efficiently answer that question by taking a look at the *"story"* I have told pertaining to that event or circumstance.

In fact, when I am honest in my review of that story, it invariably takes me to the very heart of why this event or circumstance occurred for me—specifically, my perception shifts and Power returns to where it can best serve me at this time. This sort of self-review is something you may like to try, or may already be familiar with. It can be carried out passively and actively. Passively it is something you would simply do moment to moment as challenges and internal struggles arise during the day. Actively it is something you would specifically set time aside for with the intention to recapitulate challenging past events from within your memory and the stories you told about them and/or still tell yourself now regarding those events. We'll explore this more elsewhere.

Before we move on, we'll take a look at another use of the principle that all is happening *for you* and not *to you*. What I would like to suggest is that you approach your own choices and the subsequent actions you engage in from the perspective that what you are doing is *for you* and not something you're doing *to you*. This is particularly applicable with regards to matters of self-discipline.

For instance, perhaps you have decided to exercise regularly because this is something you normally resist or forget about entirely, and you have decided it would be good for your state of wellbeing. When in a situation such as this, how often do you engage in your chosen exercise or activity with the feeling you are doing something *to you*? Making a transition to eating life-giving and health-promoting food may be another useful example. Picture the person who is resisting eating another big fat piece of cake with the feeling that they are imposing something onto themselves. At some deep level this action becomes a form of attack upon oneself, which is quite contrary to the intention behind making the resolution to eat healthfully in the first place.

A quick way to resolve this struggle is to do it *for you* and not *to you*. Exercise as an act of service for you. Eating healthily is an act of kindness *for you*, for your body, for your wellbeing, as opposed to some kind of self-punishment you do *to you*.

✷   ✷   ✷

STALKING YOUR POWER

I experience apparent energy loss, displacement, or dissipation only when I am not present to the Now, and not present to how I am managing my power. Peace, Power, and Presence are all experienced hand in hand—not one exists without the other. I realise the concept of "managing our power" may seem foreign to many, so let's take a look at what this means on the Path of Freedom as I embody and share it.

The energy that is apparently afforded to us in each moment comes through what I refer to as our life-stream. The primary function of our Body-mind is to qualify this energy in accordance with Universal intention (the Intent of Infinity, or the Will of God for those who relate to that cosmology) and literally birth it into the world—initially into our intrapersonal world, and extending from there into the world at large. In my experience much of this process of extending this energy into the world at large is dependent on the quality of my relationships with the other beings in my world and with myself in relation to those other beings. With *beings* I am referring not only to human beings, but those of the animal, plant, and even mineral kingdoms.

For people still identified with the dream and their experience of a limited sense of ego-self (of a limited separate "I") within the dream, this process of personal power dispersion takes place almost entirely unconsciously. We do, however, experience the effects of power loss, and most people, when they get real and honest with themselves, know exactly when they lose power, in relationship to whom, and what they were afraid of in that particular situation where power loss occurred.

At the most rudimentary level, stalking your power is about being attentive to, present to, and lucidly aware of when you are about to lose or relinquish power and the choices you would ordinarily make that bring that power dissipation to fruition. With this awareness, you are then in a position to make a different choice—one that does not result in power loss but rather results in the further fulfillment of intention.

At the early stages of this most basic level of stalking your power, you might start out with simply being aware of when you have already lost power—feeling the effects and taking internal note of exactly what preceded that moment of apparent[2] power loss. In this moment

---

2   I repeatedly say "apparent" because it is only at the level of appearance in the

of awareness you are able to look at what choices you made—if you are humble enough to admit that you in fact made choices that were life-taking in nature. Transcending all notions of right and wrong, as described in Chapter Nine (Being Beyond Duality), is a vital condition for such humility to safely arise. Another key is to carry out this act with feeling and intuition. It is this inner-tutor that knows all and reveals all, through feelings and inner knowing.

So you may start out noticing and acknowledging the aftereffects of power loss, re-cognising what has taken place, and becoming conscious of the choices you made. Just this simple act alone will start to redistribute some amount of your power to the Dreamer in the form of awareness. This awareness then allows an even clearer—perhaps subtle at first—vision of how you are managing your power and what choices you are making in that regard. Over time you will find that increasingly often you will premeditate acts of potential power loss and simply not go down that internal path.

BE-AWARE OF YOUR (DE)FENCES

Today I was contemplating something I read and began thinking about the act of being defensive[3]. It came to my attention that when I become defensive I am literally feeling de-fenced—like a fence has been pulled down, leaving whatever was behind the fence open and exposed. When people do not notice their defence occurring and don't check themselves on it—when they fail to stalk the power displacement that is taking place—they will act in such a way so as to establish a new fence or wall around that part of themselves that has just been exposed. This behaviour is what we commonly refer to as defensiveness. This is an important moment in which one can be aware; by being present to this fence coming down and going back up, movement and flow take place where previously there was only stagnation and stuck energy. This movement is much easier to pay attention to than the stagnation and stuck energy (which we typically become accustomed

---

dream that we experience what seems to be a manifestation of power *loss*. In reality the Dreamer—our essential Self—does not lose or gain power—rather power is placed and displaced into configurations that are more or less life-giving.

3   It should be pointed out that *defense* is spelt *defence* (literally de-fence) in UK English.

to, even numb to).

In my experience, I establish internal fences only around those aspects of myself that I judge in some way and go into denial around. When I am in denial of some aspect of myself, the energy that makes up that aspect of self is, at the apparent level, separated or fragmented out from my central identity (even if that central identity is the ego, as it is for many people). As already mentioned, it will then attract an appropriate malu, and I will over time become established in certain life-taking behaviour patterns in those areas of my inner and outer life that have any form of relationship with that which I am denying. The ego then establishes a sort of veil or fence around this aspect of self and tries to hide it not only from the outside world but also from the awareness of the Dreamer.

When someone reacts to or notices any of my life-taking behaviour patterns and points this out to me, I have, figuratively speaking, just been de-fenced. They have seen through my fence and engaged with that which was being fenced off. In a situation such as this we are each then faced with a choice. I can either attempt to reestablish this fence by going into a defensive behaviour pattern, or I can opt for transparency. Self-transparency plays an important role in our ability to experience what I describe elsewhere as Lucidity of Mind. Lucidity is something I explore in full detail in another book entitled *The Seven Empowerments*.

Simply put, we are all aiming for transparency, for this is what allows us to experience truly lucid states of Awareness whilst our attention is assembled and is here within the Dream. By lucid states of Awareness I am referring to a quality of Awareness that extends from the Dreamer into the dream identity (your apparent human self). There is, however, a balance that has to be maintained with regard to being transparent whilst maintaining healthy boundaries. These boundaries are not the fences you've just read about. Healthy boundaries are actually a natural extension of clear intention.

When we establish clear intention and remain in integrity with that intention—both inwardly and outwardly—it naturally follows that the periphery of our personal energy field forms a clear boundary. For example, when I am clear about the property my house is situated on as determined by the intention set forth in the district planning office, my property (akin to the extent of my personal energy field, or land in this example) will have clear boundaries.

I don't have to erect a fence or wall around my property to know where its legal boundaries are. Nor will I fail to notice when the neighbour's dog has stepped over my boundaries and taken a dump on my front lawn. If I should choose to erect a fence, this fence is only as effective as the legal validity of the boundary on which it has been established—put the fence just a few feet too far beyond the legal boundary line and the neighbours have every right to have it legally removed. It is not the fence therefore that defines my boundary but rather the intention that defines the extent of my property. The fence is simply a convenient and optional way of controlling what passes over that boundary.

Before we get too far off topic—yes, I've taken us on a bit of a divergence into the nature of healthy boundaries—let's now get back to the topic at hand, which is the nature of defensiveness, transparency, and healthy boundaries. To be transparent without healthy boundaries will result is a potentially lofty, ungrounded, and easily woundable personality. People in such a state tend to pick up on all sorts of distracting energies from their surroundings, and find it very hard to incarnate their Soul's intention into the world. Like a leaf blowing in the wind would be one way of putting it figuratively.

The fences many people establish around the aspects of self they are in judgment and denial of is an attempt to avoid attack. To judge some aspect of my own life-stream as wrong, for instance, is to imply that I am somehow victim to that aspect of my life-stream. To be victim to something is to imply attack is possible. Feeling that I am internally under attack (from my own deluded sense of self), I will try to establish fences or walls in order to defend myself. This war of attack and defense that is now constantly and subconsciously taking place within will without fail be projected out onto my experience of the world. The net result is that anything outwardly that has energetic relationship to or an association with that aspect of myself that is in denial will appear to be attacking me, and the ego will try to fend it away.

I've experienced situations where a person's denial has been activated and it's as if a solid and tangible, yet invisible, wall has been instantly erected all around him. This energetic wall can arise so quickly and so spontaneously because it is simply an explosive projection of the energy wall tightly bound up within the person around whatever it is he is denying and judging. Typically the person is aware that he is feeling the way he is, yet what so often happens is that his response to these feelings of denial are so engrained and habitual that he feels powerless to do anything about them.

I encourage you to stay alert to when you feel defensive. Have the humility to admit your apparent weaknesses whilst keeping the dignity to remain open to your Divinity—the perfection of your own Presence. It's important not to let the Reality of your Divinity prevent you from facing up to those areas of your being and life where you've forgotten this perfection. On the other side of the coin, it's vital not to get caught up in and identified with your apparent wounds, shadows, or issues (call them what you will) to the exclusion of your Divinity.

Being attentive to your defences is an act of Stalking your Power as outlined earlier in this chapter. When we engage in this form of self-inquiry lovingly (softly) and yet vigilantly, a great deal of power reclamation is possible and is in fact unavoidable. Through the shifts in awareness that are bound to ensue, deep beliefs about oneself and the world are seen for what they are and then released in a healthy and life-giving way. This is bound to result in a life-giving shift in your perception, which in turn results in a redistribution of Power that is more in alignment with the truth of who we are here and now, as opposed to sometime in the past.

SELFISHNESS AND SELF-CENTEREDNESS

I wish to discuss a myth my culture has bought into with regard to selfishness. We shall explore the true meaning of selfishness and how it is the only realistic way to "save the world" per se—not that the world needs saving, but I am sure you know what I mean. Let us now address two common misconceptions:
1. That selfishness is something morally wrong, which people with a conscience must avoid;
2. That living in a way that benefits the world and improves the global condition is contrary to being selfish—that self**less**ness is what is required to benefit the world and make positive change for humanity.

I observe these misconceptions getting in the way of people who would otherwise be benefiting the planet and more fully playing their part in the evolution of awareness. I observe these misconceptions getting well-intending people tied up in moralistic knots that are entirely unnecessary and avoidable.

Looking around nature I notice that all life is essentially selfish. This statement may come as a surprise to many readers, but I think it will all be clear in a moment. The word selfish literally means "toward the self." The evolution of Awareness within and through the human experience is one of increasing awareness of the nature of the self—moving from no sense of self at all, to a very limited sense of an individuated and separate personal human self, through to a much vaster sense of the one cosmic Self. As an increasing amount of Life is incorporated from the *unknown* into the known through humanity, our understanding and appreciation of the self expands. It is a journey of going from a relatively limited perception of the self to the ultimate perception and experience of the self.

Some spiritual traditions talk about transcending the self. Some postulate that there is no self. What I experience is that there is no self independent from anything else and that ultimately there is only one vast Self ineffable to the human mind in its current evolutionary state. Evolving spiritually through the human experience is not about negating the self but rather is about expanding our perception of what constitutes the self in order to incorporate an increasing diversity of the many manifestations of Life.

Some people think the self is their body, history, personality, thoughts, and emotions. Their sense of self is limited to the entity they see in the mirror and the *things* that they experience within the body they see there—what I have previously described as the ego-self. When a person believes *this is who I am*, there is no self to move toward, for we assume we are already there and being truly selfish actually becomes impossible. What results is not selfishness but rather is self-centeredness.

THE WORD "SELFISH"

Within the contemporary "Western" world mind-set the perception that being selfish is "bad" or "wrong" is highly prevalent. *Selfish* is a relatively new word in the English vocabulary. In my experience it is attributed with primarily negative connotations. What are the origins of this word?

1640, from self (q.v.). Said in Hacket's life of Archbishop Williams (1693) to have been coined by Presbyterians. In the 17c., synonyms included self-seeking (1628), self-ended and self-ful.

Let's also take a look at the definition of "self" and "-ish," as found in various dictionaries:

-ish
Suffix
1. Of, relating to, or being: *Swedish*.
2. Characteristic of: *girlish*.
3. Having the usually undesirable qualities of: *childish*.
4. Approximately; somewhat: *greenish*.
5. Tending toward; preoccupied with: *selfish*.

Self
1. The total, essential, or particular being of a person; the individual.
2. One's consciousness of one's own being or identity; the ego.

Source: The American Heritage® Stedman's Medical Dictionary

Self \Self\, *n.; pl.* **Selves**.
1. The individual as the object of his own reflective consciousness; the man viewed by his own cognition as the subject of all his mental phenomena, the agent in his own activities, the subject of his own feelings, and the possessor of capacities and character; a person as a distinct individual; a being regarded as having personality.
"Those who liked their real selves."—Addison. [1913 Webster]
"The self, the I, is recognised in every act of intelligence as the subject to which that act belongs. It is I that perceive, I that imagine, I that remember, I that attend, I that compare, I that feel, I that will, I that am conscious."—Sir W. Hamilton.

Based purely on the above definitions, and my own particular predilection for defining this word in the way that I do, the meaning of the word selfish is:

"To act in a way that tends (or moves) toward and is characteristic of the total and essential being of the individual."

As I see it, to be selfish means to live in such a way as to put the wellbeing of one's Self first. I don't actually think it is possible to be any other way than selfish, and that to try and live in a way that is selfless is folly and inauthentic. I've observed that those people who do try to avoid being selfish in the way I have defined it end up creating an imbalance in their life. This results in a loss of Power and self-rejection. There is always a self operating, even if it is in the guise of someone who is being selfless. If I am totally real and authentic with myself and my relations, how can I not act in a way that is characteristic of the total and essential being that I am (conscious of) in that moment?

I suspect that anyone who intelligently considers this proposition will have to agree—living beings are by their very nature selfish. Most living things that I am aware of live in such a way that is characteristic of their essential nature and they put their own wellbeing ahead of all else, and it is this very mechanism (if we can call it that) that maintains the integrity of the self and the species from which that "self" is derived from and is an evolving part of. In nature this does not imply that the wellbeing of one self is sought after to the detriment of the wellbeing of another self. Only humans, as far as I know, seem to behave in this way. What differs between humans and most other animals is that a human is self-conscious and this consciousness has free will[4].

I can hear some readers asking, "What about those heroic people who on the spur of the moment put their own self-interest and wellbeing aside for the sake of other people, perhaps even losing their own life in the process?" I can't claim to know what is true for each and every person making such a choice. What I can say is this: Under certain circumstances, usually of an adverse or extraordinarily challenging nature, a person's perception may shift to a similarly extra-ordinary degree. This shift in perception affords them a relatively massive

---

4 In the grander scheme of Life I don't think humans have free will quite in the way most people presume or imagine, yet I will leave this statement as it is, for the exploration of the nature of free will could occupy a book of its own.

increase in power. This increase in power empowers the heart—of some people—to eclipse their rational and separatist mind, meaning that their sense of self instantaneously shifts from one of separation to one of complete inclusivity toward the other as self. In that moment they perceive Life as it really is. In that moment they will act as though they are not putting their own self at risk for the sake of another self— because they aren't. Rather they act from the level of power that knows "There is only one Self present here, and this act is the act I, as that one self, must take right now." It is still a selfish act—an act that moves a person toward a deeper and more profound perception of the self. We say these people have acted selflessly. Selfless is to be free of the self. What I am suggesting is that this person has become free of their limited and separatist sense of self.

Then there are those people who not just in the spur of the moment act in what seems to be so selflessly, but who dedicate much of their lives to helping other people at what appears to be the expense of their own pleasure and wellbeing. I am sure Mother Teresa is one widely known example of such a person. Again, I would say these extraordinary and rare human beings have developed or surrendered into such a deeply profound sense of the true nature of the Self—the one "I" that is in all beings—that for them this is the only way they can be and live if they remain true and authentic to who and what they are—to who and what they now know themselves to be.

A Deeper Look

Here in the Dream—here in this world—it is the self (small "s") that we manifest as and operate through. It is that same limited sense of self we must transcend/transform in our awareness if we wish to awaken to a more complete and accurate sense of Self (big "S"—the Higher Self, the Spirit Self, the Christ Self, the I AM Presence, or whatever you refer to as the Dreamer). Our human self is an extension of the vaster essential Self. That Self is an extension of what some call "God," "The Supreme Source," "Infinity," "the Tao," or any number of other names. Beyond all the layers and dimensions of dreaming there is only one Awareness evolving or expanding. There is only one Dreamer. There is also only one Self, but with many interconnected, interrelated, and interdependent facets and expressions that we come to know as *your*

Spirit and *my Spirit*. We are each a unit of Awareness, just as a drop of water taken from the ocean and placed in the palm of your hand is still a unit of the whole ocean. It is only our perception that identifies it as a thing (a drop) that is no longer "ocean."

The connotations that most people in our culture project onto the word *selfish* are something I think are more accurately referred to with the word *self-centered* or *ego-centered*. To be self-centered and selfish are completely different affairs—and I accept this may be seen as a matter of linguistic interpretation, yet at least in making a clear definition of these terms we'll each know what I am referring to. Self-centeredness is the narcissistic belief that the world—and more particularly the people in the world—must revolve around me as a separate individual and my limited—often-times distorted, wounded, and dysfunctional—sense of self. It is a form of gross self-importance that never really embraces and comes to understand the true nature of Self, for the self-centered person is forever focused on the world beyond self as something separate and out there, seeking from it approval, respect, power, love, and all manner of other things that the ego believes it does not have and must obtain in order to survive. The self-centered person also focuses his or her attention on the world around the self in such a way so as to project onto that world anything and everything it does not accept and like within the self.

The self-centered person looks after the interests and perceived needs of her limited separate self as number one at the expense of the apparent *other* in the world, which is perceived as a separate "thing" out there. The selfish person, however, looks after the interests of self to the benefit of the world, which is recognised as being an extension of the collective and personal self—meaning that self and world are wholly interconnected and related, therefore what truly benefits the self will benefit the world. Because the selfish person is always moving toward the self, this sets him up to dive forever deeper into the true nature of self, for each step he takes opens him to the discovery that he is not there yet. The self-centered person, on the other hand, believes he already knows what the self is and what it constitutes and thus he becomes closed to the *unknown* regarding himself and Creation at large. It is his limited, rigid sense of self that he expects life to revolve around and pamper, and not to confront, challenge, and contradict. The self-centered person is innately a miserable person with a contracted heart and closed mind. He who is selfishly moving toward the self—delving into the vast mystery of the infinite *unknown* discoverable only through knowing thy self—is open and willing to embrace the *unknown* and the ways in which the *unknown* challenges his perception of who he is.

KNOW THY SELF

If selfishness is, as I suggest, the only integral way we can truly conduct our life in this world in a way that is impeccable and in co-operation with the intent of our Dreamer, the well-known aphorism *"know thy self"* becomes ever more important in the life of any human Being intending to wake up in the Dream and step into a place of self-empowerment and universal service. As mentioned already, to be selfish is to live in accordance with looking after the highest interests of the self, which are an extension of the highest interests of the Self, which are an extension of the interests and Intention of Infinity. People living within the limits of consensus reality, however, have a very poor notion of what is in the best interests of their *self*. Their limited ego distorts their awareness of self into something that is wholly untrue—not only inaccurate but in complete opposition to that which is true.

Let's look at a really simple example of what I mean. Drinking carbonated soft-drinks (or lolly water as my father called it when I was a child) is not in the best interests of the human *self*, yet hundreds of billions of liters of the stuff are consumed globally every year. According to a report by *Zenith International* in late 2003, total sales were predicted to reach 467 billion liters that year, equivalent to 75 litres per person on planet Earth. Soft-drinks are essentially sweet toxic poison. Only a self-centered person who has not taken the time or made the effort to find out (intuitively or intellectually) what effect soft-drink consumption has on *self* would drink the stuff. Similarly, taking recreational drugs is in 99% of cases not in the best interests of the *self* either, yet the global monetary value of the illegal drug trade is up there in the top five industries in the world (along with the weapons trade, energy trading, and pharmaceutical drugs). Again it doesn't take much effort to figure out that drug abuse, alcohol, cigarettes, and the like are not particular life-giving for *self*, yet humanity consumes vast amounts of these things every day. I could make a similar example regarding the vast majority of products found in the supermarkets where most people in the "western world" buy their so-called food only to later wonder why the self is getting sick and physically diseased. I am sure you by now get my point.

So what's going on?

The issue here is that our limited ego—our limited sense of "I"—is self-centered and as a result is self-destructive. Creative energy turned in on itself becomes the equivalent of a destructive (dis-creative) force. Our essential Self is inherently creative, yet that creative impulse is only realised and made manifest when it expands outward from self into the world in some life-giving form. A selfish person is in touch with this creative flow and with what is in the best interest of the self to let the flow unfold unhindered. A self-centered person works against that flow and in opposition to what is in the best interests for self— perhaps primarily because it approaches the world with an attitude of "what can I get from the world," as opposed to "what do I bring and express into the world?"

The more a person comes to know him or her self, the better he or she can express that self in a life-giving way. Our self-interests shift in accordance with the vibration or frequency at which our consciousness is resonating. The more our self interests are met, the higher that frequency goes. The higher it goes, the more refined and subtle our self interests become. An example of this in my life is that after doing a lot of yoga and meditation as a teenager—a practice I took up in service to the deep sense of self I felt within. By the time I was about 18 or so I found I (selfishly) no longer felt to eat meat, or drink alcohol, be in smoky bars, eat a lot of pasteurised dairy products, consistently eat chemically produced food, use synthetic skin and body care products, wear synthetic fabrics, or smoke marijuana—to name but a few of the changes that spontaneously occurred in many of my behaviours during that time. Doing the yoga and meditation was a selfish act that got me more in touch with my-self. The net result was that things I previously assumed were in my self interest were suddenly not in my self interest any more—and I let them drop from my life. I didn't fight and reject them as wrong, bad, or evil—which would be a self-centered approach—but simply let them fall away. My perception of the self expanded and thus incorporated more of who and what I am—incorporating more of the *unknown* and relinquishing that which was redundant within the *known*.

SELFISHLY SAVING THE WORLD

What prompted me to write this segment on selfishness was a discussion I had with a friend. What we were discussing was the state of the world and how massively out of balance things appear to be in the environment, global politics and war, the food industry, the medical industry, the agricultural industry, et cetera. The point my friend made was that it's important we ensure our day-to-day choices take the global situation into consideration. Choices such as where we shop, the foods and products we buy, and the like. As an example, we talked about how for her she doesn't like shopping in large supermarkets because by doing so she feels she is supporting the globalisation of our food supply. Also, she prefers to buy organically produced products (and Fair Trade products when possible) because not doing so again supports industries and ways of doing business that she doesn't agree with.

I consider myself to be someone who knows a fair bit about what is happening in the world beyond the small fraction of info published in mainstream media, as it is something I have taken an interest in since childhood. In my youth I had a disdain for watching the so-called News (I typically felt I was being deceived and manipulated), yet I've also had a big appetite for researching and understanding what is happening in the human scheme of things. With that as my background in this regard, I found it quite overwhelming to consider the idea of rationalising my every decision based on whether it supports global imbalance or not—because I am aware that this imbalance and greed-based madness is pandemic in almost all human affairs. I felt that if I went down that path I would either shut down completely, or go out into the world with a lot of aggression and start protesting and fighting the way things are (as if I was somehow a victim to it all). In my world neither of these feels like a life-giving way to live. Whilst feeling all this during my conversation with this friend, I was also aware that most of the time the decisions I am making with regard to what I buy, eat, and support in my world are in fact in alignment with what is life-giving for the world (or as far as they can be in the civic situation in which I choose to live).

So, I didn't feel that I could deal with rationalising my choices with consideration for how they impact on the world because in my experience there are too many convoluted, hidden, and conflicting factors to consider. Yet my choices are generally the ones I might come to were I doing that. I sat with this for a while and felt into what was playing out here. Then it became clear.

By being present to doing my best with recognising what is in the best interests for my self (my body, mind, and spirit) and then living selfishly (in the best interest of and *moving toward the Self*), my actions are by nature life-giving to the whole. What is healthy and life-giving for a single cell in my body must by its very nature be healthy and life-giving to the world at large. This body is, after all, a small part of the Earth that is totally interconnected with the many other parts of the Earth. It is, in fact, only our rational mind that even considers these things as "parts" rather than simply seeing it as one intelligent whole. I choose to eat predominantly high vitality, living, raw, organically grown food because in my experience the cells in my body thrive the most on this sort of sustenance. An extended effect of this choice is that it positively impacts the world in which I live. When possible, I choose to by my food at local markets or small organic shops—buying only a small amount from the supermarket. I do this because I prefer the feeling of being at a lively market and exchanging my time, energy, smiles, and money with the same people who have grown the food and produced the other products I buy there. I do this for selfish reasons—I feel good, I like it, and it adds a degree of social richness and pleasure to my life I would otherwise miss out on. This is also selfish in the sense that by connecting with these people I tend toward connecting with myself. The extended impact of this is that it not only benefits me, it also benefits the world I live in.

One could argue that making these same choices because they will benefit the planet will get the same result, and I will still benefit personally anyway. What I would like to suggest is that this approach is likely to lead to self-conflict and an underlying imbalance simply because it would be an unfathomable impractical task to try and truly know exactly what impact each personal choice is having in the world. Furthermore, trying to bring that vast array of information into every choice I make would be a huge waste of energy and again be incredibly impractical. The Path of Freedom is first and foremost practical and simple to apply. It is far simpler and more practical to know thyself and make the choices that are in alignment with that knowledge.

EMPOWERING PRINCIPLES & PERSPECTIVES

- The cause of all suffering arises through identification with a small fragment of the Mind engaged in the act of perception.

- Beliefs, and the concepts on which you base your beliefs, shape and mold your perception.

- Healing—of any authentic kind—is about the healing of your beliefs and the breakdown of disempowering concepts and their associated perceptions.

- Remember, you are completely invulnerable.

- There are no victims. There is nothing and no one to blame. Blame merely dissipates your Power.

- Most of our energy loss takes place entirely at an unconscious level.

- One Aspect of stalking your Power is about stalking the content of your own unconsciousness.

- When we feel defensive, a false belief within the unconscious has been exposed. The fence is coming down.

- To be selfish means to move toward the self. It's unavoidable and inevitable. The challenge lies in redefining that which constitutes your self.

- To be self-centerd is destructive and unnecessary. It results from our limited sense of self wanting the world to revolve around its particular point of view.

- You will "save the world" when you wake up to your true self and move toward it. This is selfishly saving the world.

- Saving the world in a self-centered way is when one tries to project onto the world one's own particular perspective. This creates conflict, not resolution.

- When you choose what is truly right for your own essential self you will be choosing what is right for the world.

Part Three

The Rebirth Of Now

rebirth, *noun*
1. A fundamental change in one's beliefs: conversion, metanoia, regeneration
2. The act of reviving or condition of being revived

now, *noun*
The present time or moment; the present

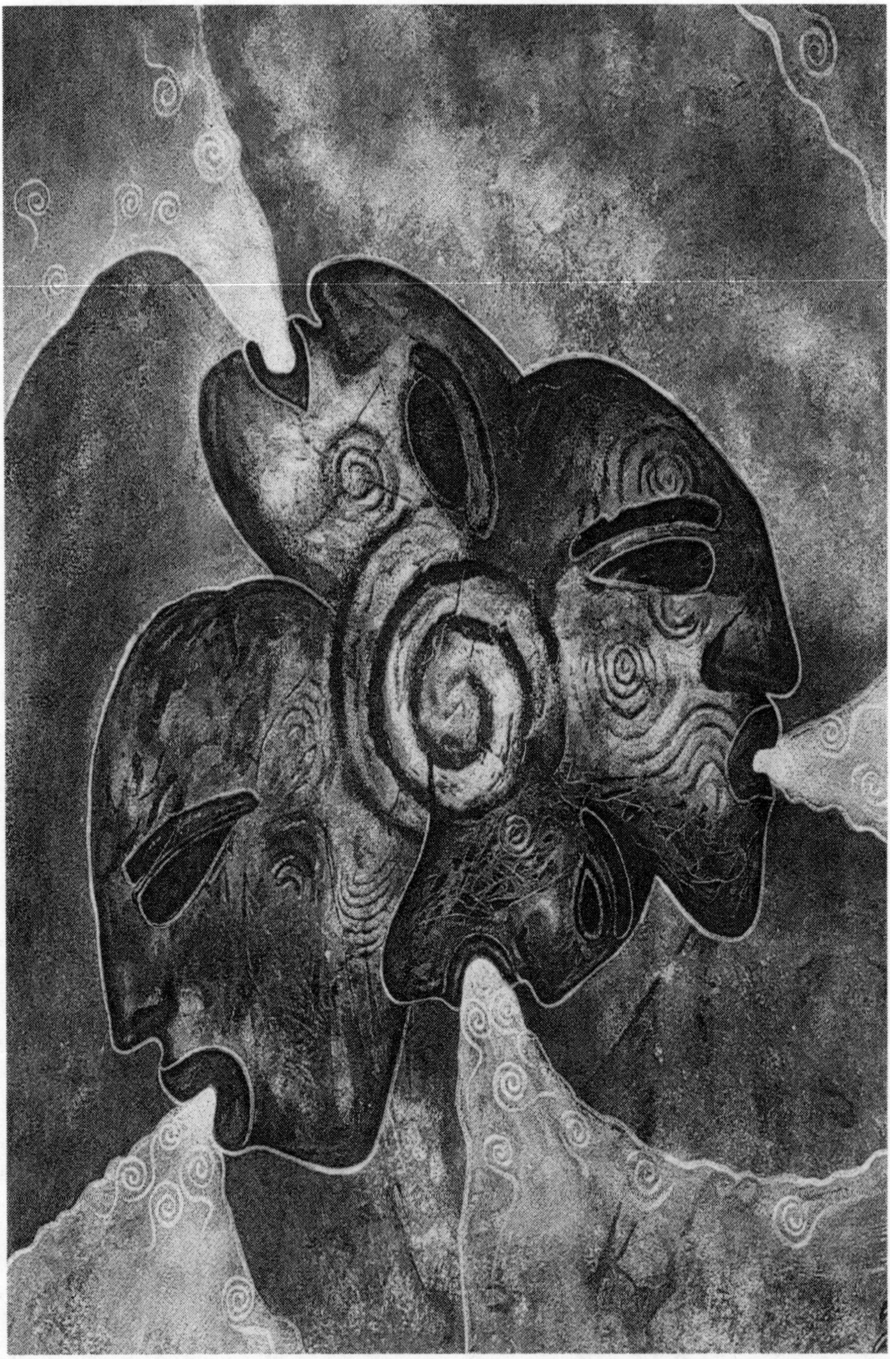

Chapter Fifteen

PEACE, POWER, AND PRESENCE

"A warrior chooses a path with heart, any path with heart, and follows it; and then he rejoices and laughs. He knows because he sees that his life will be over altogether too soon. He sees that nothing is more important than anything else."

Carlos Castaneda
A Separate Reality

Inner Peace is our natural state of Being. Actually it is our only state of Being. It can seem difficult, however, to feel this when we are too caught up in and identified with what we are doing, thinking, and Dreaming.

I'm sure you're as aware as I am that Inner Peace is something that most of humanity has forgotten how to realise and embody here within the Dream. This is neither "good" nor "bad." It simply is as it is—a natural consequence of humanity's present state of self-realisation. All experience has its purpose, and once I am truly complete with an experience, I can choose another one. Yes, if you or I don't enjoy an experience, we have the option to make a new choice—one that will result in a new outcome and a different experience. This does not imply we can always under any circumstances choose to immediately change our exterior situation, and yet always and at the very least, we can change how we approach a situation. This results in a new experience. You can choose Peace, instead of War, within yourself. You can go with the quiet voice of the Soul, instead of the loud bantering of an ego-mind that has not yet evolved beyond the illusion of separation.

For many of us, making this choice for Inner Peace may not seem easy at first. It may even appear impossible (or close to it), for the ego-mind with which the average person is presently identified knows nothing of Peace. The ego-mind, left to its own devices and believing itself independent from Spirit—is the antithesis of Peace. If there were a so-called "anti-Christ," it would have to be our limited ego. Every war ever waged in this world—be that the war between husband and wife, between siblings, between religions, between races, between friends, or between nations—has been the consequence of human beings identified with their limited ego-mind, with their misidentification of Self.

The other side of the coin here is that the Ego, as the Cosmic "I"—the "I" of Infinity—, *is* the Christ consciousness within us. The two go hand in hand—Christ and anti-Christ—and this is why it is so futile in ones approach to spirituality to negate the human ego as something bad or nonexistent. In doing so we also negate the realisation of Christ Consciousness within us. Even great modern-day spiritual texts such as *A Course in Miracles* (which in all other regards I support) fail, in my opinion, to approach the deeper nature of the Ego or the "I" in a holistic way. Negating the presently limited experience of the ego-self within ordinary man sets the up the potential for a fractured experience of self in those who don't know any better.

Walking the Path of Inner Peace is something we each must learn if we wish to be free from suffering. I share within this book and also explore in other books in this series—such as *The Seven Empowerments*—some of the simple and practical ways in which you will be able to unravel the illusions maintained by the ego-mind and start to unveil the Truth that is within you. These are the things that have worked for me during the course of my time here on Earth. These too are the things that have worked for many of our ancient ancestors. The key "secret"—secret only in light of the fact that it is so often and easily overlooked—is that You are the path of Peace, Power, and Presence.

This "path" is all about mastering your magnificence. You are a magnificent being of the universe, a great mystery, and it is your responsibility to master yourself, not for your own benefit but for the benefit of all your relations.

I'll say "yes" to that now! Will you..?

You Are the Path of Peace, Power and Presence

You are the path of your own Enlightenment. You are your own salvation—with the unwavering support of Infinity to carry you there. Let me reiterate this point, "You are the path of Inner Peace, Authentic Power, and all-pervading Presence." "Of" and not "to," for there is in Reality no going toward anything. In Reality our task is simply to Be Here Now as we truly are and to allow that to unfold and blossom as it simply and naturally intends to.

No religion, no teacher, no guru, no spiritual practice, no book, no drug or plant medicine, no external experience or form can be that path for you. There are no substitutes for the profound and delicious reality of our own Divinity. Thank God for that. The human being is a vast mystery we have barely begun to unravel.

All or any of these apparitions mentioned above (religions, teachers, gurus, and so forth) may arise in your Dream to remind you of the path within. More commonly, however, they arise through the misgivings of identification with the ego-mind and will only further trap you in illusions if you attach and project too much value to them. I am always cautious toward any path or teaching that does not completely return the aspirant back to herself. For as the historic figure Jesus is reported to have said, "I Am the way, the Truth, and the Light. No one shall pass to God except by me." Many have misunderstood this statement. The I Am that Jesus was referring to is the I Am within each and every human being—this I Am is the Presence within each of us. The accurate interpretation of this profound statement is that the "I Am within me, within you, and within every human being, is the way, the Truth, and the Light." Not one of us shall pass back into the full realisation of God except through the I Am within ourselves.

The key is this: You don't have to look anywhere except within the interiority of your own Being. Actually there is no-where else you can truly look. The experience of apparently looking elsewhere (somewhere "out there") is an illusion that goes on within your own Mind, and will continue for ever, and ever, and ever—until you call the bluff of your own ego and look to your interiority for liberation.

What you see in the world is nothing more than a magnificent, miraculous, and highly symbolic projection or extension (depending on whether you look through the eyes of the ordinary ego or the Vision of the Soul) of That which resides in your interior—within You.

> Your interiority contains all. Your interiority is the source of all. Your interiority is all.

OUR TASK

As far as I can ascertain, the task we all face is to literally re-cognise our life for what it really is; to pay attention to the symbolic nature of our experience of life; to mindfully read into the symbolic story of our Soul as it is displayed on the "screen" of the human mind—namely my experience of life and this world; and, finally, to embody the Truth that is thereafter revealed.

The Truth that is You.
This is your task.
This is my task.
This is what we have undertaken by being here on Earth…
In creation… in the Dream of all Dreams
… and living that task is the path of Inner Peace.
The path of assuming your Authentic Power.
The path of Self reconciliation through total Presence to Here and Now.
The path of Freedom.
There is really no*thing* else to do.

Herein lies the secret to Power. When you are no longer looking for or needing something outside yourself—beyond your own experience of Self—in order to complete, fulfill, or perfect you, then all things are created from within. Our deepest Power is in our capacity to create and to be aware of "I" in relation to that creation. We project out when we have forgotten what we are or feel incomplete, and then we search around in our projection for clues and missing pieces. What we project out is reflective of our unconscious state of being, and therefore it is often life-taking in consequence. When a person no longer lives under the spell of self-imperfection, then she will always turn to her own innate inner wisdom for answers. No longer is anything needed or sought after in the apparently external world. Remember, as a Divine Being you have no needs, except one—and that is the need for a mirror.

To not *need* anything from the world is a Powerful position to be in. This also encompasses not needing the world to be any particular way, as in not needing to change anyone, but rather loving and accepting people as they are. In this position no one can take anything from you, say anything to you, or do anything to you that will result in your losing touch with Inner Peace. I don't mean to imply that you won't take an appropriate course of action if someone is hurling abuse at you or trying to steal your car. The difference is that you will feel immediately from within exactly what course of action is called for in that moment, and you will then take it. No Power will be lost, given away, or swindled. Nor will you try to bargain for power. Remember, to bargain is literally to bar gain. When we bar ourselves away from gaining we can only stand to lose.

"Only as a warrior can one withstand the path of knowledge. A warrior cannot complain or regret anything. His life is an endless challenge, and challenges cannot possibly be good or bad. Challenges are simply challenges."

Carlos Castaneda

PRESENCE

A path of Freedom is a path of Presence. To simply be present to that which is here, now. I have found that by remaining present to the magnificence and mystery of Life and the many challenges I face here in the form side of Life (this world), freedom is inevitable. I've looked into a wide array of spiritual paths, teachings, religions, and New Age beliefs and schools of thought, and I have found each has its own suggestions as to what one must do in order to become spiritually aware and conscious. Many of these suggested doings get rather elaborate, even complicated to the point of being ridiculous. Many of them come with enticing promises of paranormal, psychic, and spiritual abilities. Yet what is it that gets enticed by the notion of having these abilities? Only an ego identified with a limited experience of self.

This world is so magnificent. Life is so magnificent. I have only to pause and be present to what is around me and go into a felt sense of here and now to discover such beauty, such joy, such ecstasy that the notion of needing this or that—this ability or that ability or superpower, or this thing or that thing—is nothing but laughable.

To be present to the world as it is here and now is such a—a gift to the world and a gift to oneself. All that stands between the average person and the world is their rigid identification with the thoughts and emotions playing out in their mind and body. There is nothing wrong with these thoughts and emotions, but when I identify with them as "me" I lose touch with reality. If I lose touch with reality I am no longer present to what Is, I am instead caught up in what I am projection onto my experience of what Is.

STILLNESS

> Be still in the Presence, and know That I Am God.

Presence is felt and experienced in stillness.

Some people think this means "I must have a mind free of all thoughts in order to experience this stillness and thus to be Present." These people have misunderstood. The activity of the ego-mind—the rationalising, thinking mind—does not take away from our innate stillness. The common analogy of waves on the ocean being like thoughts in the mind is so true. The presence of waves on the surface of the ocean does not destroy the stillness deep within the ocean itself. A great storm can be blowing and huge waves might appear, yet not far below the surface the ocean's stillness remains forever present. You and I are like the ocean in this regard. It's a question of whether or not I give my attention to the thoughts or to the space in which the thoughts arise. In that still, silent space I Am Present.

Why most people get tossed around by the mental activity in their ego-mind is a matter of identification. So long as I am identified with my thoughts I will struggle to shift my attention to the space in which these thoughts arise and pass away. Many people are also under the misperception that I must think in order to live. I've had weeks at a time where hardly a single thought has entered my mind and yet I was able to carry out all my daily functions and all manner of complex tasks including using a computer, preparing delicious food, driving a car, and so on. It's not our thinking that enables us to function in this world. Rather it is the still presence below the activity of the thinking mind that performs our every task with the highest degree of perfection and efficiency.

What I've just said in regard to thoughts and mental activity can also be said about gross emotions. I've met people, mostly women, who seem to believe that if they stopped being so caught up in and identified with their emotions they would somehow cease to be alive. Just as I've met many people, often-times men, who believe that if they stopped being so caught up in and identified with their thoughts they would cease to be alive. I am not suggesting the denial of thought or the denial of emotion, but rather a new way of approaching these forces.

Both emotion and thought are but waves on the ocean's surface, and with this comes a very important analogy. Right now I am on an island off the coast of Africa. Most days I have been having my lunch by the ocean, with the waves lapping just meters away from my feet as I sit there on the hot rocks in the sun. When it's really hot I'd love to slip into the deep cool water to refresh myself from the heat of the day. I've noted (through observation and past experience) that climbing into or out of that water when there is even a slight activity of waves lapping onto the rocks would be very difficult, if not decidedly painful and dangerous. When it's really calm I can slip in and out quite easily.

This gives me two immediately apparent options if I want to enjoy the deep cool ocean. I can either climb in from the rocks when the waves are very calm, or I can walk around to the beach where even relatively huge waves can be dived under or jumped over relatively safely without smashing me on something hard like the rocks. These rocks are like rigid thought-forms and stuck emotions, the hard rigidity of a mind in which I place too much importance on my particular map of the known (my view of the world) and the beliefs that go with this, and a heart closed to love and to Life. These rocks are slow to change and dangerous be around when getting in or out of the ocean. The sandy beach is like that soft embracing quality I see within a mind and heart that is open, soft, and flexible—quick, ready, and willing to change in response to Life. The ocean, with its vast ineffable depth, is like my soul, or even Infinity itself.

The waves? These are the movement of my thoughts and emotions—the waves of my human sense of self rising up from the ocean at its surface—washing up upon the shores of the form side of Life where it meets the formlessness of Infinity. Ahh… so nice to step into the water, to pause, and to be aware.

Take the time each day to pause as often as you remember. Make it a point to feel the stillness in every situation.

Being Present to Now

Pause when you next get into your car. Pause when you next walk into a shop. Pause outside the shop you're about to enter. Pause and feel. Pause outside your house when you next approach it. Pause and feel into how this moment feels. Feel the house by simply directing your attention to the house (or the car, the shop, et cetera) and remaining aware within the Body-mind—within the framework of your body. What do you feel?

The next time you go to a restaurant, stop for a moment before you enter and feel into this establishment. How does it feel? How do you feel, within your body, in relation to this establishment? If you feel light, pleasant, joyful, happy, content, peaceful, and the like, then eat there. If you don't, go somewhere else that feels better. There is no thinking required to carry out this simple act. It's all about a subtle felt-sense within your Body-mind.

When you are with other people be present to how you feel in your Body-mind. Devote some of your attention to the situation, to the people, to the conversation, whilst simultaneously devoting an equal amount of your attention to the space within the framework of your body. Be aware of the feelings you experience there. You may find it helps to pay attention to your breathing, which will naturally take you into a subtle feeling space within the Body-mind. This will provide your Attentive-mind with something tangible to be present to inwardly whilst you are also being present to the tangible reality around you.

Just to be aware. That is all.

Empowering
Principles & Perspectives

- Most people have forgotten their innate state of Peace.

- You are the path of your own Enlightenment.

- No religion, no teacher, no guru, no spiritual practice, no book, no drug or plant medicine, no external experience or form can be that path for you.

- When you no longer look for or need anything outside yourself—beyond your own experience of Self—in order to complete, fulfil, or perfect you, then all such perfection is created from within.

- Your Presence is felt and experienced within stillness.

- To simply remain aware, that is the key.

- The Body-mind is always in the now. Even though it may appear to be carrying stories about the past, it is in fact holding those stories in relation to now.

- To get present with now one only has to feel and be aware within the Body-mind.

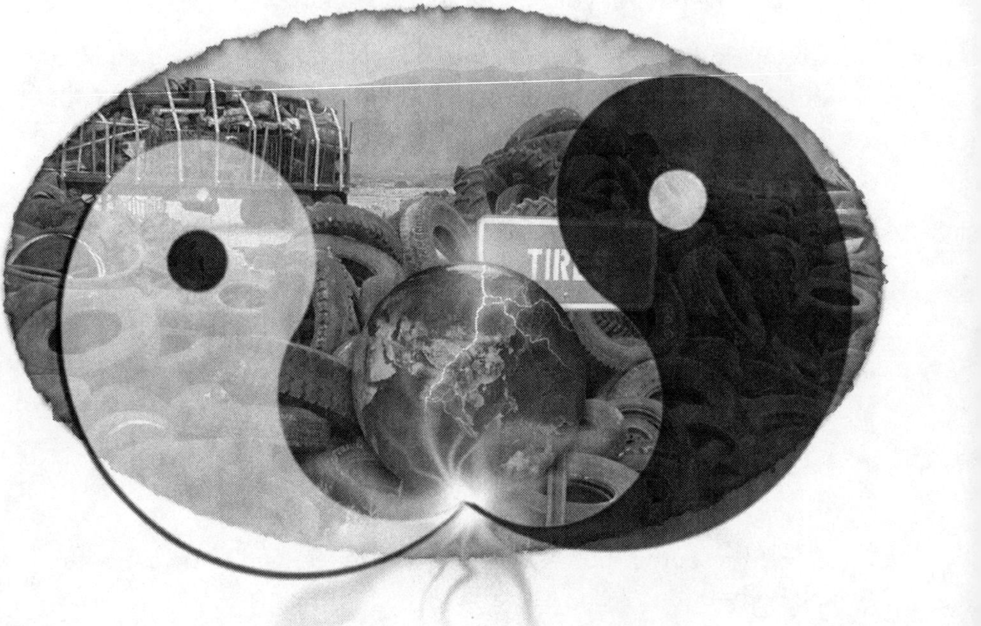
TIRE

Chapter Sixteen

KOYAANISQATSI – LIFE OUT OF BALANCE

"If we don't change the direction we are going, we are likely to end up where we are heading."
Ho Sik Pak

Koyaanisqatsi (ko'yaa nis'katsi) is a word from the Native American Hopi language. Koyaanisqatsi is the best word I can find as an appropriate name for this chapter. Translated into English it has the following definitions:

Koyannisqatsi, *noun.*
1. crazy life. 2. life in turmoil. 3. life disintegrating. 4. life out of balance. 5. ***a state of life that calls for another way of living.***

There is a beautiful movie by this name[1], one of a series of three movies that are visual and musical journeys into exploring aspects of the present-day human condition. There is a blurb from the producers of the movie that I think will eloquently set the scene for this chapter, which is as follows:

"*Koyaanisqatsi* [the movie, and this chapter] attempts to reveal the

---

1 Produced by Godfrey Reggio. Visit http://www.koyaanisqatsi.org on the Internet for further information on all three movies.

beauty of the beast. We usually perceive our world, our way of living, as beautiful because there is nothing else to perceive. If one lives in this world, the globalised world of high technology, all one can see is one layer of commodity piled upon another. In our world the "original" is the proliferation of the standardised. Copies are copies of copies. There seems to be no ability to see beyond, to see that we have encased ourselves in an artificial environment that has remarkably replaced the original, nature itself. We do not live with nature any longer; we live above it, off of it, as it were. Nature has become the resource to keep this artificial or new nature alive."

In my experience this Hopi word and the above quotation accurately sum up the present state of the world at the apparent level of reality. Everywhere I look I see the effects of imbalance—imbalance at the human level (socially, spiritually, economically, psychologically, et cetera) and imbalance at a planetary level—that result from our human activities. Having said that, I will also say that I am aware that at a metaphysical level there is an immense Perfection unfolding and working its way into manifestation here in the human realm. That which appears to be imbalance at the material and commonly recognised spiritual level is in fact one perspective on a creative flux that is playing on many levels and ultimately is in balance as a whole. Much like a tide coming in and out on the beach. When it is out we don't say that the ocean is now out of balance. Likewise, when it is high tide we don't perceive this to be an imbalance. The ocean is always in a flux that as a whole is balanced, yet simultaneously is moving (or changing tidal state) from one extreme to the other.

For practical reasons—for the purpose of evolution at the level humanity is presently at—I present this chapter from the perspective of imbalance being very real, and of our collective and individual response to that imbalance having very real and very significant consequences. As many people are primarily aware of only the physical dimension of this world, that is where many of us will have to focus our attention to restore balance[2], if that is what we wish to do. As more

---

2 In light of the fact that balance and its apparent absence are subjective, relative, and determined by one's perspective, and that in its overall totality Life is balanced, it might be more accurate to say that we are not so much being challenged to restore balance but rather to respond to the current flux of Life here on

people awaken to other levels and dimensions of their Self and reality, then attention can also be given to these deeper levels for the purpose of restoring balance.

The advent of imbalance within human culture is nothing new. As far as I can remember and determine, it may have always been like this, going on for most if not all of recorded human history[3], and I suggest that in one way or another it has been the primary cause of collapse for just about every human civilisation (if not all of them) that has existed on this planet. Some might argue that imbalance is an inherent part of evolution here on Earth, yet I disagree on two accounts: 1) Nature has an amazing capacity to create and maintain balance over long periods of time, even if within those long periods there are many shorter periods of apparent imbalance, and evolution takes place under those circumstances (although it may be accelerated by periods of adversity and imbalance); and, 2) the degree of imbalance being created by human activity today is unprecedented (within commonly accepted human history), and the evolutionary consequences (if we are to call it that) are already proving to be rather drastic, including the massive wave of species extinction occurring over the last few hundred years to present day.

THE SIXTH EXTINCTION

Is life on Earth undergoing a process of extinction? Every day a relatively vast number of species are slipping into non-existence. Many scientists are referring to this phenomena as *The Sixth Extinction*.

Scientists are warning that by the end of this century the planet could lose up to half of its species, and that these extinctions will alter not only biological diversity but also the evolutionary process itself. They state that human activities have brought our planet to the point of

---

Earth in a way that is life-giving—in a way that brings about a greater evolution of awareness than perhaps a life-taking response might bring about.

3   Unless stated otherwise, when referring to "history" the author is referring to conventionally accepted history. There is, however, a great deal of human history that conventional history does not incorporate, yet this is not the subject matter of this book and thus is not being referred to in the statements about history made hereafter.

biotic crisis.[4]

In 1993, Harvard biologist E.O. Wilson estimated that the planet is losing 30,000 species per year - around three species per hour. Some biologists have begun to feel that the biodiversity crisis dubbed the "Sixth Extinction"[5] *is even more severe, and more imminent, than Wilson had expected.*

Perspective and Context

Within this chapter we are and will be exploring some aspects of what is taking place in the world at a global level. On the one hand it may seem we are diverging from a theme thus far of the individual and our personal challenge with Power. It may seem we are jumping to something no longer about you or me as individuals, but rather about the state of the world—a world *out there*, somehow separate and apart from the individual self. Yet, in reality there is no *world out there*. As I mentioned previously, the human world that we have collectively created is separate from the Earth. As far as I can ascertain, the world is arising within the collective consciousness of Humanity and being projected into our perception and experience of the Earth. What I am unconscious of regarding the world I am unconscious of within myself. What I react toward with energy in the world, I am in fact reacting to within myself. What I deny in the world, I deny in myself. What I judge within the world, I judge within myself. One is simply a reflection of the other, as we project out the inner complexity of our stories giving ourselves the means to objectively experience our interior condition.

So as we explore this chapter and Koyaanisqatsi, I invite you to maintain openness within your body and heart and consider the possibility that the challenges we as humanity faces in the apparent world around us is in fact a projection and reflection of the challenges we face within.

---

4 Refer to http://www.actionbioscience.org/newfrontiers/eldredge2.html for further information

5 It is widely accepted scientifically that the planet has undergone five distinct periods of mass extinction, the results of various natural causes. We are presently in the heightened period of a sixth period of extinction, only this time it is the result of human activity. See the Appendix for further information

✵   ✵   ✵

Whilst the advent of imbalance and chaos within human societies is nothing new, globalisation of such imbalance may well be. The whole human story is at present going through a process of globalisation that is unfolding at an expediential rate. The Internet and computerisation are playing a significant part in supporting and accelerating this phenomenon. This process of globalisation is neither "good" nor "bad"—there are many people who believe firmly it is one or the other—for it will only be what we make of it, just like any other event in the human scheme of things. This is the first time in human *history* that we essentially have one global society, even if it appears to be a conglomeration of many societies that are still distinct and with their differences at the cultural level; environmentally, politically, economically, socially, *and spiritually* the national borderlines have been crossed and all but completely dissolved. At an economic, political, and environmental level none of the major societies on this planet today is truly independent from and unaffected by any other nation. One way or another, all the nations of the world are interdependent and interconnected in ways that can and do have deep-reaching consequences.

If England, for instance, were to collapse tomorrow, it would have far-reaching consequences in the whole world. Were China to collapse tomorrow, the rest of the world would quite likely experience massive economic challenges (I am sure you notice how many products have "Made in China" printed on them, and how vast a consumer market China is now becoming). Even the collapse of a relatively small country like New Zealand would have relatively significant global implications by virtue of the volume of products and financial commodities they trade with the rest of the world. Whilst humanity may not yet have a cohesive One World Order unifying and overseeing the global empire that exists today, it could be said that there is undeniably a great deal of *One World disorder* well established and rapidly altering the state of the planet—into exactly *what*, only time will tell. It is this disorder, should it remain unaddressed by humanity, that may eventually be the avenue through which global totalitarian control will be implemented by a relatively small collective of human beings who have the desire for such.

This whole situation of globalisation is reflecting a very important message to humanity. It is reflecting to us how completely interconnected we all are. There is no separation. What you do today affects people all over the world, even if you do it in the apparent privacy of your own home. This was always true metaphysically and now it is also true physically at a level we can witness like never before.

Humanity is in the process of integrating the knowledge that we are all connected through a collective human unconscious. Globalisation is more than simply an economic or political agenda. It is a spiritual phenomenon deeply centered in the emergence of a global human consciousness. The key question is this, "Will we collectively awaken or will we collectively self-destruct?" A number of massive global empires have come and gone before this present one you and I are a part of. Will we remember what is required to not co-create our own collective destruction yet again?

Consumption

To consume is to use up and destroy. If I do not replenish and regenerate what I am consuming at a rate equal to or quicker than my rate of consumption, it stands to reason that what I am consuming will eventually run out. There are no two ways about it. If I don't fill my glass of water as quickly as I am emptying it, the glass—short of a miracle—will run dry. So long as humanity equates consumption with self-fulfillment and satisfaction I suspect we are going to continue consuming beyond our means until the day it destroys our world.

One view of historical information indicates that all major and relatively minor empires and civilisations of the distant past eventually met their demise and descent into cultural disintegration invariably through over-use of the resources available to them, or put another way, mismanagement of the available resources. According to my assessment of the books *A Short History of Progress* by Ronald Wright, and *Collapse: How Societies Choose to Fail or Succeed* by Prof. Jared Diamond, overuse of available resources has been the cause of collapse of past civilisations. I observe that humanity has consistently failed to maintain a continuous path of social and cultural development, resulting in every major civilisation before our time reaching a point of collapse. More often than not war has also played a major if not pivotal role in the collapse of past civilisations. Faced with the prospect of running out of the things we love to consume we eventually wage war on our neighbours in order to gain control over the resources they possess. This is as true today as it was 5,000 years ago. From what I have observed, most intelligent individuals now appreciate that the wars being waged in the Middle East have little, if anything, to do with a benevolent desire to establish democracy. Even a very basic level of investigation brings to light that the wars America and its cohorts have for the past few decades been waging on the Middle East is motivated by the desire to secure control over the rich oil reserves there.

> *The world has already passed the point of no return for climate change, and civilisation as we know it is now unlikely to survive, according to James Lovelock, the scientist and green guru who conceived the idea of Gaia—the Earth which keeps itself fit for life.*
>
> *In a profoundly pessimistic new assessment, published in today's Independent, Professor Lovelock suggests that efforts to counter global warming cannot succeed, and that, in effect, it is already too late.*
>
> —The Independent, Michael McCarthy, Environment Editor. Published: 16 January 2006

Both Wright and Diamond make the point that an important defining factor in our current global empire of nations is that we have the hindsight to know what caused most (if not all) past civilisations to collapse, and we have the technology to know very clearly the present environmental and economic status of the planet and all nations. This means that whilst we appear to be heading down exactly the same path of descent due to environmental/resource mismanagement, we actually have the opportunity to learn from humanity's past mistakes and choose to avoid them. Of course, the majority of people in each nation must make that choice for it to be of real consequence.

> *Globally, 20% of the world's people in the highest-income countries account for 86% of total private consumption expenditures—the poorest 20% [consume] a minuscule 1.3%. More specifically, the richest fifth:*
>
> - *Consume 45% of all meat and fish, the poorest fifth 5%*

- Consume 58% of total energy, the poorest fifth less than 4%
- Have 74% of all telephone lines, the poorest fifth 1.5%
- Consume 84% of all paper, the poorest fifth 1.1%
- Own 87% of the world's vehicle fleet, the poorest fifth less than 1%

—Human Development Report 1998 Overview, United Nations Development Programme (UNDP)

Cultural Blindness

For much of my life, increasingly as the years go by, I have noticed the world is still relatively split or divided in its various cultural perspectives and experiences of reality. There really are so many worlds within worlds here on Earth, and yet in my experience most people don't initially have a feeling for what I mean by that when I mention it. For instance, it is very easy for those of us born and raised in English-speaking countries to assume that the rest of the world—the majority of humanity that happens to be made up of non-English-speaking cultures—is *"pretty much like us."* This is a grave and inaccurate cultural assumption that I invite you to mindfully step away from if you are at all inclined to consciously or subconsciously think and feel this way.

"One reads about the world's desire for American leadership only in the United States," one anonymous well-placed British diplomat recently observed. "Everywhere else one reads about American arrogance and unilateralism."

Jonathan Power
America is in Danger of Alienating the World, March 3, 1999

The country where I have personally found this *all-are-like-us* assumption most apparent is in America. I lived in America for 12 months during 1999/2000, and never in my life have I felt so *cut-off* from the rest of the world. Somehow I felt sociologically encapsulated in a way I was not at all used to. It was a very odd feeling that took me some time to identify the cause of. I could listen to the so-called news on the radio or television and it still left me feeling like I was inside a *bubble*—in fact I found that what my friends in America called "the news" was for me more like some form of edutainment show, and what I was being informed about seemed really insubstantial, superficial, biased, and distorted. I refer to this aspect of the USA—and it undoubtedly exists elsewhere to some degree—as bubble-culture.

The following quote from the author of a web site I found whilst doing research for this chapter sums up the experience nicely, but in someone else's words. I get the impression he also found it globally insulating living in the USA, for it is a big part of what got him looking around at other media sources, which later influenced him to create a fantastic web site—a highly informative web site on global affairs:

Around the world, even in Europe, there have long been bits of resentment or criticism of American foreign policy, even in the UK where I grew up. In addition, for many years it has been well understood outside of the US that the American mainstream media's news is often sensational and that its international news coverage is hardly international—often American-centric—leading to the effect that many American citizens know little about the outside world.

We often heard such sentiments growing up in UK, for example, though I never thought much about it and even felt most of it was ridiculous exaggeration. While I liked watching world news I never really used to be that interested in global affairs.

...all this changed shortly after graduating from University and moving to the US for my first job late 1997.

It was while living in the US that I began to see very quickly the poor quality mainstream media first hand (also being touted as the best media in the world). For example, many news reports seemed sensationalised, and what seemed like trivial issues were made into headline news while truly important global events were just not covered."

—Anup Shah, www.globalissues.org

I think this *bubble-culture* phenomenon was so readily apparent only to me as a foreigner, and that my friends there really wouldn't have known what I meant if I had tried to explain it to them. When I was young, somewhere between the ages of 8 to 12, I had begun to question the truth of mainstream media. I always felt like I was in some odd way being lied to, and when people or "things" lie to me I tend to let them be and not give them much attention. Yet whilst living in America I developed an insatiable appetite for the news—foreign news! As I mentioned, when I checked out the local and national US-derived news, it was like watching a bizarre game show or something from a surreal scene in a movie. One day I stopped to reflect on the fact that for the past week I had been watching the BBC World News via the Internet for an hour each day and scouring its web site for information on world events, and in that moment I recognised how I had been feeling—I was trying to escape from the bubble.

THE AMERICAN DREAM

If you live in America—or any of the Amero-centric "Western" cultures[6]—and you wish to wake up from the Dream, as explored in this book, then the first dream I suggest taking a sincere look at is the aptly named American Dream. The American Dream is for many—both inside and outside the borders of the USA, and both those who try to live it and those who are marginalised by it—more akin to some sort of inescapable nightmare for reasons that we will touch on in this chapter, although not in depth. I don't wish to imply that the American culture doesn't have elements to it that are life-giving (it has a great many of them), but I do wish to say that in my experience they often get undermined by a failure to humbly and honestly recognise the many that are life-taking, destructive, and completely out of harmony with the

---

6 I've never quite known how to refer to what is typically called the "Western World" because it is somewhat unhelpful and vague, outdated by the rapidly changing cultural structure of the world. I recently came across the references "Minority World" and "Majority World," the prior to denote the highly technologically developed countries, who represent a minority of the world's population, and the later refers to the less technologically developed nations who represent the bulk of the world's population. Obviously technology is not the only defining factor, but it is at least a very obvious and tangible one. Another defining factor is the degree of industrialisation and the level of commercially driven consumerism. If I use the world "Western/Westernised" it is this differentiation described above which I am alluding to.

Earth. The extraordinary level of consumption, dramatisation, ignorance, greed, superficiality, commercialisation, marginalisation of the majority world, desensitisation, sensationalism, materialism, ecological disassociation and destruction, waste, and excess it brings about in any culture that embraces this Dream is something neither this planet nor humanity can sustain and thus can no longer afford to ignore. The American Dream, like that embraced by all the westernised world, is currently being challenged to evolve into one that is more inclusive of the many facets of life and humanity it is ignorant of.

> *"The area needed to produce the natural resources to consume and absorb the carbon dioxide emitted by the average North American is almost twice the area required by the average Western European, and some five times greater than required by the average Asian, African and Latin American.*
> *'It is the consumers of the rich nations of the temperate northern regions of the world who are primarily responsible for the ongoing loss of natural wealth in the tropics' said Jonathan Loh, editor of the Living Planet Report."*
>
> —The Living Planet Report 2000, World Wide Fund For Nature (WWF)

If right about now you are thinking you would like me to back up the opinions I am expressing here with references, studies, *facts*, and statistics—and I think this would be a healthy and valid request—I encourage you to make an effort to find the information yourself. The rewards will be far greater that way and the experience far more empowering for you. I am sure anyone reading this book with the intelligence and sensitivity inherent to most human beings is able to take a realistic look at the impact the American Dream has on this planet. Of course, people who have constructed their world view almost entirely through the media and education/information channels within the American culture itself are going to have to do substantial research elsewhere. If for you that is even partially true I encourage you to spend some discerning yet open-minded time on the Internet or in a library finding what you require to make up your own mind about these matters. I am simply here to tell a story with the intention of drawing your attention toward principles and perspectives that I feel may assist you to wake up and walk a Path of Freedom.

If we all lived like Americans, we would need two additional planet Earths to produce resources and absorb wastes ... and good planets are hard to find!

Our Ecological Footprint, Gobar Times, May 2000

I include this quote from John Pilger as I feel it makes an important point for readers living in the USA wishing to wake-up to their Dream and discover a freedom *the freest nation in the world* has not yet realised:

"Long before the Soviet Union broke up, a group of Russian writers touring the United States was astonished to find, after reading the newspapers and watching television, that almost all the opinions on all the vital issues were the same. 'In our country,' said one of them, 'to get that result we have a dictatorship. We imprison people. We tear out their fingernails. Here you have none of that. How do you do it? What's the secret?'"

John Pilger – *In the freest press on earth, humanity is reported in terms of its usefulness to US power*, 20 February, 2001

CAPITALISM AND THE SUPERSTITION OF MATERIALISM

A major component of the imbalance prevalent in the world today has its roots firmly implanted in a capitalistic[7] world view that operates to the exclusion of non-capitalistic and often more inclusive ways of approaching life. Buried deep within the capitalistic drive humanity faces today, we have a rigid adherence to materialism on one hand and we have religious fanaticism on the other hand. I propose that these two apparent extremes are in fact working hand-in-hand in this world and represent the same level of thinking. We will look a little at the issue of religious fanaticism soon, but for now I wish to draw your

---

7 Defined as "An economic system based on the private ownership of capital"

attention toward the relationship between a belief in materialism and the rapid spread of capitalism around the world today.

For those who are not familiar with what materialism technically is, I provide the following definition:

> *In philosophy, materialism is that form of physicalism that holds that the only thing that can truly be said to exist is matter; that fundamentally, all things are composed of material and all phenomena are the result of material interactions. Science uses a working assumption, sometimes known as methodological naturalism, that observable events in nature are explained only by natural causes without assuming the existence or non-existence of the supernatural.*[8]

In order to capitalise (make money from) something, it must first be clearly defined and anchored within the known. Yet the known only incorporates the material/physical plane of reality in a materialist culture. No value, therefore, is given to the subtle (metaphysical) elements of Life because these are not definable in material terms and therefore not consumable. Of course within the New Age movement we have many seemingly immaterial *things* being packaged and sold for money, and I will speak to that in a moment.

People who live in denial of anything except that which can first be empirically and scientifically proven are perfect candidates for buying and consuming all sorts of stuff that is often anything but beneficial to them. Things such as pharmaceutical drugs and medical treatments that do more harm than good[9], convenience foods that are devoid of life and vital nutritional elements, 'hot' and 'in' brands that add nothing to a product except a label compared to the less popular brands, cars that have huge gas-guzzling motors and performance specifications the owner is never likely to be able to use to capacity (not even

---

8   Sourced from http://en.wikipedia.org/wiki/Materialism

9   I am not suggesting all drugs and medical treatments inflict more harm than good, rather that there are many that have this potential and therefore it is wise to always take full responsibility for the path of treatment chosen and to be present to due diligence on the matter. A smart person would not buy a house or a business without performing due diligence, so why then do we simply go along with what our health practitioners tell us without this sort of self-responsible approach? See "Death by Medicine" in the Appendix for further information.

close to full capacity) without breaking local road laws, et cetera. This list is what I would call the very, very condensed version.

Likewise, those people who identify with the so-called New Age movement who adhere almost exclusively and at times dogmatically to a world view that oftentimes ignores the pragmatic reality of a material world, along with logic, critical evaluation, and sound discernment, in favour of that which is immaterial, metaphysical, or spiritual, very often get way out of balance. This section of society is also highly susceptible to consuming all manner of weird and wonder-filled beliefs, things, workshops, readings, products, and other services that again have little if any intrinsic benefit—only serving to highlight that the materialist within them is still alive and kicking. The self-help value these New Age consumables may appear to have is oftentimes superficial and only appears real because it seems to provide an answer to something this person believes he or she is inherently missing. We literally project our own self-dissatisfaction onto these products and services in the form of believing "that this is it, the answer to what I need right now…yes, thanks, I'll take 10 of them to go."

Remember, as a Divine Being your only true need is a mirror. I know a large subculture of people who spend a relatively large amount of time and money participating in many New Age workshops related to "activating your twelve strands of DNA", "attuning your chakras to the great solar logos", attending a Wesak workshop where "144,000 Ascended Masters and Beings of Light will be (invisibly) in attendance," "aligning our meridian system to the earth grid heart matrix," and so on. I've learnt from a lot of these people that they continue to struggle to cope with the basic pragmatic realities of human life as it is in the present moment—Here and Now. None the wiser, and not significantly closer to the "enlightenment" they were seeking, for some it is common practice to ignore the fact that the expected results were not had, and they look for the next "spiritual" product or service to consume. Is having my 12 strands (some people tell me it's now 36 strands!) of DNA activated and attuned by a host of invisible beings of light of any real consequence if afterward I am no closer to living authentically, and being impeccable, empowered, and at peace in my relationships to other flesh-and-bone human beings? Is this not just another form of consumerism? Realising I am not satisfied by material consumerism I move with the same mind-set on to spiritual consumerism—what one might also refer to as spiritual materialism.

I don't wish to sound cynical, nor do I wish to imply that all this consumable stuff in the New Age culture is "bad," "wrong," or "negative." All of these things simply are as they are, and neither "good" nor "bad," but rather only what we make of them. Each has its purpose in the evolution of awareness. I know many people find they derive benefit from these sorts of beliefs and activities, and I also know that many find they must move on to something deeper that can only be found within their interiority—not out there in something I can *do* or *buy*. My intention is to invite you—if you feel attracted to various New Age beliefs now or in the future—to sincerely consider just how life-giving it really is at the proverbial 'end of the day' to approach life from a point-of-view that relies on beliefs and presupposition—be that the beliefs and presuppositions of the New Age extremes, the empiric skeptical extremes, or one of the many others I have not mentioned here (religious extremes—which includes most religions I have studied or heard of—can be appropriated to this list).

Extremes – Showing the Middle Way

> *"Science without religion is lame; religion without science is blind."*
>
> Albert Einstein
> *The New Convergence*

The *modernised* or *Westernised* culture subscribes primarily to extreme and rigid points-of-view, and if we take an honest and sincere look at the amount of destruction this sort of adherence to belief and empirical science—a science devoid of giving value to intuition and mysticism—has brought about on the planet, we'll see that there is a lot to improve in our approach, and much to answer for. Oddly, whilst most empirical scientists might not openly give value to intuition and may deplore mysticism, I think you will find that any scientist who comes up with something "new" has used his or her intuition to pluck something out of the unknown (the mystical or the occult realms) and given it form and definition here within the known.

I am not implying that those who subscribe to the New Age movement would make a better go of handling world affairs if left to their own devices than what materialists and religionists have achieved up to now. Rather I think a holistic balance between the two is both necessary *and* inevitable, which brings us to the key point of this chapter in our journey.

None of the extremes we have looked at are healthy in any way, long term. Extremes, and the beliefs one must adhere to when identifying with such extremes, are not life-giving if for no other reason than the fact that it is unsustainable. These extremes do not directly support the unfolding of Inner Peace or sustain Authentic Power—and not just the few I have mentioned, but all forms of extremism in life. It must be remembered, however, that the purpose extremes play in the human experience is one of allowing us to evolve toward a greater awareness of that which is real, that which is neither one extreme nor the other—but is residing somewhere in the space between.

A few thousand years ago a guy our ancestors decided to call The Buddha is reported to have spoken about walking the middle path. It wasn't anything new, for various Vedic teachings had been suggesting the same thing for thousands of years prior. A little later on, another chap who didn't last nearly as long as the Buddha—it's said he was fairly promptly nailed to a large cross of wood for speaking his mind (despite the people at the time expecting his arrival sometime soon)—spoke of a path into "Heaven" that was based on forgiveness and acceptance of our brothers and sisters. This guy was later referred to as Jesus Christ, and many people now claim to be following one interpretation or another of his teachings. I have found that the nature of forgiveness and walking the middle path go hand in hand. Together they allow a person to be inclusive toward a materialistic relationship to life (one that honours and does not negate our physical existence) whilst also being inclusive toward the vast array of spiritual possibilities present within New Age teachings and ancient spiritual knowledge. I will add that to be inclusive toward these two apparent polarities in a healthy and life-giving way requires an appropriate level of discernment and a pragmatic approach to reality.

PHILOSOPHICAL SKEPTICISM

Within Western philosophy there is another form of skepticism to the one we looked at previously, perhaps the purist form from which other forms later emerged, called philosophical skepticism. We will now take a look[10] at this approach to life, as I feel that for those of us wishing to wake up to the Dream it's an important perspective to have an understanding and appreciation of.

The word skeptic, also spelt sceptic, is derived from the Greek word *skeptokos* which means to look about, to consider, to examine. Skeptokos was taken, by the disciples of the Greek philosopher Pyrrho (c.360-c.270 B.C.E.), from the word *skeptesthai* meaning "to reflect, look, view." Skepticism, in this purist and philosophical form, is in my opinion a healthy approach to life and particularly to something as abstract and potentially ungrounded as spiritual knowledge.

> *"Skeptic does not mean him who doubts, but him who investigates or researches as opposed to him who asserts and thinks that he has found."*
>
> Miguel de Unamuno
> Essays and Soliloquies, 1924

For instance, as suggested in the early pages of this book, it is not my wish for you to believe anything you read in this book or to take any of it as some sort of gospel or dogma that you must either go along with or oppose. I reiterate that I am simply telling a story, with a very particular intention. Whilst this story draws on much of what we consider to be true and real, it is still only a story. I am essentially writing about aspects of reality that are mystical at best, and completely ineffable at worst (and potentially verging on incomprehensible for some people when first considered). Much of the material in this book is symbolic in nature, expressed with the intention that it inspire and motivate your Awareness in such a way so as to help you unleash your Mind from the constructs of belief, cultural and religious dogma, and ignorance—free to go within and discern the nature of Infinity for your self. Therefore I present this material for you to mentally, emotionally, and intuitively reflect on, to consider, and to look about your world in a fresh way. May you investigate and research what you have discov-

---

10 I do not wish to imply that my review of these ideas, as seen here in this book, is in any way thorough and complete. We are touching lightly on these subjects in order to awaken awareness rather than to impart certain facts or conclusive intellectual knowledge.

ered within these pages in the ways you feel inspired to in order to deepen your appreciation for life.

I have only explored these definitions of skepticism whilst researching the material for this book. What I have discovered is that according to this philosophical system of classification my own approach to life and reality could be classed as *philosophical skepticism,* of one form or another. One of the things I live and teach is to "live life inconclusively," which as far as I can discern is the basis of philosophical skepticism. I have observed in my own life that only my limited sense of ego-self draws strict conclusions and tries to impose absolutes upon a world that has no absolute nature—at least none our ordinary human senses can perceive and discern. As far as I have been able to determine there are ultimately no absolutes that can be accurately defined by the human mind. The only absolute that does exist is not definable, for it encompasses and incorporates the "I" that is trying to define it. That's not to say, however, that the absolute nature of reality cannot be felt, experienced, realised and in some way intuitively *known*. Such is the aim of many spiritual practices and paths.

The primary, perhaps only, reason the developing ego-self gravitates toward extremes and absolutes, and the creating of a reality that is conclusive, is for the purpose of identification. In living inconclusively (which is how we are at birth), there is nothing of this world one can identify with. When the human mind gravitates toward an extreme or fanatical position we invariably become identified with that particular position and the perspective on life it grants us. Our degree of power is determined by that perception. Such a person will then find her identity is in opposition to, and at some level at war against, all those who identify with a different position in the grand scheme of things. A power struggle ensues. This war takes a great deal of energy to maintain, not unlike the wars that play out in the world—which are, of course, a projection of the war within a culture of people who have identified with their particular perception of the collective dream.

Dissolving the Extremes That Hold Us Back

How can you and I notice when we are falling into the trap of swinging toward relating to life through an extreme of one kind or another?

I have found that there are a number of easy ways to do this, so let's take a look.

The Opposition of Right and Wrong

Opposition is a sure sign of a limited sense of the ego-self at play and an indication that you are taking a stance that is not in the middle ground. Only the ego will and can set up the perception that it is in opposition to something else. The Self knows no opposition, for it is the Totality, encompassing all apparent "sides" and "parts." Awareness of the Self will rapidly dissolve all forms of opposition within a person, even whilst they appear to be Dreaming of separation, i.e., lots of selves as people running around in their separate bodies, going about their separate lives. This is not achieved through denying our misperception of reality, rather it is through accepting it and opening to a deeper perspective on life.

A fast track to identifying the things you are in opposition to is to look at what in life and the world you emotionally, morally, philosophically, and even spiritually stand against—these are the things you might protest against or criticise and condemn. To go a bit deeper and see how much energy this consumes, take a look at the ways you actively avoid, judge, fight, condemn, complain about, try to convince people away from, or in some way oppose these things. What I have recognised is that all of these forms of opposition result in a dissipation of Power and a divergence from Inner Peace. It is only our ego—in its under-developed and ignorant state—that has anything to oppose and complain about. In reality there is no right and no wrong, and yet we are quite capable of believing otherwise and acting in atrocious ways whilst under the spell of that belief.

☯ ☯ ☯

Fanaticism

Fanaticism, *noun.*
1. Excessive intolerance of opposing views.[11]
2. Fanaticism is an emotion of being filled with excessive,

---

11 Fanaticism. (n.d.). WordNet 1.7.1. Retrieved December 06, 2007.

uncritical zeal, particularly for an extreme religious or political cause, or with an obsessive enthusiasm for a pastime or hobby.[12]

3. According to philosopher George Santayana, *"Fanaticism consists in redoubling your effort when you have forgotten your aim"*; according to Winston Churchill, *"A fanatic is one who can't change his mind and won't change the subject"*.[13]

For those of us walking a Path of Freedom, fanaticism is another human condition to remain mindful of. It too is something the ego-mind engages in, often to establish a false sense of security in an otherwise totally insecure world—insecure insofar as the ego can ever experience. Again we have an issue of identity playing out, for the human ego-mind typically identifies with that which it is fanatical about. I have experienced people, including myself, getting fanatical about all sorts of things and none of them really make much sense when viewed through the eyes of Infinity. Things like these:

- Certain diets and food choices (particularly things like vegetarianism, vegan diets, raw food diets, weight loss diets, stay-young-for-ever diets, et cetera) being the only acceptable/healthy way to eat
- Perfectionism through Yoga asana, and meditation practices
- Rigid adherence to Gurus, spiritual teachers, and teachings
- Rigid adherence to doing certain spiritual practices for a desired outcome
- Adhering to certain religious beliefs to the exclusion of other ways of seeing the world and approaching life

I will add that patriotism is a form of extremism and fanaticism that can be easily overlooked, because oftentimes it is so intricately woven into our cultural upbringing. There is no Power to be gained from being patriotic nor does it provide any form of Inner Peace. As far as I can tell it's basically a form of cultural mind-washing that ensures

---

12 Fanaticism. (n.d.). Wikipedia. Retrieved March 06, 2008.
13 Fanaticism. (n.d.). Wikipedia. Retrieved December 06, 2007

that the Power of a populous remains contained within the mindset of that culture or country. It keeps people identified with a tribe as their source of fulfillment and survival. Patriotism is deeply ingrained in the American Dream (perhaps more so than any other country I am aware of), and less so within other countries, though it exists nonetheless. Patriotism serves the ego-self in maintaining its illusion of separation, the many as opposed to the One. Just the other day a friend informed me that *"we won the first (world cup yacht) race last night."* It took me a moment to figure out that who he was actually referring to was New Zealand. Admittedly I've never followed competition sports and the various teams who play them, which meant I used to score really low marks for sports-related questions in the current events tests I had to sit through at the beginning of every Geography class at school.

In order to wake up to the Dream and your essential self I recommend identifying and releasing all sense of patriotism toward the country you happen to be living in or born within the borders of. "I am infinite, eternal, at one with the Supreme Source of All," and "I am an... (American, a Canadian, an Australian, a New Zealander, et cetera)." These two phrases simply don't gel. The underlying separatism of feeling patriotic and identifying with the political fiction we call *this country* or *that country* simply isn't expansive enough to allow an experience of infinity to come into being.

☯ ☯ ☯

Conflict and Offence

Elsewhere in this book we explore the nature of feeling defensive, and how this literally brings to one's attention denied aspects of Self that one has erected a symbolic fence around. Finding something or someone offensive can be read into the same way. As a Divine Being it is not possible, even remotely, for someone or something to offend me. Yet if I feel off-ended it is my own ego that has jumped off the end of reason and into a story of pain.

Attack, defense (defence in international English), and offence/offense are all aspects of conflict. Conflict or con-flict occurs when two or more people are inflicting some*thing* upon each other. The prefix "con" is a variant of "com," from the Latin, archaic form of classical Latin cum "together, together with, in combination." The word conflict is from the Latin word *conflictus* which means "to strike together." So what is it that I strike upon someone when I go into conflict with them? What is it they are inflicting on me?

In my observation people in conflict are inflicting their own repressed pain, self-rejection, and limited perception upon each other. This often happens through projecting stories, beliefs, and opinions at each other, and then feeling off-ended by what the other person projects back. All of this is possible only at the level of the small ego. Your essence has no story, no repressed self-hatred, no guilt, and no beliefs. The gift is that we can each use conflict, and all other disturbing emotional experiences, as a gateway to Reality. By noticing the emotions that arise it is possible to discern the ways in which you are suppressing your own life-force. In my own life I learnt to suppress my own Being in various stages during my childhood when I felt that was the safest way to move forward. I usually did this when confronted with some circumstances I found challenging at that time and didn't know how to handle. This resulted in my approaching life from particular perspectives that suited me then, and which only served me later through consciously dissolving them and reclaiming the power I had disowned at the time.

It occurred to me recently during a conversation with a friend that as children we typically learn to reduce our sense of Self to something relatively small and powerless. By doing this it puts the small-mindedness of the human world into a perspective we can reconcile, participate in, belong to, and relate to. How else would we make sense of the world if we were unable to meet it at the level at which it operates? Of course, it is then up to each of us—you and me—to bring into being a truer, more accurate, and more life-giving expression and embodiment of our vast, infinite nature. I call this mastering our magnificence.

☯ ☯ ☯

The Purpose of Extremes

I don't wish to suggest that extremes are "bad" or "wrong." They are not something we can ever really get away from whilst our attention is still fixated or assembled within the Dream of duality. Duality implies two parts. These two parts are inseparable, for they are two aspects of the same One thing. Within duality Awareness naturally gravitates from one polarity to the other. In the grand scheme of things this is how Awareness expands and extends. Our own Being, through which Awareness is operating, goes through exactly the same dance. So it is not a matter of ridding the world of extremes and polarities but rather a matter of identification. When I identify with an extreme—losing my true sense of self within in the process—I lose touch with what I really am, and I will eventually start to feel pain. Experiencing an extreme and identifying with it are quite different phenomena.

Ever since I was a child I have loved cold water, to the extent that I would fill up the bath tub with cold water and lie in it until it no longer felt cold (my body would eventually heat it up). I also like standing under hot water in a shower, but I then like switching it to cold and having that experience. The reason I went onto filling the whole tub with cold water as a child is that I noticed it was colder that way, for the water was warmed slightly when aerated through the shower head. Now, this is very much about experiencing two extremes, and it is something I have found very beneficial. I am aware that this behaviour seems quite unusual to many people I know and they can't bear the thought of being in cold water in that way—especially when it's below freezing outside and the incoming water is almost icy! I noticed, in those early days, that the cold was only a problem when I identified with it. "I am cold" as opposed to feeling that "I am, and this water feels cold." As soon as I identify with being cold the cold water becomes an unbearable temperature extreme that will surely make me want to switch back to the other extreme of hot water. I find that by experiencing extremes whilst remaining centered in my awareness rather than the experience, it is liberating, peaceful, and empowering. This example is a somewhat simplistic one, yet I feel it suitably illustrates the point I am making. Oddly enough I once read in a medical or scientific journal that exposing ourselves to alternating hot and cold water is beneficial for one's health and strengthens the immune system!

Another phenomenon that may help illustrate this point is that of a huge cyclone. As you know, a cyclone is an extreme weather condition with winds up to hundreds of miles an hour. Yet in the middle of every cyclone is a calm center. If you move away from that center to an extreme in any direction, the force of the cyclone is felt immediately. That same center exists within you and me, but we fail to experience the calm and Peace that is there when we've identified with the storm of human affairs around the periphery. Inner Peace is in our center at all times; we only have to train our attention to focus there and it can be felt at all times.

Just What on Earth are We Creating?

As an example of just how out of balance the human world is at present, I provide you with the following statistics on what some of the wealthiest societies of the world spend their money on.

This first table is top items of expenditure in 1998:

Global Priority	$U.S. Billions
Cosmetics in the United States	8
Ice cream in Europe	11
Perfumes in Europe and the United States	12
Pet foods in Europe and the United States	17
Business entertainment in Japan	35
Cigarettes in Europe	50
Alcoholic drinks in Europe	105
Narcotic drugs in the world	400
Military spending in the world	780
(Source: The state of human development, United National Development Report 1998, Chapter 1, p.37)	

Now compare the above to what was estimated as *additional* costs necessary to achieve universal access to basic social services in all developing countries as shown in the next table:

Global Priority	$U.S. Billions
Basic education for all	6
Water and sanitation for all	9
Reproductive health for all women	12
Basic health and nutrition	13
(Source: The state of human development, United National Development Report 1998, Chapter 1, p.37)	

World *Growth of consumption and investment* data from the World Bank for 2003[14] indicates these figures have not changed much since 1998. The situation of massive imbalance remains the same.

BELOW: The number of planets needed to sustain the world at different countries' levels of consumption (from New Economic Foundation and The Open University, *The UK Independence Report, 2006*)[15]

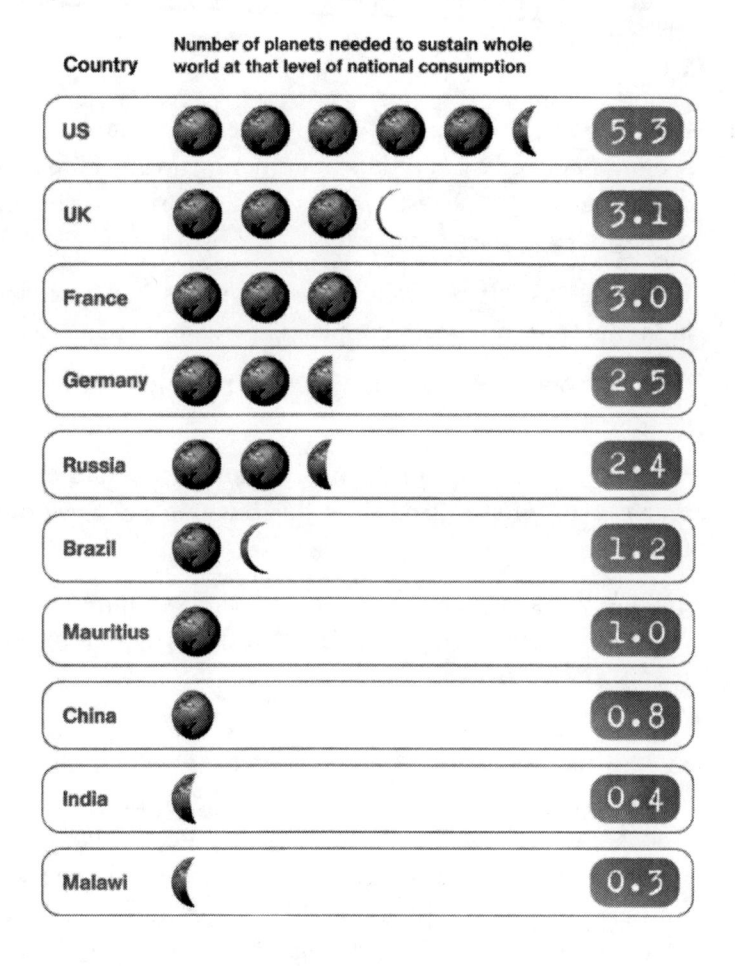

Country	Number of planets needed to sustain whole world at that level of national consumption
US	5.3
UK	3.1
France	3.0
Germany	2.5
Russia	2.4
Brazil	1.2
Mauritius	1.0
China	0.8
India	0.4
Malawi	0.3

Even by looking at what little data I have presented here, it is plainly obvious our collective way of life today is *an approach to life that calls for another way of being*. Are you ready to create that way of being now?

14 Refer to http://devdata.worldbank.org/wdi2005/Table4_10.htm
15 The full report is available from http://www.neweconomics.org

Bringing It All Home

Now is an opportunity to feel and self-enquire into some important questions. You will no doubt have your own questions so I provide the following purely as examples and for further stimulus:

- Where in my life is my Spirit calling for another way of being? What painful imbalances can I identify that are indicative of this call?
- In what ways have I unconsciously (or even perhaps consciously) been hypnotised by and thus bought into a way of life that is out of balance with the rest of the natural world, with spirit, and with my own inner knowing?
- Where do I experience conflict in my world—both internally and in my relationships with people, life, and circumstances?
- In what ways do I get fanatical and rigid in my thinking and emotions?
- In what ways do I continue to buy into the superstition of materialism and what impact does this have on my Power and my Inner Peace?
- In what ways do I get off-ended and with whom? What do they re-present to me in my world? What does my Body-mind have to say about this?

It is within and through the Body-mind that the answers to all these questions—and any you come up with—can be tapped into and experienced as a felt-sense within. Only when we—collectively and individually—face, accept, and integrate our shadows will we step into a new and more complete expression of light and illumination. So long as I suppress, repress, and deny the way I am right now, the choices I am making right now, and the role I am playing in the insanity so rife in the human world at this time, I will continue to limit my experience of Life and the discovery and fulfillment of my purpose.

"Be ye lamps unto yourselves; be a refuge to yourselves. Hold fast to Truth as a lamp; hold fast to the Truth as a refuge. Look not for a refuge in anyone beside yourselves. And those, who shall be a lamp unto themselves, shall betake themselves to no external refuge, but holding fast to the Truth as their lamp, and holding fast to the Truth as their refuge, they shall reach the topmost height."

Buddha's Farewell Message to Ananda[16]

Taking Flight

I see a great Eagle. Its two mighty wings spread out wide to each side. The right wing and the left wing, two extremes, two polarities going off in opposite directions, yet working together, for they are inseparable. Between them both is the body of the Eagle. Not separate from the wings, yet somehow not the wings either. Were someone to find just one of these wings alone they would refer to it as "an Eagle's wing." Were that person to find the body with both its wings removed they would refer to it as "an Eagle with no wings." In this way, that which is at the center is primary, and that which is to the extremities is secondary. The wings extend out from the Eagle, and not the other way around. Yet without these wings the Eagle is not truly an Eagle. It cannot fly or do anything of the activities one typically associates with an Eagle. Soaring high, watching out over the world from above, diving to catch its prey. Nesting and raising chicks. Circling on the thermal currents high up above the Earth. No, these things it cannot do without both its wings. The purpose of the Eagle and its wings are inseparable.

As I write this I am sitting in Germany. On the German Euro, and in many other official places, I see an image of an Eagle. When I speak with friends here about politics it becomes apparent that people here are very politically active—relative to my experience of people in New Zealand—and there is a strong distinction between what is referred to as the left-wing political parties and the right-wing parties. We do make these distinctions in New Zealand, yet really the difference

---

16 Reference: http://www.sacred-texts.com/bud/btg/btg94.htm

between the two is not nearly as obvious and prevalent as it is here in Germany. This, at a political level, is the manifestation of these two extremes we have explored in this chapter.

Again, I see this Eagle and I see that each wing must be present and in good health if this Eagle is to fly. The Eagle, its center, sits relatively still as the wings spread out and lift her off the ground. Up, up, high into the clear blue sky above all passing clouds. It is here in the middle that the Eagle can use the wings of extreme — the polarities of Awareness — to soar freely wherever flight and fancy might take it.

Koyaanisqatsi
1. A state of life that calls for another way of living.

"It seems to me what is called for is an exquisite balance between two conflicting needs: the most skeptical scrutiny of all hypotheses that are served up to us and at the same time a great openness to new ideas. Obviously those two modes of thought are in some tension. But if you are able to exercise only one of these modes, whichever one it is, you're in deep trouble."

Carl Sagan
The Burden of Skepticism[17]

---

17 First published in Skeptical Inquirer, vol. 12, Fall 1987

EMPOWERING PRINCIPLES & PERSPECTIVES

- Humanity is currently creating a state of life that calls for another way of living.

- As a result of our way of life the planet is currently undergoing a period of mass extinction.

- Globalisation is more than simply economic or political. It is deeply centered in the emergence of a global human consciousness.

- We are each being challenged to wake up from the hypnotically induced belief that we are nothing more noble than mere consumers. The task is to transform from living in consumer consciousness to a life of creator consciousness.

- We each contribute to cultural blindness and separation through being subconsciously identified with the one particular culture we relate to as our own.

- To be fanatical about anything is to blind oneself to or at least skew one's perception of every other thing.

- The American dream is not one the planet can sustain in its current form. Humanity is being challenged to dream a new dream—one that is inclusive of a great spectrum of life far more than our existing dream.

- The pain of extremes is to awaken us to the middle way.

- These are powerful times we live in. Dare to be bold. Dare to be courageous. Dare to be free.

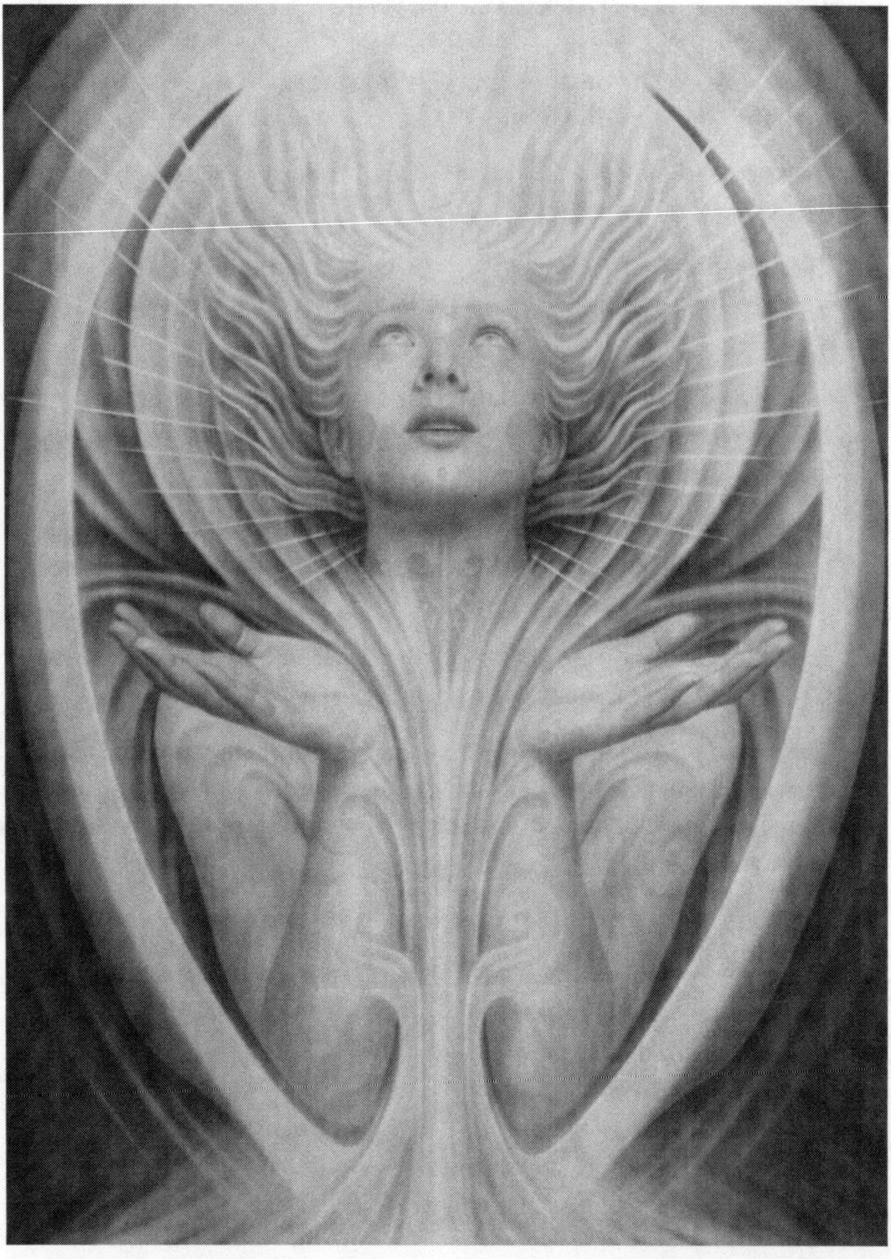

Chapter Seventeen

LOVING WHAT IS

"In love all the contradictions of existence merge themselves and are lost. Only in love are unity and duality not at variance. Love must be one and two at the same time. Only love is motion and rest in one. Our heart ever changes its place till it finds love, and then it has its rest."
Rabindranath Tagor

Are you willing to truly Love what is—right now? What would happen if you took full responsibility for your experience of life, the people in your life, and the situations you have encountered? What would happen to you and your world if you took on this level of self-responsibility? What would your life be like if in this moment you were absolutely in a place of love and acceptance with what is—right now?

I invite you to do more than just read those questions and continue on through this chapter. I invite you to pause. Breathe. Read them again. Continue to breathe and feel. Be aware of how this feels within the Body-mind, within the framework of your body.

From within the dream, a vital step necessary to waking up to the dream is to come to a place within oneself where all things are accepted and loved. Now, I'm not talking about a soft lofty ideal of love and peace and all that potentially fluffy stuff. To truly come to a place of loving what is—all of it—is hard work. I will add that it's hard work only because most people are attached to their ego-mind and its vast array of beliefs and thought-forms that keep it dissident to the experience of Reality—they are attached to their personal Lore.

Exploring What Is

I invite you to sit and make a list of all the things that you can think of that you presently do not accept as they are. Take the time now to do this. Find a quiet place where you will not be disturbed for at least an hour or two. This list includes all aspects of your present worldly situation—your financial situation, your health, your body, your self, your upbringing, other people, et cetera. Be honest. Be open. Breathe and feel and write. These are the details of what is unacceptable according to your personal Lore. In a sense, these things are what you consciously and unconsciously consider to be against your personal law or Lore.

If you're anything like me you will have ignored the activity suggested above and are reading on without doing it, thinking it's not really all that important. Perhaps you're eager to get further through the book. Of course, there is really no hurry now, is there? This book isn't about to disappear, and it doesn't contain any*thing* that is not already deeply known by you. If that is the case, I invite you, now, to reconsider, to pause, and make the list. Come on now, transformation takes knowledge *and* action! Go for it.

❂   ❂   ❂

With your list of "things against the Lore" in front of you, stand up and step back, with intention. Be very aware of your breath and then slowly and increasingly allow your body to shake. Start with the fingers and allow the shaking to move up your arms, into your body, and down your legs, until your whole body is shaking. Remember to breathe.

Now that some energy has been freed up, please sit back down and take a look at your list. I invite you to pick out a couple of items on that list that are fairly distant and low-energy for you—meaning that they don't hold much of a charge in your life right now. Then also pick a couple of items that are really present for you and hold a strong charge.

Once you've picked out four or so items from this sheet of data, write them on another clean piece of paper. With clear intention, put the first piece of paper aside and give your attention to the new sheet with the data you've recorded there.

Read over these items. Start with whatever one you feel to.

Breathe and come into a place of clear intention—"I intend to engage my awareness with the feelings surrounding this event/person/situation." Repeat that a few times to yourself, once per full breath (inhalation and exhalation).

Now on another piece of paper write down your story as it pertains to this piece of data (person, event, or situation). What is your story? What do you tell yourself and hold true in relation to this data?

Write it all down. Be as emotive and as expressive as you can be. The key is to do this with feeling, and with as little of your rational mind as possible. Go into the felt-sense of this *thing* or story within your body. This is where the unconscious resides, and this is from where your myths about the world affect you.

Here's an example…

"Joe's a fucking asshole. He always treats me like I'm a little kid or something. The wanker. Fuck, I hate it when he does that. It's like he thinks he's my father or something, treating me like a kid and not respecting me and my views on things…"—et cetera. The language you use is up to you and should be on par with what arises from the felt-sense within your body.

Whilst I don't generally encourage the day-to-day use of swearing and cursing, I will point out that you may find that letting go of all inhibitions (and socially borrowed beliefs) about such language for the purpose of this exercise could be helpful. I think harsh language such as swearing came about when people started to suppress certain emotions into a place of shadow—thus using such language can be very useful in getting these emotions back out from the shadows in which they reside. The key is then to look at what the underlying feelings are behind these harsh words. I invite you to choose words that embody and convey the actual feelings you have around this data. Hold nothing back. Put the total feeling into this.

Do this for one of the four or so items you had selected out of the main list.

Once you've written everything, stand up. Step back—with intention and awareness—and again go through the shaking process as described above. Let the shaking take over your whole body until you become the shake and cease to be the shaker. Be careful not to throw your head around too much though, as you may hurt the muscles in the neck and feel sore the next day.

Now, again—with intention—sit back down to the story you wrote.

Breathe. Feel. Come down into your belly, and read over it.

Read over it as many times as you can. At least ten times. Try to do it twenty times, or even thirty times. Each time, engage with the feelings that are expressed in that story. Remain very aware and intentional with your breathing. I'm not talking about the usual partial attempt at breathing most of us are used to—I am referring to full body breathing. Start the breath in the lower abdomen and fill that entire region up, let the upper abdomen expand, and then let the chest expand slightly but *without* raising the shoulders and collarbones more than a little at most. That's what I mean by "breathing."

Read it out loud in a normal voice. Read it in a whisper. Read it at a level of shouting. Read it silently.

Once you've read it 10-20 times, try reading it with a big smile the whole time. Even laughing if possible—of course it's possible, so try it out!

Again, really engage with the feeling behind what you wrote and read the whole story again.

Is It True?

Now ask yourself—

- Can I be sure this story is true?
- Can I be absolutely certain this story is true?
- How can I be 100% certain this is true?

Explore that for a while. Breathe with intention. Be aware of yourself reading these words and asking these questions. Give your attention to that part of You that is watching you read these words and ask these questions.

Stay with the feeling of that part of you that is watching you ask these questions. Now read over the story again, holding your attention the whole time on that part of you that can watch you sitting there reading the story. Breathe.

Turning It Around

Now I invite you to turn your story around.

Let's say Joe was one of the people in your story. Remove Joe completely. Joe does not exist. He is a role that *you* have created in order to tell this story you've just read oh so many times. So take him out of the picture. Now that Joe—or whomever you had there—has been taken out, there is only You left. So now read through the story but put you in place of Joe.

"I am a fucking asshole. I always behave like I am a little kid or something. The wanker. Fuck, I hate it when I do that. It's like my father is there, and I am feeling like a kid and not respecting myself and my views on things...."

Turn the whole story around. Rewrite it this way. Trust your innate intelligence. After reading the original story so many times, I am sure you would have found that it started to hold less and less charge for you. In fact, did you find that it started to be quite funny—more like a comedy story as opposed to the horror story it started out as?

Turn it all around and rewrite it.

A Symbolic Perspective

Also, if you feel up to it, look at the words you chose to express yourself—look at them symbolically rather than literally. I've heard it said that modern people would be wise to take their nocturnal dreams more literally and their waking dream more symbolically. Taking a look at the example I wrote...Let's look at "fucking asshole" and "the wanker." What's the story behind these words? What I see here are "fucking" and "asshole," which are both tied in with the 1st and 2nd chakras. "Wanker" is also tied in with these two chakras. These are fairly degenerate expressions of the energy from these two chakras. "Wanker" also has an element of judgment in it...it is a term used to negatively refer to someone who masturbates or makes love with themselves—which is only viewed negatively from a place of self-shame and dysfunction around one's sexuality (an expression of Life-force or vital energy). A child who views making love to himself or herself as negative or in a way that is degrading of themselves has typically picked this up through spoken and/or psychic judgment from parents, siblings, and peers. The use of these words indicates a possible displacement, or non-ownership, of energy at these energy centers, and the possibility that self judgment is harboured here.

Feel into this. Read over your rewritten story, where everything has been turned around and back in on yourself.

Bring your full awareness to the perspective that "everything is happening *for me* and not *to me*." Breathe with that for a while.

Take this perspective a step further. "Everything is being created *through me* and is not happening to me."

Feel into that. The felt-sense within your body is all-important.

Now, what is this rewritten story telling you about yourself? What does it have to say? Actually what do You (Higher Self) have to say to you? If life is nothing but a mirror, what is this story reflecting to you about yourself? If you are a Divine Being by nature, then what is this story telling you about how/where/why you've forgotten an aspect of your divinity—the aspect that's involved in this story?

Right now you might find you've just learnt something really interesting. You also might have found that this story and all the things within the story no longer hold such a charge over you. In fact they might not hold any charge at all. You may also have discovered that the person you had an issue with was in fact bringing you a gift of self-awareness. Within an organisation I work with for empowering men to lead lives of integrity and purpose, there is an exercise we do called Trust Most, Trust Least. The end result of this simple exercise is that each man discovers in a very real way that the man in the group he trusts least in fact mirrors to him something he does not trust within himself. Similarly the man he trusts most is reflecting to him some life-giving quality he does not yet fully accept within himself. The determination of whom he trusts most and least is done with no premeditation—rather he is given a few seconds to make his choice, resulting in a spontaneous and visceral selection.

Every man I have seen go through this exercise is amazed and grateful at what he discovers about himself and the secret internal relationship he had with this other man (someone he has perhaps known for only a few weeks).

THE QUICKENING

It might have taken a few hours to go through this process and you've only looked at a couple of "chapters" in your life story listed on those original pieces of paper. You might be thinking, "This is hard work...it's going to take ages to get through all this."

Because our life-story is like a woven carpet this process gets quicker, almost instantaneous at times. Once you unhitch some of the stitches in that carpet, then it will start to unravel. You've just got to be willing to be open to "Walking" around on the carpet or shaking it out (breathing, being aware, and feeling). This movement on and with the carpet will cause the holes you've made to start unraveling. I found the process got quicker and easier each time I gave my attention to it. Initially it is potentially slow and requires considerable attention, but it is not long before the unconscious mind engages with this new form of attention, and its massive ability to process outside of time and space kicks in. Now I find that most of the time, as soon as I feel myself diverging from Inner Peace, I can choose to be immediately aware of the felt-sense within my Body-mind, and I am able to incorporate into my known some*thing* that was previously unknown and unconscious. Peace returns, and awareness evolves.

Also, rather than mindlessly weaving more patterns and segments into this carpet day by day, you can—when you remember—instantly turn around events taking place that bring up energy within you. Hold the intention to stop viewing life from the place of the victim. Turn everything around by removing the "other" (whatever and whomever that might appear to be).

This process of removing the other and turning events around is something I've been exploring and applying for the last 10 years or so. I've found it to be incredibly powerful. It does require a high degree of self-honesty to make it effective, though, and a willingness to let go of old patterns and emotive habits of relating to life.

There is a teacher called Byron Katie who teaches people a process that is quite similar to the one I have described here. I was first introduced to her work when someone mistakenly thought I must have studied it. I've since discovered she has a book called Loving What Is (which influenced my choice of a name for this chapter), and a number of other books. I suggest you check out her work and her books, as it appears that what she shares has benefited many people. Her web site address is www.thework.org.

THE ILLUSION OF PROGRESS

One of the many illusions that arise through approaching reality from the perspective of a limited sense of self—through the eyes of the ego in its present condition—is that of *progress*. We live under the misperception that there is such a thing as linear progression here in the world of time and space, and that we live in a world based on cause and effect.

In reality, at a level more profound to that observed by the human senses, there is only One cause and it is unseen. All phenomena arise from that unseen cause as it extends into what we have come to know as the physical dimension. We have explored this in greater detail in Chapter Ten. I just mention it here because one of the outcomes of believing in cause and effect is that we often find ourselves living lives based on progress. For many people the measure of this progress is the amount of money and material possessions we've managed to accumulate.

Hidden within our drive for progress is often an underlying discordance or disagreement with what is. Not happy with how things are now, I strive to make them *better*. Within myself I've seen this approach to life crop up both materially and spiritually. Striving for greater monetary income, and striving for greater spiritual awareness and enlightenment. Such striving had its place in the evolution of awareness through That which I Am, and it also had its limitations. Eventually the awareness arose that enlightenment or liberation is not about taking on more of some*thing* or progressing toward a state of possessing more of some*thing*, but rather is a journey of releasing that which is not real. As I release that which is not real, that which is real, true, profound, and substantial effortlessly incarnates into the human experience.

Underlying all my illusions of progress are the innate perfection and bliss of That which I already am, always have been, and always will be. I Am That I Am. It is here that one discovers (un-covers) an experience of bliss and deep love that constantly exists and can be felt within the framework of the body, the heart, and the mind. In the body

I experience it as a blissful ecstasy. In the heart, profound love for God, Infinity, Life, and all that is. In the mind I experience it as a lucidity, clarity, knowing, and deep awareness.

Because evolution is not a linear phenomenon and does not take place at the apparent level of reality, the key to experiencing our true nature is to surrender to what is whilst simultaneously being totally present to the circumstances—the nature of—one's dream right here and now. Of course, like everything else in this book, I am by no means the first to say this. It's an ageless message that has been repeated time and time again.

With regard to being totally present to the circumstance of my life in this moment, I've found it is important to be open to the fact that my five senses can inform me of a relatively limited range of what constitutes those circumstances. One important aspect of my life circumstance here and now is the flow of intention extending into this dream—into my life—from the Dreamer.

From my own experience and through talking with people I know, I acknowledge it is not easy to let go of our attachment to the sense of linear progress and evolution and the striving and ambition that come with that. For an ego newly exposed to and affected by this revelation there are two typical, yet not especially necessary, responses:

1. I give up hope and become apathetic and despondent to the impulse of life in each moment, just making do with my situation and "getting by"; or

2. Realising that nothing and no-one really matters in the way I assumed they did, I become self-centered and indulgent living only for my own gain. With this attitude I am driven by ambition and desire with a what-the-heck attitude, none of it is of any consequence

In either scenario I am so caught up by my misperception of what life is that I miss the signals emerging from the unknown—the extension of universal intent presenting itself to me here and now. My experience of life becomes increasingly painful and difficult, and I wind up feeling like a victim to all the many things not going the way I think they should. Both of these extremes can eventually drive some people to become short-sighted, separatist toward others, and self-centered. This can lead to social retaliation and even criminal activity. At its epitome is the national leader who is willing to wage war on another nation for self-centered (collectively and individually) gains. This is usually done under the lie that it's for the greater good of the other party now blasted to smithereens yet somehow expected to be grateful for the *assistance* provided.

The remedy for this sort of madness is to love what is and forgive what is not. The question is this: are we mature enough, are we Man and Woman enough, to drop our childish stories about the world and step into the full reclamation of our divine magnificence?

In the century now dawning, spirituality, visionary consciousness, and the ability to build and mend human relationships will be more important for the fate and safety of this nation than our capacity to forcefully subdue an enemy. Creating the world we want is a much more subtle but more powerful mode of operation than destroying the one we don't want.

Marianne Williamson

EMPOWERING PRINCIPLES & PERSPECTIVES

- Freedom is only truly experienced when I absolutely love what is, right now.

- If I am to love what is I must first stop resisting it.

- To stop resisting what is I have to release the habit of projecting my stories onto the world around me.

- I may do this by owning each and every story I have about what is, through recognising that these are stories I tell and hold against my self.

- When I recognise this I can turn each story around with love, with awareness, and with my attention focused on the Body-mind.

- Awareness is all that is required to heal...to love what is.

- This is not a path. It is not something I progress along, like a journey from A to B. It is not something to struggle with. Love does not struggle.

- "Loving what is" happens here; it happens now.

- Most, if not all, of my stories about other people and situations have a symbolic element to them. These are the symbols my own unconscious is holding and they tell a much deeper story than the one my ego was previously focused on.

- The deeper story is that of my own healing. When I forgive myself—when I relinquish the stories of hatred and pain I hold against myself and have been projecting onto the world—healing is inevitable and instantaneous.

- It is the story of mastering my magnificence.

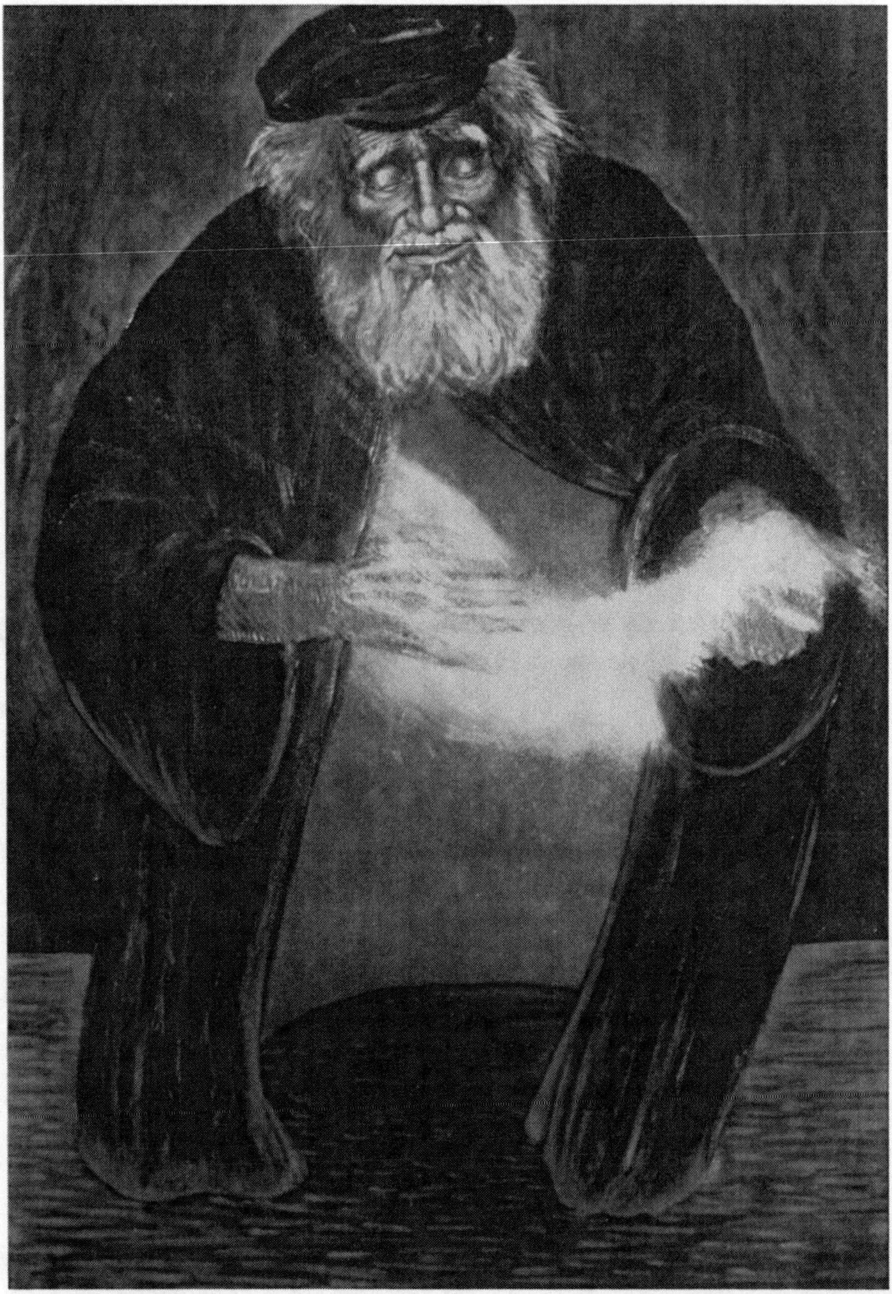

Chapter Eighteen

SETTING THE WORLD FREE

"To deny the reality of things is to miss their reality. To assert the emptiness of things is to miss their reality. The more you talk and think about it, the further astray you wander from the truth. Stop talking and thinking and there is nothing you will not be able to know."

Hsin Hsin Ming

The following topic is, in my experience, of utmost significance for people intending to establish themselves in an experience of Inner Peace and bring forth a true and accurate expression of their Authentic Power. Here we shall explore **forgiveness**—a topic that is often given some consideration in most spiritual paths, yet is all too often misunderstood, rendering it quite useless. This is, however, perhaps one of the most powerful and useful tools you and I have available to us—when understood and utilised correctly—in setting ourselves free (or rediscovering our innate freedom). With all preconceptions put aside now, when you understand what is written here, either now or sometime very soon, you will recognise and experience the power in true forgiveness.

I have often found that for those who consider the meaning of forgiveness, it is a commonly held perception that forgiveness is about recognising a wrong-doing, an injustice, or an error of some kind, and then choosing to no longer hold any resentment toward the offending party. Essentially it goes something like "You have wronged me, but I will forgive you for these wrong-doings." "You have done me an injustice, yet I am willing to not hold this against you." I am going to suggest that this is a misperception—that this is not forgiveness at all but rather just another projection of the predilection the average ego has for establishing confusion and separation.

FORGIVENESS – THE MASTER KEY

Forgiveness, as I have come to understand it, has a number of layers to it, depending on the forgiving party's degree of awareness. We shall touch on each, starting at the most superficial level and moving toward the deepest level of forgiveness.

1. To forgive is as just outlined. Someone has wronged me, it was a bad thing to do, and out of the goodness of my heart I decide to not hold it against them. "I forgive you your trespasses." This level of thinking often also displays itself as being *tolerant* toward people and situations.

2. To forgive is to realise that things are not as they seem. That what I perceive to have happened is not how things actually happened. That, in fact, everything that is happening is for the benefit of all concerned and on this basis no one can be guilty of any wrong-doing, nor can anyone be victim to such an act. Therefore, in that vein of understanding, I shall release and forgive the apparent offender of his apparent error.

3. To forgive is to release the world from my stories about it. It is about dropping the stories I hold onto with regard to the world and to all things, people, and events I experience in that world.

4. To forgive is to deeply and truly feel and re-cognise that **nothing ever happened.** N*othing* took place where I was previously thinking some wrong-doing had been performed, for in this universe, in both the form-side and formless side of Life, no individual *thing* ever truly happens. There is only one vast, integrated, and

highly intelligent whole or totality incapable of doing wrong unto itself. It is not even a question of whether something "right" or "wrong" happened, but rather that **no*thing* (no individual, independent thing) ever happened at all**. Thus there is no*thing* and no one to forgive; all is already forgiven at all times. There is simply consciousness unfolding, and I Am that Consciousness, and in that I Am whole.

Of course it is of little use to simply entertain these perspectives intellectually and then expect some sort of release or relief from the burden of all that you have been judging and labelling in the world, in yourself, and in other people. Rather, one has to discover (re-cognise) for himself or herself the deep-seated feeling of these perspectives within. This feeling is then cultivated and allowed to expand into an increasingly prominent element of your approach to the world and life itself.

Further to point 4 above, obviously some*thing* took place. If someone walks up and hits me on the head, some*thing* happened. It is our confusion about what constitutes Life, and the nature of Life, that we have mistakenly interpreted that *thing* in two ways. The first misconception is that any one observable *thing* is somehow separate and independent from the totality of Life itself. I might go so far as to accept that this *thing* is part of an interconnected chain of events, yet the misconception will remain (consciously or unconsciously) that this chain of events, that this set of circumstances is a *thing* separate and independent from myself and from the totality of Life.

The second common misconception is the belief that any one event—this *thing* I am choosing, or not choosing, to forgive—is somehow inherently significant (rich in meaning) in its own right. We use this perceived meaning to construct our stories about *things*. The mistake—the miss take on on reality—is our failure to realise that this perception is something we construct entirely based on our human conditioning. In reality no*thing* is inherently significant or with meaning outside the full and total context in which it arose—and in such a context it can no longer be seen as an independent and singular event. The whole of Life is one vast happening, and it is only for the sake of convenience we split Life up into this part and that. The more profound my grasp of the greater context in which a *thing* or event has been observed, the closer to the core I will get with regard to understanding its essential meaning.

By fixating my attention on the *thing* side of my experience — such as on an act of hatred or apparent "wrong-doing" from my peers as a child (for instance) — I miss the challenge from *Power* hidden within the much vaster and more significant no*thing*-ness of Life itself.

Physicists have calculated/estimated that of all the energy — all the stuff — in the universe, only a tiny fraction of it is in a physically manifest form, perhaps 0.1 or 0.01 percent. The remaining, let us say, 99.9% is no*thing* or non-stuff. We can see by this that in any given event or phenomena some*thing* has of course happened — the entire form-side of Life has adjusted in some way at once particular and peculiar to this event in my apparent world — yet relatively speaking no*thing* has happened.

This may seem like a tricky play on words — just as words are inherently a tricky play on reality — to someone who does not yet fathom and appreciate the sacred mystery of language and how it came into being, yet to anyone else we see that words are a play on reality, and it is our typically sterile or uncertain approach to language that has bereft us of so much meaning and understanding for Life.

Forgiveness is essentially about seeing through the eyes of Infinity as opposed to the sensory eyes of the ordinary ego. It is about seeing through the Vision of God as opposed to the perceptual sight of the human ego-mind. This "seeing" takes place primarily at the level of pure intuitive feeling. It is experienced as a deep and rich "knowing" in each moment — in the stillness of "now."

Whilst my sense of identity is based on the ordinary limited sense of ego-self, when I look out and see a person in front of me, for instance, I am still seeing what seems to be evidence of separation. Within the ego-mind I will think, "Well, here I am, and there is the other person. Therefore I am separate from this other and from the whole." Yet once I am established in forgiveness, a wholly (holy) different experience unfolds and persists — the deep knowing and tangible feeling that "I Am All that I see, I Am the witness and that which is witnessed, and All is the one creative Intelligence some call God." Every*thing*, from this perspective, is re-cognised for what it is — the Divine, creative extension of *consciousness unfolding*, and I Am That consciousness — I AM THAT I AM.

Forgiveness is, in my experience, the most direct path to this place of deep Inner Peace and to the realization of Truth that is in accordance with Reality. In fact I think perhaps forgiveness—by one name or another—is the only path to this place. For it is simply the path of letting go. Letting go, now, of the lies fed to you by malu, by parents, by social conditioning, by the influence of your ancestors deep within your bones, and by letting go of your personal Lore. The *enlightenment* that so many talk about in spiritual circles these days—and for thousands of years in various cultures and spiritual traditions—is nothing more and nothing less than an absolute letting go of that which is not real.

In the "space" created by this letting go, the *real* and the *profound* will of its own volition blossom forth. It is in our letting go that we make way for setting the world free.

One of the biggest things we each have to let go of is our misperception of the world and other people. This misperception is a projection of the misperception that we maintain within our ego-mind about the nature of self or "I." To be free of this misperception we must set the world free of this veil of illusion that is otherwise constantly maintained within the ego-mind.

✺   ✺   ✺

The Ego & Separation

The ego at its present state of evolution is invariably engaged in the perception of separation and inequality within that condition of separation. My "self" is apart from your self, and so on. The dance of language presents us with an interesting truth yet again. We only have to shuffle a couple of letters in the word "separate" to derive the words "see-a-part." To separate one thing from another is to see (perceive) them a-part and as parts.

The separatist nature of our human ego plays out in many ways—and please remember I am referring to the ego of ordinary man at our present state of evolution. The ego is typically conclusive—it tells conclusive stories about things, people, events, and life. It is typically positional. It is oppositional. It typically has something it is against and something it is for. The ego is always playing victim in some way, and the flip side is that it might also play the role of aggressor or predator. All of this behaviour and the thought-forms that create such behaviour are see-a-part in nature. This diverts my attention from the **Here** and **Now** onto something that is nothing more than a projection into the future of my beliefs and memories from the past.

There is nothing "wrong" with this dynamic per se. As Divine Beings, you and I have the capacity to create whatever we like—even the experience of dreaming up fiction that completely contradicts reality. It is not actually a question of "right" and "wrong." Rather it is about awakening to my true nature so I might experience it as fully as possible in any given moment. Through the experience of being identified with "something that is not," awareness arises of "that which is." Yet it is impossible to be aware of That which I Am when *all* my attention is caught up in identification with that which I am not, thus our mind flicks back and forth between the two. For many people the flick back to what is real happens whilst the conscious mind is asleep at night, so in their waking state they are mostly fixated on that which is not. The ego-self—whilst in a state of incompletion—is a re-presentation of that which I am not. It is an illusion. It does not in fact exist in the way we imagine it to, except within the confines of the vast Mind that I Am. The ego is a choice—a series of on-going choices and consequences. Usually these are life-taking consequences, and thus they result in pain or a loss of deep Inner Peace and a mismanagement of our Authentic Power.

Forgiveness is using the ego-mind in such a way that this series of choices and consequences is unravelled from within itself and on its own terms. It literally brings about the living awareness of that which *Is* whilst I Am here and now in the form side of Life. It is a mechanism that you and I can utilise to set the world free from error and in this way set ourselves free. The world's freedom and your freedom are one and the same—for there is only That which I Am.

It is in this way that our currently limited ego—like an immature child—is able to evolve into a true, lucid, and accurate expression of the cosmic "I," the "I" of Infinity. We'll explore this more fully in a subsequent book in this series.

Practicing Forgiveness

To truly forgive takes practice. It goes against everything the ego-mind has until now ever had you do and believe in. It goes against everything in your personal Lore. It also takes surrender and humility. Surrender and humility are necessary for healing to take place—and forgiveness is nothing more than a profound agent for healing.

What is asking to be healed?

Your Mind—that is all—for in truth **That** is **All**. It is the Mind that must be healed—and I am not referring to the subtle mental body or the human brain that many of us identify as "my mind" with its incessant thinking and mental activity. With "Mind" I am referring to something deeper and more profound.

It is this "Mind" that you will come into deeper contact with through meditation. It is this Mind that exists only in the Now. It is this Mind that is ultimately Infinity, or the Mind of God as some might call it.

To set the world free—and remember that your ego-self is also "the world"—release is all that is necessary. Release requires Awareness, which can be cultivated and brought into Being through what we experience as *practice* and *discipline*.[1] Forgiveness is ultimate awareness whilst in the human Dream, for in the moment of true forgiveness the forgiver has become absolutely aware of That which is real in this moment, here and now. There is great power in That state of Being.

The daily and moment-to-moment practice of Forgiveness may look something like this: Each time I am faced with something I don't like, that I resist, that I react toward, that I find painful, or that in any way causes me to leave my state of Inner Peace, I enquire within, "What am I asking myself to forgive in this moment? What am I here to forgive *right now*?"

The answer may most often come as a felt-sense within the body. The rational, thinking, ego-mind does not have the answer. It is what has been obscuring the answer until now. The answer is within the

---

[1] Keep in mind that the activity and discipline of personally making effort toward waking up or becoming more "spiritually conscious" is typically the ego-mind's interpretation or one-sided perception of Infinity waking up through you, as opposed to you (a limited human self) waking up to Infinity.

profound intelligence of the feminine aspect of awareness as accessed through the Body-mind. You'll feel it in the body before you think of it through the rational mind.

If after consideration, at the level of a felt-sense within the body, you think you don't know what you're being asked to forgive in that moment, then try this question, and it's likely you will find it leads you to the answer indirectly: "What would Love do now?"

The other important point is that I Am always being asked to forgive some*thing* about myself, which I may be projecting out onto the *other* I perceive *out-there*. So don't pay too much attention to "what is it about this other person I am being asked to forgive?" They are appearing in your world only to direct your attention to a place within the profundity of your own Being.

Remember, your Dream is your creation. This is your realm and you are the master of your realm. Remember that what you are experiencing is happening *for* you and not *to* you. You have invited this situation or person into your realm. Allow yourself to pause and feel the realisation of these perspectives. Are they true for you or not? The answer will come, and with this knowledge you shall set yourself free. More precisely, Infinity is establishing freedom within its own awareness through that which you have come to know as your self.

"Wherever it leads you, it will be a dream. The very idea of going beyond the dream is illusory. Why go anywhere? Just realize that you are dreaming a dream you call the world, and stop looking for ways out. The dream is not your problem. Your problem is that you like one part of the dream and not another. When you have seen the dream as a dream, you have done all that needs be done."

Nisargadatta Maharaj

Empowering Principles & Perspectives

- Forgiveness is the master key to freedom.

- Forgiveness is not about the world outside of me. It is a new way of approaching the world inside of me.

- Forgiveness is much more than recognising a wrong-doing and accepting it or passing if off.

- True forgiveness—call it radical if you like—is deeply realising and accepting and rejoicing that what I am forgiving never actually happened!

- In all of creation there is both simply and profoundly nothing but consciousness unfolding. I Am that consciousness. I Am all I see in my world.

- I have simply—and in fact quite miraculously—been perceiving (dreaming) that which I needed to dream in order to mirror to my Self that which was necessary to awaken from the dream, to awaken to Reality.

- My ego, in its current state of unconsciousness, may resist true forgiveness vehemently. This too, I may forgive and let go now.

- All forgiveness is self forgiveness.

- In forgiving myself I set myself free. In setting myself free, I am setting the world free...

...and That I Am.

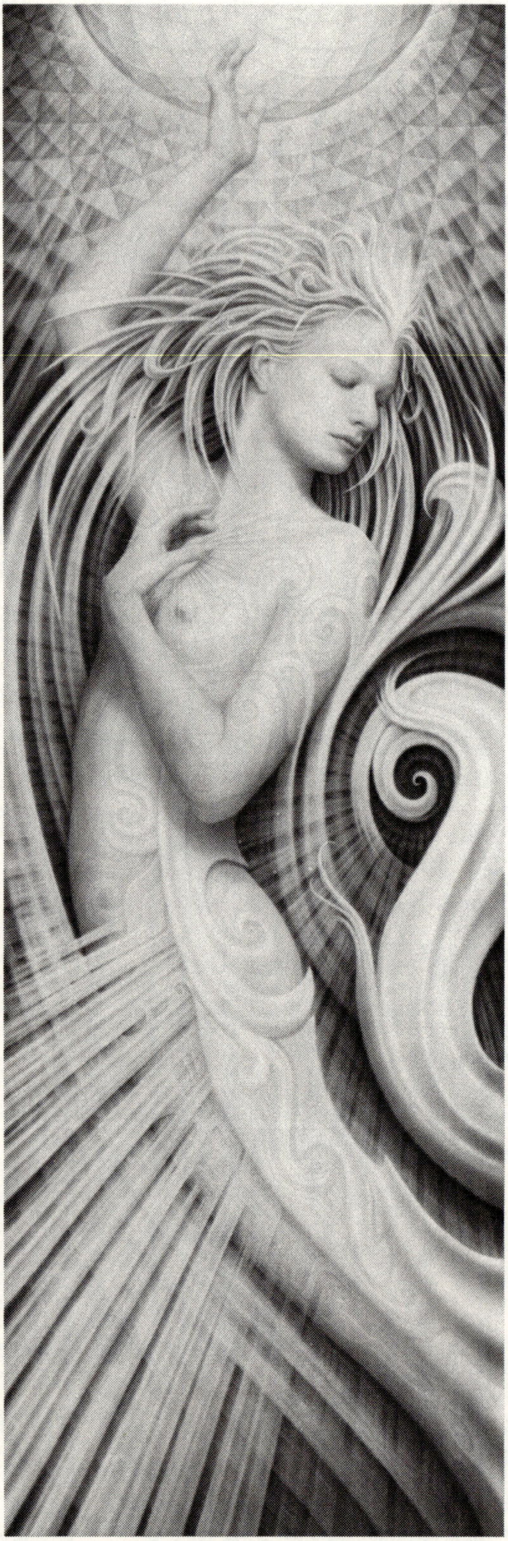

Chapter Nineteen

RESURRECTING YOUR HIGHNESS

> *"I am neither the doer nor the enjoyer. Actions have I none, now or then. I have no body, nor am I bodiless. How can there be mine and not mine? I have no flaws like attachment, Nor any suffering arising from embodiment. Know me to be the singular Self, As vast as space itself."*
>
> Avadhuta Gita
> Translated from the original Sanskrit by Georg Feuerstein

The King is calling you now. Let us revisit his realm, his story, and his resurrection. Let us take a step back now as you relax into that mystical place where so long ago the King within us all fell from its highness into the beliefs we learnt from our friend the dragon.

His eyes, still fixed on your own, have now taken on an innocence that begins to relieve much of your initial sadness, fear, and surprise. You don't know it yet, but this bony-looking man — delirious and unable to remember when he last looked into the face of another two-legged like himself — is both fighting against and surrendering into the possibility that you are some kind of angel, a gift someone has sent him, and the sheer sight of you evokes a faint yet distinct feeling of a long-forgotten time and place.

Seeing the former King relax in your presence moves you to speak to him. Neither of you can remember exactly what those first words were, for presently it all seems like the memory of a dream....

Chaos & Decline

Listening attentively to his vivid recollection of what took place before and during *the fall*, you hardly remember now that he had all but forgotten how to talk when you uttered your first words to him in the dark forest. He has recounted so much to you—all of it so important in its implications—that you have diligently committed as much as you can to pen and paper.

>...*One afternoon not long after lunch, the Queen came running into the castle complaining of a small black dragon roaming the North-facing garden. When the King came down to see what all the commotion was about, the Queen was adamant that he remove this dragon from the Kingdom so she may continue with her day outside. The King was not at all sure what threat the dragon actually posed, as he could remember no past experience with such things. He asked the Queen about this, and she remarked that she recalled dragons were dangerous creatures that could not be trusted and were renowned for bringing harm to humans and the human realm. None the wiser, the King took her word for it.*
>
>*Unafraid, and taking this request in his stride, the King went out into the garden, and just as the Queen had described, there was a small black dragon lurking around. He'd never seen a dragon before, and he hardly had time to consider what the dragon looked like before it gave him a quick look deep into his eyes, leapt into the river, and started swimming upstream toward the mountains. He never would have thought a dragon could swim, yet then again he'd never really thought much about dragons at all. The Queen, however, seemed to recall quite a bit of information on such things, and she was clear that this dragon was not of this world and should not be here at all. She was adamant it must be followed and removed from the Kingdom.*
>
>*Determined not to disappoint his Queen—as any true man would for his beloved—he set off from the stables and followed the dragon on horseback, keeping a close watch on it from the riverbank. The two of them made their way North like this for several miles before the King noticed they were now entering the foothills, and the vast mountains of the North towered high above in a way that was far more visually awe-inspiring than the view from his Castle further South.*
>
>*Strangely, and unexplainable by the King, there was a well-estab-*

lished tree growing on a small island—barely big enough for just the tree and a little surrounding turf—right in the middle of the river. While he didn't come up this way often, he came up from time to time yet was sure he'd not seen this island before. Without time to consider all this any further, he watched as the dragon made its way up onto the small island, climbed up the tree, and wrapped its tail around the trunk. Identifying the one brightly colored fruit hanging from a branch, he was now aware that this was in fact a pomegranate tree. Just how it came to be here he did not know, yet here the tree stood in the middle of the river with the dragon settled in its branches.

Knowing that the dragon could, and quite likely would, at any time make its way back down the river right into the castle gardens—causing further displeasure for the Queen—he figured he must get onto the island and somehow get rid of the scaly intruder. With this intention in mind, the King considered his options for getting over to the island, and determined that a nearby tree if felled would land in the river and provide a crossing from the bank he was on.

Pulling a large axe from his rucksack—a smart King such as this one always travels well prepared even when departing in such haste—he chopped down the tree and as anticipated it fell down into the river straddling the West bank and the edge of the small island.

Steadying himself on the island he confronted the dragon and demanded it leave his kingdom immediately. The dragon smiled slyly, as dragons do, and calmly refused. With this response, the King threatened to kill the dragon if it did not leave. The dragon pointed out that surely the King would use his sword to kill him. "Indeed I would," the King agreed. The dragon remarked that if the King killed him in this way, his blood would in all likelihood flow into the river and devoid it of life-force—as dragons are not of this realm and, for reasons unknown to Man, their blood is toxic to life here. As the King really knew very little about dragons, he listened to all this with open ears and assumed it might in fact be true. Before the King had time to really consider this possibility, the dragon held out a clawed hand containing seven seeds and made him an offer.

"If you eat these seven seeds from the fruit of this pomegranate tree, I will leave your kingdom and not return, if that is what you want. I promise you too, that each of these seeds will develop in you the knowledge of the seven empowering laws of this realm in which you live. You have nothing to lose but your ignorance."

Having never heard of these seven empowering laws, the King felt curious and wanted to know more. He wasn't so keen, however, on eating the seeds, so he enquired further. "What exactly are these seven empowering laws you speak of; will you tell me more?" And that is precisely what the dragon did....

"There exists in Creation," said the dragon, "a thing called time, and within time there exists what is called past and future. Situated between the two is a brief gap, negligible compared to the rest, and that is called the present. This limited gap in time is where you have been living since your inception, and let me tell you there is a great deal more pleasure to be had in the vast expanse of past and future." The dragon went on to teach the King about time and about the past and future in a way that made it all sound very alluring and desirable.

The next law the King learnt about had to with his personality, his image, and his identity — things he had not consciously considered before now — and how important this identity is, and how important it is for other people to have the **right** opinion of his image. Not knowing what the dragon meant by **right** and the implication that people might have the **wrong** impression of his so-called identity, he enquired into the nature of right and wrong. The dragon talked for many hours on this topic alone. The whole notion of right and wrong was previously unknown to the King, but in the way the dragon explained it this concept really started to make sense to him. The King was amazed to learn of all these new things. He was really starting to quite like this dragon and all its wisdom in the ways of the world.

The dragon went on to explain the next law stating, "There is an amazing thing called belief and with mastery of the skill of **belief** you can have and create anything you like — even that which previously was not real." Astounded, the King asked how such a thing is achieved. "You only have to believe it and so it shall be. Belief is a construct you can create within your mind. What is more, with belief and memory of your past, you can create the Lore of this land and establish yourself as the sovereign ruler of this creation. No longer will you be subject to the laws of nature and the Almighty." The dragon went on to show the King how to create perceptual constructs within his mind, how to utilise the power of belief, his memory, and how to create his personal Lore.

"Now," said the dragon, "your image and your Lore must, of course, be defended. These things will give you great power over the many beings in your world. Take heed that you are not the only King in these parts. No, there are many Kings, and out of greed for your power they will try to attack and oppose you; they will even try to take it from you, leaving you weak and defenceless." The King was quite shocked by this thought. He had never felt weak or in need of defence before. Yet he thought he understood the implications of what the dragon had to say.

"Your only sure protection is to attack them first, and with the power of your belief you can keep them separated out from your kingdom." The King stated he had never had to think about all this before and was convinced that would not be necessary. The dragon assured him it would, and that with his words—used in certain ways—he could ensure his relations would approve of him, and if they choose to reject him, there were words he could use that would tear them down and keep him safe and under the protection of his personal image and Lore. Discovering how to use language in these ways and more...the fifth law was taught to him that day.

"Because you may not always win your battles with the other kings who attack you, it is important you know how to avoid feeling the pain of having your image attacked and beaten. It is inevitable that with so much power other kings will victimise you, and believe me it will hurt if you don't have protection." The dragon proceeded to teach the King in the ways of projection and denial. He taught that through the mastery of projection it is possible to deny and avoid the effects of your relations causing you pain. "The trick is to close your (spiritual) eye—the one situated in the center of your forehead—and simply use your imagination to project back at the world those things that cause you pain."

The King knew not of pain thus far in his life, yet agreed that it sounded undesirable, and protection from such things would be necessary should it arise. So he promptly took to heart the lessons on projection and denial.

In the closing hours of this long lecture, the King was not sure exactly what ensued. He recalls getting tired, eventually losing all awareness of the day and evening now behind him in the newly discovered past. If he was told the seventh law he certainly didn't remember it...sleep overcame him.

Upon awakening in the morning, or so it seemed, the King found *himself sitting where he remembered sitting the day before. In front of him was the dragon. The dragon asked, "Are you hungry for more?" whilst handing him seven juicy pomegranate seeds. "I went to see your Queen in the night," the dragon added, "for she was concerned about your whereabouts, that being your first day and night apart. She knows you are safe; we talked for some time; she ate seven of the same delicious seeds I now offer you; and she is eager for your return."*

The King noticed himself having feelings he was not at all acquainted with. Feelings that felt connected to hearing of the Queen's concern and his not telling her where he was. Passing these feelings off as insignificant, he was aware of his hunger and thirst. The dragon again offered him the seeds, and as if somehow reading his mind, spoke to his thoughts about the Queen. "Do not concern yourself about the Queen. She was displeased with you, yes, although I spent the early hours of the morning with her in your bed fulfilling her womanly desires, and all is well."

Immediately outraged and no longer trusting the dragon in the slightest, and without the Queen nearby to consult on the matter, the King rashly swung his sword at the dragon's outstretched hand. The dragon was swift to retract his hand, yet it was not quick enough, for the sword struck a slight blow flinging the seven seeds into the air and deeply cutting the tip of its claw.

With a rush of adrenaline in his body the whole world suddenly seemed to slow down, and the King watched the seven seeds and one piece of the dragon's claw slowly glide through the air. Each seed landed somewhere along the banks at the river's edges. Within moments of the seeds touching the ground, the ground in each location began to shudder, rumble, and split apart. Not at all sure what was going on, the King could only stand and watch in dismay.

Where each seed landed, a stream broke away from the main river, seven new streams in all. Much of the water that previously flowed down the main river was now forging new streams out to the West and East of this river. You are so engaged in what happened to the seeds and the visible streams they created, that the King almost failed to see what became of the dragon's claw. The claw flew up high, high into the air, almost out of sight, almost into the clouds. Arriving at the peak of its ascent, the claw dropped now, down, faster and faster, all the way down, now, until it hit the river with an almighty splash. Far from being "out-of-sight, out-of-mind," the river began to swirl into a turbulent whirlpool. It took him a moment to understand what was going on here, but then he realised the claw had hit the bottom of the river and forged a hole deep in the Earth, all the way down as far as you might imagine. Much of the river went underground, deep into the darkness within, and forged its way down to the ocean, just as it has always done, except now it flowed underground, unseen, and hidden from the King's eyes, and hidden from his Kingdom.

What water remained flowed now through the seven small tributaries, out across the land. The main river all but completely dried up.

A large splash of water startled the King back to the present moment as the dragon dived, with his bleeding claw, back into the main river, heading North, and disappeared from sight. Relieved to see the back of it, he returned to the castle and his Queen—although not entirely sure what to make of all that had recently come to pass between the dragon, himself, and the river.

✴   ✴   ✴

In your notes you have recounted how the King made his way back to the castle. He noticed that the mighty river that had been flowing from the high mountains through his land had waned in size considerably—only the smallest trickle still made its way to the castle—and the seven new streams were dispersing the river's waters out across the land. They did not, of course, flow to and under the castle in the way the mighty river had all these years. The castle had considerably less power than ever before, with nearly all of the power generating water vanishing further upriver before it could be utilised here at the castle.

The King described how the high tower had always been accessed via an elevator—being so high that stairs were considered impractical and were not installed when it was built. This elevator relied on a waterwheel to engage with a pulley system that lifted it with ropes. With the water supply depleted, the result was a waterwheel that didn't function, so now the King couldn't go up the high tower anymore, and this resulted in him losing the vantage point of vision he once had over all his land. Without the help of the power the river once generated in the bowels of the castle, the King and Queen found it took a lot more time and personal energy to maintain the castle and the small surrounding gardens. Less water also meant their gardens had to be made smaller and smaller each ensuing year.

The King explained that daily his relationship with the Queen deteriorated under the strain of finding it harder and harder to maintain the life and ways they had been living. She was not able to attend to the Earth and nature in her gardens due to the lack of water flowing through the Kingdom. Silently she blamed the King for this situation. Oddly, and just as silently, the King blamed the Queen for sending him off to banish the dragon in the first place. The tension mounted between them and they were no longer able to co-operate in a life-giving way. They fell out of love.

The King explained that their love had always been based on co-operating intelligently, in a way that is life-giving for all concerned. Yet they became so preoccupied with a disdain for their depreciating situation that such co-operation all but disappeared entirely.

The King also explained that the dragon continued to live in the Kingdom, and despite many attempts to track it down, he was never able to catch it. Whenever the King approached, the dragon would jump into one of the many streams and quickly swim away. All these streams interconnected up in the foothills by the little island with the pomegranate tree, so the dragon could get around much of the King's land without ever stepping onto dry ground. Aside from simply using these streams to hide, the graver issue was that the dragon's wounded claw never properly healed and continued to bleed ever so slightly. The dragon's blood, life-taking to humans and most beings of this Earthly realm, would drip into whichever stream he happened to be hiding within, tainting the water and the surrounding land.

> *I built dams in many of the rivers as a way to stop the life-taking water from flowing through the kingdom. With the dams I could control the flow of water from whichever river, or rivers, were affected by the dragon that day. These dams formed lakes and from the lakes came more small streams. Eventually I had these dammed too, yet I could see it was a losing battle. With so many dams and rivers and streams, it became impossible to keep watch on them all. Over time I simply left the gates of each dam closed, as this caused the water to overflow into the surrounding land, and at least not come toward the castle.*
>
> *I thought the dams might help with capturing the dragon, or at the*

very least confine it to the North toward the mountains. His only safe passage within close vicinity of the castle was via the seven streams, and by damming them in the North there was not enough water for him to come and go by. Of course, this meant even less water flow through the Kingdom and drought ensued in most places.

The King also shared, with obvious sadness and a heavy heart, the many challenges he and the Queen faced during the period of decline. He spoke of how after the fall, as he called it, their relationship took a fall of its own.

Because of our terrible troubles, the Queen and I argued almost constantly, until eventually we were no longer on talking terms. Her sadness at this eventually caused her to fall sick, and one day she slid into a deep coma. After seeking council with the very best herbalists and healers I could find, it became apparent that her coma was incomprehensible to them all. Even though our recent times were troubled and we seemed to fight all the time, the Queen's absence left me desperately alone. Strangely, at first I felt great relief from the tension that had been day and night playing out between us. Yet it wasn't long before I remembered from deep within my mind and heart the loving union we once shared, and I then felt only remorse. Still, I had the Kingdom to attend to so I put these feelings aside and got on with it. What else was I to do?

Deranged and struggling with my inner torment, I felt I didn't want the Queen in the castle constantly reminding me of this loss, so I had her moved to a Pagoda in what remained of the South garden. That was where she liked to be the most, tilling the soil and nurturing new life into healthy vegetables and plants and fruit-bearing trees, so that was where I thought she should be now. What's more, I seldom if ever went out there by that stage, so I figured she could rest peacefully and undisturbed, and cease reminding me of my loss. I had given up hope that she might come out of the deep coma she was in, yet I couldn't bring myself to end her life at will.

My thoughts soon moved on from obsessing about my loss of the Queen; there were more pressing issues arising every day and needing my attention. You see, because I had not been able to monitor what was happening on the boundaries of the kingdom—which was previously accomplished by viewing it from the tower—the Queen and I had been sharing the now tedious task of checking on the perimeter of our realm by foot and horseback. We had to build a stone wall around the perimeter but this required maintenance to keep it strong. With her now gone I could not maintain it on my own. Somehow she had always seemed to know just which segments of wall needed our attention and we would simply go there, repair what was needed, and return home. First without the high tower and then without her help this task became impossible.

The walls, which seemed to increasingly require maintenance, slowly deteriorated. It was not possible for me to walk to every section of my boundaries and assess their condition. Portions of the walls broke down completely in many places, and wild animals, thieves, and rogues began to make their way into my realm. Over time I went quite mad with fear and anxiety constantly trying to ward them away from the castle.

My horses began to die from lack of healthy water, what with the life-taking influence of the dragon's blood in the streams, and my servants too eventually left the Kingdom in search of food and drink. I was alone, vulnerable for the first time in my long life, under attack and on constant defence. It wore down my spirit. On my own without my army or my Queen, with complete loss of control of my realm and complete loss of any intuitive Feminine access to the unknown, it wasn't long before I began to lose all sense of reason. I felt like a stranger in a strange land—in the very place I once had full dominion of and used to call "home," and, without my consciously noticing it, madness set in.

That, my friend, was when I mindlessly wandered off into the black forest, leaving the dragon and my lifeless Kingdom behind. I had truly fallen from the fortitude of what once was.

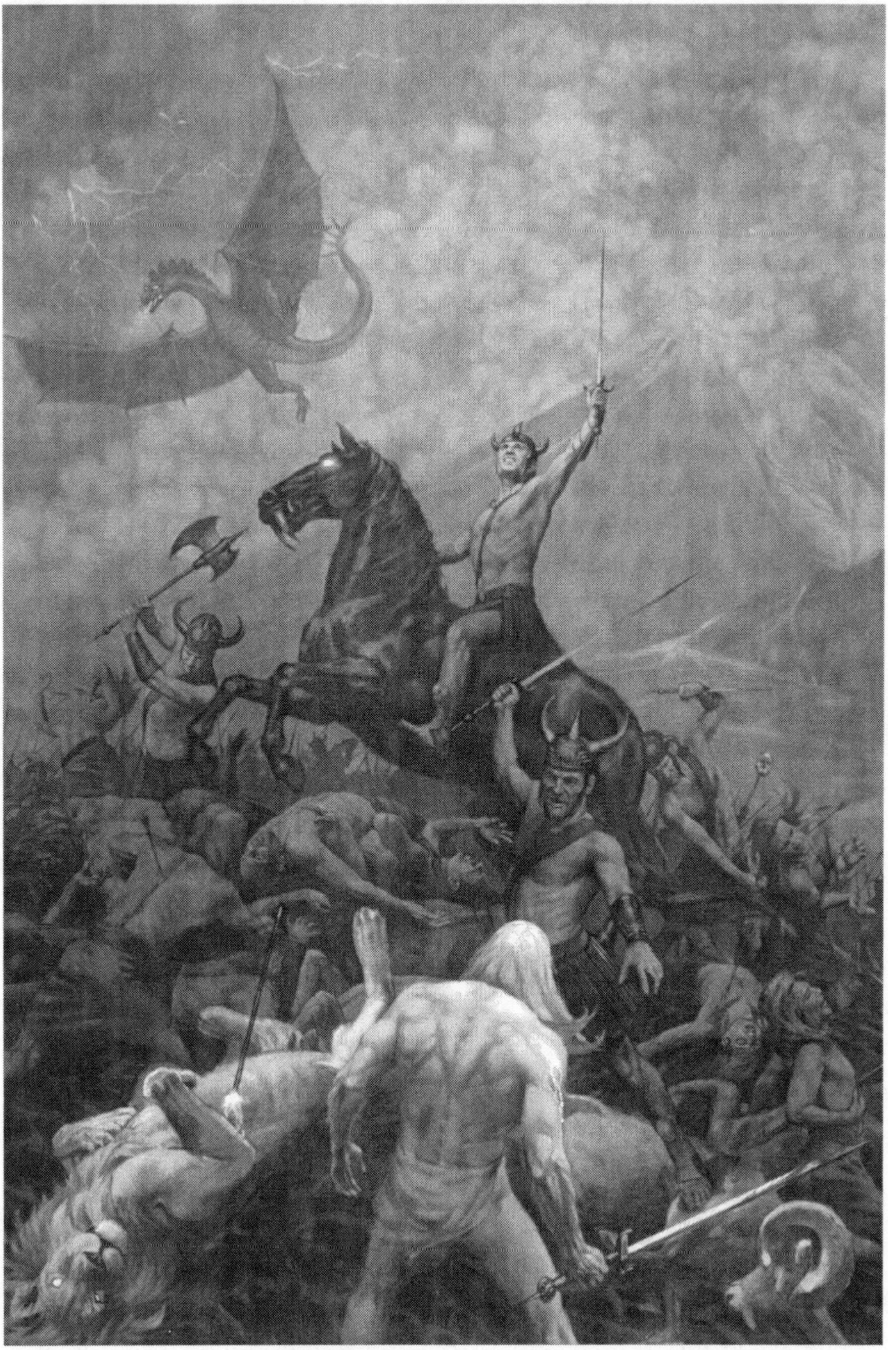

The Resurrection

The journey described by the King in our story symbolises many aspects of how you and I—the "Son" or Creation/Extension of Infinity—have come to be in a world of so much apparent suffering and degeneration. Just today whilst listening to the radio I heard an advertisement for a fund-raising event intended to assist the estimated 150 million children living on the streets without a place to call "home." When I consider that the majority of the financial wealth on this planet is in the hands of less than a few thousand people, it certainly is a rather odd world we are collectively creating here on Earth to have so many homeless, and hundreds of millions more starving. I am sure anyone watching humanity from an entirely objective stance—let us imagine Beings from another planet watching from outer space—would consider the human world to be quite mad.

Rising up out of this Dream of the fall, which we are each living in at present, is something that only you can do within your world. No one can do it for you, and you cannot do it for anyone else. We must also not forget the interrelatedness of all things, the effect of which being that each person who rises up out of humanity's present condition of collective consciousness—where most of life and living is lived out in unconscious realms of the human mind—and awakens to who and what he is as a Divine Being actually adds momentum to the collective making that same transition. There is nothing radical about waking up, in the sense that this is where the whole of humanity is heading anyway. If, shall we say, 10% of the global population rises into a more expansive, encompassing, and loving state of consciousness, the "mass" or "quantum stuff" of that 10% will exert a subtle force of inspiration on the remaining 90% in that same direction or toward that same shift in consciousness.

There's encouraging news in that last point, the news being that not every human being has to go through the same kind of "battle" for full and true consciousness that the sort of people drawn to a path of freedom—like you and me—must go through. There are enough pioneer spirits incarnating on this planet to swing the whole planet into a full resurrection of consciousness toward freedom rather than greed and suffering. Whether you know it or not, you are one of those pioneer spirits; otherwise you wouldn't have been drawn to, let alone be reading, a book of this nature. I am quite certain, however, that you are fully aware of this fact already.

✹   ✹   ✹

Your brightly shining face in the dark forest somehow reminded me of my own image in a time since past. The jolt of that reminder was enough to set me back toward reclaiming what I had forgotten I once had.

Upon my return to the Kingdom I was immediately aware of what had to be done. As I have said — and I repeat myself to make these events clear in your mind — my listening to the many lies told to me by the dragon and the loss of coherency in the One stream flowing down from the mountains were the beginning of my descent into madness. Once the stream split into eight separate branches, the water dissipated, making very little of it available to the energy system within the castle. My rash reaction to the dragon and the effect of his life-taking wound made any one or more of the streams toxic from time to time, yet there was really no way to tell just which stream it was in from one moment to the next.

What is more, by damming up the rivers to ward off the dragon and his toxic influence on the water, I blocked the flow of Life from the high peaks of the mountains in the North. This left my kingdom barren and thirsty, and in a state of despair.

It was necessary to reunite the eight streams and restore the river to what it once was — for the loss of coherency in the stream was the beginning of my descent into madness. With the river back to its former glory and power restored within the castle, I could again light the castle from within. I was also able to elevate myself and reach the top of the tower. From my renewed vantage point — one that endowed me with the eagle-vision over my realm — I could carefully follow the movements of the dragon and figure out its habits. It was then only a matter of setting a well-orchestrated trap. Once captured, the dragon agreed to leave if I released it in the mountains, and this I did.

After some time with the river restored to its former glory, the gardens around my castle were again brought to life with much-needed water. Most of the plants the Queen had tended there so long ago had left a wide array of seeds before they died off in the drought. Of course I didn't figure all this out until much later. You see, I had in fact completely forgotten about the Queen in her coma, just as I had forgotten about the incredible beauty of her many garden beds. It wasn't long, however, before these seeds sprang into life and the lush greenery I had all but forgotten was beautifully restored. The sight of this stirred something deep within me, deep in a place I didn't even know I'd lost touch with. Yet it was like I was taking my first full, deep, and soul-enriching breaths in years.

The sight of these plants blossoming into a full array of amazing flowers brought me to my senses. Something about the sight, and, yes, the smell, brought the recognition of my former Kingdom back to me. It was at this moment I remembered the Queen still resting in a coma inside the Pagoda, in the South Garden. Little did I know that she too, recognising the smell of these blossoms—all so familiar to her Being—was stirring from her coma. She was standing there when I arrived.

It took us some time to get reacquainted, yet not as long as I had anticipated considering how long ago we last stood face-to-face with our full senses intact. The love, of course, instantly flowed between us—what our minds had long since forgotten, our bodies remembered perfectly and without falter. Daily our bodies embraced in love, opening both my heart and her mind to the full former glory of our union. I couldn't begin to tell you what a relief this was, and just how much I began to recognise about myself from that time on.

Under the radiant love of our co-operation and sharing, harmony was restored. Once as good as dead, my former self as King and Master of my realm was healthily restored. Balance—one I hardly had the sensibility to remember I had lost—was gracefully regained. I can see, now, with hindsight that this entire fall and resurrection I went through served a deep and profound purpose—although I cannot yet fully comprehend the full extent of its ramifications. I can sense that my awareness of Life has grown greatly, and I feel a great deal more powerful and at peace than ever before. The peace I feel now is experienced deep within the body, as is the awareness I have now gained.

Restoring Balance

It is this balance that we each must restore within our inner and outer world—the outer being an extension of the inner. On your path to Peace, Power, and Presence, I encourage you to start relating to your world and the way you experience it as your own individual and sovereign realm or Kingdom in which you are the sovereign ruler. Keep in mind at all times that the purpose of this realm is the evolution of Awareness, this and the manifestation and fulfillment of Love—Love being the natural outcome when your actions are in alignment with your true nature. As a result your Kingdom accurately reflects your true nature. Love is most practically made manifest through the principle of *intelligent co-operation*—with yourself and all the other beings within your Kingdom. Each is there as a gift from Infinity.

Taking this to heart now, I invite and encourage you to take full responsibility for your past—for all your actions and your every experience—and for your future, for all that is yet to unfold. Above all else take responsibility for this moment—Here and Now—for only in this aspect of your reality is Love felt, expressed, and experienced. Responsibility is quite literally my ability-to-respond. How are you responding to Life at this time? In what areas of your realm, your Kingdom, could you step into greater intelligent cooperation if you knew exactly how to do that, right now? Which areas of your realm are reflecting fear to you? Any? Which areas bring about pain? Look far and wide. Look close, within, at the profundity of your inner being, your emotions, and your body. Again, I invite you to take responsibility for your world as it is, right now.

This is not to say that you, with your attention fixed primarily on the human experience—as it is for all human beings—have and can consciously dictate exactly what unfolds in your world. To suggest this would be to dismiss the profundity of Life, of which you and I are just one part. Rather it implies a disposition toward life and toward your world that is open to what unfolds, without blame, condemnation, or judgment of any kind. The river splitting into eight streams is a metaphor of our own life-stream being fragmented and consequently being dispersed out across our realm. This also relates to the fragmentation that occurs when our primary energy centers (typically called chakras) are not functioning as a unified whole. The castle—our essential core Self here in the Dream—ends up with very little life-force flowing through it as a result.

We use that life-force to maintain our awareness. We use that life-force to elevate our perspective to what my friend (a Huna Shaman-priest) calls "Eagle Vision." It is this *Eagle Vision* that affords us a clear and all-encompassing perspective on our realm, like an eagle sawing high up above the Kingdom, and swooping down with great precision to engage with what really matters. I have found that without this degree of vision—without lifting my perception up from time-to-time beyond the confines of the human collective ego—it becomes very difficult to be clear on the true nature of all that is unfolding in my world. It also becomes very difficult to maintain healthy boundaries that are supportive of my realm and the intention manifesting through me into that realm.

Eagle Vision is vital if you intend to track down the *dragon* and come to understand its movement and its ways, and know how to capture it. This dragon is the equivalent of life-taking spirits inhabiting one's Mind and creating toxic or life-taking feelings, beliefs, perceptions, and the many outright lies that we live with every moment of every day. What's more, when my life-stream is fragmented into many smaller streams spreading out all over the place, this dragon (perhaps plural "dragons" is more appropriate) has so many places it can "hang out" that tracking it becomes very difficult.

One aspect of bringing these many streams back into one coherent flow is to bring all of my personal energy centers—called chakras in some traditions—into coherent harmony. Some people working in the self-help field talk about having the head and the heart work together, whereas I say that most people are energetically, emotionally, and spiritually split—perhaps literally, perhaps metaphorically—into more than just these two rudimentary *parts*. Each of the streams in the story of our King represents one of the seven chakras or energy plexuses anchored within the physical Body-mind that we each utilise to process (and create) our perception of reality with. For most people, these seven energy centers get fractured further, with many smaller streams flowing out into our realm, particularly into past and present relationships that are dysfunctional and heavily influenced by malu. You will recall the bulk of the water was diverted underground. Humans also have a number of other energy plexuses spatially located above the head. Until we start waking up to our true nature, the energy of these upper centers operates almost entirely unconsciously. This energy flows through us and plays out in ways that are unseen and unconscious. Often the expression of this life-force comes out through a shadow self we don't like or accept. Whilst we are still asleep to our true nature, the bulk of our life-stream is flowing into the dark hole under the Earth, created by the dragon's claw.

This results in relatively little life-force making it right down into the flesh and body—failing to in-carn-ate—and we lose consciousness at the physical level of our being, meaning that we also lose Eagle Vision over our physical being and our physical realm. We also lose this degree of vision and perspective/clarity when experiencing our strong and most basic emotions. This is one condition under which physical disease may manifest and require outside assistance to "manage" (much of our contemporary medical system approaches *health* as a matter of carefully controlled "disease management"). For many, consciousness is also lost at the astral (emotional), mental, and spiritual levels of their Being. In my experience, it is the clear and congruent incorporation of these aspects of Self that ultimately provides us with on-going access to Eagle Vision.

❈   ❈   ❈

Reinstating your Self—both the masculine and feminine polarities of awareness—as the caretaker and creator of your realm is vital to Inner Peace. It is vital to Authentic Power. It is also vital to the fulfillment of the Universal Intention that brings all of Life into Being. How can we be Authentically Powerful when unable to manage even our own basic expressions of life-force—as emotions, thoughts, and a physical body? Loss of consciousness on these levels inevitably results in denial and addiction of one form or another (some obvious and some much less so), and again there is little sense of Authentic Power in someone who has in a big way handed his spirit over to addictive and habitual behaviour. There is nothing "wrong" in that scenario, for its purpose is always to awaken us to how and where we lose power—yet it is undeniably painful. In reading the above points it is vital to remain clear of the mentality that says this is "right" or "wrong," or that points a finger of blame or guilt. Every*thing* is perfect. Every*thing* is exactly as it should be. When I put my hand into a fire it is perfect—as it should be—that my hand starts to feel pain. Only in this way do I become *aware* that fire burns and a burnt hand just ain't a lot of fun. It's not supportive to the manifestation of Life that I am.

Some great news for us all is that not one of us is alone here in this story—rather we are in fact al-one. All-one in an intelligent universe that is perfectly configured toward and by the highest fulfillment of Love that any human being might imagine. Actually, the Truth is that the I AM in you and me is not "in" an intelligent universe...it "is" the intelligent universe. The intelligence of all Life is the I AM in you and me—experienced as the profound sense of "I" or a state of non-dual Awareness within us when we are quiet and still enough to notice it.

In the next chapter we shall now explore what this means in more detail.

EMPOWERING PRINCIPLES & PERSPECTIVES

- Right now I am being challenged to restore the balance in my world and to reinstate my Power.

- Responsibility is quite literally my ability-to-respond. How am I responding to Life at this time?

- I dreamed my fall from Heaven, and I have it within my capacity to dream my resurrection. In fact, I am the only one who can.

- I use my life-force to maintain awareness here in this world. When this life-force is dissipated my awareness naturally withdraws.

- Without awareness I am like someone stuck in a room with no windows and with all the lights turned off. I stumble into and trip over the things in the room. It hurts and yet never seems to end.

- When I call back my energy—when I call back my soul—from the many things I have bought into which no longer aid me in mastering my magnificence, my awareness returns. It's that simple.

- When my awareness returns I experience a new perspective on life, a new way of perceiving. That new perception grants me access to more Power.

- That Power enables me to create an even more empowering perspective.

- This is the "upward" spiral of resurrecting your Highness.

- Choosing a higher perspective through increasing awareness grants me what one might call Eagle Vision.

- From the perspective of Eagle Vision I have a clear view of my realm, my Kingdom, my world, my self.

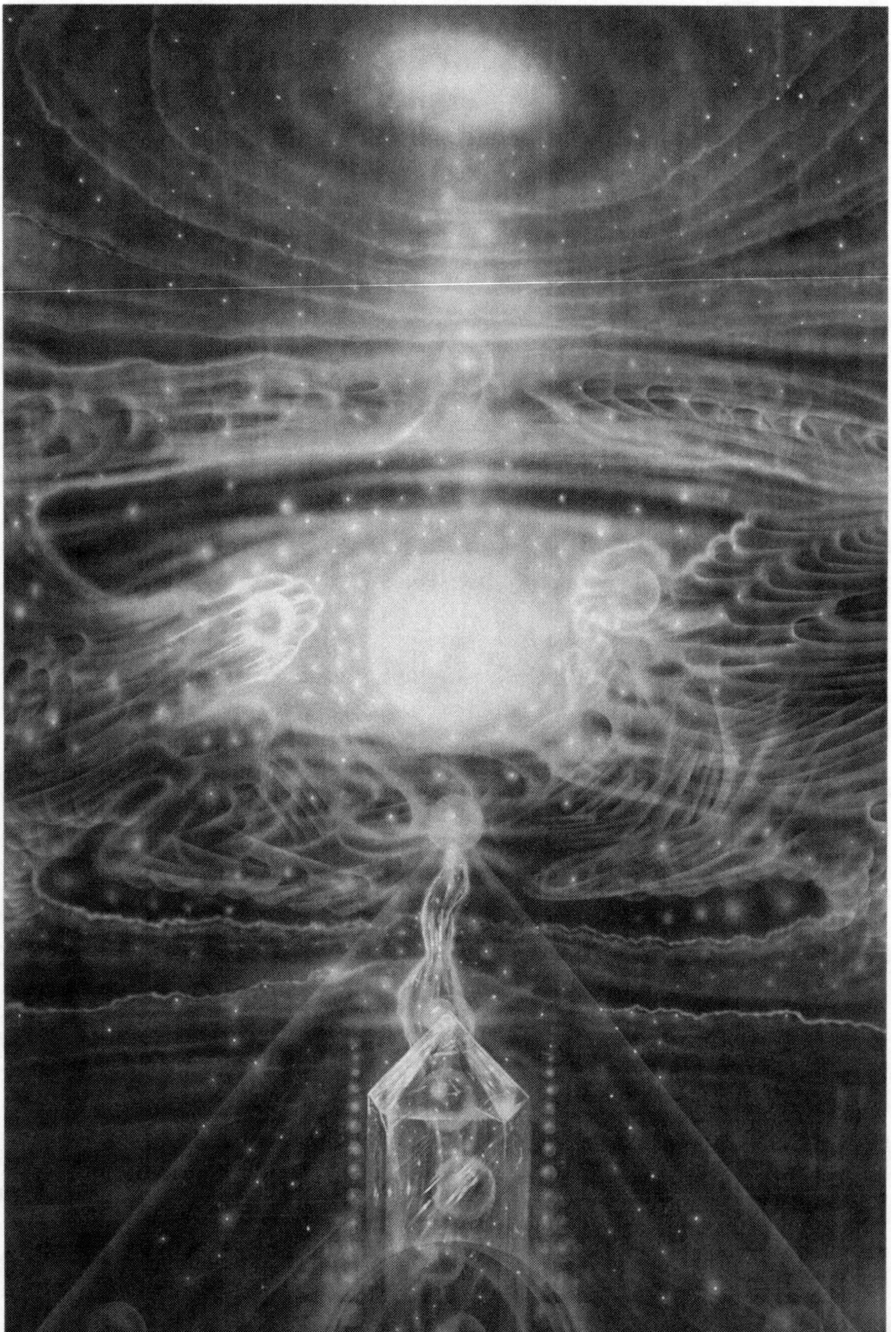

Chapter Twenty

The Intelligent Universe

"All matter originates and exists only by virtue of a force...We must assume behind this force the existence of a conscious and intelligent Mind. This Mind is the matrix of all matter."
Max Planck
Nobel Prize-winning Father of Quantum Theory

We exist within a wholly intelligent universe. Intelligence permeates all things and all non-things (such as the apparent space in between the things). This might be a challenging concept to grasp for someone who is not clear on what I mean by this use of the word "intelligence." Let's take a look at this word. Intelligence, as I use it here, refers to:

- The capacity to organise information—to structure the *stuff* of the Universe—in a way that is conducive to the fulfillment of Universal Intention in the most efficient way possible
- The recognition and creative application of knowledge
- Accordance with Reality
- That which orientates itself with Life and therefore is life-giving in nature

I am suggesting the Universe, along with everything in it, is permeated with these qualities of intelligence. This means you and I are also permeated with these qualities. We are, in effect, all genius—although most people are still discovering that about themselves and others. The implications of this point are that we each have immense creative talent and ability that, for the most part, are yet to be discovered (remembered) and tapped into. Time and time again I have seen situations and learnt of cases where people who previously thought they were either stupid or simply deficient in intelligence and creative capacity expressed great genius and creativity when they relinquished all such limiting beliefs about themselves.

"Mind and intelligence are woven into the fabric of our universe in a way that altogether surpasses our understanding."
Freeman John Dyson (1923)
An English-born American physicist and mathematician, famous for his work in quantum mechanics and nuclear weapons design and policy

COSMIC SELF-AWARENESS

The universe is permeated with awareness. The whole universe arises out of consciousness. Materialists believe and maintain that the material universe gives rise to consciousness—such as the consciousness within a human being that they say arises within the brain. They have not yet been able to prove this using the methodologies and scientific processes they are so fond of, but scientists are trying pretty hard to do so. Using my own process of self-analysis and observation, the assertion that consciousness is a product of the brain is not how I experience it, and I understand this is also not the experience of many people—often mystics and sages—who have explored their inner nature throughout the ages. The brain arises within a localised field of consciousness that one might recognise as "I." The brain and the rest of the human body have manifested in an intelligent and organised fashion out of this field of consciousness. It is that field of consciousness with which the DNA in the developing zygote and the resulting foetus in the womb is attuned. Through this relationship of resonance, the field of consciousness determines what portions of the code within the DNA are exposed and thus available for amino-acid synthesis. Thus a heart cell developed into a heart and not a liver because of the intelligence—the in-form-ation—transferred to it by the field of consciousness manifesting as Man. A heart arises where it does, just as a liver arises where it does, just as a brain and nervous system arises where it does, all in accordance with the originative field of consciousness in which it arose. This is literally a marriage between spirit and matter. Matter—the mother—is literally inspired or inspirited into giving rise to the many forms of life within this great orb we call Earth.

Human beings are a great mystery, and I think two of the greatest mysteries of the Human being are awareness and perception. It is through the human being—although I am not suggesting it's limited to this particular form—the universe gains self-awareness. You and I are quite literally the (re)turning point on which the universe—on which Infinity or "God" if you like—is turning back to face itself, and through doing so Cosmic Self-Awareness arises. You and I exist on the cutting edge of the consciousness of the Supreme Source, and it is an act of intelligence that brought this about.

Humanity and this world and the Earth through which this world arises are not mistakes. They are not the result of some error of a cosmic scale or a fall from the heavens as many religious and esoteric schools of thought often suggest. I find this to be an immature perspective on reality that I feel only arises from an ego-self which has not yet evolved to a point of inclusivity toward all Life—a human ego-self hypnotised by the perceptual illusion of multiplicity. Only if I live under the illusion of separation will I believe and maintain that the human experience and this physical universe in which we exist is some form of mistake that has separated out from God, Infinity, or the Totality. All is arising from the ineffable Supreme Source, and all has already *returned* to that source.

That which is playing out through the human experience is perfect. It is whole, beautiful (filled with beauty), and of Divine origin. It is the result of an immense and rich intelligence ordinary man is not yet able to fathom—not for lack of the capacity to do so, but simply the lack of readiness. Right now, more than ever before, humanity is faced with an extraordinary opportunity to take a quantum leap in consciousness. Such a leap is required in order for us to step into a more complete experience of the love and perfection that we are. This leap is in fact already occurring, and it is correct to say it has already taken place. Whatever happens, and however the events of the next decade or so play out, I assure you it is all intelligently and divinely orchestrated. This intelligent universe knows no error.

The "I" of Infinity

Throughout this book I have endeavoured to portray a perspective of the human ego and the "I" within Man and Woman that does away with the concept that the ego is a problem; a mistake; a negative attribute we must do away with; a fragment of the human psyche we must fix; and any of the many other ways in which I see the ego talked about and defined. Even when people suggest these very ideas—be they "enlightened" or not—there is an awareness of an "I" there when they do so. It may be a very impersonal sense of "I," but there is an "I" none-the-less.

It is as Alan Watts used to say and ask, "Who is it that knows there is no ego?" Who it is that knows there is no ego is in my experience a transformed sense of the same "I" that was previously experienced as the limited and immature human ego that has in effect gone. Not gone in the sense of destroyed, but gone in the way a seed disappears when it germinates into a seedling; and the seedling disappears when it develops into a plant. Enlightenment is not a process of eradicating this thing we call an "ego," rather it is the natural unfolding of the limited human awareness of ego-self into a experience of a more complete awareness of the Cosmic "I"—the "I" of Infinity. The whole notion of the ego—the "I" of our Being—as some kind of fault or error is dualistic and schizophrenic in nature.

As we each move into a greater experience of the intelligence and the genius within ourselves we will discover that the "I" within us is the "I" of Infinity, and this too is the "I" of Intelligence. As I have said time and again, the human being is a great mystery. It is a mystery that cannot be solved from within the mystery; it cannot be solved in a rational way. A very important aspect of this mystery is the awareness of "I" each human being has within. In trying to do away with this "I," to split away from it, is pure folly that only serves to take that individual further away from what it means to be alive, what it means to be Human, and what it means to Be.

LOVE AND TRUTH

We exist in a wholly (holy) intelligent universe. Within the human experience, the highest form or expression of intelligence is Love. True Love is in total accordance or congruency with Reality. Fear, on the other hand, would have to be one of the lowest forms of intelligence, insofar as fear is an absence of love[1]. Love, therefore, empowers and uplifts, whilst fear disempowers and drags down. Love is life-giving; fear is life-taking. Love, and the mastery of love, is the most direct (and really the only) way through and out of suffering and illusion. Fear is love mis-qualified through a lack of attunement to reality.

Love and Truth are one and the same. Truth is an expression of and the adherence to Love. Love is an expression of and adherence to Truth. Truth is that which is in accordance with reality. That which is in accordance with Love is Truth. In the dictionary one definition of truth is "conformity to reality or actuality." As Love is the highest reality, this suggests to me that Truth is the conformity to Love—for as already mentioned, everything is an expression of, and is permeated by, Love. What this implies is that reality is loving in nature. This means you and I are always loved—we always are love. It makes me smile to think that once upon a time I used to look for love "out there" somewhere—usually in girlfriends, parents, and people I liked.

From one perspective disease, pain, and suffering are the consequence of diverging away from love, away from the truth of your Being. Because you and I are love, it is accurate to say the degree to which I experience pain is the degree to which I have diverged from re-cognition of my Authentic Self. This brings us back to what was described near the beginning of this book—I make life-taking choices only in the areas of my world (or my Kingdom) where I have forgotten my true nature—where I am asleep to the reality of who and what I Am. The consequence of a life-taking choice boils down to an experience of pain. This may be anything from slight divergences away from experiencing absolute Inner Peace right through to massive physical, physiological, and/or emotional pain. The purpose of the pain is to grab your attention—to break its connection with what you have had

---

1 More accurately, although still in very simple terms, fear is a misqualification of love. We won't explore that here for the sake of brevity.

it habitually fixated on—to realign your awareness with Universal Intention, and provide a means to re-cognise the reality of That which "I Am"—namely Love. Of course, pain is not our only avenue to awakening. We can *consciously* walk a Path of Freedom, a path with heart, and awaken through the bliss, joy, and excitement of consciousness rather than the pain of unconsciousness.

Every day I see that more of the world is choosing to wake up in this way rather than the painful way of the past. More and more we are graduating from the school of hard knocks to the school of Reality consciousness. As mentioned above, the apparent absence of physical health can also typically be defined as the result of diverging from Love and the reality of myself as love. So dis-ease is what results from a lack of intelligence—a divergence from Love—and it is the Body-mind's way of restoring balance. I have said a "loss of intelligence" and yet I would like us to go deeper into this and see it from another perspective. You see it is also accurate—in fact more accurate—to say that a greater degree of intelligence is being called into being. If my liver is breaking down due to my abusing it through excess anger and alcoholism it appears that the intelligence of my liver is being compromised, when we view the liver and even the human being as something separate and apart from all-that-is. In reality the human being is not something separate and apart from all-that-is, and thus in reality the liver breaking down (as the case may be in this example) is in fact a push from the unknown for an increase in intelligence within and through that apparent individual. A higher expression of Life, a greater expression of intelligence, is emerging from the unknown into that person's *known*.

Continuing with this example of a failing liver, and entirely from the perspective of the liver: When my liver is able to maintain homeostasis (balance) and is functioning in accordance with the loving intention that has brought my body into being, then it is acting intelligently. If my liver fails to act intelligently, I may experience disease of the liver—a lack of ease within the liver. An important point to remember here is not to take disease personally and definitely not to get into a guilt trip over it. I have found there's nothing to be gained by judging myself for my experience. Instead, may we all celebrate our magnificence as we awaken to Totality within us.

Now, a liver-benefiting herb, such as milk thistle (Silybum marianum), is also the manifestation of a particular quality or expression of intelligence. This herb is an expression of an intelligence that is closely related (similarly configured) to the intelligence—to the original intent—embodied by the liver when it is healthy. I can therefore take that herb into my body in order to restore this intelligence within the liver—but only if I am open to the new awareness of myself that milk thistle will help awaken within my consciousness. Milk thistle is great for helping protect the liver and also for helping the liver to regenerate. If healing takes place, then it could be said that my liver (and my body) and the milk thistle have intelligently co-operated—an act of love. If a healer or herbalist was involved in my decision to take a particular herb for a particular state of dis-ease, then she too has imparted her intelligence—her healing wisdom—to me. The healer and I have conspired to engage in an act of *intelligent co-operation*.[2] This brings me to the next point I'd like to share with you in this chapter.

Intelligent Co-Operation

Love, as expressed and experienced here in the human world, at the most pragmatic level is expressed as **intelligent co-operation**. For a man and woman (or any two people) to be in a loving relationship, they must co-operate intelligently for the relationship to be a mutually joyful, empowering, and life-giving one. This is akin to the intelligent co-operation that takes place when a few doses of milk thistle extract help restore the wisdom/health/integrity/intention/reality of my liver.

I cannot co-operate intelligently with that which I judge, fear, condemn, envy, despise, or wish to manipulate and control. All of these mental conditions lead only to the perception—and thus the experience—of separation. Separation obscures the "co" in co-operation, and as separation does not exist in reality, it is also not an expres-

---

2   I must add that this is a very basic exploration of this topic. I trust it is enough to provide many clues as to the nature and purpose of disease, healing, and the agents of healing. If health and healing is a topic of particular interest to you please let me know via email or my website. I may eventually write a small book that explores this field in greater depth if the interest is there.

sion of intelligence—rather it is the result of ignorance. Therefore I cannot love or be loved by that which I judge or go into relationship with from a mind-set of separation.

I am certain all people wish to experience more love in their lives. We all would like to know how to be more loving—both toward ourselves and other people. Some people perhaps don't realise this is what they are seeking, but I think they seek it nonetheless. They feel the pain inherent to a state of not loving, yet they do not understand what it means to love. Bringing it back to the understanding of its being about intelligent co-operation can make it a great deal easier to put into practice.

The implication of what we have just explored is the more I intelligently co-operate with the people and things I have a relationship with, the more love I experience and the more Inner Peace and Power I resurrect within my world. The more Present I am to the relationships I have, the more those relationships will flourish. The first step is to intelligently co-operate with your Self and with the Intentionality that is driving that Self into Being here in this world. The next step is to extend that intelligent self-co-operation into all your relations. Self-co-operation may sound like a contradiction of terms. Where is the "co" in "self?" Remember that from one perspective we are made up of three distinct spheres of consciousness or "selves." So cooperation in this regard is the cooperation between the body-mind, attentive-mind, and spirit-mind—and the cooperation between that total human self and Infinity.

The art of intelligent co-operation is embodied in what I refer to as Empowered Relatedness, and it is a topic I will elucidate more fully in Volume III of this series of books. In my experience human relationship—and in fact all forms of relationship a human being can create and experience—is a significant aspect of our awakening and freedom. With the world being such a complete and profound mirror to us as human beings, there is really no limit to what I can learn about myself through my interaction with that world, and especially with other human beings. The keys are an open heart and the humility to surrender into deeper awareness of that which is being revealed moment to moment through my relationship with all the people in my life—with all my relations.

With these simple keys our awakening is right here and now...not just as a possibility but as an unavoidable inevitability. An intelligent universe would have it no other way!

THE BOOK OF LIFE

I've often heard people jokingly talk about how "God didn't give us an instruction manual when we were born," and other remarks to that effect. Some say it is as though we were put into a spaceship—spaceship Earth—without a flight and operations manual. We have to blindly fumble around and try to figure out what's what—at a material level and eventually at a spiritual level. When a human being starts to awaken to the spiritual nature of reality they may develop an interest in religion or some other form of spiritual teachings and path. Following the line of thought just touched on, I can see how in a way most spiritual traditions provide—and often even openly claim to provide—the average person with the instruction manual he or she previously lacked. Whether it is the Holy Koran, the Bhagavad-Gita, the Holy Bible, or some other spiritual text, the person now has what might be referred to as a spiritual instruction manual, and also an instruction manual for how to live a "good" life.

I've looked into a wide variety of the many religions in this world, both common ones and not so common ones. I've also delved into a wide range of spiritual texts and teachings. Yet I've not come across any religion[3] and only relatively few spiritual texts that I consider to provide that proverbial "instruction manual" for life in a form that is in accordance with a Path of Freedom. The vast majority of spiritual teachings I am familiar with all inevitably establish a way of approaching life that is inherently based on separation as a truth. They establish and support within the human being a kind of psycho-spiritual split that fractures the holistic and intelligent nature of both the Universe—Life itself—and the human being arising within that Universe. The result is a teaching—an approach to Life—that veils a person's experience of Inner Peace, establishes and/or maintains a life-taking displacement of Power, and ultimately incapacitates that person's ability to be

---

3   Here I am referring to religions as they are commonly taught, in their contemporary form. Many of the religions I have looked into do appear to me to have a core essential understanding that is typically quite different from the contemporary interpretation of that understanding.

fully Present to what Is right now. For this reason, since I was a child, I've never chosen to take any religion and the majority of spiritual teachings particularly seriously. Consequently my search took me elsewhere. What I discovered through that search was nothing short of miraculous, and has left me in complete awe at the perfect and intelligent nature of Life.

What I've discovered is that it's as if every human being is born not into the world without a book (the instruction manual on how to live a life of Peace, Power, and Presence) but that the world we are born into and experience from moment-to-moment *is* the book. We simply haven't known how to read it, and, not even knowing about the language and ways it uses to communicate with us, we haven't recognised the book of life as a book at all.

THE STORY OF TRUMAN

Imagine, if you will, that a child is born; this child at the age of around two is with his parents far out at sea on a ship. The year is 1721 and they are making a long voyage to a faraway land. Unfortunately misfortune strikes the ship in the form of a massive rocky reef whilst the ship is sailing past some uncharted islands. The ship is severely damaged and eventually breaks apart and sinks. Sometime later the young boy serendipitously washes up on an island in a little wooden crib, with his head resting on a rather hard and rectangular pillow. You see, when his parents put him into the crib as the ship was going down, they wanted to try and ensure their child—if he survived this ordeal—would grow up with access to all the keys necessary to know about life and about himself, to better understand who he is. His parents were people of Knowledge, and they wanted to maximise the chances of their child also growing into a man of Knowledge. They had grabbed one particular book from their cabin—a book his Father had in fact written himself—that contained all the key information about Life, the human spirit, and about where the child was from; they wrapped it in a large cloth and made it into a kind of makeshift pillow. Carefully the Father propped the child's head up on the pillow whilst his Mother tied him safely into the crib with some ropes she took from off their luggage. When finished they floated their child out to sea. On the side of his crib is carved the child's name in large letters; a word they are still just able to make out and read as the ship jolts and finally sinks to its new place of rest taking them with it. The child's name is Truman.

Truman eventually washes up on an island, as children do in stories such as these, and miraculously he, the crib, and the book have survived the unknown period of time they spent floating across the vast ocean—the deep unknown abyss that now lies between him and his loving parents and that will surround him in every direction for the rest of his life. Fortunately this island is lush with everything Truman might require for his survival. It has trees laden with fruits to eat, springs of fresh water to drink from, and warm tropical weather by day and by night. Perhaps most importantly of all, shortly after his arrival Truman is discovered by a tribe of people living peacefully in the forests, and these people take him in as one of their own. This is a race of people who have had no contact with the modern world, and whilst they can speak they have not yet developed or even considered the notion of reading and writing.

About 7 years after his arrival on the island Truman's new family makes preparations for a day trip. As they each pack some dried fruits and skins filled with water onto their backs, Truman detects an air of seriousness and importance to what is about to unfold. This feeling persists as they walk mostly in silence for many hours until eventually they arrive at a beach. Truman does not recall having ever been to this beach before, although in some strange way it does feel vaguely familiar. His family explains to him that this is where he came from, that this is where they first found him, and not only him but a few other things. One of his family members, who he had previously noticed disappearing into a cave in the cliffs, returns to where they have gathered and presents Truman with what looks like a little wooden boat. Inside the boat are some ropes and some kind of a substance that feels incredibly soft yet also very strong—he's not seen fabric since arriving on this island. When he picks up this soft bundle he of course finds the book. Truman has no idea what this object is as he curiously strokes the cover, feeling as he does so the distinct markings embossed into the leather in which it is bound. As to what this is, his family of course has no better idea than he does. He opens it and touches the pages with his fingers, and notes all the little black lines, dots, and squiggles that are like much smaller versions of the markings on the front. Except that there aren't just a few of these shapes inside the object, but thousands and thousands of them. He does not know about numbers and how to count, so to him it simply looks like a near infinite array of these strange little markings. The markings inside the book don't look or feel nearly as impressive as the ones embossed on the front though, with their shiny golden colour, larger size, and distinctive raised feeling under his touch. He follows their lines with his hands outlining these shapes, "T H E B O O K O F L I F E."

Truman keeps this heavy book and his crib, which he notices also has a few markings on the side that look like the shapes T R U M A N. Of course these people do not call it a book as such; they have their own name for it and that name changes over time depending on how it is being used, but these are not words I can represent in English so I'll just refer to it as a book. Over the following years Truman tries using this book for many different purposes. He uses it to prop other objects up with, to sit on, to rest his head on, to etch markings on with bits of charcoal; he removes pages and wraps things with them; he finds he can also soak the removed pages in water and they can then be stuck onto things where they will magically remain even once they've dried. On many occasions he even tries wiping himself with a page or two after he empties his bowels, and blowing his nose when it is runny. He also discovers that the pages are particularly good for burning and for taking a flame from the main village fire to somewhere else where he wants to light one.

On more than one occasion when someone annoys Truman, he uses the book to wallop them on the head with, which is particularly effective at knocking them unconscious for a while, or at least sending them running. Over time this leads to the discovery that he can wrap the book up in the material it was first found in, and then securely tie this together with the ropes he'd found in the little boat. Truman figures out this contraption is really good for swinging around at high speed and that in this way it makes an even more effective tool for hitting people over the head with and knocking them unconscious. Whenever Truman doesn't get his way with someone he simply wallops them with his swinging book bundle. This gives him a sense of control in his world and in his relationships with the islanders.

Truman's tribe is not used to weapons, and now that he has one, he soon gets himself into all manner of trouble. He also quickly rises to a position of power because people are afraid of him. After a while many of the tribe's men are not happy about this, and following Truman's example, they fashion ropes of their own out of plant fibres and they secure these onto hand-sized rocks. They too now have weapons with which to wallop people and Truman's stint at being the all-powerful leader soon comes to an end. Fighting and quarrelling was not previously commonplace among the villagers—not before Truman started wielding his book with such speed and accuracy. Over time the islanders fall out of feeling as happy and as at Peace—which had been their natural state for as far back in time as the tribe could remember. Conflict, pain, unhappiness, and violence are so new to this tribe that it is almost too late before the wise elders finally recognise and understand what is going on and where this will lead.

The elders call a meeting with the whole tribe—about 220 people in all—and they ask Truman to give them his book. They explain that this book has caused more problems than they care to remember and that it must be returned to the cave at the beach where Truman was first found. Everyone, including Truman, agree this is a good idea, so that is what they do. Not that this makes them any happier, but it certainly prevents the tribe from experiencing further decline.

Many years come to pass and not long after Truman first begins to notice grey hairs appearing on his head and in his beard, something very significant is unfolding unbeknownst to him and the other islanders. Far from their village a ship arrives and anchors out to sea near the island, and from that ship rows a small boat of explorers. Both the ship and the small row boat have the symbols "H.M.S. DISCOVERY" carved into their stern. The explorers land on the island and begin to explore—that is, after all, what explorers do. One of the first things they investigate is a cave at the base of the cliffs because they know caves are places where humans tend to store things and create paintings, and where they take shelter and make fires. There are, however, no paintings in this particular cave. Much to their disappointment there are also no remnants of past fires or any signs of past or present habitation for that matter. The explorers are making their way back out to the daylight to search further afield when the man who is deepest into the cave shouts out loud, exclaiming his discovery of something most certainly man-made.

Laid out on the large oak desk in the captain's study, it barely resembles the book a small child's head had once rested on far out at sea all those years before, and since it was last held by its authors hands this book is now short of well over half of the many pages it had once contained. What is more, those pages lucky enough to have survived are tattered, torn, and dirty. Despite the book's rough condition the ship's captain, after carefully cleaning and studying the book over many days in his cabin, is able to make out and read a great deal of what it contains. He is, shall we say, no less than completely amazed at the message before him. Here is a discourse on Life and the human self so rich in meaning, so intelligent in its composition, and so profound in its implications that reading it awakens in him an immediate and timeless state of consciousness where he recognises the oneness of all life. The captain awakes to a new awareness of Reality as if all his life he'd been in a half sleep without knowing it.

He knows in that moment he must find the people who put this book into the cave, or at least their descendents. He is certain that for a people to place such a book deep in the back of a cave they must have *fully* realised and understood all that was contained within it. If the author is not alive then perhaps he'll be fortunate enough to find one of the author's enlightened descendants to whom he can express his thanks. He thinks from the book's condition that it has certainly been thoroughly studied over the course of perhaps many hundreds of years. He says to himself, "I must find the race of people on this island who surely reached such a place of collective understanding and enlightenment that a book such as this had no further value and was merely cast into the back of a cave."

The captain and his crew waste no time setting off into the interior of the island and it is not long before they discover the islanders. What they find, however, makes it starkly apparent to the captain that these are not the people he is looking for. He recognises these people as a race related to those they'd spent many months with on another island in this region, not more than a year earlier. Yet somehow their demeanour is different. Unlike what he had witnessed on the other island, here there is not a smile to be seen on any one of their faces and they are often unfriendly toward one another. They are especially unfriendly toward the captain and his crew, as if they had learnt to distrust outsiders. On the other island they had been welcomed, for the people there had no past experience of foreigners and had no reason to distrust them. Pondering the situation, the captain figures they must seek deeper into the interior of the island, that there must be another race or group of people here somewhere from whom this book had been produced. He asks the islanders who else they share this island with. With a look of surprise they explain this is their island; no other people live here.

It is at about this time the captain recognises one man who looks different from everyone else, from everyone but the captain and his crew that is. For although his skin has gone a dark leathery brown from a lifetime of exposure to the sun and the elements, Truman is quite obviously not of the same race as the other members of this tribe. The sailors can see that Truman is one of their own kind, or some race very similar to their own. The captain converses with Truman in the language of the tribe, and it is eventually revealed that Truman arrived here in a tiny little boat.

The captain was not prepared for what happened next. As he pulls the book out from his leather knapsack the islanders jump back in fear; some of them run and hide in the bushes. Truman, however, stands there motionless for a while whilst he watches the book emerge in its entirety. During this brief moment he realises he still doesn't know what this object is, and that he'd discovered a great deal of things he could use this object for but it really wasn't particularly suited to any of them. Even swinging it on a rope and clouting people over the head with it proved to be less effectual than using a rock on the end of a rope. Breaking Truman's mental wandering, the captain asks if they know who the creator of this object is or where it had come from.

"That *thing* is mine" says Truman. "It is nothing but trouble, quite useless, and it created a lot of struggle in my life. It helped me rise to power within the tribe, and it also brought me down, taking the tribe down with me." With surprise, the captain asks if he knows where he came from and if he knows how to read the language from that place... from his source. Truman, sadly, does not as he only learnt how to say his name and a few words with which to identify his all–but-forgotten parents. Now, it is in this moment the captain becomes lucidly aware, aware that what has just unfolded is a very important lesson. Thinking out loud, he says to his companions, "This village has had in its midst a book containing the greatest wisdom I have ever seen, and yet they not only have no idea how to approach the wisdom within this book, they actually don't even know what a book is. Such intelligence right there in front of them yet without their recognising it as such, it brought about an experience of nothing but pain and struggle." The captain smiles as he ponders this thought and he reflects on how this reminds him of something from his own life—his life before he found and read this book.

✺ ✺ ✺

So Truman and his island friends had in their possession all that was required to awaken their consciousness to the highest states of Cosmic Awareness, to open them to the most profound of human and spiritual mysteries—they had all but one important thing. The only thing they were lacking was the simple understanding of how to approach what was there in front of them in such a way that it would reveal to them its almighty intelligence and compassionate wisdom.

We truly do live in an intelligent universe, and one of the most significant implications of this intelligence is that it makes no mistakes. Therefore we as human beings are not simply drifting through time and space destined to struggle and suffer through an onslaught of things that appear to happen to us, and for no apparent reason. Rather we have at all times around us—what I've called your Personal Dream Configuration—exactly what is required to awaken our awareness to profound Inner Peace, Power, and Presence. The spiritual traditions of the past have tried to teach people how to live their lives; to teach them what is right and what is wrong; and to give them some form of cosmology that is comprehensible to the peoples' level of thinking at that time. I have no doubt this served a life-giving purpose, and I also have no doubt that purpose is now a thing of the past, and we must now learn not about the specifics of *how* to live but about ways to approach the life we are already living.

"The whole history of science has been the gradual realisation that events do not happen in an arbitrary manner but that they reflect a certain underlying order, which may or may not be divinely inspired."

Stephen W. Hawking

Empowering Principles & Perspectives

- You exist in a wholly intelligent Universe. This intelligence permeates all-that-is, including you—all of you.

- The Universe is permeated with Awareness. Matter arises out of consciousness; not consciousness out of matter.

- The human ego is not an error to be corrected. It is the seed of the Cosmic "I" within the human being.

- Love and Truth are synonymous.

- We make life-taking / life-negating choices in the areas of our dream where we have forgotten our divine nature.

- We are each born not with a "book of life," but into "the book of life." Life itself—all that we perceive—is in every moment reflecting to us a magnificent story. That is the story of who we are, what we are, and where we come from.

- The challenge is to recognise Life as such and to remember how to "read" it.

- When we approach Life with ignorance of its true nature and function, this brings about pain, dissipates our Power, and obscures Inner Peace.

- When we approach Life with respect and understanding for what it is, Peace, Power, and Presence are unavoidable and immediately realisable.

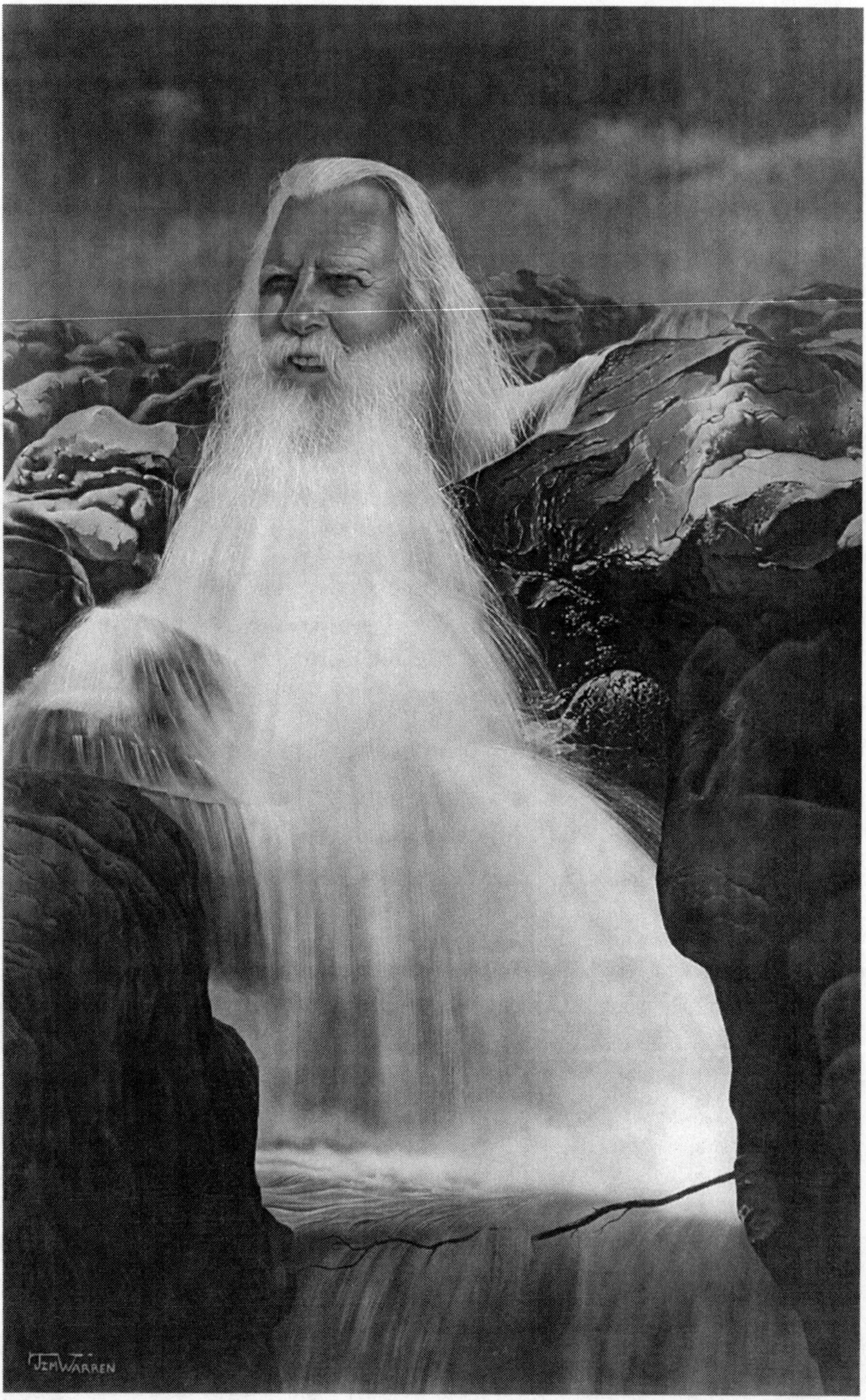
JIM WARREN

Chapter Twenty-One

HEALING PRINCIPLES AND PERSPECTIVES: AN OVERVIEW

"The aim of life is self-development. To realise one's nature perfectly—that is what each of us is here for."
Oscar Wilde
Irish dramatist, novelist, & poet (1854 - 1900)

This story is soon coming to a close, and yet in its own peculiar way it will never close as such, for this is a story born from the womb of Infinity, a story that is forever open, new, and endless. One way or another this story—laid out here before in the pages of this book—is also now a part of you and your story. Whether you reject or accept it, this story is now part of the illusive mystery that constitutes what you identify as yourself. Just as you are without conclusion, this is a story without conclusion, for it is a story about the evolution of awareness...the impersonal Awareness of what some call God, and the seemingly personal awareness of you the reader and me the writer.

Is this a true story? Is it true for you? What I can say is that the content within these pages is a true account of how I experience reality—a true account of a little of what I have discovered and realised in my time here within the eartH|Heart. It is a true account of some of what I was birthed into this world to share and impart because that is what was called for.

You may discover now, or sometime in the future, or perhaps you realised this already, that this is also an account of a deeper reality that is in part or in whole true within you, a deep knowing you consciously or unconsciously feel and experience in your sojourn with Life through Earth, through the Heart. My own feeling on this is that you and I share something at some intangible level that we may perhaps struggle to put our finger on exactly, yet which if we were to meet in person we'd most certainly feel and notice—and perhaps in reading what I've shared you already feel this connection now. It's not necessarily a direct connection between *you* and *me* as such, but rather that you and I are both connected to the same some*thing* at the more profound levels—if not all levels—of our magnificent beings.

Many people believe fact and fiction are mutually exclusive and separate from one another. In the culture I was raised in we speak of fact and fiction in this way, one being the product of the imagination—fanciful and unreal—and the other being an account of direct observation and discernment of that which is *real* and *actual*. I am going to suggest that fact and fiction are actually mutually inclusive of one another—not wholly mutual, however, as one is a subset of the other. That which we refer to as fact is a subset of that much vaster field of possibility we call fiction. Fact is born from fiction. The known arises from the unknown; the unknown arises from the unknowable. The form side of Life we experience from day-to-day arises from Life's formlessness. The form arises from the void, and returns thusly to the void. Not an empty sterile void but a potent vacuity devoid of matter and form, yet wholly and entirely rich in Power and potential and creative possibility. Such is the beauty and magnificence of That which we are in essence. All that arises into the known—into the form side of Life—must first pass through the imagination. First the imagination of the Dreamer and then through the imagination of Man.

Shared within this book is a Way. A Way of approaching reality that I have discovered within my own life and, through self-application, has proven its efficiency in waking up the Human self to greater freedom, greater Inner Peace, and greater Power. A Way that when embodied and understood takes us **away** from that which is life-taking and toward that this is life-giving at a rate far greater than many other ways so popular in the human world today. A Way through which I have found it possible to clear away my grievances, my judgments, and the causes of suffering in my world. A way to freedom. A way to deep bliss. A way to happiness. A way to awaken that which was unconscious into that which is conscious. I don't claim this to be **my** way in terms of ownership or origin, yet it is my way in terms of what I live and prosper from each moment, each day.

It is my wish that some or all of this Way also integrate into your way, for experience has shown me that if more human beings lived this Way, and approached reality this Way, there would be far more peace on Earth than I see arising from all the other ways many people are commonly living and conducting their lives. I don't perceive fault or error in those ways, for all ways ultimately lead to the same destination, and all ways have their own inherent beauty and magnificence. I offer this Way simply because it has already fulfilled one of the two things I wanted in this life, and in sharing it I trust it will fulfil the other, namely to discover my own innate freedom within the interiority of my Being, and to help all my relations awaken to the same within themselves.

> *"Imagination is more important than knowledge. For while knowledge defines all we currently know and understand, imagination points to all we might yet discover and create."*
>
> Albert Einstein

THE WAY OF NO WAY

This Way I have shared with you—this Way of approaching life and Reality— is in fact the Way of No Way. It is the Path of No Path. I have not offered you a prescription on how to live your life. I have not offered you rules to live by. I've not presented you with an external path to walk along, nor have I offered you external practices to apply and attempt to master. My intention has simply been to draw your attention to the profound, beautiful, and truly magnificent Reality of your own Being. It is my wish that in being attentive to what lies in the depths of your interiority, in the depths of the Self—your True Self—you will discover, on your own accord, The Way. Your Way.

You are the Path of Your Awakening

"However many holy words you read, however many you speak, what good will they do you if you do not act upon them?"

The Buddha

Even if everything you have read within these pages was familiar to you—and I am sure at least some of it has been—the application of it all starts right here and now. This Way is not a journey of progress taking us from point A to B, where one can be ahead or behind. Rather it is a moment-to-moment approach to Life, right now! Actually it is not simply an approach to Life, it is the approach of Life. I am either living it now—aware of that now—or I am not aware of it now. I am either being true to this Way or I am not. I am either conscious and present and aware now or I am not. It is for this reason that in essence no one person is any further ahead than another on this path. We walk it together. We heal together. We celebrate our magnificence together, as one. For this is not a path out there in the world, it is simply the path inherent within the inner depths of what it is to be Human. The late Jiddu Krishnamurti said, "Truth is a pathless land." I agree wholeheartedly with the entire content of the powerful speech in which he made this statement[1], and yet I must elaborate on the use of this word "pathless". Our encounter with reality is pathless in the sense that there can be no prescribed path to get there, and there is in fact nowhere to get to. We must simply arrive to where and what we already are. In this regard I say you are the path. No institution, organisation, teacher, guru, or religion can be the path for you. You are the path of the unfolding reality of your own Divinity, and it is up to you to walk that path in such a way that your truth aligns with reality. This path is an inherent quality of your own essential nature. Where you are unconscious of your essential nature—unconscious of your Divinity—you will experience pain and an absence of Inner Peace. That is all. This is a path with no beginning and no end, yet so long as there is movement—so long as there is life—there is a path along which you can't help but walk, and

---

1 This statement was made in a speech given in 1929 when Krishnamurti announced the dissolution of the Order of the Star—the organisation that had been built around him by Theosophists who believed him to be the vehicle through which the Christ or Maitreya was returning.

that path exists within the interiority of your own essential nature.

You and I, we are like two legs on the one body, walking side by side, in the spirit of intelligent co-operation as we unveil that which is True and Real about our own essential nature. It's a noble journey, and yet utterly humbling. When I use the word humble I am not referring to what this word has come to mean in terms of a lowly or inferior state. The word humble is derived from the Latin word *humilis* which literally means "on the ground," and is derived from *humus* which refers to "earth." For me it means to be with one's feet on the ground, down to earth, and pragmatic—to arrive at what is real.

It is my sincere wish that you make this journey with a knapsack filled with the most valuable of treasures and the most sustaining of foods. There is only so much you can take with you from your excursion through these pages. It is here in this chapter I wish to review with you the most important Principles and Perspectives we have explored together. Some of them I have touched on only briefly, doing them minimal justice really, yet it is my wish that you use what I have given you—in the way of a reminder of what you already know—to further explore the many great treasures awaiting you within your Mind, Being, and Eternal Presence.

- You are not a composite of fragments, part ego, part spiritual being of light, part human, and the like. There is no bad ego to overcome within yourself, just perception shifting and expanding, Peace to express, Power to embrace, Presence to embody.

- You are Divine. That is your True Nature. Every*thing* is Divine for that is the true nature of All.

- As a Divine Being you are whole, complete, and at One with your Creator.

- Therefore, you have no needs, bar one—your only need is that of a Mirror. Even this *need* is being met right now through the mystery called perception, and it is displayed in the world you perceive around you.

- This world is akin to a Dream. It is a construct within the Infinite Mind of your essential and impersonal self...the Dreamer.

- The Dream, like all dreams, is filled with symbols, archetypes, morals, and lessons. Therefore this Dream provides you with the perfect mirror—exquisitely reflecting to you the content of your Mind.

- Our purpose in this Dream is to master our own expression of Authentic Power, from a state of Inner Peace. The more consciously and lucidly we Dream, the more our Presence here in the world will heal all our relations. That is our vocation...our Divine Calling.

- How you go about healing the world and all your relations will be beautifully unique and deeply inspired—it will manifest as the most wondrous expression and extension of the Real You, the Dreamer.

- You can only lose that which is not real. Therefore hang on to no*thing* and embrace all *things*. Most of all, embrace the unknown, that which is beyond the level of thinking that turns the totality of Life into separate things.

- You are a circle—whole and complete. Not a set of dots or points along the line making up that circle.

- You can attack, oppose, and conquer only that which is not real. Therefore create and support that which is real, rather than opposing that which is not real.

- Belief is only required for that which is not real. That which is real is directly recognised and it works.

- Responsibility follows consequence. I am responsible for that which I experience, for all that I experience is the result of the choices I am making right now. Own the consequences of your actions that affect you. Shift your perception to the degree made possible by your capacity to respond in this moment.

- Realise there is only One. Ultimately all *things* are of consequence to me to some degree, so ultimately I am responsible for it all to some degree. Don't take this statement personally. Don't make it a burden. Sit with it.

- There is no "right" or "wrong." There is no "good" or "bad." All dualities are written into your personal Lore (your List Of

Rules in Error). There is only that which is life-giving and that which is life-taking. As both are an expression of Life, fulfilling the purpose of That Life, all is ultimately life-giving.

- Love is the most powerful force in Creation. When you give up your personal Lore you will discover your innate virtues. Living according to your virtues and not the rules established by a limited sense of self will move you into living in Love.

- Authentic Power is silent, it is invisible, and it extends out into your world from the core of your Being.

- To find your Authentic Power you only have to look and be aware within your interiority. If I don't look within, then I will go without.

- There is only One Power... and That I AM

❈   ❈   ❈

As you reach out to return the King's worn notebook to a small gap you've spotted on the shelf between the many other books you keep there, a loose piece of paper falls to the ground. Picking it up, you cast your eye to the last few pages of his well-worn notebook. You had not looked at the end of the book until now, for his notes finished only part way through.

You find another loose piece of paper tucked between the last few pages of the King's notebook, the same in appearance to the first. You sense the peculiarity of not having noticed these pages before, and wonder upon the fact they hadn't fallen out until now. Hmm...yes, well, putting that thought aside...with a smile of eager anticipation you sit with these two pages, feeling somehow so precious, and read them to yourself...

With harmony restored and my memoirs in good hands, the Queen and I both felt strongly called to the mountains. Since the resurrection of our Kingdom we had walked in those parts of our realm on numerous occasions, as they were always a source of inspiration for us, providing the perfect environment for re-creation activities. In fact we made our way there quite regularly after the challenge with the dragon. Yet...we both felt this journey would be our last. Taking nothing but a small knapsack that held a copy of our joint memoirs and a little water for the hike, we set off to the far North. We passed by the pomegranate tree and took with us one of its fruit as we entered the foothills. We chose the river as our path, feeling drawn to find the spring from which it ultimately must pour forth.

The journey was long, yet not as hard as one might think. The love between us was always a source of great strength, and was even more so in the presence of these mystical mountains. Many days and nights were spent ascending, enjoying the ever-expanding view of our realm by day, and watching in awe the wondrous starry sky by night.

✦ ✦ ✦

The Top of the Mountain

This entry I feel is my last.

I sit here at the source of the great river that has been the life-blood of my Kingdom and our realm for what seems like eternity, yet also just a flash of time within infinity....

Hungry from our climb, the Queen and I each took a handful of seeds from the pomegranate, and enjoyed their sweet juices. As we looked into each other's eyes I felt as if a veil—not noticed until now—was being lifted from my eyes and cleared out from my mind. I cannot find words to express it...

...a smile on her face and wonderment in her eyes, she too was feeling what I could see.

In that eternal yet brief moment—Here, Now—it all became so clear...yet...to write...what words to express it...?

The dragon...an ally...the seeds...?

Intention...it was all the intention...Infinity...

These mountains...the world...?

The dragon's lies...?

None of it...?

Yet...it all seemed so...so real...so very real...

Not even this...?

...just a Dream...Creation...?

A Dream...Lucidity...Balance...Awareness...ah...

...Yes...That...yes...

...I Am...

All of it...a Dream...dreaming,

Forever Expanding Awareness...in...

... in Liberation

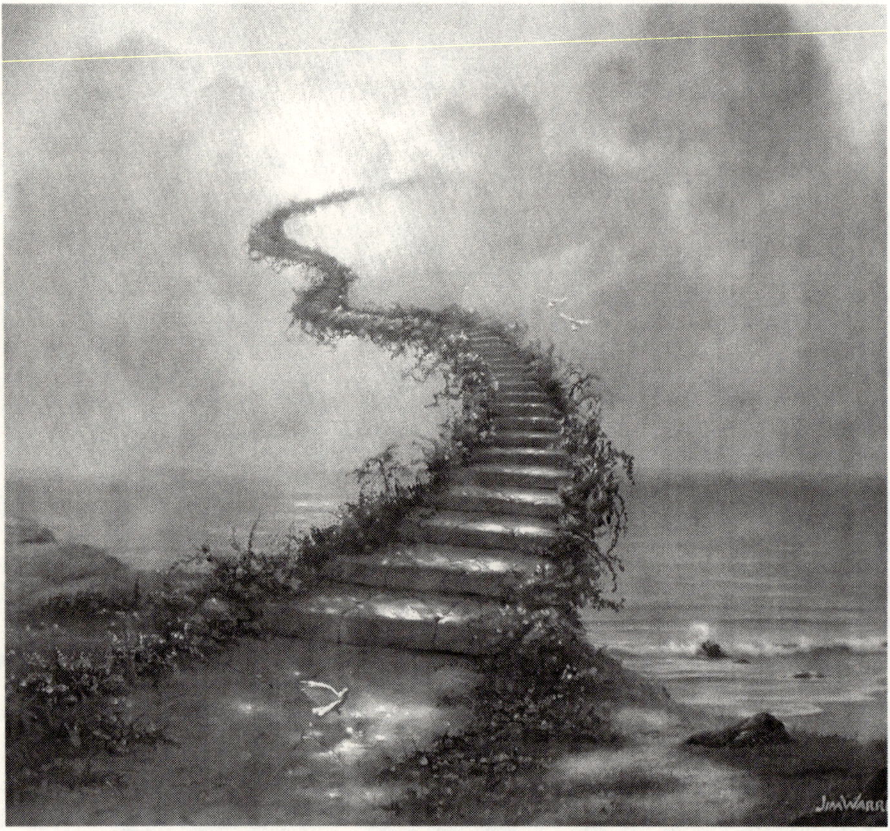

Ωmega

FROM NOW TO INFINITY

"Just as the highest and the lowest notes are equally inaudible, so perhaps, is the greatest sense and the greatest nonsense equally unintelligible."
Alan Watts

I give thanks that this story is now complete in your world and in mine. It is a wonderful gift that that you have journeyed with me this far. Your Presence brought you from the Alpha point on page one to this Omega point, in perfect accord with your Path of Freedom and in alignment with your Power inspiring itself into Being. This is all in accordance with the Intent directing your life.

Together we have walked with courage and with an unwavering Love of the Truth. May you take from these pages all that in your experience is life-affirming, supportive, and truly reflective of the magnificence of That which You Are. May you leave the rest behind and give thanks for that which has been received.

Know now that you are the One you have been looking for. You are the authority you've been seeking to look up to, to aspire to, to learn from, and to be led by. Know that the time to take the next step is now. Know now that you are the saviour you knowingly or unknowingly seek in the Enlightened Beings, the leaders, and the heroes and heroines of this world. You are the one you've been waiting for. Your only challenge is to re-cognise All that You Are…and in Truth it is now so.

I bless you on your travels hereafter; from Now to Infinity…. May we rejoice and rejoin within Volume II in this series of books...an exploration of *The Seven Empowerments*.

Jonathan Evatt
www.jonathanevatt.com

ABOUT THE AUTHOR

Jonathan Evatt was born and grew up in The Land of the Long White Cloud—Aotearoa / New Zealand. He is a contemporary yogi, mystic, mentor, and spiritual pragmatist. He has been exploring, testing, and applying a wide array of spiritual, scientific, philosophical, aboriginal, and Inner knowledge since childhood.

He lives with one Intention that has been with him ever since he first began to seriously consider, "What is it I wish to do in this world?" He was 13 and deciding what subjects he might study at school. None of the subjects that were offered, and no career path he was aware of in society elicited any sense of passion within him. All he felt was the intention to realise, live, and express the power and reality of Love, as made known to him through the unfolding Awareness within his own consciousness. So this is what he did.

This intention expresses itself in two ways, firstly to be free—to be liberated from the many bonds and illusions that would otherwise bring about suffering and the absence of true Love—and secondly to help people awaken to the same realisation within their own lives. With this intent Jonathan lives a Life of Freedom and shares in that freedom with all his relations.

From the age of 13 through 29 Jonathan used much of his time to explore the nature of reality, the nature of freedom, the way the human mind and spirit function, the cause of pain and suffering, and the ways to heal these causes. He has travelled extensively both visiting and living in more than 22 countries on all major continents of the world—meeting and living with a multitude of healers, spiritual masters, spiritual seekers, gurus, yogis, and people gifted with their own unique appreciation and understanding of Love and Reality.

Since his early teens Jonathan knew the writing of this book would unfold, along with the others in this series. It was just a matter of timing, which he felt was not in his hands. Every action taken with impeccability has its perfect moment of expression in time.

That time is now. That perfection is here. May the dance begin....

You can find out more about the work and sharing of Jonathan Evatt on the Internet at
WWW.JONATHANEVATT.COM

Appendix

General references cited

Ho'ala Huna Wisdom, as taught by Lono Ho'ala
Lono and Lani are two wonderful people who live and share a clear and direct understanding of ancient Hawaiin Huna wisdom. They openly share what has proven itself to support people in waking up to their Divine nature. Contact them online if you feel inspired to. I am sure they'll be happy to connect.
On the web at: www.hunawisdom.com

The Mankind Project: *Changing the world one man at a time*
The Mankind Project is doing fantastic work in the field of empowering men from all walks of life to step up and into an experience of the empowered masculine, both in their personal lives and in service to the world.
On the web at: www.mkp.org

The UK Independence Report, by Andrew Simms (New Economics Foundation policy director), Dan Moran, and Peter Chowla
"The UK Interdependence Report: How the world sustains the nation's lifestyles and the price it pays" cites some very interesting information pertaining to our rate of consumption that is unsustainable.
Redirection link: www.inspiredearthpublishing.com/ref-ukindependence

Global Issues (web site), Social, Political, Economic and Environmental Issues That Affect Us All
Here your will find over 550 articles, mostly written by the very dedicated Anup Shah. "The issues discussed range from trade, poverty and globalization, to human rights, geopolitics, the environment, and much more. Spread over these articles, there are over 7,000 links to external articles, web sites, reports and analyses to help provide credence to the arguments made on this web site." (Quoted from his 'about' page). This site is a fantastic source of

information on a wide range of global issues. Anup Shah has done us all a great service in compiling so much information into such a usable web site. Pay him a visit for more info.
On the web at: www.globalissues.org

References cited to books and authors

Biology of Belief, by Dr. Bruce Lipton
This fantastic book presents Dr. Lipton's truly pioneering work in the field of genetics and conscious human evolution. Please make a point of reading this book, and/or attending his lectures, or viewing them on video.
On the web at: www.brucelipton.com

Death by Medicine, By Gary Null, PhD; Carolyn Dean MD, ND; Martin Feldman, MD; Debora Rasio, MD; and Dorothy Smith, PhD
A controversial report showing from official medical data how the medical system may be a major cause of death and disease in America.
On the web at: (search the net for "Death by medicine" to get info)

Molecules of Emotion, by Dr Candace Pert
This book details Dr. Candace Pert's pioneering research on how the chemicals inside our bodies form a dynamic information network, linking mind and body. She offers a great deal of wisdom and insight from a grounded, well researched, and body-conscious approach to reality. Candace Pert, Ph.D., is a Research Professor in the Department of Physiology and Biophysics at Georgetown University Medical Center in Washington.
On the web at: www.candacepert.com

Who am I?, by Ramana Maharshi (a.k.a. Bhagaván Ramana)
"Throughout the history of mankind spiritual giants have appeared on very rare occasions to exemplify the Highest Truth. Guiding followers by their conduct in every moment of their live, Bhagavan Sri Ramana Maharshi was such a giant. Unique in our time, He perfectly embodied the ultimate truth of Self-realisation, or complete absorption in the Supreme Itself" [quote from the website]
On the web at: www.arunachala-ramana.org

References cited to further topical information

Energy Anatomy and Healing
Caroline Myss is an expert in this field. Her work is widely available through her books, lectures, videos, and audiobooks. Discover the wealth of wisdom she has to offer by visiting her website.

On the web at: www.myss.com

Anthroposophical science—Rudolf Steiner
The late Rudolf Steiner was a true innovator and genius in many key areas of human endeavour. Much of the collection of his lectures and books is available freely online.

On the web at: www.rsarchive.org

Energy Healing—Barabara Ann Brennan
Barabara Ann Brennan is an expert in the field of Energy healing. She has established schools in the USA and Europe. She is author of the popular books "Hands of Life," and "Light Emerging."

On the web at: www.barbarabrennan.com

The Sixth Extinction
"As long ago as 1993, Harvard biologist E.O. Wilson estimated that Earth is currently losing something on the order of 30,000 species per year — which breaks down to the even more daunting statistic of some three species per hour. Some biologists have begun to feel that this biodiversity crisis—this "Sixth Extinction"—is even more severe, and more imminent, than Wilson had supposed."

Redirection link: www.inspiredearthpublishing.com/ref-extinction

Gaia Community Online
This is an online community of fantastic people who genuinely want to make a positive difference in the world. I quote the following from the site:

"We're a little different than most social networks. We're here for a purpose—to inspire and empower you to be the change you want to see in the world.

We're a community of individuals committed to supporting each other in being our highest selves. We aspire to live at our greatest potential, seeing the best in others and encouraging them to do the same. We're here to discover our purpose and to contribute our gifts to the planet. We're here to live authentically.

In short, we're here to change the world. Even though we think it's already a pretty amazing place to be."

On the web at: www.gaia.com

Christopher Evatt
Christopher is a pioneer of Inner Leadership for positively transforming businesses and lives. Using his methods, people unlock enormous inner power and capabilities for their sustained well being and for extraordinary accomplishment. He is a highly inspiring speaker and advisor; his ideas are adopted by government departments and multinational companies. From leaders to economists, from educationalists to students, from a world champion ice skating team to those recovering from health challenges, all who work with him gain outstanding benefits from his life tools and deep wisdom. If you want guidance in applying the essential message of Peace, Power, and Presence, whether it be into the business and governmental arenas or in one's personal life, then Christopher Evatt is the one to call on.

On the web at: www.chrisevatt.com

REFERENCES CITED TO OTHER BOOKS BY THE AUTHOR

The Seven Empowerments, **by Jonathan Evatt**
This is Volume II in the Wisdom for a Life of Freedom series. It is due to be published in late 2008 / early 2009. Here the author, Jonathan Evatt, explores the seven primary principles and approaches to reality that have proven themselves to be empowering to the Human Spirit as it awakens from lies, illusions, and deception—the bitter fruits of unsciouisness. The Seven Empowerments builds upon, in a practical way, the knowledge laid down in Peace, Power, and Presence.

On the web at: www.inspiredearthpublishing.com/sevenempowerments

Empowering Relationship, **by Jonathan Evatt** (title subject to change)
In Empowering Relationship, Volume III of the Wisdom for a Life of Freedom series, Jonathan will take you on a journey into the nature and beauty of true relatedness. Recognising that love is, at its most practical level of expression, the art of intelligent co-operation, you will discover how to both empower your relationships and be empowered by your relationships—with yourself, other people, life, and All-That-Is.

On the web at: www.inspiredearthpublishing.com/relationship

Living beyond The Secret, **by Jonathan Evatt**
This is an ebook due for publication in 2009. In this deeply inspired work Jonathan elucidates what he considers to be the missing and oftentimes distorted information pertaining to the Law of Attraction as popularised by the movie The Secret (2006).

On the web at: www.livingthesecret.tv

THE ARTWORK AND THE ARTISTS

As you will have noticed, there is a wonderful selection of exquisite artwork throughout this book. This artwork has been graced upon these pages out of pure kindness and support from the artists involved. To see more of their art—and to see it in splendid full colour which will absolutely delight you—please visit the web sites listed below:

Andrew Forrest
Andrew Forrest is an extremely talented visionary artist and musician whose works reflect a Divine inspiration and love for the great wonders and mysteries of existence. His brilliant use of colour to intensify the viewers reaction to his subjects, has only now become accessible to the public at large after more than ten years in private collections. Andrew can be contacted directly by email at this address: andrewforrest13@hotmail.com
Redirection link: www.inspiredearthpublishing.com/forrest

A. Andrew Gonzolez
Andrew Gonzolez is an award-winning figurative artist whose work has been exhibited in several countries. Influenced by idealism in the mystical, visionary, and esoteric traditions, he describes his work as contemporary Tantric or Transfigurative Art that explores the dramatic union of the sensual & spiritual. His work is akin to a revival of classical neoplatonic ideals centering on the figure as temple & vessel sublimed by transformative forces:
On the web at: www.sublimatrix.com

Jim Warren
Jim Warren is one of the most successful & versatile artists in the world today! From the wild & whimsical to the sweet & sensuous, for over 35 years Jim Warren has been painting his way into the hearts and minds of people the world over. Already considered a "living legend of the art world", Jim continues to surprise and amaze. Is available online at:
On the web at: www.jimwarren.com

Prof. Philip Rubinov Jocobson—Artist, Writer, Philosopher, Teacher
Philip's paintings have been exhibited internationally in more than 90 exhibitions and his writings have been read worldwide. Recognized as a central figure in both the Fantastic and Visionary genres' of art, his versatile works range from a mystical precisionism to an intuitive abstraction. His renowned international painting seminars: "Old Masters-New Visions" were established in 1997.
On the web at: www.rubinovs-lightning.com

Jonathon Earl Bowser

Jonathon's limited-edition prints and collector's plates are now represented by many galleries internationally, and his original paintings are in public and private collections across North America, Europe, and Asia. Jonathon's web site has an excellent selection of his best work, including his unique figurative-landscape paintings that he calls Mythic Naturalism - images looking for the mysterious poetry of which the natural world is made.

On the web at: www.jonathonart.com

LOOKING FOR MORE? THERE'S PLENTY OF IT!

Visit the publisher's web site for links and references to a wide array of inspiring and transformational books, web sites, scientific studies, audio books, and more.

www.inspiredearthpublishing.com/moreinfo

CONNECTING WITH JONATHAN ONLINE

Jonathan has a web site at:

WWW.JONATHANEVATT.COM

You can freely enjoy over 300 pages of articles, along with many blog entries, podcasts, and videocasts.

Sign up to Jonathan's free newsletter for updates and empowering information.

You can listen to recordings of his piano music (played intuitively):
WWW.JONATHANEVATT.COM/MUSIC

A contact form is available on his web site for sending him a message. Feedback and contact with a positive intent is always welcome.

Social Networking Links

Gaia Community:	http://feal.gaia.com
Facebook:	www.jevatt.com/facebook
Online Video (YouTube etc.):	www.jevatt.com/videolink

Index

A Course in Miracles, 292
Assemblage point, 79
Assumption
  about life, 51
  cultural, 308
  of right & wrong, 129
  of separation, 93
  reclaiming attention from, 248
Astral body, 82
ātman, 86
Attention
  as related to Attentive-mind, 86–112
  first, 238, 239, 245, 249
  reclaiming, 183
  second, 238, 239, 245, 249
  third, 238
Awareness, 41, 67, 219
  of defences, 274–277

Balance
  restoring, 366
Baseline state, 133
Basic Self, 82
Belief, 64
  and our dream configuration, 123
  as Personal Lore, 127–135
  cellular attunement to, 84
  freedom from, 77
  healing of, 267–288
  Huna perspective on, 267
  in attack, 271
  in guilt / sin, 271
  in more than one power, 56
  in separation, 55
  not required for reality, 52, 67
Blame
  loss of power via, 269
Body-mind. *See* Tri-part self: Body-mind
Boundaries
  personal, 275
Breathing
  an exercise, 229–231

Capitalism, 312
Castaneda, Carlos
  on self-reflection, 250
Cause and effect, 207–208
Cellular memory
  as aspect of Body-mind, 83
  skeptic's view on, 83
Chakras
  and the life-stream, 368
  as aspect of Body-mind, 85
Challenges
  embracing them, 263–264
Choice
  of experience, 291
Choices
  for you not to you, 272. *See also* Events: for you not to you

Christ, 56
Collective
  awakening, 364
  dream configuration, 75. *See also* Dream: dream configuration
  world views, 153
Collective Consciousness, 67
Conflict
  transforming, 321–322
Consumerism, 306–307
  New Age, 314
Corruption
  human affairs, 158
Culture
  American, 308–311
  blindness, 308–310
  bubble, 309

Defensiveness, 274–277
Denial
  health use of, 59–60
Discernment
  in relation to Attentive-mind, 87
Discontent
  acting from, 227
Disease, 56, 147
  and power, 215
  as punishment, 216
  collective, 216
  collective thought-forms of, 216
  new level of power, 217
  not from outside, 215
  resolution of, 218
Dream, 31, 32, 34, 61, 115
  American, 310–311
  approach to, 137
  lucidity, 128
Dream configuration, 66
  Collective, 75
  Personal, 115–125
    defined, 123
  role of Spirit-mind, 89

Dreamer, The, 64
Duality
  right and wrong, 63
  dissolving, 319

Earth
  connection with Body-mind, 86
Ego. *See also* Ego-self / ego-mind
  and conclusiveness, 318
  and fanaticism, 320
  and forgiveness, 344
  and opposition, 319
  and progress, 338
  and separation, 347. *See also* Separation
  and stillness, 296
  and the dreamer, 111
  anthroposophical view of, 101
  as anti-Christ, 292
  as hydrogen, 101
  as primordial, 102
  as the Christ, 292
  as the sun / son, 102
  confusion about, 94
  deeper mystery of, 88
  definition, 63
  denial of, 45
  error of denying it, 88
  identification with, 88
  in animals, 100
  mistaken identity, 38
Ego-self / ego-mind. *See also* Ego
  as agglomeration of stories, 139
  relationship between, 87
Emotions
  within Body-mind, 83
Energy
  emotional, 142, 146
  emotional, owning it, 263
  in relation to issues, 260
  provided by Body-mind, 85
Enlightenment, 347
  See Path: to enlightenment

Etheric body
  as aspect of Body-mind, 82
Events
  for you not to you, 176, 180, 255, 259, 270–272, 350
  an exercise, 336
Evolution of Awareness, 81. *See also* Purpose
Excuses
  for unhappiness, 232
Exploring
  what is, an exercise, 332
Extinction
  sixth, 303
Extremes
  dissolving, 318–322
  political, 327
  purpose of, 315–316, 322–324

Fanaticism, 319
Feelings
  clarity of, 220
  compared to emotions, 66
  defined, 66
  within Body-mind, 83
Feminine, 154
Forgiveness
  in depth, 344–347
  living it, 349–350

God
  as vengeful, 271
  creative power of, 58
  redefining, 37, 40–43, 61–62
  self as extension of, 37
God Is, 143
Good and bad. *See* Duality: right and wrong
Gossip, 140
Great White Light
  falsity of, 174

Healing. *See also* Medicine: life as and curing, 218
  and humility, 260
  and reality of oneness, 180
  and shadow projection, 184
  as intelligent cooperation, 378–379
  beliefs and perception, 267–288
  of perception, 52
  principles and perspectives, 391–399
  the world, 161
  through forgiveness, 349
  through relationship, 131
Heart
  discernment with, 87
  inclusivity through, 281
  path with. *See* Path: with heart
History
  freedom has no, 140
Homeostasis
  as function of Body-mind, 83
Humility
  and healing, 260
  word definition, 395
Huna
  name of Attentive-mind, 86
  name of Body-mind, 82
  perspective on belief, 267

"I", 35
  am fully responsible, 257
  and Atma, 93
  and the mask it wears, 93
  as Christ Consciousness, 292
  deeper look at, 97
  dreamed experience of, 177
  ego evolving into, 348
  is the same in all beings, 122
  knows no separation, 244
  limited sense of, 93, 273, 284
  of Infinity, 92, 376

power to be aware of, 294
the seed of, 218
I Am Presence, 89
Ignorance
accepting in oneself, 156
Illusion, 32
definition of, 33
Inner Peace. *See also* Peace
and extremes, 316
and opposition, 319
defined, 225–226
Intelligence
definition of, 373
deterioration of in Body-mind, 85
Intention, 47
alignment with, 219
in boundaries, 275
Introspection. *See also* Self-reflection
compared to self-reflection, 232
Invulnerability, 268

Judgment
and loss of power, 214
God's lack of, 62
mistaken denial of, 59–60
releasing, 259
replacing, 146
Jungian psychology
conscious mind, 86
subconsious / unconscious mind, 83
super conscious, 89

Karmic cellular memory. *See* Cellular memory
Katie, Byron, 337
King (the story) [sorted by page #]
Chaos and decline, 353–361
Closure, 397–398
Into the forest, 361–362

Once upon a time..., 162–163
The fall, 164–167
The Resurrection, 364–366
Knowing, 220
Known, 39

Language
English, 78
Lies, 228
about who you are, 75–77
Life
form side of, 137
has no opposite, 65
meaning of, 137
Life-giving, 62
Life-stream
and chakras, 368
fragmented, 268
Life-taking, 62
Lipton, Dr. Bruce, 84
Lono (in Huna), 86
Lore
definition of, 127
experiencing the pain of, 132
exploring, an exercise, 332
in conflict with reality, 132
inheriting, 130
recognition of, 129
regulating our world with. *See* Lore
veil of maya, 134
Lose, 51
Love, 130
as intelligent co-operation, 379–380
call for, 142
false, 131
is your nature, 167
most powerful force, 131
permanence of, 131
stories of, 141
what is, 331–341
Lower self, 82

Malu
  and victim consciousness, 269
  arising of, 192, 268
  as allies, 193, 268
  attraction of, 275
  definition of, 105–107
  in relationships, 142
  not identifying with, 247–248
Mana, 215
  in relation to Body-mind, 82
Mares, Theun
  on third attention, 238
Masculine, 154
Materialism, 312
Matter
  arising of, 374–375
Maya, 32, 34. *See also* Illusion
Meaning
  of life, 137
Media
  American, 309
Medicine
  defined, 256
  life as, 255–265
Memory
  as aspect of Body-mind, 83–84, 84
Middle Self, 86
Mind, 37, 65
  lucidity of, 220
  the nature of, 81
Mirror
  our only need, 111, 214, 295, 395
Moment
  Latin meaning of, 140

Need
  of a mirror. *See* Mirror: our only need
  of something outside self, 294
Needs
  and self-centeredness, 282
  of the ego & the dreamer, 111
New Age
  -ism, 314–315
Now
  living in, 147

Objectivity. *See* Perception: Objectivity
Oneness
  reflection, 252

Pain
  not suffering, 132, 133
  of our personal Lore, 132
  purpose of, 132
  wallowing in, 133
Path
  of enlightenment, 293
  of freedom, 63, 66
    a practical path, 286
    in relation to fanaticism, 320
    in relation to feelings, 66
    in relation to Presence, 295
    in relation to wounds, 39
  with heart, 66
  you are it, 293, 394–395
Patriotism. *See also* Separation: and patriotism
  and Inner Peace, 320
  creates separation, 321
Peace. *See also* Inner Peace
  at your center, 324
  prerequisite for, 133
Perception, 34
  fluidity of, 219
  gift of, 139
  healing of, 52
  objectivity, 176
  of reality, 67
  phenomenon of, 155
  unique, 153
Personal history, 140
Personal Lore, 35

Pert, Dr. Candace, 84
Philosophy
  of reductionism, 80
  skepticism. *See* Skepticism: philosophical
Physical body
  arising from consciousness, 85
  as aspect of Body-mind, 82
Polarization
  with projections, 142
Politics
  hidden agendas, 157
  new way required, 159
Power
  and disease, 215
  authentic, 202
  false, 200, 204–205
  from within, 202, 294
  gaining, 209–211
  losing, 214–215
  only one, 221
  powerlessness, 211–213
  product of perception, 134, 139, 208
  stalking, 273–274
  to take next step, 134
  within the Tri-part self, 218
Presence
  developing, 298
  to what is, 295
Progress
  illusion of, 338–340
Projection, 35
  of the unconscious, 294
  suppressed positive, 185
Purpose
  alignment with, 219
  of life, 47, 137
  of pain, 132
  of the dreamer, 47

Quantum
  field, 91
  field and Mind, 65
  field of information, 89
  glue, 131
  particles, 156
  physics, theories of, 32
  stuff, 152
  time and space, 94

Rational mind
  as aspect of Attentive-mind, 86
Reality
  and truth compared, 67
  creating it, 123
  different experiences of, 57, 79
  false perception of, 137
  mirror nature of, 181, 232, 336, 380
    turning it around, 335
  objective, 155
Relationship
  clearing issues, 261–262
Rules. *See* Lore

Self
  -centeredness, 277–286
  know thy, 283
  limited sense of, 278. *See also* Ego
  transcending, 278
  transparency, 275
  true, 281
Selfish
  life is, 278
  misunderstood, 277
  word definition, 279
Self-reflection
  explained, 250–251
  folly of, 181–183
  stepping out of, 251
Separation, 55–56
  and patriotism, 321
  fixation on, 183

from God, 38
human as separate, 80
illusion of, 199, 270–271
in religions, 381
perception of, 270, 319, 346, 347
Shadows
  gold, 184
  integration, 326
Skepticism
  empirical, 156
  philosophical, 316
Sobriety, 220
Space
  at quantum level, 94
Stalking
  power, 273–274
Stillness, 296–298
  in the breath, 230
Stories
  all fiction, 140
  clearing them, 261
  in our interiority, 140
  internalisation of, 178–179
  life-force consumed by, 147
  love stories, 141
  maintaining perception with, 128
  moral of, 174
  objectivity on, 177
  reaction to, 140
  replacing them, 145
  suppressing, 173
  telling them, 138, 140
  unravelling them, 175, 179–181
Story, 63
Success, 205–207
Symbols
  within Body-mind, 83

Time, 53–55
  at quantum level, 94
  outside of, 140
Tolle, Eckhart
  Pain body, 83

Toltec (references to), 42, 79, 105, 134, 155
  art of dreaming, 238
Tri-part self
  Attentive-mind, 86
    connection with Spirit-mind, 89
    power manifested through, 220
  Body-mind, 82
    stories within, 147
  correct context of, 79
  Spirit-mind, 89
    connection with Attentive-mind, 89
    in fulfilment of your purpose, 89
    power manifested through, 219
    stories within, 147–148
Triune self. *See* Tri-part self
Truth
  and reality compared, 67
  discernment of, 87

Uhane, 86
Unihipili, 82
Unknown, 39
  and discernment, 87
  and the heart, 88
  and the life-stream, 106
  emerging, 132
  incorporation of, 76, 95
  mapping of, 86

Victim consciousness
  and blame, 268–269
  letting go of, 257–260
  the perception behind it, 270
Virtues, 130
Vision
  and attention, 247
  eagle, 367, 365–368
  holding for another, 194

of God, 143, 183, 346
of the human heart, 144

Warrior, the
  as an archetype, 43–45
  challenge of, 46–47
  masculine or feminine?, 45
  's approach to
    being superior, 44
    good and bad, 211
    life, 44, 211
    pain, 133
    projection, 231
Way, the
  of approaching reality, 392
  of no Way, 393
Who am I
  as a self enquiry practice, 73–75
Wholeness, 79
Words. *See* Language
  limits of, 47
  purpose of, 68
World
  as mirror. *See* Reality: mirror nature of
  of love, 131
  created by humanity, 154
  fixation on ego-self, 88
  imbalance, 324
  more than meets the eye, 157
  not the Earth, 152
  setting free, 143, 343–351
  trapped within, 155

Changing the Dream

Have you benefited from the knowledge within this book? If so, I am very grateful to receive your help in making this knowledge available to other people who might also benefit as you have. The more this wisdom spreads and awakens within humanity, the faster we will change the global dream in a way which is life-giving. I am sure you agree it's time we started dreaming a new world; one in which all Beings are empowered into living a Life of Freedom.

You can kindly assist in these simple yet important ways:

- Rate the book and leave a review on one or more Amazon web sites, such as Amazon.com, Amazon.co.uk, Amazon.ca
- On the Amazon product page for this book tick the Search Tags you find relevant and add new ones if you think of some.
- Write an article on Amapedia.com about this book. You'll find the link for this on this book's Amazon.com product page.
- Include this book in Listmania lists on Amazon.
- Write a review on any other online book store you use.
- Tell your friends about this book. They can preview it on Amazon and also at http://books.google.com
- Write articles and reviews for your favourite magazines.
- Use blogs, social networking, Digg, social bookmarking, and the other great Web 2.0 online tools to spread the word.

The following are eay links to this book at online bookstores:
Amazon.com   http://tinyurl.com/PPP-USA1
Amazon.co.uk   http://tinyurl.com/PPP-UK2
Bookdepository.co.uk   http://tinyurl.com/PPP-Global

If you live outside the U.K., Canada, and America then The Book Depository may be the best place to buy this book (and most other books) online, because they have free shipping to many countries.

Printed in the United States
140400LV00001B/10/P